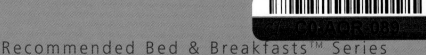

Recommended
BED&
BREAKFASTS™

The South

Carol and Dan
Thalimer

Guilford, Connecticut

Copyright © 2000 by Carol and Dan Thalimer

Recommended Bed & Breakfasts is a trademark of The Globe Pequot Press.

Cover illustration by Michael Crampton
Cover and text design: Nancy Freeborn/Freeborn Design
Illustrations by Mauro Magellan and Duane Perreault

Library of Congress Cataloging-in-Publication Data
Thalimer, Carol.
    Recommended bed and breakfasts. The South / by Carol and Dan Thalimer.—
1st ed.
        p. cm—(Recommended bed & breakfasts series)
    Includes index.
    ISBN 0-7627-0494-2
        1. Bed and breakfast accommodations—Southern States—Guidebooks. I. Title.
II. Series. III. Thalimer, Dan.

TX907.3.S68 T49 1999
647.9475'03 21—dc21   99-040233

Manufactured in the United States of America
First Edition/First Printing

To the Geigerettes
who always go the extra mile

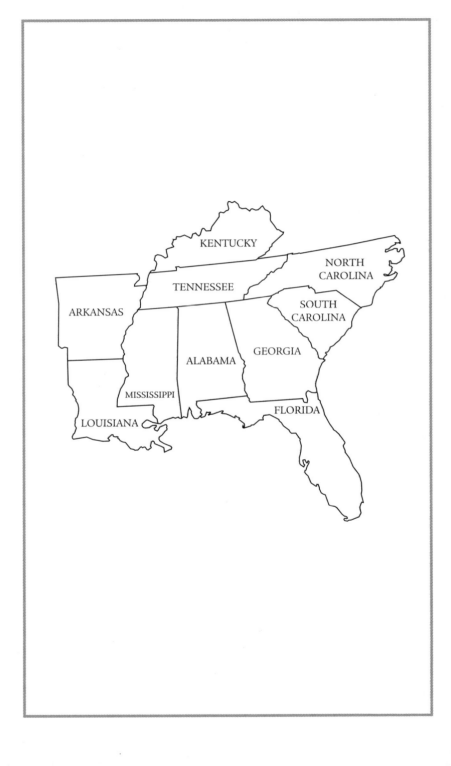

Contents

Acknowledgments

As always: Laura Strom and Paula Brisco for continuing to believe in and put up with us; Ann and John Thalimer for serving as research assistants; Karen and David Wiseman, Williams House B&B Inn, Hot Springs, Arkansas; Judy Peters, The Gables Inn, Hot Springs, Arkansas; Janice and Glenn Wall, Highland Place, Jackson, Tennessee, Sam and Mike Hossom, the Log House, Russellville, Kentucky.

A Few Words about Visiting Southern Bed and Breakfasts

Bed and Breakfast: *Two things children never make for themselves. (That's why most of us adults like to get away to a bed and breakfast once in a while.)*

What's the South best known for? That famed Southern hospitality for one, its home cooking for another, its antebellum architecture for still one more. You can experience all of this and much more at the region's burgeoning variety of bed and breakfasts. Why do so many travelers search out bed and breakfasts instead of staying at motels, hotels, or resorts? Diversity, intimacy, and individual pampering come immediately to mind.

There's a fine line between a bed and breakfast and an inn, and the terms are often used synonymously. For our purposes, we define a *bed and breakfast* as having ten or fewer rooms. (We describe establishments with more than ten rooms and/or a restaurant on the premises in our book *Recommended Country Inns: The South*.) Sometimes a hostelry doesn't fit neatly into one or the other category; in these cases we've made an arbitrary decision about where to put it.

Twenty years ago, there were only about 2,000 bed and breakfasts nationwide. Then Jimmy Carter initiated tax incentives for the restoration of historic buildings. Many old derelicts were saved, but new owners often found their new mansions too expensive to maintain without some income, so they were opened as bed and breakfasts and/or special-events facilities. Now there are tens of thousands, so you have almost unlimited choices, but that makes your job of finding the right one even harder.

Whether you have a pleasant experience at a bed and breakfast is highly dependent on whether you're matched up with the right B&B for *you*. Do you want a historic city mansion filled with museum-quality antiques? Do you want a rustic cabin in the woods, or a farm vacation? Do you want to be around a lot of other people, or do you want to be alone? In this guide we've described each B&B as accurately as we can, so you'll know whether it fits your needs and desires or not.

B&B owners are generally gregarious, openhearted folks who love to get to know all kinds of people. Most of them are well traveled and know what they like in a lodging; that's what they try to provide to you. Many B&B guests are very similar in personality, so it's a good match. Spend a night or two at a bed and breakfast and share a little of your life. We suspect you'll thoroughly enjoy yourselves and perhaps make some new friends. Indeed, if new B&Bers have a good first experience, they generally become B&Bers for life. The repeat rate at B&Bs is extremely high.

We've personally visited the majority of these B&Bs, although we haven't stayed overnight in all of them: Such an undertaking would be time and expense prohibitive. Therefore, we can only report on our impressions and what the owners have told us about their offerings. Sometimes we've interviewed current guests to get their impressions. Other B&Bs included in this guide have been so highly recommended by those near and dear to us—family, friends, business colleagues, travel agents, other travel writers, and even B&B owners we know very well—that we simply couldn't leave them out even though we didn't have the opportunity to visit in person. In these cases we've had extensive conversations with the innkeepers.

Just because we didn't list a bed and breakfast that you may know and love doesn't mean there's something wrong with it. It probably means we don't know about it, haven't had time to visit it, or haven't had it personally recommended to us by someone whose judgment we trust. We follow up on reader suggestions, so if you find a wonderful bed and breakfast, let us know about it through the publisher. We'd also like to have feedback on the B&Bs included in this book. Although we generally choose for inclusion in the guide bed and breakfasts that have been in business for a while and have a solid reputation, things can change. If an establishment's quality declines, you're bound to be disappointed. We don't ever want that to happen, but if it does, be sure to let us know so we can check out the problem and perhaps remove that B&B from the next edition. We can't revisit all these B&Bs every two years in addition to finding new ones, so your comments are invaluable to us.

Sweet dreams!
Carol and Dan

No B&B has paid to be in this guide. Any opinions expressed are strictly those of the authors. When studying this guide, keep in mind that because of the lengthy research, writing, editing, and publishing process required before a book makes it to the bookstore, some of these bed and breakfasts may no longer be in business or may have changed significantly. Certainly new ones will have opened. This guide is meant to give you ideas about B&Bs you might want to investigate further.

How to Use This Bed-and-Breakfast Guide: The ABCs of Bed-and-Breakfast Stays

Alphabet soup. We've arranged the bed and breakfasts in this guide as follows: The ten Southern states are listed alphabetically, followed by an alphabetical list of the towns within each state, then a similar list of the B&Bs within each town (where there's more than one). The maps at the beginning of each chapter show you where the B&Bs are geographically.

Beds. Naturally you'll want a heavenly night's sleep, but sometimes the terms *antique bed* and *good night's sleep* are not synonymous. An antique bed is part of the ambience at a historic bed and breakfast, but only the rare genuine custom-made period frame can accommodate a king-size mattress. Don't despair. Some owners have created king-size beds from two antique twins; some use period reproductions instead of the real thing so they can offer king-size beds. Most authentic old bedsteads, however, can be modified to accommodate a queen-size mattress, and that's what you'll find in most historic B&Bs. Antique beds of any size can also create an uncomfortable problem if you have a night of passionate lovemaking in mind—they often squeak and groan.

Booze. Liquor-sale laws vary from state to state, county to county, even city to city. Many areas of the South are dry. It's the rare bed and breakfast that has a liquor license, and some insurance companies may dictate whether a bed and breakfast can even offer complimentary alcoholic beverages. In our litigious society more and more owners are worrying about liability, so fewer and fewer B&Bs are offering any alcoholic beverages at all. If an evening cocktail or wine with dinner is important to you, it's a good idea to travel with your own supply. We've noted the few B&Bs that don't allow you to bring alcoholic beverages onto the premises.

Breakfast. After your room, the next most important consideration in choosing a B&B may be its breakfast. The morning repast can range from a true continental breakfast—juice, roll, and coffee—to a groaning Southern plantation breakfast with all those artery-clogging specialities. What each bed and breakfast serves may be dictated by local regulations. Some will try to accommodate individual requests and dietary restrictions, although you need to notify them in advance so they can have the appropriate ingredients on hand. Some B&Bs serve at a specific time, others during ceratin hours, others whenever the guest requests. Make sure you know what the custom is at a particular B&B when you make your reservation if the time breakfast is served is important to you—for instance, if you want to sleep in. A few B&Bs offer breakfast in bed, and we've noted them.

Business travel. Increasingly, business travelers are opting to stay at bed and breakfasts instead of hotels. To attract business travelers, many B&Bs are adding amenities specifically for them: desks, in-room telephones (often with voice mail and/or data ports for computer hookup), fax and copier services. Although we've noted the basics in each writeup, be sure to ask if there's something else you need; the innkeepers may be able to supply it.

Children. As much as we love staying in B&Bs, and as well behaved as our own children were—at least away from home—we would never have taken them to 90 percent of B&Bs when they were young. For the most part, these are people's homes, and they're often filled with museum-quality antiques and priceless family heirlooms and memorabilia. Many B&Bs just aren't set up to accommodate extra guests in their bedrooms. Unless an entry tells you explicitly that children are welcome, it's best to call and ask about facilities and guidelines when you are traveling with children under age sixteen. Don't ever just arrive with a child and expect to be accommodated. We provide an index of especially family-friendly B&Bs at the end of the book.

Decor. Although we describe furnishings and decor in order to whet your appetite, B&B owners are constantly redecorating and upgrading, so don't be disappointed if the exact room we describe has changed.

Designations Best Buy
For some entries, you'll see the Best Buy symbol—meaning rates are less than $100 per night. National statistics tell us that the average price of a hotel room in 1999 is $110. We think a room at a bed and breakfast that costs less than this and includes breakfast and lots of extras is a real deal.

Fireplaces. Many historic homes have a fireplace in every room, but the owners are sometimes not allowed to operate them because of insurance restrictions. We've tried to indicate when they are decorative only, wood burning, gas-log, or other usage.

For Sale. It seems to us that at any one time, 50 percent of all B&Bs in the United States are for sale. Several in this guide are on the market. Don't let that stop you from enjoying a particular B&B. The current owners know that if they want to get top dollar, they need to keep their reputation at its highest level. Just be aware that if you're making reservations for a time far in the future, the owners we describe here, and possibly the decor and furnishings, may have changed.

Heat and air-conditioning. Unless otherwise noted, all properties described in this guide have heat and air-conditioning. Most are central rather than individually controlled.

Location. Keep in mind that B&Bs are often located in transitional neighborhoods. Once grand and exclusive, these enclaves deteriorated over the years as the homes became too expensive to maintain and as modern folks sought out simpler lifestyles. The resurgence of historic preservation and restoration is now breathing new life into these areas, however, with the result that sometimes an exquisitely restored home sits next door to a derelict or a commercial establishment. We've tried to indicate situations where the surroundings may be less than ideal by noting "Transitional neighborhood." But we haven't recommended any B&Bs, no matter how wonderful, if we thought the neighborhood was unsafe.

Payment. Most bed and breakfasts accept at least some credit cards; we indicate those that do not. If you aren't paying by credit card, some B&Bs may require that you pay for your entire stay far enough in advance for the check to clear. Traveler's checks are generally accepted, and cash is always a big hit.

Pets are rarely allowed at B&Bs, so assume pets are not allowed. We note the few exceptions. There may be, and in fact usually are, one or more resident pets, so if you have allergies, ask.

Rates given are the basic room rates from the lowest to the highest, but they are subject to change. There will undoubtedly be state and local taxes added to the amounts we list, just as there are at hotels and motels. Rates often vary by the season and the day of the week, so always be clear about the rate for the time of your visit. Also ask about discounts.

Reservations and cancellations. Don't ever just show up at a bed and breakfast and expect to get a room. You'll almost surely be disappointed. For one thing, it will likely be full. For another, if you're not expected, no one may be home. Almost without exception B&Bs have stringent reservation, deposit, and cancellation policies. You will almost universally be expected to guarantee your reservation by credit card, or to send one (or more) night's deposit. There may also be a cancellation fee, no matter how far in advance you cancel.

Reservation services. Some B&Bs, particularly in cities such as Savannah, Georgia, where there are so many, belong to a reservation service. Others belong to a service so they don't have to be waiting by the telephone every hour of the day. The price is the same for you whether you make the reservation directly through the B&B or through the service. (It's the owner who pays if the reservation is made through the service.) The advantage of using a service is that if a particular B&B is full, they can make another recommendation.

Shared baths. Properties that have shared baths often provide robes for their guests, but not always. Either ask when you make your reservation or bring a light robe just in case.

Signage. The vast majority of bed and breakfasts we describe are located in private homes whose owners don't want strangers knocking on their doors at odd hours, so many have no signage at all, or else signs so discreet you might miss them. Be sure to take your directions with you when you travel. A small bone we have to pick with B&Bs is that when you arrive, you often don't know where to park, which door to go to, and whether you should ring the bell or just walk in as you would at a hotel. When there are no signs, we recommend that you park in a spot where you're not blocking the street or driveway, and then go to the front door. This is a person's home, so ring the bell.

Smoking. For insurance purposes and for the comfort of other guests, bed and breakfasts are almost exclusively nonsmoking indoors, so unless we make note of an exception, assume that smoking is not allowed inside. A few establishments don't even allow smoking on the porches. We've noted that in the writeup, too.

Special events. Many B&Bs supplement their income by hosting special events such as luncheons, weddings, corporate meetings, and the like. This can be disturbing if you had an ultraquiet getaway in mind, so you might want to ask when you make your reservation whether any events are scheduled during your stay.

Suites. The word *suite* is one of the most misused in the entire hospitality industry, whether by cruise ships, hotels, or bed and breakfasts. A suite can be anything from an extra-large room with a sitting area to a full apartment. If a separate sitting room is important to you, make sure that's what you're getting.

Telephones and televisions. Some B&Bs have neither, most have them in common rooms, others have them in every room. Each writeup indicates whether you'll find these modern conveniences.

Wheelchair access. The majority of bed and breakfasts are located in historic multistory homes that are unlikely to be modified for wheelchair access—nor are they required to be under ADA laws because of their small size. We note those bed and breakfasts that are wheelchair accessible, fully or in part. Still, even at those B&Bs where a first-floor room is accessible, it is rare to find a fully accessible bathroom with safety bars and a step-in shower.

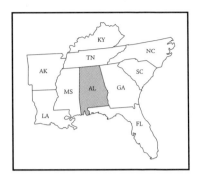

8

19

14

10

65 59

7

11 1

Birmingham 20 Anniston

21

2 59

1

5 13 65

20 3 17

Montgomery 16 85

4

65

31

15

Mobile 6

10

12

9 18

N

Alabama

Numbers on map refer to towns numbered below.

1. Alexander City, Mistletoe Bough, 2

2. Aliceville, Myrtlewood, 3

3. Auburn, The Crenshaw Guest House, 5

4. Eufaula, Kendall Manor Inn Bed and Breakfast, 6

5. Eutaw, Kirkwood Plantation Bed and Breakfast, 8

6. Fairhope,
Bay Breeze Guest House, 10
Church Street Inn, 13

7. Fayette, Rose House Inn, 14

8. Florence, Wood Avenue Inn, 15

9. Gulf Shores, Beach House Bed and Breakfast, 17

10. Leesburg, the secret Bed and Breakfast Lodge, 19

11. Lincoln, The Governor's House Bed and Breakfast, 22

12. Magnolia Springs, Magnolia Springs Bed and Breakfast, 23

13. Marion, Myrtle Hill, 25

14. Mentone, Mountain Laurel Inn, 27

15. Mobile,
Molly Young's Bed and Breakfast, 30
Towle House, 32

16. Montgomery, The Lattice Inn, 33

17. Opelika, The Heritage House Bed and Breakfast, 35

18. Orange Beach, The Original Romar Bed and Breakfast Inn, 37

19. Pisgah, The Lodge on Gorham's Bluff, 39

20. Selma, Grace Hall Bed and Breakfast, 41

21. Talladega, Historic Oakwood Bed and Breakfast, 44

Mistletoe Bough

497 Hillabee Street
Alexander City, Alabama 35010
(256) 329–3717 or (877) 330–3707

WEB SITE: www.bbonline.com/al/mistletoe/

INNKEEPERS: Jean and Carlice Payne

ROOMS: 5; all with private bath (1 down the hall), decorative fireplace, TV, clock radio; some with ceiling fan and/or robes

ON THE GROUNDS: Veranda, gardens

RATES: $85 to $125 double, including welcome refreshments and full breakfast

CREDIT CARDS ACCEPTED? No

OPEN: Year-round

HOW TO GET THERE: Directions will be given at the time of booking.

The Grand Lady of Herzfeld Hill—that's how this imposing Queen Anne Victorian was known in its heyday at the end of the nineteenth century. Built in 1890 by the Reuben Herzfeld family, it continued to house descendants for more than a hundred years. Among the most spectacular architectural characteristics are the round rotunda on the wraparound veranda and the whimsical turret.

Jean and Carlice Payne bought the house in 1993 and lavished their love and attention on its restoration. Following guidelines of the Department of the Interior, their efforts were rewarded with placement of the house on the National Register of Historic Places.

The distinctive decorating style creates a relaxing environment that's perfect for lingering and unwinding. Among the outstanding details are stained-glass windows, a grand staircase, original oak and pine woodwork, and brass chandeliers. Elegant common rooms and guest chambers are decorated with an eclectic mix of traditional, Victorian, and European antiques. Decorated in American traditional antiques is the gentlemen's parlor; the ladies' parlor is done in American Victorian antiques. There are both formal and informal dining rooms. Guest rooms feature high ceilings, tall windows, and king-, queen-, double-, or twin-size beds—some of which are romantic four-posters.

You'll know you're in for warm hospitality and pampering from the moment you arrive to welcoming refreshments. A variety of goodies are available throughout your stay. A delicious country buffet breakfast—perhaps an entree such as French toast filled with fruit or preserves, omelettes, or eggs Benedict, accompanied by fresh fruit, hot curried fruit, and home-made muffins and jellies—is served in the formal dining room using fine china, crystal, silver, and linens. And oh yes, you'll have "the best grits you ever put in your mouth," according to Jean. Many of the herbs used in the recipes or as garnishes are from Carlice's garden.

While away some time in the formal parlor, relax out on the veranda, or stroll through the acre and a half of gardens, azaleas, camellias, gardenias, and fruit, pecan, and magnolia trees.

What's Nearby Alexander City

"Alex City," as locals call it, is known for its hometown company, the Russell Corporation. Many athletes—from Little League to the National Football League—sport clothes manufactured by Russell. You, too, can dress like a pro and shop at the Russell Textile Mills. Wear your new T-shirt and sweats to Lake Martin, a great spot for boating, fishing, swimming, and other athletic pursuits.

Myrtlewood Best Buy

602 Broad Street
Aliceville, Alabama 35442
(205) 373-8153 or (800) 367-7891

WEB SITE: www.bbonline/al/ myrtlewood/

INNKEEPERS: Johnie and Billy McKinzey

ROOMS: 4; all with private bath, TV, telephone; a ramp into the house and 1 suite wheelchair accessible

ON THE GROUNDS: Sunporch

RATES: $50 double, including breakfast; additional person $5

CREDIT CARDS ACCEPTED? Yes

OPEN: Year-round

HOW TO GET THERE: From Tuscaloosa, take Highway 14 into Aliceville. Turn right onto Broad Street and go 4 blocks up the hill to Myrtlewood, which is on your right.

In 1909 the Horton family, one of Aliceville's founding families, built this lovely home for their family of eight children. In 1919 they sold it to the Duncan family, who lived here for fifty-seven years. Then the house sat empty for many years until the McKinzeys bought and restored it. Since 1993, they've shared their home with bed-and-breakfast guests.

Typical of a middle-class home of the turn-of-the-century period, the house is a substantial two story with a full-length veranda. Although it lacks the ostentatious exterior ornamentation that the very wealthy lavished on their homes, inside you'll find high ceilings, hardwood floors, decorative moldings, tall windows, and beautiful fireplaces that attest to the opulence of the period. Among the outstanding architectural features are an unusual staircase and generous use of stained glass. To this background Johnie and Billy have added Oriental carpets, dramatic window treatments, decorative borders, crystal chandeliers, and opulent Victorian-era antiques. In complete contrast, the bright, cheery sunroom upstairs is filled with wicker and floral fabrics. This is a great place for guests to gather to get to know each other and to enjoy the views of downtown.

Guest accommodations are offered in spacious rooms with sitting areas. Some of the bathrooms feature claw-foot tubs. The Honeymoon Suite boasts an ornately carved bed.

Breakfast can be whatever you want it to be. Those who like to sleep in and splurge when on vacation can opt for the full plantation breakfast; early risers who are watching their waistlines might prefer an early continental breakfast.

During World War II, Aliceville was the site of a German prisoner-of-war camp. POW artifacts and other items of local historical interest are on display at the nearby Aliceville Museum.

What's Nearby Aliceville

Aliceville is home to the only World War II German prisoner of war museum: The Aliceville Museum and Cultural Arts Center remembers the thousands of German prisoners who were held at Camp Aliceville, the present-day Sue Stabler Park. If museum-going is not your thing, perhaps you'll enjoy the area's antiques stores. Or try the Tennessee-Tombigbee Waterway for water sports and general fun in the sun.

The Crenshaw Guest House

Best Buy

371 North College Street
Auburn, Alabama 36830
(334) 821-1131 or (800) 950-1131

E-MAIL: crenshaw-gh@mindspring.com

WEB SITE: www.crenshawguesthouse.
com or www.auburnalabama.com

INNKEEPERS: Fran and Peppi Verma

ROOMS: 6; all with private bath, cable
TV, VCR, clock radio, cassette player, direct-line telephone with computer data port, well-lit study desk, ceiling fan; some with kitchenette

ON THE GROUNDS: Verandas

RATES: $48 to $85 single or double, including continental-plus breakfast

CREDIT CARDS ACCEPTED: Yes

OPEN: Year-round

HOW TO GET THERE: From I–85, take exit 51 and follow US 29 into Auburn, where it becomes College Street. Continue past the university and 3 blocks past downtown. The B&B is on your left.

Shaded by venerable old oak and pecan trees, the stately Wedgwood blue Crenshaw Guest House—itself on the National Register of Historic Places—is located in the Old Main and Church Street Historic District just blocks from Auburn University. These trees were probably planted by Bolling Hall Crenshaw, an Auburn University mathematics professor, when he built the house around 1880. Professor Crenshaw was not only an instructor but also an author of mathematics textbooks that earned him international recognition. Overlooking other imposing homes in the historic district, the gingerbread-trimmed, wicker-filled front porch welcomes guests inside and makes an ideal spot for early-morning coffee or a refreshing cold drink at the end of the day.

Inside, 12-foot vaulted ceilings, burnished heart-pine floors, graceful proportions, spacious rooms, rich hardwood trim, and dozens of other late-Victorian details are hallmarks of the turn-of-the-century era. Decorative mantelpieces, transoms, and brass ceiling fans reflect a bygone, less-hurried way of life. Antique furnishings in the public and guest rooms complement the period ambience without sacrificing comfort and convenience. This is not such a formal museumlike house that you're afraid to sit on the furniture;

you can believe that a real family lived here. Victorian-style bathrooms, which feature claw-foot tubs with gleaming brass and porcelain trim, have been discreetly modernized to provide every convenience.

The crown jewel at the Crenshaw Guest House is the Bay Room, a two-room suite named for the bay windows in both the parlor and bedroom. A beautiful two-tiered mantel trimmed in Dutch blue tilework is the centerpiece of the Victorian parlor; an ornately figured mantel anchors the bedroom, which has a queen and a twin bed. The Oak Room features a queen and a double, and the Walnut Room has a queen. Guests in the main house get a room-service breakfast.

To the rear of the main house is a humble carriage house, which was Professor Crenshaw's personal hideaway where he read, prepared lessons, and authored his textbooks. With an addition, the carriage house now provides two more guest accommodations. The extra seclusion, casual and eclectic furnishings, and well-appointed kitchenettes make these rooms ideal for longer-term stays. Guests in these suites receive a daily complimentary breakfast basket.

What's Nearby Auburn

Auburn is home to Auburn University, which is a popular place to visit. Tour the Auburn University Historic District and stroll past the brick nineteenth-century buildings. A highlight of the campus is Donald E. Davis Arboretum. You'll enjoy the lake and red Japanese maples and magnolia trees, among other lovely plantings.

Kendall Manor Inn and Bed and Breakfast   Best Buy

534 West Broad Street
Eufaula, Alabama 36027
(334) 687–8847; fax (334) 616–0678

E-MAIL: kmanorinn@aol.com
WEB SITE: www.bbonline.com/al/kendallmanor/
INNKEEPERS: Barbara and Tim Lubsen
ROOMS: 6; all with private bath
ON THE GROUNDS: Upstairs and downstairs porches, sunny private deck

RATES: $84 to $109, including full breakfast, welcome beverage, afternoon tea, fresh flowers, a sweet with turndown service; additional cost for dinner (by reservation)

CREDIT CARDS ACCEPTED? Yes

OPEN: Year-round

HOW TO GET THERE: Follow US 431 to Eufaula; at Broad Street, turn west. The B&B is in the third block on your right.

Eufala is one of the most beautiful towns in the South, with a collection of more than 700 preserved and restored historic buildings—many of them Italianate in style. We've always thought Kendall Manor was the most beautiful structure in town, indeed perhaps in the South, and were overjoyed when it opened its doors as a bed and breakfast.

Kendall Manor, a National Register of Historic Places treasure, is the quintessential wedding-cake Victorian, built in the 1860s when cotton was king. An architectural masterpiece in the Italianate style, its majestic two stories are festooned with columns and porches, and the mansion is crowned with a graceful towering belvedere—a tall addition put there not for its striking good looks, but to let hot air escape from the house. Do yourselves a favor and make the climb to this tower: From its tall windows, looming 75 feet above the street, you can see for miles in every direction.

Kendall Manor's belvedere is very special in another way, too. Over the more than one hundred years since the house was built, guests have gathered in it to see the view and enjoy the cool breezes, but also to leave behind graffiti—names, salutations, and anecdotes, which have never been scrubbed off or painted over. In fact, graffiti is not a dirty word here. As guests, you'll even be invited to leave your own mark by adding your remarks to the collection. Inns, more likely than not, have guests books in which guests are encouraged to leave comments. This is the only one we know of where you're induced to leave a permanent record of your visit directly on the house!

Named one of the Top Fifty All-American Getaways by *Condé Nast Traveler*, the bed and breakfast offers a warm welcome and the gracious ambience of the Old South as well as exquisite accommodations, delicious food, and exceptional attention to detail. Public rooms and guest chambers showcase 16-foot ceilings, gold-leaf cornices, Italian marble fireplaces, and ruby-colored glass windows; each is opulently decorated in the lavish Victorian style with antiques, period reproductions, and ornate fabrics. Large, light, and airy, with high ceilings and numerous windows, guest rooms blend history with modern amenities and personal touches. Each is individually decorated and, in addition to king- or queen-size beds, the well-appointed rooms feature cozy sitting areas and spacious baths.

After an exceptional night's sleep in your romantic bedchamber, you might be tempted to lie in bed indefinitely, but the wafting aromas of home-made breads and muffins and a special blend of freshly ground coffee will draw you out of bed and down to a delicious full breakfast, which might include an entree such as eggs Kendall, orange French toast with berry sauce, or gingerbread pancakes, accompanied by coffee, tea, fruits, and juices.

To make your Kendall Manor experience even more special, arrange ahead of time to have a romantic, multicourse gourmet dinner for two served by candlelight in the Manor Dining Room or in front of the fireplace in the Original Kendall Dining Room. After a stay here it will be difficult to reenter the twentieth century.

What's Nearby Eufaula

Eufaula is the second-largest historic district in Alabama and is much admired for its stately Southern mansions and historic treasures. If you're here in April, get details about the Eufaula Pilgrimage—an annual event that includes home tours, antiques shows, and concerts. A must-see home is the Shorter Mansion, a grand Neoclassical Revival mansion. You may take a guided tour through the home, and see the antique furnishings, displays of period wedding dresses, and state memorabilia.

Kirkwood Plantation Bed and Breakfast

111 Kirkwood Drive
Eutaw, Alabama 35462
(205) 372-9009

E-MAIL: krkwd@bellsouth.net

WEB SITE: www.kirkwoodplantation.com

INNKEEPER: Sherry Vallides

ROOMS: 6; all with private bath, clock, TV, telephone, decorative fireplace, and balcony; limited wheelchair access

ON THE GROUNDS: Screened porch, gardens, woods

RATES: $89 single, $99 double, including full breakfast, afternoon refreshments, tour of house

CREDIT CARDS ACCEPTED? Yes

OPEN: Year-round

HOW TO GET THERE: From I-20/59, take exit 40 (Highway 14), drive 2.5 miles east, and turn left onto Kirkwood Drive.

Let's start right off with superlatives. Kirkwood is the most photographed house in Alabama—perhaps in the entire South, perhaps the entire country. What makes Kirkwood so extraordinary, in addition to its classical Greek Revival style and massive Ionic columns, is its oversize belvedere.

"What's a belvedere?" you might ask. It's an addition perched on the roof of a house, barn, or other structure. If it's square, it's called a belvedere; if it's dome shaped and on a round base, it's a cupola. We twentieth-century folks may think of them as purely decorative, but they really served a useful purpose as an early method of air-conditioning. Of course, the more opulent the house, the larger and fancier the belvedere or cupola was likely to be. And Kirkwood's belvedere is the biggest and fanciest we've ever seen. Like the mansion itself, it has a veranda and columns all the way around.

Kirkwood's story is a romantic one—right up to the present time. Just prior to the Civil War, Foster Mark Kirksey, a bachelor and successful cotton merchant, bought ninety-seven acres on which he began construction of a grand Greek Revival home, importing luxuries such as eight Carrara marble mantels from Italy and Waterford chandeliers from Ireland. Colored panes of glass around the door represent the four seasons. Kirksey married in 1860 when the house was almost complete, but when the Civil War broke out, construction came to an abrupt halt. After the war federal occupation troops commandeered the parlor, and there forced Southerners to sign an oath of loyalty to the Union. Kirksey's fortunes were never regained, and the construction was left incomplete.

Descendants continued living in the mansion until 1953—by which time the downward spiral of deterioration was almost fatal. Kirkwood remained abandoned until 1972, when Roy and Mary Swayze fell in love with it. They left their home in Virginia and devoted ten years to the restoration project, scouring the South for old materials such as slave-made bricks and heart-pine beams and flooring, as well as locating craftsmen who could do the intricate plaster cornicework. It took one month per room to repair the ornamental moldings. Mary told us that fourteen-month project of reconstructing the belvedere was "like putting a puzzle together." The Swayzes used the unengraved sides of rejected Union tombstones to replace the marble steps and found appropriate ornamental ironwork to install the never-completed second-floor balcony. Then the hunt began for period furnishings and accessories to complement the few remaining original pieces. In 1982 First Lady Nancy Reagan presented the Swayzes with an Honor Award from the National Trust for Historic Preservation for their outstanding work in bringing this wonderful old mansion back to life. After Roy's death Mary, her daughter, and her granddaughter, opened the house for tours and as a bed and breakfast.

Since August 1998 the mistress of Kirkwood has been Sherry Vallides, an energetic go-getter we met several years ago when she was running tours in Marion, Alabama. Even so, as a visitor you'll feel as if you're the master or mistress of the entire estate. You can relax on the verandas or screened porch, stroll the eight acres of grounds, enjoy the public parlors on the ground floor, or shoot a game in the third-floor billiards room; by all means make a trip up to the belvedere to enjoy the view.

Sherry's major contribution to the continued life of Kirkwood is the conversion of additional rooms to bed-and-breakfast accommodations, each with a private bath. She's also freshened the paint and added period wallpapers.

What's Nearby Eutaw

Eutaw hearkens back to another era. Its fifty-three antebellum structures decorate the downtown historic district. Many of the sites are listed in the National Register of Historic Places. Eutaw is close to the Tombigbee and Black Warrior Rivers, and the area is popular for water sports, golf, tennis, biking, and hiking. There is a greyhound racetrack there, too.

Bay Breeze Guest House

742 South Mobile Street
(mailing address: P.O. Box 526)
Fairhope, Alabama 36533
(334) 928–8976; fax (334) 928–0360

WEB SITE: www.bbonline.com/al/
baybreeze

INNKEEPERS: Bill and Becky Jones

ROOMS: 4 (with 3 in main house, plus
1 cottage suite); all with private bath;
some with TV; cottage suite with
telephone, small kitchen, and wheelchair access

Jubilee

An incredible and largely unexplained natural phenomenon occurs only within a 20-mile area near Daphne, Alabama. For some reason all types of sea life come to the surface at the same time in a shallow place where they can be easily caught. Imagine scooping up armloads of shrimp, lobsters, and other sea delicacies with little effort. It's no wonder that this bounteous occasion is called Jubilee!

The curious occurrence is most likely to happen once or twice between May and September and between midnight and dawn. Of course, no one wants to miss it, so locals take turns patrolling the beaches at night; if they see things beginning to happen, it's their duty to let everyone else know by banging on pans, blowing whistles, ringing bells, or whatever other means they can. Once alerted, everyone rushes out with gigs, washtubs, nets—anything that allows them to scoop up the bounty of the sea. Bonfires are lit and Jubilee becomes one big beach party, with the leftovers taken home for future feasting.

It's speculated that Jubilee may be caused by quick changes in the amount of fresh water meeting salt water (for instance, after a heavy rain), which changes the oxygen level and forces sea life to the surface. Others claim it has something to do with the position of the moon. Most folks don't question why—they just enjoy.

ON THE GROUNDS: Private pier, decks, and beach on Mobile Bay

RATES: $100 single or double; $120 suite, including full breakfast in main house; $10 each additional person in suite

CREDIT CARDS ACCEPTED? Yes

OPEN: Year-round

HOW TO GET THERE: From I–10 take US 98 toward Fairhope and exit right onto Scenic/Alternate Highway 98 at the WELCOME TO FAIRHOPE sign. At the third traffic light, turn right onto Magnolia Avenue. Go 4 blocks and turn left onto South Mobile Street at the municipal pier. Bay Breeze Guest House is about a mile farther, on your right.

Becky Jones wrote saying that some of her guests thought Bay Breeze Guest House deserved to be included in this guide. "We are very special, too," she added. So we checked it out. The inn, the location, and the Joneses are, indeed, special.

The inn sits on a three-acre site right on the shores of Mobile Bay. The grounds are filled with mature shrubs and trees that give you a feeling of being in the woods. The stucco building was built in the 1930s and has been variously remodeled and enlarged over the years to accommodate the family's changing needs. It works beautifully as an inn.

The entire downstairs—a sitting room with fireplace, glassed-porch bay room, living room, and kitchen—is devoted to guests. (The Joneses have private quarters upstairs.) Most of the furnishings in the main house are family heirlooms going back as far as five generations. The mix of wicker, stained glass, and hooked and Oriental rugs produces a homey feel no designer could duplicate. "And everything has a story," Becky says.

However, Dan's favorite "room" isn't a room at all, but the 462-foot private pier on Mobile Bay. The sunset over the bay can't be beat.

The cottage suite is newer. It has pickled white-pine walls, old brick floors, vaulted ceilings, and lots of generously sized windows. It is well equipped for the handicapped, with wide spaces to accommodate a wheelchair, grab bars in the proper places in the bathrooms, and flexible shower wands. The cottage is decorated with just the right combination of antiques, Oriental rugs, new sofas, and good beds. You feel comfortable but not overwhelmed with stuff. Becky has been careful to keep the suite light and spacious.

As a hostess, she knows how to find out what you like and provides it without apparent effort: a special jelly, a particular bread or coffee or drink. And if you come back again, she'll remember what you liked and have it ready for you.

What's Nearby Fairhope

Fairhope is a breath of fresh air. Its downtown area is literally blooming with flowers. Some downtown sites include art galleries, eateries, boutiques, and antiques shops. Fairhope Pier is a popular place to walk and jog. You'll also enjoy Fairhope's public beaches, rose gardens, and park.

Church Street Inn

51 South Church Street
(mailing address: P.O. Box 526)
Fairhope, Alabama 36533
(334) 928-8976

WEB SITE: www.bbonline.com/al/
churchstreet

INNKEEPERS: Bill and Becky Jones

ROOMS: 3; all with private bath

ON THE GROUNDS: Porch with rockers,
garden courtyard, bicycles

RATES: $85 single or double, including continental breakfast

CREDIT CARDS ACCEPTED? Yes

OPEN: Year-round

HOW TO GET THERE: From I–10, take exit 35 onto US 98. Drive about 8
miles and exit right on Scenic/Alternate Highway 98 at the WELCOME TO
FAIRHOPE sign. At the fourth traffic light, turn right onto Fairhope
Avenue. Go 1 block, and turn left onto Church Street. The inn is the
white stucco house right at the next corner.

Most of us like staying at small B&Bs because we feel at home. This
restored 1921 house, listed on the National Register of Historic Places,
went directly from being a home to being an inn with virtually no
changes. Becky's mother lived here until she needed extra care. When she
moved out she left everything: the furniture, the knickknacks, even the
dishes. And almost all that was left now welcomes guests, who pore over the
scrapbooks and family pictures as though they were reading a novel.

It's better than a novel. Becky's mother had three husbands. Their pictures are all here. A portrait of Becky's mother commands your attention
from its position over a white brick electric fireplace. You'll see a striking
resemblance to Becky. And in the window seat you can browse through the
family memory book for glimpses of first boyfriends, family pictures, World
War II ration books, even letters.

In case you are wondering, this is the same Bill and Becky who own the
Bay Breeze Guest House, where they live, but you won't be neglected here.
The Joneses take care to have enough help so that there's always someone
around.

The guest rooms, larger than average, are named after great-grandchildren of Becky's mom. Laura Leigh's Room is furnished in period oak; Ellen Elizabeth's contains the Jenny Lind bedroom suite of her great-grandmother; Ashley Ann's Room, on the second floor, contains her great-grandmother's spool furniture.

Like most of the buildings in Fairhope, this one is stucco. Becky says the old buildings were usually made of stucco because a local pottery produced large tiles. It seems almost anyone could do a fair job of putting up a house with them, covering the tiles (and their little mistakes) with stucco. They had another reason for using stucco: Even today, it keeps a building cool in summer and warm in winter, so you're comfortable inside.

What's Near Fairhope
See page 12 for what's nearby Fairhope.

Rose House Inn

325 Second Avenue Northwest
Fayette, Alabama 35555
(205) 932-7673 (ROSE) or
(800) 925-ROSE

E-MAIL: Treasure@Fayette.net
WEB SITE: www.bbonline.com/al/
rosehouse/

INNKEEPERS: Diane and Dennis Fisher

ROOMS: 10; 8 with private bath (1 with a whirlpool), 2 share a bath; all with cable TV, telephone, ceiling fan; 2 with decorative fireplace; two telephone lines, voice mail, computer access; limited wheelchair access

ON THE GROUNDS: Wraparound porch, walking distance to downtown

RATES: $55 to $90 single or double, including continental-plus breakfast; additional person $10

CREDIT CARDS ACCEPTED? Yes

OPEN: Year-round

HOW TO GET THERE: At the intersection of Highway 43 and Highway 18, turn right onto Highway 18 West. Pass through three traffic lights. After the third light, turn onto Second Avenue Northwest and proceed until you approach a four-way stop. The Rose House Inn is on your left before the stop sign.

One of the oldest houses in Fayette, the Rose House Inn is also the only individually listed National Register property. Built on four acres in 1898 by Edward Rose, it is an excellent example of a Queen Anne Victorian cottage with features such as the telltale wraparound porch, a hexagonal turret with a bell-shaped tower, and imbricated woodwork on some of its gables. The newly constructed Rose Cottage blends well with its sister; in addition to a porch, it also boasts a tower.

Tastefully decorated, mostly in Victorian-era antiques, the interior ambience is that of the turn of the century. Many guests are particularly interested in the large collection of Thomas Kinkade lithographs.

Between the main house and the cottage, ten guest accommodations are available. Each has its own distinctive personality and is tastefully decorated with period antiques. The queen among the rooms, the Honeymoon Suite, boasts a king-size canopy bed and a two-person whirlpool tub.

Breakfast is a substantial meal of fruits and juices, muffins—perhaps the specialty sausage-cheese muffins—cereals, grits, eggs, and hot beverages.

Located only 2 blocks from downtown, the Rose House Inn is within easy walking distance of restaurants, shops, and businesses. In fact, this convenience to downtown makes the Rose House Inn popular with business travelers, and the Fishers know how to treat them right. Each room has a work space, there are two telephone lines with voice mail, and a modem is available for computer communications.

What's Nearby Fayette

You'll certainly enjoy downtown Fayette and its antiques shopping. While you're in town, visit the Fayette Art Museum and Fayette County library. The Guthrie Smith Park is also in the area. Fayette also offers opportunities for fishing, golf, and tennis.

Wood Avenue Inn (Best Buy)

658 North Wood Avenue
Florence, Alabama 35630
(256) 766-8441; fax (256) 766-8467

INNKEEPERS: Alvern and Gene Greeley

ROOMS: 5; 3 with private bath, 2 share, 3 with ceiling fan; all with gas-log

fireplace; clock radio and hair dryer available on request; Rose Room wheelchair accessible

ON THE GROUNDS: Veranda, gardens; public tours of the house are conducted on Tuesday

RATES: $64 to $97 single or double, including full breakfast, afternoon/evening refreshments

CREDIT CARDS ACCEPTED? Yes

OPEN: Year-round

HOW TO GET THERE: From I-65 take AL 72 west into Florence, where it becomes Tennessee. Continue to Wood Avenue, where you turn north and go 5 blocks to the B&B.

Everyone in Florence breathed a big sigh of relief in 1990 when Alvern and Gene Greeley bought the house at 658 North Wood Avenue and began to restore it. The imposing Queen Anne "High Victorian" with the red roof and both square and octagonal towers had been a familiar landmark in town since 1889, but it was deteriorating and many feared that the distinctive structure would be lost. Local folks were mighty pleased that it would become a bed and breakfast—in fact, many have come to stay for a special occasion.

Victorian splendor at its best describes the opulent Wood Avenue Inn—an exceptional and unusual example of the style. Originally known as the Crossland-Karsner House, the residence was built for G. W. Karsner, superintendent of a local cotton mill. (W. A. Crossland was the architect.) The C. L. Smith family occupied the house the longest and began the long tradition of offering hospitality and good food. During the building of nearby Wilson Dam, there was a severe shortage of housing, and locals were asked to open their homes to the workers. The Smiths boarded as many as twelve at a time, later boarding teachers from the Teachers College (now the University of North Alabama) across the street. It was during this time that they became well known for the quality of their food.

Emphasis has been placed on maintaining as many of the original architectural details as possible while providing today's modern comforts. Inside, 14-foot ceilings, heart-pine floors, twelve fireplaces, a majestic staircase, pocket doors, and appropriate furnishings create a time warp—you almost expect to hear the latest news about the dam's construction, or that Woodrow Wilson has been elected president. In addition to the public rooms, spacious porches and beautiful gardens with wisteria arbors and antique roses offer perfect spots for relaxation.

Five romantic guest rooms display elegant antiques, period reproductions, and special decorator touches while still providing the utmost in comfort. Each boasts a gas-log fireplace. Three chambers feature a private bathroom and a private breakfast area as well. Charm and peace and quiet are ensured by the absence of telephones and television. Popular with honeymooners, the downstairs Rose Room features a king-size rice-carved four-poster bed you have to use steps to climb into, paneled walls, a bathroom with a claw-foot tub to which a ring shower has been added, a sunporch, and a separate sitting room. Another particularly striking bedchamber is the Bird Room. Other rooms include the Roosevelt, a more masculine room favored by businessmen; the more feminine Cameo Room, which is a favorite of professional women; and the Blue Room.

Enjoy the scrumptious breakfast—which might consist of any one of thirty-five combinations—in the dining room, or indulge in a private meal in your room. Crepes are a house specialty, but you might be served fruit tarts with lemon sauce, pastries, omelettes, quiches, or sculpted baked apples.

Whether they're celebrating a romantic evening or visiting Florence on business, the Wood Avenue Inn prides itself on pampering its guests.

What's Nearby Florence

It's not Italy, but it definitely is a kind of Renaissance town. To get a perspective of the city, visit Renaissance Tower, which overlooks the Wilson Dam, and offers an aquarium and restaurant. Florence has a number of museums, including the Indian Mound and Museum and the W. C. Handy Home and Museum. In October, visit the Alabama Renaissance Faire at Wilson Park for dancing, music, and Renaissance fun.

The Beach House Bed and Breakfast

9218 Dacus Lane
Gulf Shores, Alabama 36542
(334) 540-7039 or (800) 659-6004

WEB SITE: www.bbchannel.com

INNKEEPERS: Carol and Russell Shackelford

ROOMS: 5; all with private bath, ceiling fan; TV on request

ON THE GROUNDS: Porches, hot tub

RATES: $450 to $1,390 (three, four, or seven nights) double, including breakfast, snacks, beverages, afternoon wine and cheese; for a single deduct $25

CREDIT CARDS ACCEPTED? Not at this time

OPEN: Usually closed from mid-December to mid-January, but dates change, so be sure to ask

HOW TO GET THERE: From I–10 (exit 44), follow AL 59 south to Gulf Shores. At the fourth traffic light after the bridge over the Intracostal Waterway, turn right (west) onto FL 180 (Fort Morgan Parkway). When you see the Meyer Real Estate office on your left, continue approximately 0.7 mile and turn left onto Veterans Road. Take the second left, onto Dacus Lane. The Beach House is on your right at the end of Dacus Lane.

For us, there is no better place to be rejuvenated than at the beach. We like to stay right at the water's edge so we can step outside our door to swim, sun, take long walks, or search for shells. We want to be able to open the doors and windows so we can see the waves crashing, hear the soothing sounds of the sea, and watch the vivid displays of color as the sun rises or sets. The delightful Beach House Bed and Breakfast, near Gulf Shores, fulfills our every requirement and desire—even things we hadn't previously realized we wanted. Owners Carol and Russell Shackelford provide an intimate, friendly atmosphere with lots of amenities to spoil you outrageously. Their philosophy is to balance "leaving you alone" with "taking care of you."

Perched on high dunes directly on the shores of the Gulf of Mexico, the rambling, three-story house sits on the last lot before the Bon Secour National Wildlife Refuge, guaranteeing that the vast stretch of dune-backed beach next door will never be developed. Although the house is new, the natural-wood, tin-roofed exterior is reminiscent of grand turn-of-the-century beach houses. A huge screened porch wraps around the front of the first floor—a perfect place to get out of the sun and to socialize with your hosts and fellow guests. Outdoor stairs lead to the hot-tub deck, where you can soak away your tensions. A smaller second-floor screened porch with wicker, hammocks, and hanging chairs is another favorite retreat.

Inside, ample use is made of pine, ceramic tile, and beaded board. Round timbers rise through all floors of the house like the masts of old sailing ships. The large, open living room/kitchen has a wall of windows looking out onto the Gulf. Comfortable seating induces guests to settle in, and a large library table is a great place to play games or put together a puzzle. In the kitchen area a guest refrigerator is stocked with lemonade, juices, and soft drinks; there's also an ice maker and coffeemaker. Bookcases in the living room and up the stairways on all three floors are laden with books and magazines on every subject. What you happily won't see are televisions and telephones. In fact, the Shackelfords advertise their home as a "no phone, no TV, no shoes zone." Instead they provide kites and floats, beach chairs, and even flip-flops.

All five luxurious guest rooms have their own distinct personality indicated by their names: Nags Head, Cape May, Key West, Cumberland Island, and West Indies. All boast fabulous views, pine floors, Oriental rugs, and ceiling fans (air-conditioning is used in particularly hot weather). Private baths are large; all are amply supplied with plush towels and bathrobes. Beds are king or queen size and feature premium mattresses topped with plump featherbeds, down pillows, and luxury linens. Two of the rooms open onto the second-floor porch. The two suite-size rooms on the third floor feature seating areas and private whirlpools; one has a private deck.

Firmly believing that a one-night stay simply isn't sufficient in which to unwind and get all the benefits of the ocean, beach, and fresh salt air, as well as the inn itself, the Shackelfords require a minimum three-night stay.

What's Nearby Gulf Shores

Gulf Shores is a beautiful retreat on the Gulf of Mexico—and a relatively new retreat at that: The town of Gulf Shores was not listed on Alabama's official highway map until the 1960s. Gulf State Park Resorts is a great recreation area. You'll find white sandy beaches, a restaurant, golf course, fishing pier, campsites, and tennis courts. And if you visit in October, check out Gulf Shores' National Shrimp Festival.

the secret Bed and Breakfast Lodge

2356 Highway 68 West
Leesburg, Alabama 35983
(256) 523–3825; fax (256) 523–6477

E-MAIL: secret@peop.tds.net

WEB SITE: www.bbonline.com/al/thesecret

INNKEEPERS: Diann and Carl Cruickshank

ROOMS: 4, plus 2 cottages;
all with private bath,
TV, VCR, ceiling fan,
desk, and telephone
jack; no wheelchair
access in the main house

ON THE GROUNDS: Rooftop pool; twelve acres

RATES: $95 to $135 double, including full breakfast; each additional person $25

CREDIT CARDS ACCEPTED? Yes

OPEN: Year-round

HOW TO GET THERE: At the traffic light in Leesburg, turn right. The inn is 2.4 miles on your right. Turn right at the sign and follow the road 0.2 mile to the top of the mountain.

Psst! Come a little closer. We want to whisper something in your ear. Promise you won't tell anyone; it'll be our little secret. You can enjoy one of the most spectacular views in Alabama from the rooftop pool of this secluded getaway. Overlooking Weiss Lake, the vista stretches to Rome, Georgia, to the east; Gadsden, Alabama, to the west; and Weisner Mountain and beyond to Mount Cheaha, the highest point in Alabama, to the south. All we can say is, Wow! Located near the Lookout Mountain Parkway, the rustic thirty-five-year-old mountaintop lodge offers everything you need to get away from it all. The stone lodge itself was built as a private home in 1965. Being hidden from view earned it its current name.

It's Not a Secret Anymore

When Carl Cruickshank retired from the outdoor-advertising business several years ago, he drew a circle on a map within a 100-mile radius of Atlanta and looked for water. He found what he was looking for in northeastern Alabama's Weiss Lake, and after several visits, purchased a fishing camp there. He was thoroughly enjoying his retirement and fishing almost every day until the night he stopped by Muffins 50s Cafe for dinner. The rest, as they say, is history. Diann and Carl will love to tell you all about what led them to creating the secret.

One wing houses four vaulted-ceilinged guest rooms, which each open onto decks. Two have panoramas of the lake and mountains, while the other two look into the forest and down a shady mountain road. Named for the feelings you'll take away from them, the Tranquility and Serenity Rooms boast king-size mahogany rice beds and private balconies leading to the rooftop pool; the Remembrance and Enchantment Rooms feature queen-size iron beds. For those who desire even more privacy, a cottage, perfect for a longer stay or two couples, has a kitchen and laundry facilities as well as a queen-size bed and daybed/trundle bed. A small, steep-roofed "Hansel and Gretel" cottage called the Sugar Shack boasts a fireplace and two-person whirlpool tub surrounded by mirrors.

Rivaling the view and the pool is the mammoth common area with its 22-foot tongue-and-groove vaulted ceiling, gargantuan stacked-stone fireplace, and tall windows. Diann and Carl have great senses of humor, and you'll find lots of it in this special room. A life-size mannequin sits in a chair, stuffed animals line the staircase, and a doll collection occupies a display cabinet. But the biggest conversation starter is the 8-foot chair they built. When adults climb into it, they look like Lilliputians. You'll want Diann or Carl to take your picture in it to remind you of your quirky visit to the secret. If it's your anniversary, they'll give you a large cutout heart to hold; if it's your birthday, you'll hold a cutout cake for your memento photo.

For years we've been saying that someone should invent a table that revolves like a lazy Susan. Well, someone has come close. This 12-foot dining table had to be built in place; a gigantic lazy Susan is necessary if guests are to reach all the breakfast treats. Morning repasts vary—one day it might include biscuits and gravy, eggs, sausage, juice, and hot beverages; another day, pecan pancakes, eggs, sausage, and fruit. Carl makes a mean apple French toast, too.

When guests aren't lounging in or around the pool, there are twelve acres of forest land filled with white-tailed and fallow deer, a pair of albino wallabies, llamas, a fox, raccoons, peacocks, muntjacs, and squirrels to wander. Ask about the Kissing Tree, where it's another tradition to get your picture taken.

What's Nearby Leesburg

The Leesburg area offers lots of recreational attractions. Visit Noccalula Falls, Little River Canyon, Yellow Creek and Little River Falls, DeSoto Falls and DeSoto Falls State Park, and Weiss Lake. All kinds of outdoor options await you, including fishing, skiing, sailing, boating, rock climbing, hiking, walking, and bird watching.

The Governor's House Bed And Breakfast

Embry Cross Road
(mailing address:
500 Meadowlake
Lane, Talladega 35160)
Lincoln, Alabama 35160
(205) 763-3366;
fax (256) 362-2391

E-MAIL: gaineslaw@aol.com

WEB SITE: www.hotel-intel.com/prophome

INNKEEPERS: Mary Sue and Ralph Gaines

ROOMS: 4; 2 with private bath; all with radio, desk, and ceiling fan; limited wheelchair access

ON THE GROUNDS: Tennis court, antiques shop, swimming pool, boat ramp, fishing pier

RATES: $75 to $150 double, including full breakfast; reduced rates for renting the entire house

CREDIT CARDS ACCEPTED? Not at this time

OPEN: Year-round

HOW TO GET THERE: From I-20, take exit 165 and go south 2 miles to Embry Cross Road. The Governor's House is on your right.

The stately Greek Revival Governor's House gives new meaning to the term *mobile home.* The house was built in 1850 in nearby Talladega by Alabama Governor Lewis Parsons, but Mary Sue and Ralph had it moved to their Meadowlake Farm in 1990. Completely restored and furnished with family antiques, heirlooms, and quilts, the house now serves as an elegant bed and breakfast.

In many cases a B&B's allure is the house itself, or its owners. In the case of the Governor's House, you'll find all this and even more—the peaceful, bucolic setting, the farm animals, the varied things to do. Located on a knoll overlooking Logan Martin Lake, the house sits amid rolling green pastures, split-rail fences, and grazing cattle. We could spend our days endlessly strolling down the winding farm road, fishing in the bass-stocked pond, taking a pontoon-boat ride on the lake, sitting on the veranda, or feeding the horses, chickens, ducks, and pet goats. Browsing through the Horse Barn Antique Gallery, located in a former pig pallor, is a pleasant way to while away some time as well. Type-A personalities can enjoy the lighted plexipaved tennis court and even make arrangements for private instruction.

Mary Sue and Ralph become not just hosts but friends with their guests, who often return because they like being treated like home folks. Both enjoy reading, antiquing, tennis, and boating—though Lord knows how they find the time, what with being farmers as well.

Awaken to the sounds of cows lowing and birds chirping. After enjoying coffee and juice on the veranda, you'll be summoned by a dinner bell to a typical farm breakfast of fresh fruit and juice, eggs or a cheese soufflé, grits, a breakfast meat, fresh-baked biscuits, and sweet rolls with homemade jellies and strawberry butter. If that doesn't keep you going all day, a guest refrigerator is stocked with juices, cheese, breads, wine, and soft drinks. Afternoon tea and a dessert are served. If you don't want to leave the idyllic property even for meals, the Gaineses will also prepare lunch and dinner for an additional fee.

And here's another little extra: The Gaineses' son-in-law operates a veterinary practice nearby. If you're traveling with a pet, you can have it boarded there.

What's Nearby Lincoln

Lincoln offers a lot of outdoor activities, like bicycling, canoeing, fishing, golfing, and hiking. If you have the need for speed, take a quick ride to Talladega, home of the International Motorsports Hall of Fame and Talladega Superspeedway. You'll enjoy exhibits of vintage cars, drag racers, and motorcycles.

Magnolia Springs Bed and Breakfast

Best Buy

14469 Oak Street
(mailing address: P.O. Box 329)
Magnolia Springs, Alabama 36555
(334) 965-7321 or (800) 965-7321

E-MAIL: msbbdw@gulftel.com

WEB SITE: www.bbonline.com/al/magnolia
or www.bbhost.com/magnoliaspringsbb

INNKEEPER: David Worthington

ROOMS: 4 rooms and 1 suite; all with private bath, alarm clock, ceiling fan, cable TV, and telephone with data port; ask about pets

ON THE GROUNDS: Porches, manicured grounds

RATES: $94 and up double, including full breakfast and afternoon refreshments; extended-stay discounts; rates may be higher and a minimum stay required for holidays and special events

CREDIT CARDS ACCEPTED? Yes

OPEN: Year-round

HOW TO GET THERE: From US 98 in Magnolia Springs, take County Highway 49 south at the Conoco station. Go 4 blocks and turn right onto Oak Street between the Moore Bros. Fresh Market and the Magnolia Springs Community Center. The B&B is 0.2 mile ahead on your right at the corner of Oak and Jessamine; it's identified by a large sign.

This venerable hundred-plus-year-old house has a long hospitality tradition. From 1913 into the 1930s, it operated as the Sunnyside Hotel, better known to locals as Mrs. Harper's; even after the hotel closed, Sunday dinner was served here well into the 1950s. What could be more natural than that the home now serve as a bed and breakfast? Energetic innkeeper David Worthington treats every guest like a valued friend and serves as a walking advertisement for area restaurants and attractions. He's been in love with the area since he vacationed here with his uncle as a child.

Approached by a canopy arch of old oaks and surrounded by plenty of others, the one-and-a-half-story cottage features steep gables and a wraparound veranda made from heart pine and enhanced by turned posts and balusters. Inside, walls and ceilings are constructed of rare beaded yellow heart pine. Mostly stained rather than painted, the floors are of heart pine, and the woodwork is curly pine. All the balusters, rails, and newel posts are original, as is the wavy glass in the windows. The excellent restoration work has earned the house a place on the State Board of Historical Homes and the National Register of Historic Places.

Guests rooms, one of which is on the first floor and four of which are tucked up under the eaves (and therefore characterized by little nooks created by the sloping ceilings), are named for the current and past owners. Located on the first floor, the McLennan Suite is named for Christopher McLennan, who built the house in 1897. It features a beautiful iron king-size canopy bed and a bathroom with the original claw-foot tub and an elephant trunk toilet with a water closet. The Harding Suite, which has a separate sitting room, is named for the former owners who operated the Sunnyside Hotel, the Cowen Room for Mrs. Harding's sister and her husband who inherited the house after her death, the McNair Room for a couple who owned the house in the 1980s, and the Worthington Room for the present owner. Bedding in these rooms range from queens to a double and a twin; furnishings are an eclectic mix of antiques and contemporary pieces. Fresh flowers grace the rooms, and there's a book swap for guests who enjoy reading.

Guests gather for relaxation and conversation in the formal great hall, where a magnolia print hangs over a fireplace surrounded by overstuffed furniture; the bright and airy Florida room; the dining room, where a full breakfast is served; or on the veranda. David serves a full home-style repast or a light breakfast, depending on guests' desires. The neatly manicured grounds make a pleasant stroll, and it's 1½ blocks from the Magnolia River.

Magnolia Springs is located at the headwaters of the Magnolia River. From earliest times the community has been accessible by small craft and steam packets. Because of the natural springs and abundant fish and wildlife, the area attracted settlers early on. In the 1890s Magnolia Springs began to attract the attention of winter-weary Northerners. Magnolia Springs remains a quiet community tucked away off the main road. The mail is still delivered by boat to those lucky enough to live along the river.

What's Nearby Magnolia Springs

Magnolia Springs offers great art galleries, golf, hiking, and sailing. Visit the Magnolia River and Mobile Bay. Enjoy the local antiques shopping. And venture out to nearby towns such as Point Clear, Fairhope, and Gulf Shores.

Myrtle Hill

303–305 West Lafayette Street
Marion, Alabama 36756
(334) 683–9095

INNKEEPERS: Wanda and Gerald Lewis

ROOMS: 6 rooms, 4 with private bath; all with decorative fireplaces, mid-1800s antiques, clock; some with TV

ON THE GROUNDS: Verandas, ample grounds, gardens

RATES: $85 to $95 double, including full plantation breakfast served in the formal dining room and refreshments all day

CREDIT CARDS ACCEPTED? Yes

OPEN: Year-round

HOW TO GET THERE: From I–59, take exit 97, Centreville–West Blocton. Go south on AL 5 into town. One block past the caution light, turn right onto West Lafayette.

We came to Marion on an odyssey: We were doing research for several books and articles, as well as searching for Carol's roots. Although her family was from Fort Deposit near Montgomery, her uncle attended the Marion Military Institute (before going to West Point) and all her great-aunts attended Marion's Judson College (the only remaining women's college in Alabama). The family ties made us more than welcome everywhere we went in Marion. In fact, when the folks at the Alabama Women's Hall of Fame at Judson learned we'd inherited china decorated with historic campus buildings from the aunts, they gave us a matching cup and saucer. Alabamians are like that; they want to know who your people are—not for snobby reasons—but to find common ground.

Myrtle Hill was just one of the gems we found in Marion. The stately 1840 Greek Revival mansion features a hip roof and four pillars supporting full-length first- and second-floor verandas. The floor plan is unusual for the period in that the upstairs and downstairs halls are to one side of the house rather than centrally placed. Myrtle Hill was built for George D. Johnson, a brigadier general in the Confederate States of America. Before the Civil War Johnson served as the mayor of Marion and as a representative in the Alabama Legislature. After the war he served as the commandant of cadets at the University of Alabama, superintendent of the South Carolina Military Academy (the Citadel), and later an Alabama senator.

Current owners Wanda and Gerald Lewis—Gerry is the current commandant at MMI—have lovingly restored the mansion and furnished it with elegant eighteenth- and nineteenth-century antiques. They live in an equally lovely mansion next door, so guests have the complete run of Myrtle Hill. We easily fell under its spell, imagining ourselves as master and mistress of all we surveyed. We tried the formal parlor for a while, but just like at home ended up relaxing for the late afternoon and evening in the comfortable, informal enclosed sunroom.

The palatial upstairs guest room in which we stayed boasted a private bath and a 1700s tester bed custom-made for Baron de Graffenreid that's so high it takes a three-step stool to climb into. Other bedchambers may have tester or heavily carved beds. No matter which room becomes yours, you'll enjoy high ceilings, hardwood floors, period art, and a sofa or love seat. Some rooms have decorative fireplaces as well, which add to the romantic period ambience.

The next morning we awoke to delicious aromas from the kitchen; Wanda was preparing a bountiful breakfast. The dining room, dominated by a magnificently carved and gilded mirror, was set for a formal plantation breakfast. A crisp white tablecloth accentuated with Battenburg lace provided the backdrop for a fresh floral arrangement and exquisite china, silver, and crystal. As Wanda bustled in and out with various courses, she regaled us with some ghost stories about the house. We won't spoil them, so be sure to ask her. Morning menus might include omelettes, a breakfast casserole, or blueberry pancakes accompanied by grits, fruits, juices, and nut breads.

Perched on a hill, the five-acre property is shaded by (naturally) stately myrtles, and other aged trees, with ample space for Victorian gardens and a new water garden with a small waterfall. If we hadn't been so busy with other pursuits, we'd have spent daylight hours wandering the grounds or relaxing in the rockers on any of several upstairs and downstairs porches.

Wanda and Gerry are very helpful in suggesting places to go, things to see, and not-to-be-missed places to eat. Among the latter are the Gateway Inn for a substantial lunch buffet, or Del's Tea Room and Interiors for antiques shopping and a light lunch.

What's Nearby Marion

Get to know Marion, and visit Judson College, the Marion Military Institute, and the Marion Genealogical Library. You can tour the Alabama Women's Hall of Fame and the Alabama Military Hall of Honor. Marion also offers a host of unique antiques shops.

Mountain Laurel Inn

64 Road 948/East River Road
Mentone, Alabama 35984
(256) 634-4673 or (800) 889-4244

WEB SITE: www.bbonline/al/mli
INNKEEPER: Sarah Wilcox
ROOMS: 5; all with private bath and TV
ON THE GROUNDS: Porches, seven acres

RATES: $85 to $125 single or double, including full breakfast; ask about winter and weekday discounts

CREDIT CARDS ACCEPTED? Yes

OPEN: Year-round except December 23 through 25

HOW TO GET THERE: From AL 117 in Cloudland, Georgia, you'll see a MENTONE CITY LIMIT sign on your right. Look for the Moon Lake Baptist Church on your left. Turn past the church onto East River Road (County 165). At the stop sign, look for signs to the B&B.

We consider a secluded setting surrounded by natural beauty profoundly romantic, and the Mountain Laurel Inn filled the bill for us. Not only is the inn nestled in deep woods just a short stroll from a bluff overlooking the dramatic Little River Canyon and DeSoto Falls, but it's located next to the tiny, rustic Mentone Wedding Chapel, and one of the guest rooms is the especially romantic Bridal Room. Just think—you could have a small private wedding at the chapel, then spend your honeymoon at the Mountain Laurel Inn, named for the lush stand of laurels clinging to the bluff below DeSoto Falls. In fact, making things perfect for newlyweds is Sarah's mission.

Rustic with a touch of class describes the ambience. Sarah lives in a contemporary home that blends right into the landscape; four guest rooms and a two-room suite are located in a separate guest house. Guests come over to the big house for a delicious full breakfast and are encouraged to use the inviting great room to watch television, borrow something to read from the well-stocked library, play games, or get to know Sarah and fellow guests. A former storage building is in the process of being converted into another tempting place to relax. A porch, several windows, and doors have been added; the building will have a refrigerator, microwave, game table, and fireplace.

Cozy rooms in the guest cottage are simple but nicely decorated, and offer basic modern conveniences: private baths and television. In addition to the Bridal Room, you'll find the Wildflower, Ski, and Deer Rooms. Three of the four have queen-size beds, the fourth a pair of twins. The suite has a king-size bed, a trundle bed, and a small kitchen. Each opens onto a deeply shaded porch with rockers where we sat with tea and coffee and a good book, but found ourselves drinking in the scenery and watching the wildlife rather than reading.

We spent time hiking through the seven-acre property, peeking into the wedding chapel, taking the ten-minute walk to beautiful DeSoto Falls, and just sitting on our porch rocking. All that fresh mountain air and exercise guaranteed that we slept like babies. In the morning we awoke refreshed to find carafes of tea and coffee waiting on our porch to be sipped while we got ready for breakfast, which is served family-style in the main house. Guests begin the meal with a special bread, such as zucchini, carrot, or lemon, followed by an entree like breakfast pizza, egg and sausage casserole, or eggs rancheros.

The Mentone area has a large concentration of summer camps, and it was when Sarah attended Camp DeSoto as a teenager that she fell in love with the natural beauty of the region and vowed to come back permanently. In addition to running the B&B, she's also now the camp's accountant. She sends out a newsletter with gossip about the inn and the Mentone area, one of her recipes, comments guests have written, and a quirky column from her golden retriever, Baxter, whom Sarah says even gets mail from past guests. Baxter takes his job as guest relations manager very seriously. He'll be more than happy to guide you to the falls.

What's Nearby Mentone

Mentone is a great site for outdoor excursions. Visit DeSoto Falls State Park, Little River Canyon, and Sequoyah Caverns. Attend the May Rhododendron Festival and October Colorfest Festival. Explore the Cloudmont Ski and Golf Resort. Try mountain biking and horseback riding. And don't forget to visit the local antiques stores and restaurants.

Other Recommended B&Bs in Mentone

Mentone Inn Bed & Breakfast, a small mountain hotel built in 1927, offers 12 rooms, cabin, private baths, and full breakfast; Highway 117, Box 290, Mentone, AL 35984; (256) 634-4836 or (800) 455-7470. *Mentone Springs Hotel,* an 1884 Queen Anne Victorian hotel, offers 9 rooms and 1 suite and a 3-bedroom cottage that sleeps six; 6114 Highway 117, Mentone, AL 35984; (256) 634-4040 or (800) 404-0100. *Raven Haven* offers 4 rooms with private bath and full breakfast in a contemporary home; 651 County Road 644, Mentone, AL 35984; (256) 634-4310.

Molly Young's Bed and Breakfast

Best Buy

504 Church Street
Mobile, Alabama 36602
(334) 438-9478

INNKEEPERS: Darlene Lane and Mary Odell

ROOMS: 4; all with private bath; TV and clock radio on request

ON THE GROUNDS: Veranda

RATES: $85 to $110 double, including full breakfast and afternoon refreshments; discount for multinight stay; ask about single and corporate rates

CREDIT CARDS ACCEPTED? Not at this time

OPEN: Year-round

NOTE: Transitional neighborhood

HOW TO GET THERE: From I-10, take the Canal Street exit and go straight ahead to the second traffic light, which is at Church Street. Turn left. The bed and breakfast is in the middle of the fourth block on your right.

A quaint picket fence with a scalloped top and ancient trees frame Molly Young's, located in the East Church Street historic district—a neighborhood on its way back up from sadder days. Painted in the authentic Victorian manner, the charming two-story house with a wraparound veranda and a small upstairs porch is a soft green with several bright accent colors highlighting the windows, moldings, spindles, and other architectural details.

The turn-of-the-century home is named for Mary Ailey "Molly" Young, Darlene's great-aunt (her grandmother's sister). Born in 1880, Molly was the third of eleven children in a family of farmers, quilters, and Old Harp singers. She was quilting one afternoon in 1899 when one of her younger brothers began teasing her with a Civil War gun. What started as a game ended tragically when Molly was shot and killed. This house was built the same year.

Inside Darlene and Mary have successfully re-created the excess that was so typical of the Victorian era—rich dark colors, stained-glass windows, multiple patterns of fabrics and wallpaper, furniture and accessories packed into every nook and cranny, patterns painted onto moldings and ceilings. The decor, true to the period, could be described as eccentric or quirky. We hardly knew where to look next.

Guests love to gather and relax in the comfortable charm of the Victorian parlor, which is well supplied with games and books. Of course, in nice weather you might prefer to lounge in the rockers or old-fashioned porch swing on the front veranda, where you can catch some of the refreshing breezes that come up from the Mobile River not far away.

Each guest room features a dramatically draped bed, a small sitting area, and a bathroom with a claw-foot tub and a pedestal sink. Every bed—two are doubles and two have been modified to accommodate queen-size mattresses—is a masterpiece. One is an 1830 tester, another a four-poster, yet another an elaborate Renaissance bed with a 1-foot headboard, and last but not least an 1870 walnut Eastlake bed with a mirror incorporated into the headboard. Most often requested for honeymoons is the front room, which has access onto the second-story porch. Darlene and Mary fill its voluminous mosquito netting with balloons for honeymooners. They tell us that one ultra-romantic couple had delivered ahead of time a large basket of rose petals for Darlene and Mary to scatter on the bed and in the bath before they arrived. They'll be glad to help you create your fantasies.

You'll greet each day with a full Southern breakfast served family-style in the dining room. Tantalizing treats created from old family recipes include such dishes as tomato gravy with hot sausage, creamed salmon on toast, and smothered chicken legs that never fail to elicit requests for seconds, as well as fresh fruit, something sweet, chicory coffee, and the ever-present bowl of grits.

What's Nearby Mobile

Mobile is known for its enormous oak trees and springtime azaleas. In March the city showcases its azaleas in the annual Azalea Trail Festival. You'll enjoy historic districts, like the Church Street area, DeTonti Square, and Oakleigh Garden. Learn all about Mobile's history at the Museum of Mobile. You might also tour the decks of the battleship U.S.S. *Alabama.*

Towle House

1104 Montauk Avenue
Mobile, Alabama 36604
(334) 432-6440 or (800) 938-6953

E-MAIL: TOWLEBB@aol.com

WEB SITE: www.towle-house.com

INNKEEPERS: Carolyn and Felix Vereen

ROOMS: 3; all with private bath, TV, telephone, ceiling fan

ON THE GROUNDS: Sundeck, patio, gardens

RATES: $85 single or double, including full gourmet breakfast and afternoon refreshments; discount for multiple nights

CREDIT CARDS ACCEPTED? Yes

OPEN: Year-round

HOW TO GET THERE: From I-10, take exit 26B, US 90; go west on Government Street to Hallett Street. Turn north and continue 1 block to Montauk. The B&B is on the corner.

Carolyn and Felix offered us Southern hospitality at its best in their beautiful historic home. The large lot abounding with azaleas, dogwoods, and seasonal flowers is a perfect backdrop for the 1874 Italianate mansion. Amos Towle built the structure as the Towle Institute, a boys' school; it served as classrooms and quarters for boarding students as well as his home. The school continued until 1893 when Towle retired.

Constructed of heart pine and cypress, the mansion features beautiful floors, high ceilings, traditional moldings, and large windows that admit plenty of light. Furnished with antiques and embellished with Oriental rugs and lacy window treatments, the Towle House exudes Old South charm.

Elegantly appointed guest rooms are named for flowers found on the grounds: Rose, Magnolia, and Azalea. The largest and most luxurious—and therefore most popular—is the Magnolia Room, which features a four-poster rice bed and a formal sitting area. The Rose Room boasts a queen-size four-poster rice bed, lovely mirrored armoire, and sitting area. A high-back carved bed is the focal point of the Azalea Room, which overlooks the garden and the courtyard. Created to preserve the spaciousness of the guest rooms, the bathrooms feature showers.

Although the Towle House has a lovely formal parlor, our choice for the most pleasant place to relax is the Florida room. This informal, glass-enclosed space incorporates the rear stairway, so a portion of the room is two stories high. For those who love light as much as we do, this room has extra-special charm.

In addition to a delicious gourmet breakfast of juice, fruit compote, an egg main dish or pancakes with a breakfast meat, and rolls or sweet rolls served in the formal dining room, the Vereens offer evening wine and hors d'oeuvres. Honeymoon and anniversary couples receive a special surprise.

What's Nearby Mobile

See page 31 for what's nearby Mobile.

The Lattice Inn Best Buy

1414 South Hull Street
Montgomery, Alabama 36104
(334) 832–9931 or (800) 525–0652

E-MAIL: Michaelp41@aol.com

WEB SITE: www.members.aol.com/ latticeinn

INNKEEPER: Michael Pierce

ROOMS: 4; all with private bath, radio, clock, desk, fan; 2 rooms have computer hookups; 2 rooms wheelchair accessible

ON THE GROUNDS: Porches, decks, patio, hot tub, fish pond, lap pool

RATES: $75 to $85 double, including full breakfast, cookies, fruit basket; additional person $5; discount for three-night stay or longer

CREDIT CARDS ACCEPTED? Yes

OPEN: Year-round

HOW TO GET THERE: From I–85, exit at Union Street and go west on the service road to Hull Street. Take Hull south to the inn; it's on your right between Maury and Earl.

Hurry to the Lattice Inn while Michael Pierce is still there, because the inn is for sale. Affectionately known as the Cookie Man, Michael is so famous for his homemade oatmeal chocolate chip cookies that he's published the *Meet the Cookie Man* cookbook. He'll be missed. New owners will have big shoes to fill.

Michael bakes about 2,000 cookies a month and leaves them in old-fashioned apothecary jars in the guest rooms; he'll also send a bag with you when you leave. In addition to cookie recipes, the cookbook also includes recipes for his most popular dishes, including breakfasts, breads, main dishes, soups, and salads. Many are from treasured family recipes and are accompanied by helpful hints and delightful anecdotes.

The Lattice Inn is a very good example of not being able to tell a book by its cover. The totally nondescript 1906 cottage, distinguished only by its lattice-enclosed porch, is located in the historic Garden District. That's where "ordinary" stops, however. The inside, which features 12-foot ceilings, is beautifully decorated and the grounds are especially inviting, with the added attractions of a lap pool, hot tub, sundecks, and gardens. The Lattice Inn has been singled out with such awards as the Mayor's Hospitality Award and one of the Top 25 America's Favorite Inn Awards. It has also been recognized as offering some of the best gourmet coffee in Montgomery. A testament to Michael's hospitality philosophy, "to be attentive without intruding on guests' privacy," is the large percentage of return guests.

On the main level two bedrooms feature high ceilings and tall windows. The William J. Room, which was the original master suite, has a decorative fireplace, a four-poster bed Michael built himself, matching bed coverings and window treatments, and a sitting area with a love seat. Its bathroom boasts an original claw-foot tub, a basin built into an antique chest, and a separate walk-in shower. Aunt Myrtle's Bedroom was the original dining room. She loved cooking and entertaining so it seemed only natural to name this bedchamber for her. This special room features a wood-burning fireplace, an intricately carved mahogany four-poster bed, and a modern bath with a corner shower and pedestal sink. Downstairs on the garden level, Lucille's Hide-A-Way and Lynn's Place are smaller and have lower ceilings, but they feature private entrances and a television and small refrigerator. The beds in Lucille's can be configured as two twins or a king. The headboard of the king-size bed in Lynn's is an antique door. These rooms can be turned into a suite by closing the door to the hallway. Personal touches in all the rooms include fresh flowers, cookies, and fruit.

Guests may like to gather in the formal living room or the library—both with fireplaces—or on the lattice-trimmed porch, but it's the backyard that appeals to most. Several levels of decks provide space for the lap pool and hot tub and lead down to an Oriental meditation garden. Dimly lit lanterns and flickering candles along the path during the evening hours will turn you into a hopeless romantic. So will the steam rising from the hot tub to drift across the moon.

Breakfast varies according to Michael's mood. Although he says he never sticks to a recipe, whatever he creates is magnificent. Your morning repast might feature delicious oven-baked French toast with blackberries, sausage, and Waldorf salad—or any number of other imaginative dishes.

What's Nearby Montgomery

All the world's a stage, and the men are merely players at the Alabama Shakespeare Festival. Hundreds of thousands of visitors from all over the world flock to this Alabama stage, which claims to be the fifth largest Shakespeare festival in the world. The multi-million-dollar complex performs everything from the Bard to Tennesse Williams. Also visit the Montgomery Museum of Fine Arts, which exhibits American art.

The Heritage House Bed and Breakfast

Best Buy

714 Second Avenue
Opelika, Alabama 36801
(334) 705-0485

INNKEEPERS: Barbara and Richard Patton

ROOMS: 5; all with private bath, telephone, and cable TV; computer access via phone in room; limited wheelchair access

ON THE GROUNDS: Gift shop in carriage house

RATES: $65 to $85 single or double, including full breakfast and refreshments; corporate rates

CREDIT CARDS ACCEPTED? Yes

OPEN: Year-round except Christmas Day

HOW TO GET THERE: From I–85, take exit 62 toward Opelika. Turn right onto Sixth Street. Continue to Second Avenue, turn left and go 2 blocks. The B&B is on the corner of Eighth Street and Second Avenue. Park in the back.

The first thing that caught our eye was the stunningly beautiful semicircular portico supported by six soaring fluted columns topped by ornate Corinthian capitals. Behind the columns is the gorgeous redbrick Neoclassical Revival Heritage House, a one-of-a-kind mansion in Opelika.

The house was built by the W. E. Davis family around 1913 or 1914 to serve as a residence and, in its declining years, as an antiques shop. In choosing to preserve the house, Barbara and her son, Richard, had to determine how to make it pay for itself. They decided to make it a comfortably elegant home with spacious bed-and-breakfast guest rooms, as well as a special-events facility. In addition, they operate Heritage House Gifts, an upscale boutique, in their carriage house.

When we entered the front doors, we stepped into a formal reception area well suited for social functions. Then we took in the hardwood floors, high ceilings, and Craftsman-style architectural details. Furnishings throughout the house are period antiques and reproductions, many of them for sale. In addition to the formal parlor and dining room, the downstairs is occupied by a cheery sunroom and one of the guest rooms.

A stately staircase leads to the second floor, where there are four more romantic guest chambers. One boasts a canopy bed; the other three have four-posters. The bathing arrangements are pretty romantic, too. One room sports a whirlpool tub, one a claw-foot tub, and one—incredibly—two claw-foot tubs. Two of the upstairs bedrooms have access onto a shared balcony above the porte cochere. The long central hall on this floor leads out to the balcony under the portico. Either of these outdoor porches makes a wonderful private retreat.

Richard handles the gourmet breakfasts. In addition to essentials such as hot beverages, juice, and a breakfast meat, he might fix such entrees as baked Mexican eggs or one of several different kinds of French toast—caramel, pecan, or orange. He'll also prepare grits on request. Guests can choose to dine informally in the cheery sunroom or more formally in the stately dining room with its lovely ceramic-tile fireplace.

In our extensive search for exciting B&Bs to write about, we often find that elegant historic homes are so overdecorated that there seems to be scarcely a square inch of unembellished wall or floor space. Sometimes your eye and your mind can't find a place to rest. The only small criticism we have of the Heritage House, and it's purely personal, is that it leans too far the other way—the look is very understated, almost spare.

Be sure to browse through the gift shop and get a cup of gourmet coffee. There'll surely be some real finds you can't live without.

The Original Romar House Bed and Breakfast Inn

23500 Perdido Beach Boulevard
Orange Beach, Alabama 36561
(334) 974-1625 or
(800) 487-6627

E-MAIL: original@gulftel.com

WEB SITE: www.bbonline.com/al/romarhouse/

INNKEEPERS: Jerry M. Gilbreath, owner; Darrell Finley, innkeeper

ROOMS: 6 rooms, 1 cottage; all with private bath, clock radio, ceiling fan

ON THE GROUNDS: Hot tub, deck, beach, hammock, swing, courtyard with fountain

RATES: $79 to $129 double (depending on season), including full breakfast and afternoon wine and cheese; additional person $20; two-night minimum stay on weekends; rates higher during holidays, festivals, and special events

CREDIT CARDS ACCEPTED? Yes

OPEN: Year-round

HOW TO GET THERE: From I-10, go south on AL 59. Turn left onto AL 182. Go 4.1 miles to the inn.

The Original Romar House is our idea of the ultimate sandcastle. Our friends Karen and Ron Sliwa, who lived next door to us for eighteen years, stayed at this B&B when they visited the Alabama Gulf Coast. They loved it and the area so much, they up and moved to Orange Beach. After seeing this B&B for ourselves, we can understand what captured their hearts. It's casual and funky, not prim and proper. This is the place for a perfect beach getaway; a place where you can let your hair down and put your feet up. Best of all, it reminds us of the beach cottages we used to go to with our grandparents—low-slung frame construction, wrapped with porches. In fact, Jerry says, "I wanted it to remind people of their old family vacation houses—vacation the way it used to be and should be." Charming as the house is, the real draw is, of course, its beachfront location.

One of the oldest houses along the coast, Romar House was built in 1924. There weren't even any roads here then. Spurgeon Roach was so determined to build here that he had to have the lumber floated down the beach pulled by a mule team. Roach took the first two letters of his last name and combined them with the first three letters of his friend Carl Martin's last name to create the name Romar House. In time, as the area started to develop, Romar Beach took its name from the house. Jerry bought the house in 1980, restored it, and opened it as Alabama's first seaside inn in 1991. He's been assisted by Darrell as innkeeper since 1996.

Jerry scoured the country for materials and accessories with which to restore and improve Romar House. Primarily decorated in art deco style, its eclectic charms include stained-glass windows, an 1800s tiger oak bar from a New Hampshire inn, cypress doors and wainscoting from a turn-of-the-century New Orleans home, brass sconces from a Washington, D.C., home near the White House, and a fountain from a French castle. The front door is from Australia. Old Chicago bricks were used for the walkway to the beach.

Each guest room is named for a local festival and has a queen-size bed, along with an original bedroom set from the 1920s. The popular Shrimp Festival Room, for instance, is done in shrimp and coral tones and features oak trim and stained glass; the Sea Oats Festival Room is done in pink and teal. You get the idea. In all there are four doubles, one single, one suite, and one cottage.

Breakfast—which might include fresh fruit, eggs, and biscuits and honey one day and peach pancakes, hash browns, and bacon the next—is served either in the dining room at a table handcrafted of heart pine by the original owner, or out on the spacious deck. When guests need to come in out of the sun, they gather in the Purple Parrot Bar, where complimentary wine and cheese are served at sunset and drinks are available on the honor system.

Stroll along the beach collecting seashells, curl up in a swing or hammock to read a good book or take a nap, relax in the outdoor hot tub, listen to the palm trees rustling in the wind, smell the salty air, let the Gulf breeze caress you. What more could you ask?

What's Nearby Orange Beach

Charter boats at Orange Beach marinas offer sunset cruises and fishing trips. Orange Beach is next to Gulf Shores, where you can golf, fish, swim, and play tennis at the Gulf State Park Resort.

The Lodge on Gorham's Bluff

101 Gorham Drive
Pisgah, Alabama 35765
(256) 451–3435

WEB SITE: www.thebluff.com

INNKEEPERS: Bill, Clara, and Dawn McGriff, owners

ROOMS: 6; all with private bath, single or double whirlpool tub, clock, desk, ceiling fan, working fireplace; 4 with private shuttered porches; telephone by request. Wheelchair access only to common areas and dining room

ON THE GROUNDS: Porches, decks, gazebo, lawn games

RATES: Rooms $120 to $175, including full breakfast; additional person $10

CREDIT CARDS ACCEPTED? Yes

OPEN: Year-round

HOW TO GET THERE: From Pisgah, follow Jackson County Road 58 for 2.2 miles. Turn left onto County Road 357 and go 1.2 miles. Turn left onto County Road 457. Follow it 0.7 mile and turn right onto Main Street.

This sounds like a tall tale, but it's for real. In 1992 Bill and Clara McGriff and their daughter Dawn set out to develop a complete town on 186 acres they owned on a 1½-mile bluff overlooking the Tennessee River in the foothills of the Appalachian Mountains. They started with a few houses, shops, a wedding pavilion, and a performance amphitheater where summer theater, storytelling, and chamber-music performances are given periodically.

Next came the lodge high atop Sand Mountain, with its long back porch yielding spectacular views. Now, don't get the idea that this is a rustic mountain log cabin with knotty-pine paneling. Rather, it's built in the style of a grand Southern mansion, with columned verandas wrapping around both the first and second floors of the white clapboard structure and a belvedere perching on top. Inside, common rooms feature cream-colored clapboard walls, hardwood floors, and enormous fieldstone fireplaces. Oriental carpets and traditional furnishings give a touch of elegance.

Six spacious guest rooms boast king- or queen-size beds, whirlpool tubs, sitting areas or separate sitting rooms, and gas-log fireplaces. Hardwood floors gleam in the light admitted through tall windows and French doors out onto the private, shuttered verandas. The focal point of each room is a graceful white mantel against a stacked-stone chimney, but carefully chosen furniture, rich fabrics—often handcrafted—and interesting art and accessories give each guest chamber a feeling of both elegance and intimacy. Deserving of special mention are the Owens and Roden Rooms. These rooms have cathedral ceilings with exposed beams, double-size whirlpool tubs, and separate sitting rooms. The lodge supplies every comfort for a very special Appalachian hideaway.

Breakfast, a substantial meal, features a buffet of fresh fruits and juices, egg dishes or a casserole, cheese grits, and biscuits. Dinner is available to guests by request at an additional fee.

A visit to Gorham's Bluff might make you a permanent residence. The new town is built in the tradition of the small towns that thrived in the United States at the turn of the century. Three-hundred-and-fifty residential homesites are grouped into six neighborhoods and are all in close proximity to the town green, post office, shops, and meeting house. A workshop district attracts artists, who live and work there. There's even an assisted living facility. Prescribed setbacks, building heights, roof pitches, and overhangs ensure a consistent look. Front porches are even required to encourage residents to extend themselves from the privacy of their homes into neighborhood activity. Swimming pools, garden pavilions, tennis courts, parks, and lakes are spread throughout the community.

What's Nearby Pisgah

Pisgah will feel like home to the outdoor enthusiast. Lace up those hiking boots and explore Pisgah's hiking trails. Bring your bicycle and ride through downtown. Or break out your fly rod and go fishing at Weiss Lake or in the Tennessee River.

Grace Hall Bed and Breakfast

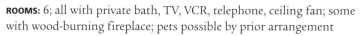

506 Lauderdale Street
Selma, Alabama 36701
(334) 875-5744

E-MAIL: adman@wwisp.com

WEB SITE: www.olcg.com/selma/
gracehal.html or www.traveldata.
com/inns/data/alstbb.html

INNKEEPERS: Joey and Coy Dillon

ROOMS: 6; all with private bath, TV, VCR, telephone, ceiling fan; some
with wood-burning fireplace; pets possible by prior arrangement

ON THE GROUNDS: Verandas, courtyard

RATES: $79 to $99 double, including full breakfast, afternoon refreshments, and a tour of the mansion

CREDIT CARDS ACCEPTED? Yes

OPEN: Year-round

HOW TO GET THERE: Take Highway 80 West to the Selma city limits, then
take Business 80 West. Cross the Pettus Bridge and go four traffic lights
to Dallas Avenue. Turn left onto Lauderdale. Grace Hall is on your right.

A consummate example of the delightful eclecticism that pervaded Alabama architecture in the middle of the eighteenth century, Grace Hall combines elements of the older neoclassicism with newer Victorian trends.

Grace Hall was built by Henry Ware in 1857 at a cost of $29,000—a princely sum in those days. In 1863 Madison Jackson Williams, who became mayor of Selma, purchased the property. Only two years later Williams stood on his front porch to give an encouraging speech to bedraggled Confederate troops embarking on the Battle of Selma—one of the last battles of the Civil War. Two days later Union officers of Wilson's Raiders imprisoned Mayor Williams and took possession of the house for their headquarters. Considering that 60 percent of Selma was burned to the ground by Union troops, the fact that the mansion was occupied by federal troops probably ensured its survival. After sitting empty for three years, the mansion was purchased by Anna Evans for use as a boardinghouse.

The astute reader will be asking by this time, "Who was Grace?"—after whom the house was named. It seems that Mrs. Evans enlisted her niece Eliza Jones and her family to help run the boardinghouse. Grace Jones, who was born in the house on October 4, 1898, was Eliza's daughter. Miss Grace resided in the house for eighty years until it was condemned and she was forced to give up her lifelong home. As the longest resident of the house, it seemed only appropriate to name the mansion for her. After the house was condemned, the local historical society assumed the responsibility for finding someone to restore it; they found Joey and Coy, who purchased it in 1981. Their prodigious restoration effort took five years, after which the Dillons opened Grace Hall as a bed and breakfast and special-events facility. Grace Hall has hosted many notable guests, including a former first lady and stars of stage and screen.

As soon as you step through the front door and say your hellos to the Dillons, turn around and look back at the glass surrounding the front door. When the sun shines through, what looked like dark glass from the outside is revealed to be a brilliant ruby color with floral designs etched in. Drink in the high ceilings, burnished hardwood floors, Oriental carpets, opulent Victorian furnishings, crystal and brass chandeliers, and graceful fireplaces. We were particularly impressed with the collection of large gilt-framed mirrors, some of them practically floor to ceiling, and with the paintings.

Sumptuous accommodations are offered in the main house and adjacent two-story servants' quarters, with full-length verandas on both floors. Opulent guest chambers in the main house are spacious and high ceilinged; those in the servants' quarters are more cozy, but none the less elegant. Beds—some of which are ornately carved canopy rice beds—are queen or king size; bathrooms have showers.

Lovely English gardens wrapping around the mansion invite you to wander, absorbing the quiet setting as well as the delightful sights and aromas. Discreetly hidden from the street between the two houses is a New Orleans-style courtyard with a central fountain—an ideal place to sit with morning coffee, a cool drink, a good book, or the love of your life. We arrived on a pleasant afternoon when the weather just begged us to sit outside and enjoy a glass of wine. As Carol was reclining on a wicker chaise with a book, a friendly feline resident hopped up on her chest, inserting himself between her face and the book, as cats are so wont to do. We loved it; it reminded us of home and our own pets.

Old Miss, Miz Eliza, Pappy King, and Other Residents of Grace Hall

Anna Evans purchased Grace Hall after the Civil War to run as a boarding-house. Known as Old Miss, she brought with her Pappy King, an old black man who had worked on the Evans plantation and felt that at his advanced age, he didn't want emancipation. Mrs. Evans also enlisted the aid of her niece Eliza Jones. This trio, along with a former boarder named Mr. Satterfield and an unidentified spirit, have been known to appear to the current owners, Joey and Coy, and their guests.

Joey and Coy first encountered Miz Eliza in the summer of 1982 while they were photographing their renovations to the house. When they got the film developed, one of the exterior pictures showed a figure standing in one of the windows. They dismissed it as a trick of sunlight or shadow. But after the house was restored and opened to the public, three small children wanted to know who was the beautiful lady in the white gown. They had seen her on the upper stairway with a small black dog. Grace Jones, who had lived in the house eighty years, said it was her mother with Barney Doolittle, who never left her side. Miz Eliza has been a frequent visitor, especially when children and young ladies are in the house—perhaps because she had four daughters of her own.

Another guest got up during the night and went out to sit on the porch overlooking the fountain. She saw the figures of a white-haired lady and an old black man. It is believed that these were Old Miss or Miz Eliza and Pappy King.

Several times guests have seen a gentleman in early-1900s dress. Coy has seen him himself. This apparition is believed to be Mr. Satterfield, a prominent attorney who boarded at Grace Hall from the late 1800s to 1923. He was in love with Miss Mary, one of Miz Eliza's daughters, but he was much older than she and they never married.

The last ghost is unidentified. In May 1994 Fox television came to Selma to record ghostly sightings for its program *Encounters*. A psychic stayed at Grace Hall and encountered Old Miss, Miz Eliza, Pappy King, Mr. Satterfield, and one other gentleman spirit, who held him down one night so he couldn't get out of bed.

Other than this last ghost, who has never been encountered by anyone else, all the spirits are benign. Perhaps they're just keeping a close eye on their old home.

Historic Oakwood Bed and Breakfast

715 North Street East
Talladega, Alabama 35160
(256) 362-0662; fax (256) 362-7168

WEB SITE: www.bbonline.com/al/oakwood

INNKEEPERS: the Woods family and Sam, the cat

ROOMS: 3; 1 with private his and her baths; all with TV, clock, ceiling fan

ON THE GROUNDS: Porches

RATES: $49 to $89 double, including full or continental breakfast; gift certificates

CREDIT CARDS ACCEPTED? No

OPEN: Year-round except Thanksgiving and Christmas

HOW TO GET THERE: From I–20 traveling west, take exit 185, AL 21. Go 20 miles and turn left into the B&B driveway, which is identified by a sign. Traveling east, take exit 168, AL 27. Go 10 miles and turn left at the courthouse square. The B&B is 0.8 mile on your right.

Constructed in 1847 by peg-and-auger method, this lovely white frame home is considered one of the finest examples of pure federal-style architecture in Alabama. Its massive hand-hewn heart-pine framing secured by large square iron nails remains perfectly sound after more than 150 years. The perfect symmetry of the dignified federal motif is evidenced by two nine-over-nine windows flanking identical French doors on both stories and giant Doric columns framing the doors and the hidden-support balcony.

Among the three guest rooms, the Bowie Suite, named after Captain and Nancy Bowden Bowie who moved into the house as a newly married couple in 1849, is the most popular and most requested as a honeymoon suite. Gleaming hardwood floors, Oriental carpets, high ceilings, the huge 20- by 20-foot size, a queen-size four-poster bed, and his and her bathrooms create a romantic getaway fit for a king and queen. Her bath features a tub and a bidet; his has a shower. Much more casually furnished, the Remson and Woodward Rooms share a bath with a tub/shower and twin sinks. This pair of rooms is ideal if family or friends are traveling together. If a couple or business traveler rents only one of the rooms, the other is not rented so you'll have a private bath. More feminine, the Remson Room is decorated with floral wallpaper and pastel colors and features white wicker accents and a white iron double bed and matching daybed. The more masculine Woodward Room is decorated with a geometric wallpaper and deeper colors. It features wooden twin beds.

The upstairs sitting room contains a common telephone and a small refrigerator stocked with soft drinks and bottled water.

What's Nearby Talladega

After visiting Talladega's International Motorsports Hall of Fame and Talladega Superspeeday, slow down a bit and take a leisurely tour of the Silk Stocking District. The district's historic homes, like Heritage Hall, are recognized in the National Register of Historic Places. You can also visit Talladega College and nearby DeSoto Caverns Park. Your children will be climbing the walls, because the park encourages kids to climb DeSoto's cave walls.

Other Recommended B&Bs in Talladega

Orangevale Plantation, an 1852 Greek Revival plantation home on a working livestock and fruit farm, features 7 rooms with private baths, and full breakfast; 1400 Whiting Road, Talladega, AL 35160; (205) 362-3052. *Somerset House Bed and Breakfast* offers 4 rooms with private baths and full breakfast in a turn-of-the-century home in the Silk Stocking Historic District; 701 North Street East, Talladega, AL 35160; (205) 761-9251 or (800) 701-6678.

Arkansas

Numbers on map refer to towns numbered below.

Arsenic and Old Lace

60 Hillside Avenue
Eureka Springs, Arkansas 72632
(501) 253-5454 or (800) 243-LACE;
fax (501) 253-2246

E-MAIL: arsniclace@prodigy.net

WEB SITE: www.eureka-usa.com/arsenic

INNKEEPERS: Phyllis and Gary Jones

ROOMS: 5; all with private bath, whirlpool tub,
TV, VCR, robes; 4 with fireplace; 3 with private
balcony or patio; 1 room has wheelchair access

ON THE GROUNDS: Gardens, steps from a trolley stop

RATES: $125 to $165 double, including full breakfast, refreshments, and
golf, tennis, and swimming privileges at the Holiday Island Country
Club; additional person in Patio Suite $15

CREDIT CARDS ACCEPTED? Yes

OPEN: Year-round

HOW TO GET THERE: On North Main Street (AR 23), find the quaint railroad
station at the northern end of town. Across from the railroad station,
turn onto Hillside Avenue and go up the hill 0.7 mile. The B&B is on
your right.

Although lace does indeed billow from the window treatments as well as
draping the canopy of one of the beds, rest assured there's no arsenic in
the elderberry wine—or anything else here, for that matter. You will live
to tell the tale of a wonderful stay in this beautiful bed and breakfast.

This striking Queen Anne Victorian with 1,000 square feet of wraparound verandas fits in so well with all the other mansions in the historic
district that we were astounded to learn that it's only seven years old. It was
built in 1992 by Jeanne Simpson Johnson from a set of hundred-year-old
blueprints, though, so it is authentic—it had to be to pass muster with the
Historic District Commission. Ms. Johnson built it to be a bed and breakfast and filled it with imported wallpapers, crystal chandeliers, original
works of art, and antiques. Outside, she created elaborate rock walks and
walls and perennial gardens. Her attention to detail includes reproduction
tin ceilings, antique doors, mantels, and stained-glass windows, combined
with all the modern comforts and conveniences.

Ms. Johnson obviously had a sense of humor, what with naming her
B&B for the comic play by Joseph Kesselring and movie of the same title

starring Cary Grant. In case you're a little vague about the plot, it's about the Brewster sisters, two charming elderly spinsters who dispatch lonely aging gentlemen with tea or elderberry wine laced with arsenic. Ms. Johnson incorporated movie memorabilia such as original marquee prints, a window box, a door labeled PANAMA CANAL, and elderberry wine. The B&B rapidly became well known for its architectural and garden beauty.

Phyllis and Gary, who both took early retirement from IBM, bought the B&B lock, stock, and barrel in 1994, as well as the wooded lot next door so it can't be built on. They've added fireplaces, whirlpool tubs, private balconies, expanded gardens, and a waterfall emptying into a deep pool filled with water plants and fish.

The three-story home cascades down a hillside so that all three levels have wonderful views—in particular from the octagon-shaped Tree-Top Suite. This extra-special guest room occupies the turret and is two stories tall. Two levels of windows make you feel indeed as if you are perched in a tree house. The ultimate in luxury, the room features a fireplace by the king-size brass canopy bed; the bathroom boasts a whirlpool tub for two. Privacy abounds in the Patio Suite on the lower level. Floral bed coverings on the queen-size bed and daybed give the room a garden feel. Guests here luxuriate in the warmth of the fireplace or the whirlpool tub. The other guest rooms are the Monet, Chantilly Rose, and Library. Each has a distinct personality in keeping with its name, as well as its own special amenities. Naturally, every bedchamber has a copy of *Arsenic and Old Lace* to play on the VCR. Sweet dreams!

A hearty three-course breakfast of such gourmet treats as baked eggs with three cheeses and poached pears with honey and nutmeg is served in the dining room or breakfast room overlooking the gardens. Refreshments are served in the afternoon, and there's always something to munch on.

Phyllis and Gary seem to have boundless energy. Phyllis is active in many local and state organizations, including being president of the state B&B association. On the side, Gary operates Golden Age Aircraft, Inc., making safety inspections of antique aircraft. Sometime in the future, after they retire from the B&B business, the Joneses plan on buying a sailboat and sailing around the world.

What's Nearby Eureka Springs

Eureka Springs is a Victorian-era town built around its sixty springs, which many folks believe to have magical healing powers. Its winding and hilly streets have earned it the nickname Little Switzerland. Some say that its outstanding Victorian architecture makes it a San Francisco in miniature. Of the 230 streets, none cross at right angles, and there's not a traffic light in town. Filled with wedding chapels, the village is known as the Wedding/Honeymoon Capital of the South. *Time* magazine has called its historic architecture a "Victorian national treasure."

Given Eureka Springs' permanent population of less than 2,000, it's astounding to know that more than a million visitors pass through every year, and that it has more than 3,000 guest rooms. We're convinced that every home in town is a bed and breakfast. Streets are lined with crafts shops, galleries, antiques shops, cafes, and restaurants. Essentially a walking town, it offers a trolley to help visitors get around.

Other Recommended B&Bs in Eureka Springs

Angel at Rose Hall features 5 rooms with private baths and a dramatic tower in an elegant Victorian mansion; 56 Hillside, Eureka Springs, AR 72632; (501) 253-5405 or (800) 828-4255; www.the-angel.com. *Bridgeford House Bed and Breakfast*, an 1884 inn, offers rooms with private baths, and full Southern breakfast, children welcome; 263 Spring Street, Eureka Springs, AR 72632; (501) 253-7853 or (888) 567-2422; www.webeureka.com/bridgefordbb.

Foxglove Bed and Breakfast

229 Beech
Helena, Arkansas 72342
(870) 338-9391 or (800) 863-1926

WEB SITE: www.bbonline.com/ar/foxglove/

INNKEEPER: John Butkiewicz

ROOMS: 7; all with private bath (4 with whirlpool tub), telephone, cable TV, clock radio, hair dryer, bath amenities; some with fireplace, desks; fax and computer available

ON THE GROUNDS: Verandas

RATES: $69 to $109 double, including full breakfast, afternoon refreshments, candies in the rooms; additional person $20

CREDIT CARDS ACCEPTED? Yes

OPEN: Year-round

NOTE: Transitional neighborhood

HOW TO GET THERE: From I-40, take US 49 east toward Helena, then follow US Business 49 into town. Turn right onto Beech. At the next intersection go straight ahead into the driveway.

Built in 1900 by Elmer West, this stunning Queen Anne Victorian remained basically unchanged until 1994, when conversion into a bed and breakfast began. Although ten bathrooms were added, changes were still quite subtle, and extreme care was taken to match the interior and exterior trim. Like many old dowagers, this one is showing some exterior wear around the edges. In fact, the entire exterior could use a good scraping and a coat of paint. Inside, however, everything is in exquisite condition.

Listed on the National Register of Historic Places, the mansion is filled with handsome antiques and features original stained-glass windows and among the most beautiful floors we've ever seen. Not only are they original hardwood planks or parquet, but they have intricate inlaid patterns of various woods. We were immediately taken with the unusual, built-in, bilevel, semi-circular bench at the foot of the staircase. On the stair side is an upholstered bench, on the foyer side is an upholstered banquette. We also loved the fretwork that stretches across the foyer. Throughout the house quarter-sawn woodwork and ornate fireplace mantels embellish the spacious rooms.

John has made the most of the spacious mansion's rooms, turning even the former parlors and dining room into guest chambers so that he can offer more rooms than most B&Bs. All feature modern marble bathrooms (four boast whirlpool tubs), and most have antique beds modified to fit queen-size mattresses. A few period reproduction beds permit John to offer some king-size accomodations.

Huge pocket doors separate the foyer from two elegant bedchambers that occupy what used to be the double parlors. In one is an ornate brass bed with posters that merge into a curved canopy topped with a crown—obviously a room fit for royalty. The other former parlor features a carved tester bed. The former dining room sports a highly carved king-size bed and a whirlpool tub. Upstairs some of the rooms will accommodate additional travelers—one has a daybed and the other is a two-bedroom suite, which offers a queen-size bed in one bedroom and a double and three-quarter bed in the other.

Breakfast is served in a casual dining area off the beautiful kitchen. John wanted the two rooms to merge so he can talk with his guests while preparing the morning repast of eggs and ham, bacon, or sausage served along with fruit and biscuits. In good weather guests like to gather on the verandas.

What's Nearby Helena

Helena marks the first bridge across the Mississippi River south of Memphis. A raft of casinos on the Mississippi side of the river attract thousands of visitors. In October Helena hosts the King Biscuit Blues Festival, the third largest blues festival in the world. With 125,000 people descending on the town, you need to have made your reservations far in advance. Helena was the site of a Civil War battle on July 4, 1863—a bad day for the South. It was one of three battles lost that day; Gettysburg and Vicksburg were the other two. Remains of Battery C are only 50 yards behind the B&B, and the town has a Confederate cemetery.

Magnolia Hill Best Buy

608 Perry Street
Helena, Arkansas 72342
(870) 338–6874; fax (870) 338–7938

WEB SITE: www.bbonline.com/ar/magnoliahill

INNKEEPERS: Jane and James Insco

ROOMS: 8; all with private bath, cable TV, telephone, clock radio, luggage rack

ON THE GROUNDS: Verandas, screened porch, hot tub

RATES: $75 to $95 single or double, including full breakfast, snacks, and beverages

CREDIT CARDS ACCEPTED? Yes

OPEN: Year-round

NOTE: Transitional, commercial neighborhood

HOW TO GET THERE: From I–40, take US 61 to US 49 toward Helena. When it splits with US Business 49, take the business route. At Columbia Street, turn left and go 1 block to Perry Street. Turn right. The B&B is on your left at the next intersection.

The setting will capture your heart before you even set foot inside. This gracious Queen Anne mansion, which was built in 1895 by cotton merchant and Confederate captain Charles Lawson Moore, perches high on a hill on a large grassy lot shaded by venerable old trees. Multiple gables, a tower with a conical roof, a wraparound porch, and a porte cochere are guaranteed to get your attention. You've heard the real estate term *street appeal*. Magnolia Hill has it in abundance. It's no surprise that the house is listed on the National Register of Historic Places.

Jane greeted us warmly and told us she wanted us to feel as if we had traveled back to the turn of the century to visit in the home of a favorite relative or friend. In a well-to-do home of that period, she explained, we'd have been waited on by servants. At present-day Magnolia Hill, she said, she's the servant. We'd prefer to think of her as a gracious hostess, and in fact, her discreet pampering is one of the pleasures of staying at Magnolia Hill.

During its proud history, the house has served as a private home, Presbyterian church, and cadet club for World War II soldiers. With such a checkered background, it's amazing that the house retains so many original features. The entry hall walls are covered with the original broadcloth topped with a stenciled border. Portraits of the original owners of the house bestow their blessings on the current use of their home. Massive pocket doors separate the foyer from the formal parlor and dining room. Carefully preserved and restored original hardwood floors, ornate mantels, ceramic tiles, period antiques, and carefully selected decorative arts such as the collection of museum-quality Japanese porcelains with lithopane images grace the public rooms and guest chambers.

Eight antiques-filled guest rooms occupy the second and third floors. Although each has its own special charm, each features a firm mattress, satin sheets, a modern private bath, and all the comforts and conveniences discriminating travelers expect of larger properties. With so many rooms, we can't describe them all here; suffice it to say that they have hardwood floors, Oriental or Aubusson carpets, brass or heavily carved beds, sitting areas, dramatic window treatments, warm, rich colors, and appropriate period-inspired wallpapers. Most of the beds are queen size, although there are also a few doubles and kings. Some feature bay windows and claw-foot tubs. You can step through the floor-to-ceiling window in the Ruby and Blue Room onto a private porch. Cathedral ceilings crown the third-floor rooms. The stunning Honeymoon Suite, located in the circular tower, boasts a circular bed romantically draped with gauzy fabric.

Jane gets your day off to a good start with a sumptuous, three-course Southern breakfast. If you stay several nights, she'll outdo herself with yet another creative dish such as chocolate gravy on homemade biscuits, three-cheese-stuffed French toast, pumpkin pancakes with praline sauce, herbed eggs with Brie, or an egg and sausage dish. To enhance your dining experience, the morning repast is served on the William and Mary dining table using exquisite antique china. On nice days you might prefer to have a more casual meal on the screened porch. Afternoon refreshments are served, and the informal sitting rooms have a coffeemaker, microwave, and small guest refrigerator, as well as being stocked with snacks and beverages. Among Jane's other special touches are fruit and chocolate selections in each room. As an extra added attraction, there's a hot tub on the screened porch.

Oh, and just one more thing. The house reportedly has a benevolent ghost named Jasmine. She obligingly opened an armoire door to prove her presence to us.

What's Nearby Helena

See page 52 for what's nearby Helena.

The Gables Inn Bed And Breakfast

318 Quapaw Avenue
Hot Springs National Park, Arkansas 71901
(501) 623-7576 or (800) 625-7576

E-MAIL: gablesn@ipa.net

WEB SITE: www.bbonline.com/ar/gablesinn/

INNKEEPERS: Judy and David Peters

ROOMS: 4; all with private bath, TV, VCR, telephone, ceiling fan

ON THE GROUNDS: Verandas, stone patio, landscaped grounds

RATES: $69 to $89 double, including full breakfast, snacks, sweets, and soft beverages; Sunday through Thursday, corporate single rates are $65; ask about extended-stay rates

CREDIT CARDS ACCEPTED? Yes

OPEN: Year-round

NOTE: Transitional neighborhood

HOW TO GET THERE: From the center of downtown where US 70 and AR 7 cross, take Central Avenue north to Market Street and turn left. Turn left again at Quapaw. The Gables is at the next corner on your right.

Our kudos to innkeeper Judy Peters for offering to coordinate our entire Hot Springs itinerary, phoning and e-mailing all the B&Bs there that we'd be dropping by for a tour and a visit with the innkeepers. Her initiative, enthusiasm, and service-oriented philosophy told us right away why she and her husband, David, do such a good job presiding over the charming

Gables Inn, a stately turn-of-the-century home sitting regally on a corner lot in the Quapaw Historic District. From the moment we pulled up outside and saw the many gables, wraparound front porch, bay windows, and stained-glass windows, we knew we were in for a treat in the Victorian tradition.

We stepped into the foyer and traveled back in time ninety-five years to a period when gleaming hardwood floors, burnished woodwork, a winding staircase, high ceilings, and massive pocket doors were integral parts of any home. When we admired the hanging light fixture, the light on the newel post, and the stained-glass window on the staircase, Judy was proud to point out that they are original to the house. An ornate archway capped with decorative wooden scrollwork leads into the formal parlor, where the light fixture and leaded glass, as well as a chaise longue, are also original. A wood-burning fireplace is the focal point in the less formal study. Among the appealing original architectural details in the dining room, where a full breakfast is served, is the plate rail above the paneling. Be sure to poke your head into the kitchen to see the fully operational replica of an old-fashioned cast-iron stove on which the Peterses do their cooking. You'll also find sweets, snacks, and complimentary beverages.

Upstairs is an informal guest sitting room where early-morning coffee is served. Oversize windows overlooking the gardens, a well-stocked guest refrigerator, telephone, and a television make this a popular retreat. Four charmingly decorated guest rooms each display their own distinctive personality and feature either king- or queen-size beds. Custom-made stained-glass windows in the transoms were designed to complement the decor of each room. The Governor's Room features a four-poster cannonball king-size bed and a comfortable sitting area in the bay window. The original master bedroom of the house, it was connected to the nursery, which now serves as the bathroom. Lillian's Room is the most romantic, with its satin and crocheted bedspread and throw pillows, king-size brass bed, and angel and dove accents. A note of whimsy in this room is the collection of Barbies. The focal point of Terri Lynn's Room is the queen-size brass bed with its fancy draped treatment at the head. The fainting couch makes a perfect place to read. Monogrammed robes are provided to guests in the Sunshine Room because they must come out into the hall to reach their private bath, which boasts an old-fashioned claw-foot soaking tub.

Breakfast is an elegant meal served on china and crystal in the dining room. The entree might be pancakes, a ham and cheese omelette, or stuffed French toast accompanied by fruits, juices, and hot beverages.

Judy and David are nothing if not creative; they've devised a dozen packages for very special two-night stays. Among the features of these packages might be a fresh floral arrangement, candles, gourmet chocolates, a dinner cruise, admission to the Hot Springs Tower, show tickets, a round of golf and cart rental at the Belvedere Country Club, or horseback riding. The most popular amenity, however, is a deluxe thermal bath/whirlpool with a mineral wrap and a massage for two at the historic Buckstaff Bathhouse. Super-romantics can have their wedding, reception, and honeymoon at the Gables.

What's Nearby Hot Springs

Hot Springs is famous for its flying banners that read HOT SPRINGS—BOYHOOD HOME OF BILL CLINTON. President Clinton spent his formative years in Hot Springs, and many of his old favorite hot spots are marked with signs saying BILL CLINTON ATE HERE. Another historical figure, Al Capone, was a well-known regular around town during the Prohibition years. Capone and his gang visited the gambling houses and bathhouses, which are now tourist attractions at the 4,800-acre Hot Springs National Park visitors center. Besides horse racing and hot baths, Hot Springs is also known for its fine arts center and weekly Gallery Walk, when twenty-five art galleries open their doors to visitors who may mingle with local artists.

Another Recommended B&B in Hot Springs

Lady of the Lake, a 1950s-era ranch house, offers rooms with views of Lake Hamilton from the decks; 301 Stearns Point Road, Hot Springs, AR 71913; (501) 760-1341.

Prospect Place Best Buy

472 Prospect Avenue
Hot Springs, Arkansas 71901
(501) 318-0385 or (877) 318-0385

E-MAIL: prosplace@mail.snider.net

WEB SITE: www.bbonline.com/ar/prospectplace/

INNKEEPERS: Mary Medley and Terry Miller

ROOMS: 4; all with private bath, clock, ceiling fan; 2 with decorative fireplace

ON THE GROUNDS: Veranda, patio

RATES: $75 to $105 single or double, including full breakfast and afternoon refreshments; two-night minimum on weekends; mid-week corporate rates and special packages available

CREDIT CARDS ACCEPTED? Yes

OPEN: Year-round

NOTE: Transitional neighborhood

HOW TO GET THERE: From the downtown intersection of US 70 and AR 7, go west on Grand Avenue to Hawthorne and turn right. Continue 4 blocks to Prospect Avenue. Turn right; the B&B is on your left.

Mother and daughter Mary Medley and Terry Miller, ably assisted by Terry's teenage children, graciously open their beautiful Queen Anne Victorian home to bed-and-breakfast guests. Built in 1900 at the foot of West Mountain in a neighborhood that is now part of the Quapaw-Prospect Historic District, the mansion showcases a wraparound veranda and a circular three-story tower covered with fish-scale shingles. Built in 1900 by the Robert Strauss family, the house passed into the Cooper family, who operated the Kindercoop kindergarten here for thirty years. Many a local has fond memories and stories to tell about attending this kindergarten.

Terry welcomed us warmly and gave us the grand tour beginning in the foyer, which merges into a circular tower that holds a grand piano—original to the house—for the pleasure of any guests who play. Even the foyer boasts a wood-burning fireplace. Adjacent to the foyer through French doors is the graciously furnished parlor, equipped with a TV, VCR, and comfortable seating. This room's fireplace has fluted pillars and an ornamental overmantel. Another wood-burning fireplace warms the dining room, where a full breakfast is served. This substantial repast might feature an egg casserole, pancakes, or French toast accompanied by breads, biscuits, fruits, juices, and hot beverages. Coffee is available a half hour before breakfast, and many guests enjoy having it on the veranda or out on the patio.

A graceful staircase with white risers and natural steps ascends from the foyer to the second-floor guest rooms. The premier room is the Moonlight Suite, a spacious, elegant room done in navy blue. This room frames a brass king-size bed and a wicker sofa, but it is the footed tub in the bathroom that's most popular with romantics. This elegant bath has decorative columns and a wall of windows overlooking the gardens. An opulent Victorian settee fills the round tower portion of the Turret Room, which features a brass queen-size bed. Wedgwood accessories and a king-size bed with an upholstered headboard highlight the Haven. Both the Turret and the Haven have baths with huge step-in showers. Robes are provided for guests in the Nook to take the few steps into the hall to their private bath. Being the original bathroom in the house, it is the largest. The bed in the Nook is double-size iron.

What's Nearby Hot Springs

See page 56 for what's nearby Hot Springs.

Spring Street Inn

522 Spring Street
Hot Springs, Arkansas 71901
(501) 624–1901 or (800) 284–8780

WEB SITE: www.hotspringsusa.com/
springstreet-inn

INNKEEPERS: Cheri and August Ericson

ROOMS: 4; all with private bath, cable TV, VCR, iron, ironing board, clock radio, telephone, ceiling fan, bath amenities, flashlight, fresh flowers

ON THE GROUNDS: Verandas, stone patio

RATES: $85 to $125, including full breakfast and afternoon snacks and beverages; two-night minimum stay some holidays and weekends; ask about rates for extended stays

CREDIT CARDS ACCEPTED? Yes

OPEN: Year-round

NOTE: Transitional neighborhood

HOW TO GET THERE: From the intersection of US 70 and AR 7, take AR 7 North to Spring Street (just before the visitors center). Turn right onto Spring. The house is in the third block on your right. Parking is in the rear.

Appropriately enough, this ultra-romantic bed and breakfast opened its doors to guests for the first time on Valentine's weekend 1999. One of Hot Springs's treasured historical homes, it underwent a two-year renovation for its new function in life. Built in 1905 for local clothiers Simon and Rosa Meyers, the handsome home is located across the street from national forest land and one of the city's famous bathhouses.

Gracious hosts Cheri and August have created an elegant retreat for discriminating travelers and were only too glad to give us the grand tour,

Hot Springs

The naturally hot water from the springs from which the town takes its name have been used by humans as far back as 10,000 years ago. The springs reached the peak of their popularity at the turn of the century when dozens of opulent bathhouses were built—most of which survive, although only a few are open. The entire area, town and all, became a national park in 1921. The historic spa city is surrounded by lakes and the Zig Zag Mountains, which can provide endless hours of outdoor recreation. What could be better at the end of a long day of hiking or horseback riding than to soothe aching muscles by luxuriating in a steam, soak, and massage at the historic Buckstaff Bathhouse (501–623–2308). The price of $30 plus tip is incredibly reasonable. Thus refreshed, you can enjoy the wide variety of restaurants, shows, and nightlife the town offers.

explaining what they'd retained and what they'd changed. Although the ambience is formal, with elegant antique furnishings and beautiful bedroom settings, the B&B provides a relaxing atmosphere for a perfect getaway. Guests love to gather around the fireplace in the parlor, in the upstairs sunroom (stocked with snacks and drinks), or outside on the verandas or patio. A magnificent Empire buffet is the focal point of the dining room, where there are individual tables so romantic couples can dine totally immersed in each other.

All but one of the generously proportioned bedrooms feature a queen-size bed and all the modern amenities. The Magnolia Suite, which was the original master bedroom, boasts a majestic four-poster rice bed, a sitting area, and a private porch, but the pièce de résistance is the bathroom, which could have come right out of a bridal magazine. Beautiful columns and Grecian-style tilework set off a double-size whirlpool tub; there's also a separate shower, and a sink in an antique dresser. In the Fountain Room, so named because it overlooks the patio fountain, the focal point is the Louis XIV bedroom suite. Its bathroom has an original claw-foot tub to which a brass shower has been added. Named for its view of the Hot Springs Mountain Tower, the Tower Room features antique oak furniture and a bathroom with an oversize shower. Perfect for a business traveler, the Jockey Room has a double bed and is decorated with racing prints.

What's Nearby Hot Springs

See page 56 for what's nearby Hot Springs.

Stitt House Bed and Breakfast Inn

824 Park Avenue
Hot Springs, Arkansas 71901
(501) 623-2704

E-MAIL: stittbb@hsnp.com
WEB SITE: www.bbonline.com/ar/stitthouse/
INNKEEPERS: Linda and Horst Fischer
ROOMS: 3 rooms and 1 suite; all with private bath, bath amenities, robes, TV, clock radio, iron and ironing board, hair dryer; some with desk; limited wheelchair access
ON THE GROUNDS: Verandas, heated swimming pool, landscaped grounds
RATES: $100 to $120 single or double, including full breakfast, snacks, and beverages; additional person $20; ask about the Pamper Yourself Getaway package; two-night minimum stay on weekends, three-night on holidays and special weekends
CREDIT CARDS ACCEPTED? Yes
OPEN: Year-round
NOTE: Transitional, commercial neighborhood
HOW TO GET THERE: Take AR 7 through downtown. You'll pass the Arlington and Majestic Hotels; go another 0.5 mile until you see a STAX gas station on your right. The Stitt House is the second house past the station. Turn into the driveway at the end of the white wall with the black iron fence.

At the Stitt House you'll be pampered with exceptional service, because Linda and Horst know the hospitality industry forward and backward, inside and out. Contrary to popular opinion, that famed Southern hospitality isn't restricted to born-and-bred Southerners. Both natives of Germany, the Fischers have extensive backgrounds in the hotel and restaurant industries. They welcomed us as if we were old friends who'd come to visit, and delighted in chatting about the house and showing off its most outstanding features.

A true estate, the white-frame manor is the oldest surviving house in Hot Springs—built in 1875, it's on the National Register of Historic Places. It perches majestically at the apex of two shaded acres filled with some of the city's oldest magnolias as well as rare Chinese ginkgos and Japanese tulip trees. Sitting well back from busy Park Avenue and still surrounded by its original iron fence, the villa is almost invisible from the street. The eclectic architecture showcases Italianate and neoclassical elements such as uneven roof lines, interesting window protrusions, a roomy wraparound porch, and gingerbread.

Inside, the Fischers have been careful to maintain the house's original details—woodwork, ceiling medallions, a hand-carved oak staircase, imposing fireplaces, elaborate mahogany and cherry mantels, hearths and fireplace surrounds of intricately designed Italian ceramic tiles, and pine and oak floors. Tall windows, some with leaded or etched glass, fill the house with light and provide lush vistas of the grounds. The Fischers have made no major changes except the addition of bathrooms.

Large, gracefully proportioned public rooms and guest chambers with high ceilings are cleanly squared and beautifully furnished. European artifacts such as Linda's rare-plate collections and nineteenth-century Mechelen pieces accent many rooms. Downstairs, guests can enjoy the big double parlor with its bay window and gas-log fireplace or the smaller library, which features a Baccarat chandelier and another gas-log fireplace. Upstairs, there's an informal guest sitting room with a stocked refrigerator and fresh fruit always available.

Named for the Fischers' four children, the striking guest rooms feature private baths and all the modern amenities, but are decorated differently to create distinct personalities. Although these rooms are furnished in antiques, a concession to modern-day life has been made by featuring period reproduction beds so guests can enjoy the comfort of a king-size mattress. Hong's Hideaway, tucked behind the library on the first floor, features a hand-carved French bedroom suite, a sitting area in its bay window, a desk, and a claw-foot tub. The focal point of Michael's Manor is a grand mahogany four-poster bed. A full-tester iron bed in two-room Kai's Korner is adorned with a Battenburg lace bedspread and bed curtains. Loc's Loft, a favorite of honeymooners and other ultra-romantics, boasts a whirlpool tub, a separate glass-enclosed shower, and skylights.

Although many bed and breakfasts offer their guests the opportunity to eat breakfast in the dining room, out on the porch, or even in their rooms, the Stitt House is one of the very few that offer a true breakfast in bed. The night before guests sign up for what they want for breakfast, when they wish to dine, and where they want to be served. Other nice touches include crisp hand-ironed all-cotton sheets, a welcoming beverage, and nightly turndown service with gourmet chocolates.

What's Nearby Hot Springs

See page 56 for what's nearby Hot Springs.

Vintage Comfort Bed and Breakfast

Best Buy

303 Quapaw Avenue
Hot Springs National Park, Arkansas 71901
(501) 623–3258 or (800) 608–4682

E-MAIL: btberg@ipa.net

WEB SITE: www.bbonline.com/ar/vintagecomfort/

INNKEEPER: Bill F. Tanneberger

ROOMS: 4; all with private bath, clock radio, coffeemaker, makeup mirror, ceiling fan; 1 room has a desk and a phone outlet

ON THE GROUNDS: Verandas

RATES: $75 to $90 double, including full breakfast and afternoon refreshments; $15 per additional adult in the room; $10 for additional child age six through fourteen in the room

CREDIT CARDS ACCEPTED? Yes

OPEN: Year-round

NOTE: Transitional neighborhood

HOW TO GET THERE: From the downtown junction of US 70 and AR 7, go north on Central Avenue. Turn left onto Market Street, then left onto Quapaw Avenue. The B&B is on the corner of Quapaw and Market.

The telltale signs of Queen Anne Victorian style are the wraparound veranda and the tower, although the architectural embellishments on the exterior and interior of this house are much more subdued than some flamboyant homes of the period. Spacious rooms, high ceilings, and hardwood floors characterize both the public and private rooms. We entered directly into the formal parlor—somewhat unusual for houses of the period, which more typically have a foyer. The most interesting features of this lovely room are the coffered ceiling and elegant staircase rising to the second floor.

Bill is a genial host who wants graciousness, hospitality, and casual comfort to be the key ingredients he offers. You won't find the overdecorated look so common in historic houses, but rather furniture that invites you to sit down and relax with your fellow guests or in a solitary pursuit with a good book or a puzzle. For instance, the informal parlor, where the original owner gave tap-dancing and violin lessons, is filled with leather and wicker and sports a large-screen television along with an assortment of books and games. Simple farm furniture fills the dining room, where a full breakfast—casserole, muffins, fruits, juices, and hot beverages—is served.

Guest chambers, all which have queen-size beds, are named for a previous owner's daughters and granddaughters. One of the most popular is the Debrah Ann. Warm and spacious, it features a four-poster bed, a large bath with a claw-foot tub, and a private screened porch with an old-fashioned swing and wicker furniture, including a chaise longue. The Leah Anne's queen-size bed with an upholstered headboard and an additional twin-size iron and brass daybed with a trundle make it ideal for travelers who don't want to share the same bed or those vacationing with children. A light-toned bird's-eye maple 1920s-era bedroom suite gives the Courtney Elizabeth Room its special charm. Its private bath is reached via the hall. Three large windows allow the sun to drench the Lynn Helen Room with light. Decorated in country charm, it offers an additional single daybed and a desk. In the upstairs hall guests will find toiletries to use, for those they may have forgotten, as well as an iron, hair dryer, and games. A guest refrigerator on the back porch is stocked with mineral water and soft drinks.

Ask Bill about several creative two-night packages that include various activities in the area.

What's Nearby Hot Springs

See page 56 for what's nearby Hot Springs.

Wildwood 1884 Bed and Breakfast

808 Park Avenue
Hot Springs, Arkansas 71901
(501) 624–4267

E-MAIL: wildwood@ipa.net

WEB SITE: www.bbonline.com/ar/wildwood

INNKEEPERS: Karen and Randy Duncan

ROOMS: 5; all with private bath, ceiling fan, clock radio

ON THE GROUNDS: Veranda

RATES: $85 to $95 double, including full breakfast and always-available refreshments

CREDIT CARDS ACCEPTED? Yes

OPEN: Year-round

NOTE: Transitional neighborhood

HOW TO GET THERE: Take AR 7 through downtown, passing the Arlington and Majestic Hotels; go another 0.5 mile until you see a STAX gas station on your right. Wildwood is the first house past the station.

Despite its stereotypical Queen Anne Victorian style—steeply pitched gables, a turret, a wraparound porch, stylized chimneys, and ornate gingerbread—Wildwood isn't your typical Victorian-era bed and breakfast. We'd describe the current treatment of its classical interior adornments as funky. Some floors are painted vibrant colors such as red; some walls have quirky faux finishes; some showers or tubs are incorporated into the bedroom rather than the bathroom. Those looking for unsurpassed elegance and luxury won't find it here, but the artsy and those with a good sense of humor will find it very comfortable.

Built on a hillside, the pink palace was constructed in 1884 for Dr. Prosper Harvey Ellsworth and his wife, Sarah, who named the property Wildwood. They created a showplace for their wealth that incorporated 15-foot ceilings downstairs and 14-foot ceilings upstairs, ornate cherry, walnut, and mahogany woodwork, hand-painted English ceramic-tile surrounds on the fireplaces, elaborate plaster ceiling medallions, and lavish use of stained-glass. The oblong, triangular, and pentagonal spaces here permit two to three exposures and four to five windows for each room. Each of the main downstairs rooms features a different wood; massive walnut and cherry pocket doors separate the rooms. The cherry staircase is accented by two large stained-glass windows that Sarah designed and had produced in Italy. There's a dumbwaiter and a hidden pass-through in the dining room. Innovative features included speaking tubes, indoor plumbing supplied by a windmill, and an early version of air-conditioning that uses a network of ducts. Construction cost $40,000—a vast sum in those days.

Although the house sat empty for thirty years, its outstanding architectural details, original light fixtures, and even furnishings were salvageable. Fortunately for Karen and Randy, the magnificent hand-rubbed woodwork had never been painted or varnished. Their restoration efforts were rewarded with the 1993 Arkansas Excellence in Preservation through Restoration Award.

Guest rooms, which are more traditionally decorated, are named for Karen and Randy's grandchildren, as is the Grace Elizabeth Music Room. Often used as a bridal suite because of its rounded shape and antique high-back half-tester bed, the Stephanie Suzanne Room is decorated in forest green. Get Karen to show you the hidden safe incorporated into the mantel over the fireplace. The Don Wade III features lavender and violets, a cherry high-back bed, and a private porch. Pretty in pink, the Hannah Faith boasts a private porch, a king-size bed, and a daybed that can be turned into two twins. Bright and yellow as sunshine, the Kensie Danae is cheerily decorated with sunflowers and a queen-size brass bed. Its bath has an antique claw-foot tub. Light and homey in peach and green, the Braeden Lee has a canopy bed and lovely private porch with an old-fashioned porch swing.

What's Nearby Hot Springs

See page 56 for what's nearby Hot Springs.

Williams House B&B Inn

420 Quapaw Avenue
Hot Springs, Arkansas 71901
(501) 624–4275 or (800) 756–4635

E-MAIL: willmbnb@ipa.net

WEB SITE: www.bbonline.com/ar/ williamshouse/

INNKEEPERS: Karen and David Wiseman

ROOMS: 2 rooms and 3 two-bedroom suites; all with private bath, TV, VCR, clock radio, robes, extra pillows and blankets, iron, ironing board, hair dryer, ceiling fan, telephone available on request

ON THE GROUNDS: Verandas, patio, gardens, antiques shop for guests only

RATES: $85 to $135 single or double, including early-morning coffee, full breakfast, snacks, and beverages; $40 for second bedroom in the two-room suites; midweek and extended-stay discounts available; ask about the Honeymoon/Anniversary Package

CREDIT CARDS ACCEPTED? Yes

OPEN: Year-round

NOTE: Transitional neighborhood

HOW TO GET THERE: From AR 7 (Central Avenue), turn west onto West Grand Avenue, then right onto Orange Street. The B&B is at the intersection of Quapaw and Orange, with signs to identify it. Don't be confused by the number 220 on the front steps; that was Dr. Williams's telephone number.

Masterfully constructed, this historic district jewel was built for Dr. Arthur Upton Williams, a prominent physician and businessman. It was the first home in Hot Springs to have electricity. Although old photographs show that the tower and porte cochere of the 1890 mansion have been modified and some of the fretwork and gingerbread removed, this is still an exceptional house. Constructed of brick with a wraparound first-floor veranda and a smaller second-story veranda, the Williams House has an additional and unusual feature—a three-story brownstone tower copied from the one at Aukland Castle in England. In fact, a stonemason who worked on the original was brought over to create this one. The house remained in the family until the mid-1970s. Another previous owner opened the house as a bed and breakfast in 1980—the first in Arkansas. Karen and Dave have owned it since 1996.

We entered the 6,500-square-foot mansion from the side door off the porte cochere into a lavish formal sitting room with a black marble fireplace and a magnificent staircase. This room, which could easily double as a ballroom, features a grand piano and stunning antiques. A narrow back hall serves as a guest pantry and refreshment area; there's a small refrigerator with mineral water and wine as well as a coffeemaker and a selection of teas and coffees.

In addition to Karen and Dave's private quarters, two other spacious downstairs rooms have been converted into the luxurious suite where we stayed. The bedroom is in the circular part of the tower and features a carved queen-size bed with a dramatic draped treatment at its head. Since we visited, a double-size whirlpool has been added to this suite. The sitting room features an 11-foot pier mirror, a comfortable seating area, a desk, and a game table. Guests in this suite can request a private candlelight breakfast in their sitting room.

Upstairs is another large sitting room in what was Dr. Williams's billiards room and a porch with a hammock. Two pairs of commodious guest chambers each share a bath, making them ideal for families or friends traveling together. (If only one room of a suite is rented, the other is not so that single guests or couples can have a private bath.) Of special note is the enclosed sunporch off the guest chambers, which features wicker furniture and a daybed.

The Ghost of Dr. Williams

The Williams House has survived at least four forest fires. During the 1913 fire, which burned fifty blocks of Hot Springs, Dr. Williams hired help to protect his home. He had water drawn from a well on his property and placed workers with buckets at several locations on the roof and in the attic to douse any fireballs that might land on his house. The roof never caught fire. Another fire-fighting strategy in those days was to dynamite buildings in the path of the fire. During one fire, Dr. Williams, shotgun in hand, confronted anyone who wanted to dynamite his home. The Williams House and several others in the neighborhood were spared.

Although Dr. Williams died in 1923, many believe that his spirit still remains in the house to protect it. Previous owners and guests have reported unexplained occurrences such as a hall light that goes off by itself, sounds of someone in heavy boots walking in the attic, big stacks of boxed books moving mysteriously, seashells in a hard-to-open curio cabinet being rearranged. One travel writer who stayed here reported hearing a gruff voice shouting orders to "keep those buckets moving." When a recent fire broke out near the Williams House, innkeeper Dave Wiseman reported hearing footsteps in the attic. Is Dr. Williams still on guard?

The quaint former carriage house, a three-story structure, contains two more accommodations—a suite and a guest room. The Carriage Suite, which occupies the former hayloft, is an extra-large room with a sitting area, a queen-size four-poster bed, a large bathroom with a claw-foot tub/shower, a smaller second bedroom, a small refrigerator, and a coffeemaker. The Carriage Room features a queen-size brass bed. Its large bathroom has a daybed for an additional guest.

Breakfast is a festive meal served in the sun-drenched dining room. Our repast included a fresh fruit dish, juice, a mouthwatering herbed egg and cheese croissant, sausage, and freshly baked muffins. Guests who stay more than one night might devour raspberry-stuffed French toast or an egg and sausage dish. In addition to the large porches, guests like to gather on the patio in the garden, where there's a grape arbor, fish pond, fountain, and statuary connected by a brick walkway.

What's Nearby Hot Springs

See page 56 for what's nearby Hot Springs.

The Empress of Little Rock

2120 Louisiana
Little Rock, Arkansas 72206
(501) 374-7966

E-MAIL: hostess@TheEmpress.com

WEB SITE: www.TheEmpress.com

INNKEEPERS: Sharon Welch-Blair and Robert H. Blair

ROOMS: 5; all with private bath, ceiling fan, clock radio, featherbed, robes, telephone with data port; TV on request

ON THE GROUNDS: Verandas

RATES: $115 to $175 double, including full breakfast; additional person $50; ask about special packages

CREDIT CARDS ACCEPTED? Yes

OPEN: Year-round

NOTE: Transitional neighborhood

HOW TO GET THERE: From I-30, take I-630 West and exit at Main Street. Turn left onto Main and take it to 22nd, then turn right. The B&B is 1 block ahead at the corner of Louisiana and 22nd.

Outside and in, the Empress is one of the most stunning examples of the flamboyant Gothic Queen Anne Victorian style we've ever seen. In fact, the National Trust for Historic Preservation calls it the best example of ornate Victorian architecture in Arkansas and the most important existing example of Gothic Queen Anne in the region. We'd been hearing about the house for years and we weren't disappointed.

The grandeur of the mansion was an example of one-upmanship. James H. Hornibrook came to town from Canada after the Civil War, but because he was a liquor importer and a saloonkeeper, he and his family were shunned by Little Rock's high society. When a competing saloonkeeper built a grand home, Hornibrook vowed to build the most extravagant dwelling in the state. Completed in 1888 using Arkansas materials exclusively, the home cost a staggering $20,000. Hornibrook certainly showed everyone, but he didn't get to enjoy his home very long; he died of a stroke at his front gate shortly after the mansion was completed.

We hardly know where to start in describing this venerable dowager, but let's try curbside. The Empress sits on a large corner lot where it can display two grandiose sides to the world. A brick facade rises from a stone foundation. Gables, ornate chimneys, bay windows, and porches protrude everywhere, but the focal point is the circular three-and-a-half-story pagodalike tower. Be sure to note the generous use of stained-glass, brackets, and gingerbread.

We entered through massive double doors into the foyer—the first level of the tower—to be greeted by the twittering of finches in an ornate Victorian birdcage. From there we got intriguing glimpses into the ladies' and gentlemen's parlors as well as the grand double staircase. It immediately became evident that there's not a single square or rectangular room in the mansion—many of the rooms are hexagonal, others defy description.

We simply drank in all the architectural elements and decorating schemes. The parquet floors are oak and walnut, the staircase walnut, pine, oak, and cypress. Beautiful fireplaces are adorned with ceramic-tile surrounds and ornate mantels—all but one original Eastlake. As we started up the grand staircase, we noted that it was bathed in multicolored light and looked up to see an 8-foot-square stained-glass skylight. In the upstairs hall, fixings are available for coffee service. Five magnificent guest chambers open off the hall.

The centerpiece of the James H. Hornibrook Room is its working fireplace with an extra-large surround. The room is furnished with a Renaissance Revival mahogany bedroom suite, the crown jewel of which is the 10½-foot half-tester bed modified to accommodate a queen-size mattress. This room's spacious adjoining bath has the original fish-footed tub with an unusual mahogany rim and an old-fashioned water closet.

Next door in the tower is the ultra-romantic John Edward Murray Room, named for the youngest brigadier general in the Confederate Army (he was an Arkansan). This room boasts a king-size bed created by combining two antique Austrian twins. One of the most interesting accents in this room is the ornate cradle. A full-size four-poster bed dominates the Eliza Bertrand Cunningham Room, named for the first Caucasian resident of Little Rock. The Petit Jean Room is filled with military and naval relics and features a queen-size Empire high-back bed; the Washburn-Welch Room has as its centerpiece a French walnut bed that can be configured as a king or two twins.

Be sure to make a trip up the last of the staircase to the third-floor card room. It's said that Hornibrook had a perpetual card game going here.

Although the windows are stained-glass, one was left clear so he could watch for raids on his establishment.

Early risers can choose a continental breakfast, but unless you're on a strict diet, we suggest waiting for the formal candlelight breakfast served in the dining room.

What's Nearby Little Rock

If you're looking for a good museum, then look no farther than Little Rock. You can visit the Arkansas Arts Center and its six galleries, museum school, and children's theatre. You can tour the Children's Museum of Arkansas and try your hand at the interactive hands-on exhibits. For some out-of-this-world fun, visit the Little Rock Planetarium at the University of Arkansas. If you'd rather just talk to the animals, check out the menagerie of birds, reptiles, and fish at the Little Rock Zoo.

The Hotze House

1619 Louisiana
Little Rock, Arkansas 72206
(501) 376–6563; fax (501) 374–5393

INNKEEPERS: Suzanne and Steven Gates

ROOMS: 5; all with private bath, telephone, computer connection, desk, cable TV; 4 with gas-log fireplace

ON THE GROUNDS: Verandas

RATES: $90 single or double, including full breakfast, snacks, and beverages; ask about special-occasion packages and corporate rates

CREDIT CARDS ACCEPTED? Yes

OPEN: Year-round

NOTE: Transitional neighborhood

HOW TO GET THERE: From I–30, take I–630 West to the first exit (1A), Main and Center Streets. Follow the access road to Main. Turn left over the interstate to Seventeenth Street. Turn right and go 1 block, then turn right again onto Louisiana. The B&B is in the first block on your right.

ometimes the measure of a hostelry is the type of guests it attracts. The Hotze (pronounced hote-ze) House attracts great ones. When we dropped by for a tour, it was a guest who showed us around and sang the praises of both the bed and breakfast and its owners.

When this magnificent neoclassical mansion was built by Peter Hotze in 1900, it was the most expensive and elegant home in Arkansas. Located in the Quapaw Quarter Historic District only 2 blocks from the Governor's Mansion, it is often mistaken for the official residence. Everything about the Hotze House is grand—the imposing exterior of light yellow pressed brick with a green slate roof, the monumental semicircular portico supported by two pairs of 30-foot-tall fluted Ionic columns, the steps and balustrade of Batesville marble, the size and architectural details of the interior, the 8,500 square feet of living space, the intricately patterned mahogany, walnut, oak, and birch parquet floors, and the mahogany and oak woodwork. Still, we can only imagine how much more impressive it was originally, because the interior was designed by Louis Comfort Tiffany. In fact, it's reported that Hotze gave Tiffany a blank check. Steve tells us that the last Hotze descendant died in 1974, and the mansion and contents were put up for auction several years later; each Tiffany light fixture was sold for more than the mansion itself. The magnificent staircase is a work of art. It was carved from one enormous mahogany tree cut down in South America and shipped to Little Rock so all the grains would match.

Some of the cavernous downstairs public rooms are sparsely furnished because they are often used for special functions, but a gracious sitting room has comfortable seating and a grand piano. More comfortable for guests is the bilevel upstairs sitting room, which has a raised area where you can sit and look out the front windows. A buffet in this room is outfitted with an instant hot-water dispenser, and there's a generous selection of coffees, teas, and hot chocolate as well as ice, fruit, cheese, crackers, soft drinks, and complimentary beer and wine. Be sure to stop in the upstairs conference room to see the tapestry covering the walls above the paneling.

Generously proportioned and grandly decorated guest rooms feature king- or queen-size beds—some of them heavily carved rice four-poster or tester beds—along with all the modern creature comforts. Suzanne says a lot of research went in to determining authentic colors for the guest chambers; the results are burgundy, mustard, dark green, and steel blue. All but one have gas-log fireplaces. Many of the bathrooms have antique sinks, and some sport claw-foot tubs.

A full breakfast is served in the baronial dining room or the bright, airy conservatory, which is where most guests prefer to dine. This delightful sunny room features leaded-glass windows all the way around and a floor of hand-painted white Italian tiles splashed with colorful designs of red, yellow, and green; the domed ceiling alternates clear and turquoise panes of glass. Cast-iron bistro chairs, tables topped with plaid cloths that pick up the colors in the tiles and glass panes, as well as numerous plants create a festive turn-of-the-century atmosphere. (It's no wonder the Victorians spent so much time in their conservatories!) Breakfast might consist of French toast, waffles, buttermilk pancakes, frittatas, or fluffy Cajun omelettes accompanied by a fruit dish such as a poached pear stuffed with lemons, raisins, and pecans.

Peter Hotze, an Austrian immigrant, had a fascinating life, including fighting on the side of the Confederacy in several Civil War battles and being taken prisoner. Obviously, he was an extraordinarily successful businessman as well. Be sure to ask your hosts more about him. The Gateses are pretty fascinating themselves: Their travels as businesspeople working for IBM helped them create a bed and breakfast that meets the needs of other business travelers.

What's Nearby Little Rock

See page 70 for what's nearby Little Rock.

The Josolyn House (Best Buy)

501 North Palm Street
Little Rock, Arkansas 72205
(501) 666-5995 or (877) 567-6596

E-MAIL: JJB0705@aol.com

WEB SITE: www.josolynhouse.com

INNKEEPERS: Cindy and Joe Bures

ROOMS: 1 suite and 1 single room with shared bath, cottage with private bath; all with clock radio, flashlight, TV, bath amenities, luggage rack, telephone; limited wheelchair access

ON THE GROUNDS: Porches, deck, landscaped grounds

RATES: $69 to $89 in the house, $129 for the cottage, all including full breakfast, afternoon refreshments, evening turndown service

CREDIT CARDS ACCEPTED? Yes

OPEN: Year-round

HOW TO GET THERE: Take I–630 to exit 4, Fair Park Boulevard. Go north on Fair Park, which becomes Van Buren when it crosses Markham, for 0.8 mile to Lee Avenue. Turn right and go 4 blocks to North Palm. The B&B is on the corner of Lee and Palm. Park in the driveway in the back, which is entered from Lee.

indy's bubbly personality is just the first attraction that got our attention at the Josolyn House. Although you arrive as a visitor, Cindy wants you to leave as a friend or, better yet, one of the family. Then there's the house, of course, and the beautifully landscaped grounds. The neat, trim Craftsman-style stucco cottage was built in turn-of-the-century Hillcrest—Little Rock's first suburb. Another big plus here is the attention to detail, which means even the smallest things are just right.

Cheerful guest accommodations furnished in antiques and reproductions are offered on the lower level of the main house and in a newly constructed cottage that blends so well with the house, you'd swear it's original. The two guest rooms—one a queen, the other a single—and kitchen in the main house can be configured in various combinations. Both bedrooms have private entrances as well.

The spacious Queen Guest Quarters has a comfortable sleeping area and a sitting area with an entertainment system, an old-fashioned free-standing gas-log fireplace, and a large selection of games; rental includes the use of the microwave and refrigerator in the kitchen. The Single Guest Quarters is the perfect place for a businessperson traveling alone, or it can be combined with the Queen Room to provide accommodations for an additional family member. These two accommodations share one bathroom. You can rent the single room with the bath or the entire suite, but if only one is rented, the other remains empty so strangers won't have to share a bath. The cottage, which was just being completed when we visited, will obviously be popular with honeymooners. The large, airy, cathedral-ceilinged bedroom is dominated by an iron four-poster tester bed draped in diaphanous fabric, a freestanding gas-log fireplace, and a double whirlpool tub. This love nest also boasts a full bath with a corner shower as well as a hospitality room with a refrigerator and microwave. Stained-glass windows and Tiffany-style lamps and chandeliers complete the romantic ambience.

Guests are welcome to come upstairs in the main house to use the formal parlor and to visit with Cindy and Joe. In cool weather you might want to sip a cup of hot chocolate by the fireplace, but in warm weather you'll be more likely to take a glass of ice-cold lemonade out on the wicker-filled front porch or the more casual back deck. Both are good vantage points from which to enjoy the grounds and watch the birds visiting the feeders or bird-bath. Cindy says watching the sunset from the front porch is spectacular.

Attention to details here means taking into account all the amenities you may need or wish. It means the best-quality sheets, plump pillows, luxurious bed coverings, ample drawer space for unpacking, generous closet or armoire space for your hanging clothes, a writing desk stocked with stamps, envelopes, and pens, and turndown service with homemade chocolate treats. A savory breakfast might include apple lasagna, ham and asparagus frittata, or bird's nests—phyllo dough filled with spinach, eggs, Parmesan cheese, green onions, and hollandaise sauce. Our mouths watered just hearing about this specialty. Cindy assures us that after you taste it, you'll never want eggs Benedict again.

Surrounded on two sides by a stacked-stone wall, the grounds have been beautifully planted with trees, shrubs, annuals, and perennials punctuated with an arbor, but our favorite was the whimsical "flower bed"—an iron bed frame planted with flowers.

What's Nearby Little Rock

See page 70 for what's nearby Little Rock.

Pinnacle Vista Lodge

7510 AR 300
Little Rock, Arkansas 72223
(501) 868-8905

E-MAIL: pinnacle@arkansas.net

WEB SITE: www.pinnaclevista.com

INNKEEPER: Linda Westergard

ROOMS: 2 rooms and 1 suite; all with private bath; 2 rooms with data port

ON THE GROUNDS: Barn, trails, pond, fishing

RATES: $89 to $115 single or double, including breakfast, snacks, beverages; additional person in suite $15; ask about the two-night Romantic Getaway package

CREDIT CARDS ACCEPTED? Yes

OPEN: Year-round

HOW TO GET THERE: From I–430, take the Cantrell exit and go west about 7 miles. Turn right onto AR 300. The B&B is about 0.75 mile on your right.

A country haven at the edge of the city, this rustic home, which sits on twenty-three acres in the shadow of Pinnacle Mountain, offers the simple joys of rural life. We arrived in the spring just at the end of daffodil season, when thousands of the cheery yellow flowers bloomed around the house. The surrounding fields were seas of yellow or light blue wildflowers waving in the breeze. We knew right away that this would be a perfect spot to unwind.

Built in the 1930s and suitably weathered as well as being shaded by old trees, the three-story log lodge blends into the landscape. Inside, the expansive great room contains a comfortable sitting area grouped around a stone fireplace, a raised dining area, and what we can only describe as a play area. Dominating this section of the room is an old-fashioned bar with barber chairs pulled up to it, but there's also a player piano, a turn-of-the-century Brunswick pool table, a pinball machine, a jukebox, and a popcorn cart filled with the freshly popped snack. This is a great place to gather with your fellow guests, as is the large front deck. When you want some alone time, there are swings overlooking the stocked fish pond, a barn, and trails meandering through the property. You can even pick your own wild blackberries. Some guests like to use the barbecue grills, so they don't have to leave the property even to eat.

When it comes time to tuck yourselves in for a quiet night of deep, country slumber, the lodge offers three guest accommodations—two rooms and a two-room suite. These cozy chambers have hardwood floors covered with simple area rugs and are filled with early-nineteenth-century, 1920s, and wicker furnishings, hand-stitched quilts, and country accents. The Greenery can be configured with twin beds—which can also be made into a king. The most interesting piece in the Victorian Rose Room, which features a small private deck, is a sofa built into a massive oak library cabinet. Nana's Retreat has a separate bed/sitting room that has an iron daybed with a trundle. In addition to a large private deck, this suite has a closet outfitted as a snack center with a small refrigerator, microwave, and coffeemaker—ideal for a family or two couples traveling together.

What's Nearby Little Rock

See page 70 for what's nearby Little Rock.

Twelve Oak Inn and Riding Stable

6925 Highway 300
Little Rock, Arkansas 72212
(501) 868-4812

INNKEEPER: Ruth Ann Robinson

ROOMS: 4; 2 with private bath; all with TV, VCR, telephone; pets and horses welcome; wheelchair accessible

ON THE GROUNDS: Porches, stables, paddocks, riding lessons, trail rides, pond

RATES: $69 for shared bath, $89 for private bath, single or double; additional adult $10; children $5

CREDIT CARDS ACCEPTED? Yes

OPEN: Year-round

HOW TO GET THERE: From I-430 on the western side of Little Rock, take the Highway 10/Cantrell Road exit. Go west 7 miles and turn right onto AR 300. Twelve Oak is just ahead on your left.

Whether you're traveling with your kids, your pets, or even your horses, you'll find a perfect place to bed down at Twelve Oak with its homey, ranchlike atmosphere in a country setting. How many places can you find that provide stables and pasture for your equine companions? Where else can you awaken to see horses outside your window or hop out of bed for an early-morning ride? For horse lovers, this is a comfortable working horse ranch in the heart of Arkansas, yet within a few minutes' drive of Little Rock.

The simple low-slung, one-story ranch house sports a deeply shaded full-length veranda with plenty of wicker where you can sit a spell. Inside, the decor is eclectic but definitely has a western flavor. The great room, which serves as both living and dining room, is full of surprises. A saddle, equine art, chamois-soft deer hides, antlers, and an elk skin attest to Ruth's background as a rancher and wilderness adventurer, but modern art, brocade-upholstered furniture grouped around a fireplace, and a grand piano impart a semiformal air. Hardwood floors and a beamed ceiling complete the picture.

Guest rooms also have western names and themes with heavy wood furnishings, quilts, and ranch or horsey accessories. Both the Rancher and Branding Iron have queen-size beds and private baths as well as a special feature: The Rancher has a private entrance and Branding Iron sports a woodstove. The Trail Boss with its king-size bed and the Round-Up with two double beds share a bath, making either or both perfect for a family or friends traveling together. A full country breakfast will get all you cowboys and -girls off to a good start for an active day. *Casual friendliness* and *accommodation* are the bywords here.

What's Nearby Little Rock

See page 70 for what's nearby Little Rock.

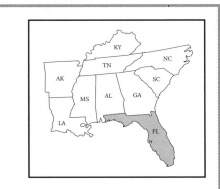

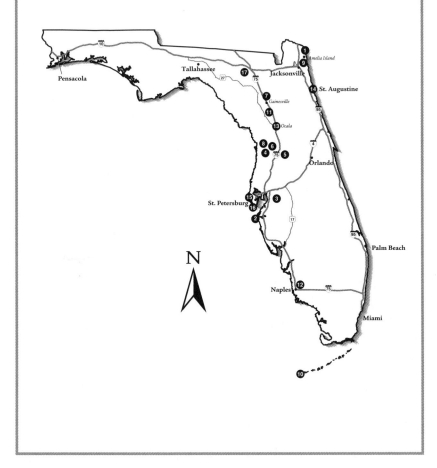

Pensacola

Tallahassee

17 Jacksonville

1 Amelia Island
9

14 St. Augustine

7 Gainesville
11

13 Ocala

8
6
4 **5**

Orlando

15
St. Petersburg **16**
2

3

Palm Beach

12
Naples

Miami

10

N

Florida

Numbers on map refer to towns numbered below.

1. Amelia Island,
   The Amelia Island Williams
      House, 80
   The Bailey House, 82
   The 1735 House, 83

2. Anna Maria Island/Holmes
   Beach, Harrington House Beachfront Bed and Breakfast, 84

3. Brandon, Behind the Fence B&B
   Inn, 86

4. Brooksville, Verona House
   B&B, 88

5. Bushnell,
   Cypress House Bed and
      Breakfast Inn, 90
   Veranda House Bed and
      Breakfast, 92

6. Floral City, The Cottage at
   Shadowbright, 94

7. Gainesville,
   The Magnolia Plantation, 95
   Sweetwater Branch Inn Bed
      and Breakfast, 97

8. Inverness,
   The Lake House Bed and
      Breakfast, 99
   Magnolia Glen Bed and
      Breakfast, 101
   Running Deer Lodge, 102

9. Jacksonville, House on Cherry
   Street, 104

10. Key West,
    Center Court Historic Inn and
       Cottages, 105
    The Curry Mansion Inn, 107

11. Micanopy,
    Herlong Mansion, 109
    Shady Oak Bed and
       Breakfast, 111

12. Naples, Inn by the Sea, 113

13. Ocala, Seven Sisters Inn, 114

14. St. Augustine, Casa de la Paz,
    116

15. St. Petersburg,
    Bayboro House, 118
    Bay Gables Bed and Breakfast,
       Garden, and Tea Room, 120
    Mansion House Bed and
       Breakfast, 121
    Sunset Bay Bed and Breakfast,
       123

16. St. Petersburg Beach, Pasa
    Tiempo Bed and Breakfast
    Inn, 125

17. Wellborn, McLeran House Bed
    and Breakfast, 127

The Amelia Island Williams House

103 South Ninth Street
Amelia Island, Florida 32034
(904) 277-2328 or (800)
414-9257; fax (904) 321-1325

E-MAIL: topinn@aol.com

WEB SITE: www.williamshouse.com

INNKEEPERS: Richard Flitz and
Chris Carter

ROOMS: 8; all with private bath, TV, and telephone; 2 with two-person soaking tub; 2 with Jacuzzi; 3 with two-person shower; 1 with wheelchair access

ON THE GROUNDS: English walking gardens, bicycles

RATES: $145 to $225 single or double, including gourmet full breakfast

CREDIT CARDS ACCEPTED? Yes

OPEN: Year-round

HOW TO GET THERE: From I-95, take exit 129 and head toward Amelia Island/ Fernandina Beach on Highway A1A. Go 14 miles. When the road narrows to two lanes, go through the next two traffic lights. At the next corner, turn right onto Ash Street. The inn is on the corner of Ninth and Ash.

This place has been raking in the raves steadily since it opened in 1994. It's been shown on television, written up in newspaper stories, and featured with full-color photography in slick magazines. Everyone who has tried to write about it has been a little boggled, because journalists are trained to avoid superlative adjectives. Yet the place seems to demand them. The inn, comprised of two of the oldest houses in Amelia Island, has Civil War history, guest rooms decorated with perfect taste in an assortment of fine antiques, gourmet breakfasts prepared to look as good as they taste, and skillful, involved innkeepers.

Dick and Chris opened the Williams House, built in 1856; then, a couple of years later, they acquired the next-door Hearthstone, believed to have been built about 1859. Each house has four guest rooms, but all the common spaces are in the Williams House. Guests receive keys to their own rooms and to the Williams House, so they'll find it easy to treat the two buildings as a single inn.

Both buildings required extensive renovation to bring them back to their earlier grandeur. After that, the furnishings and decorating command your attention. Although every room is luxurious and has its own priceless antiques, it's the Versailles French Room in the Hearthstone that astonishes guests. It has a white marble fireplace and a huge, turn-of-the-century headboard of baby blue antiqued with gold. The bathroom is 14 by 16 feet, done in white marble with an Oriental carpet, a two-person Jacuzzi, a two-person shower, and a crystal chandelier in the arch. Dick calls it "decadent." When they first see the Versailles Room, guests often exclaim, "Oh my god!" And by the time they get to the bathroom, they're exclaiming phrases that don't usually get written into guidebooks. The first guest who ever stayed in the room wrote an entire page in the guest book. Another guest wrote a challenge to those who followed to help maintain the room in prime condition, because "we will be back." But plan way, way ahead if you want this room, because it's popular. One man who wanted it for his wedding anniversary, and was willing to be flexible about when he and his wife took it, still found the room booked solid for more than a month.

It would be no penance to stay in one of the other opulent rooms. Some of their names—the Leonardo da Vinci Italian Room, the Manchurian Dynasty Suite, and the Chinese Blue Room, for instance—give you a clue to their themes and nature. All the rooms live up to the red and gold formal dining room, where breakfast is served at a 12-foot inlaid wood table with Chippendale chairs. There is a fireplace, a mantel of hand-carved mahogany, and a 5-foot European crystal chandelier that matches another one in the living room. In this dining room breakfast is served on fine antique china, sterling silver, and crystal.

Some of the other remarkable pieces at the inn are a robe worn by the last emperor of China, Japanese watercolors from 1597, and a lamp that once belonged to Napoleon III. Such elegance fits the beginnings of the Williams House; it was built by a wealthy banker who had Jefferson Davis as a guest and kept some of his personal items during the Civil War. During Yankee occupation, the building became a hospital for Union troops. Still later, the home was a safe house for runaway slaves. The secret room where they hid is still here.

What's Nearby Amelia Island

Amelia Island boats 13 miles of quiet sandy beaches—and it's one of the only resorts along the Atlantic where you can ride a horse on the beach. Seahorse Stable offers horseback rides daily, which last about one and a quarter hours. You can also explore the island's creeks, marshes, and rivers aboard guided kayaking tours.

The Bailey House

28 South Seventh Street
Amelia Island, Florida 32034
(904) 261–5390 or (800) 251–5390

E-MAIL: bailey@net-magic.net

WEB SITE: www.bailey-house.com

INNKEEPERS: Tom and Jenny Bishop

ROOMS: 10; all with private bath and TV; some with whirlpool tubs;
1 with kitchen

ON THE GROUNDS: Verandas, bicycles available

RATES: $105 to $175, single or double, including full breakfast

CREDIT CARDS ACCEPTED? Yes

OPEN: Year-round

HOW TO GET THERE: From I-95 or US 17, take Route A1A to Amelia Island.
Stay on A1A. In Fernandina Beach on Amelia Island, A1A becomes
Eighth Street. Turn left onto Centre Street and left again onto Seventh
Street. The Bailey House is on the left corner at Seventh and Ash Streets.

Unlike some antiques-filled Victorian inns, the Bailey House at Fernand-ina Beach on Amelia Island has a homey, lived-in feeling. You feel that it would be okay just to walk in and sit down.

The Bishops have a fine collection of Victorian antique furniture, but they've arranged it carefully so that no room seems too full and you never feel as if you're bumping into knickknacks everywhere you turn. Conse-quently, you're able to give a lot of attention to some special pieces. We were charmed by the working pump organ, and mentally conjured up all kinds of stories about the old wicker bath chair. A 150-year-old crystal chandelier in the large turret of the parlor is a focal point. The Bishops have worked steadily at upgrading everything about the Bailey House, which is listed on the National Register of Historic Places.

Each of the ten guest rooms has its own special features: a king-size bed with a hand-carved headboard in the Rose Room; an antique footed tub (and separate shower) in the Country Room; imported marble fireplace and two-person whirlpool in the French Garden; and towels and sheets coordi-nated with the color scheme in each room. Oriental rugs throughout tie everything together.

Breakfast is spread on the marble-topped buffet in the dining room bay window for guests to help themselves to in the morning. In addition to the usual coffee, juice, fruits, and homemade granola, the Bishops feature bran muffins with nuts and raisins.

Fernandina Beach on Amelia Island has had good food for a long time, and in recent years some great new places have been added. For lunch, Bretts, an old favorite, serves salads, soups, good breads, and pasta creations. Snugg Harbor is a popular favorite these days for seafood, and the Beech Street Grill, kind of a coastal bistro, receives the Bishops' special, enthusiastic recommendation. An added bonus—all these restaurants are within walking distance of the inn.

What's Nearby Amelia Island

See page 81 for what's nearby Amelia Island.

The 1735 House

584 South Fletcher
Amelia Island, Florida 32034
(904) 261-4148 or (800) 872-8531;
fax (904) 261-9200

E-MAIL: frontdesk@1735house-bb.cc

WEB SITE: www.1735house-bb.com

INNKEEPERS: The Auld family

ROOMS: 5 rooms and 1 suite in lighthouse; all with private bath and TV

ON THE GROUNDS: Cooking and laundry facilities, beachfront

RATES: $130 to $165 single or double, including continental breakfast

CREDIT CARDS ACCEPTED? Yes

OPEN: Year-round

HOW TO GET THERE: Amelia Island is near the Florida/Georgia border. Take the Yulee exit from I-95 onto Route A1A and follow the signs toward Fernandina Beach. The inn is on A1A.

You don't find many places like the 1735 House at the beach these days. It's a Cape Cod-style inn, directly facing the ocean, furnished with antiques, wicker, neat old trunks, and some bunk beds just right for kids.

Maybe there will be no room at the inn, and you'll stay instead in the lighthouse. Its walls are covered with navigation maps. As you enter, you can either step down into a shower and bath area or take the spiral stairs up to the kitchen. A galley table and director's chairs make a good spot for playing cards, chatting, or ocean gazing as well as eating. The stairs keep spiraling up to a bedroom with another bath, and finally up to an enclosed observation deck, which is the ultimate spot for drinking in the ocean views.

Wherever you stay, in the evening all you have to do is tell the staff what time you want breakfast and they'll deliver it right to your room in a wicker basket, along with a morning paper.

The physical setup is uncommon, but the staff have the true inn spirit. They'll give you ice, towels for the beach, bags for your shell collection or wet bathing suit, and just about anything else you need. All you have to do is ask.

The staff are full of helpful recommendations about good eating places, of which there are many on Amelia Island, too. The Down Under Seafood Restaurant, under the Shave bridge on A1A, is in keeping with the nautical mood of the inn and the lighthouse. The seafood is all fresh from the Intracoastal Waterway. There's a boat ramp with a dock, and the atmosphere is correspondingly quaint. You can enjoy cocktails and dinner.

If staying at the 1735 House gets you in the mood for more inns, you're welcome to browse through a large, well-used collection of books about inns in the office.

What's Nearby Amelia Island

See page 81 for what's nearby Amelia Island.

Harrington House Beachfront Bed and Breakfast

5626 Gulf Drive
Anna Maria Island/Holmes
Beach, Florida 34217
(941) 778-5444 or (888) 828-5566;
fax (941) 778-0527

E-MAIL: harhousebb@mail.pcsonline.com
WEB SITE: www.harringtonhouse.com
INNKEEPERS: Jo and Frank Davis

ROOMS: 11 rooms and 1 cottage; all with private bath, cable TV, desk, telephone, small refrigerator; some with ceiling fan; 1 with whirlpool tub; 2 rooms with wheelchair access

ON THE GROUNDS: Bicycles, kayaks, swimming pool, beachfront, equipment and games, gift shop

RATES: $129 to $239 double, including full gourmet breakfast and refreshments; two-night minimum stay on holidays and weekends

CREDIT CARDS ACCEPTED? Yes

OPEN: Year-round

HOW TO GET THERE: From I–75, take exit 42B (northbound) or 42 (southbound) and go east on Manatee Avenue, Route 64, over the causeway to Anna Maria Island. Turn right onto County Road 789, Gulf Drive. The Harrington House is on your left on the beach side.

You don't have to go to an anonymous, cookie-cutter motel or high-rise hotel, nor do you have to rent an entire house, to get beachfront accommodations. At relatively undiscovered Holmes Beach on the Florida Gulf Coast's Anna Maria Island, bed-and-breakfast accommodations are offered in a charming restored 1920s multilevel stucco home and adjacent 1940s one-story cottage located on one and a half acres directly on the Gulf of Mexico and both surrounded and separated by thick stands of pines. The Harrington House is a place of casual elegance, where antiques and eclectic furnishings combine with floral patterns in the wallpapers, window treatments, and bed coverings to create old Florida charm.

Although every guest room is different, each is light and summery, with a soft romantic touch and a cozy feel of home. Eight rooms are found in the Main House, four in the Beach House. Many have French doors leading to balconies overlooking the pool and the Gulf of Mexico. A variety of bedding sizes ranges from twins to several kings created from two twins. Among the most popular are two found in the Beach House. The Surfside has a four-poster bed, wraparound walls of windows, and a deck. The Gulfside has a king-size wicker bed, whirlpool tub, and deck.

What's important here isn't what the houses and decor look like, but everything you can do. Watch stunning sunrises and sunsets. Listen to the soothing sounds of the ocean lapping against the shore. Walk all or part of the 7 miles of white sand beach. Take moonlight strolls hand in hand with your honey. Kayak with the dolphins. Take a tour of the island by bicycle. Splash in the pool. Soak up some rays on the pool deck or the beach. Revel in the gracious hospitality. But most of all—bask in the tropical surroundings and tranquillity. This is a bed and breakfast where you'll stay around all day rather than running off for sight-seeing and shopping.

Morning coffee is set out at 7:00 A.M. for early risers. A good stiff walk on the beach or a few laps in the heated pool will work up an appetite for a breakfast that might consist of stuffed French toast, eggs Benedict, omelettes, frittatas, or pancakes with strawberries and whipped cream and all the accompaniments. A refrigerator well stocked with cold drinks is a welcome respite from the heat of the day.

Although the weather's great here year-round, there are those occasional chilly or overcast days. These are the times to curl up with a good book and a mug of hot chocolate by the fireplace in the great room with its 20-foot open-beam ceiling. When night falls, take the pecky cypress staircase to your room.

What's Nearby Anna Maria Island/Holmes Beach

Anna Maria Island was founded by the father of the Fig Newton, Charles Roser, who sold his popular recipe to Nabisco. Anna Maria is adjacent to Holmes Beach, where you'll be treated to international cuisine. Not to worry—you can work off the calories by swimming, jet skiing, or sailing. Of course, shopping is great exercise, and there are plenty of stores to see at Holmes Beach.

Behind the Fence B&B Inn

Best Buy

1400 Viola Drive
Brandon, Florida 33511
(813) 685-8201

INNKEEPERS: Carolyn and Larry Yoss

ROOMS: 3 rooms, 1 suite, 1 cottage; all with private bath, phone, TV, VCR

ON THE GROUNDS: Swimming pool

RATES: $59 to $79 double, including breakfast, afternoon tea, and evening snack; guest microwave and refrigerator; additional person $10 extra; children younger than ten free

CREDIT CARDS ACCEPTED? Not at this time

OPEN: Year-round

HOW TO GET THERE: From I–75, take exit 49, US 301 South. Instead of following 301, though, stay on Bloomingdale. Turn left onto Countryside, then left again onto Viola. The B&B is on your right.

Located close to historic Ybor City outside Tampa, this bed and breakfast is full of surprises. To get there, we drove through a neighborhood of brick ranch homes probably built in the 1950s; we were sure we'd made a mistake somewhere with the directions. Lo and behold, we came upon a large fenced, heavily wooded lot shaded with pines and oaks. Once we pulled into the driveway, we could have sworn we'd left west-central Florida far behind for the New England of yesteryear, because before us sat a saltbox-style home we were convinced was built in the 1700s or early 1800s. Acutally, the house is only twenty-two years old, but the lumber used to construct it was salvaged from nineteenth-century buildings located as far away as Michigan. This ambitious project was undertaken after Carolyn and Larry's unsuccessful search for an appropriate house in which to showcase their early American and Amish antiques.

Inside, they've enhanced the nineteenth-century ambience by scouring Hillsborough County for old staircases, doors, windows, and other authentic antique architectural elements. The great room, for instance, has paneled walls, a beamed ceiling, and a circa-1825 Ohio mantel. Furnishings, which are primarily Amish antiques, are perfectly suited to the period evoked by the house. Baskets, hand-dipped candles, tin lanterns, and dried-herb wreaths or bundles of dry herbs reinforce the look of a simpler time. Larry built one of the sofas in the great room. A folk-art-style portrait of Carolyn painted by one of her daughters hangs over this couch.

Simply furnished guest rooms feature pencil-post beds, primitive armoires, and straight chairs, complemented with homespun bed linens and curtains, shutters, and rag rugs. In addition to rooms in the main house, the Yosses offer two accommodations in a cottage separated from the main house by a swimming pool designed to resemble a lagoon. This cottage, which has a deeply shaded front porch, was fashioned from lumber salvaged from late-nineteenth-century Tampa Bay buildings scheduled for demolition.

Breakfast consists of homemade sweet rolls from Amish recipes and pastries from a nearby berry farm. Herbal tea is served in the afternoon, and on chilly evenings you can enjoy popcorn served by the fireplace.

The Yosses are so enthusiastic about the early-1800s lifestyle that they open the B&B to school tours and invite spinners, weavers, and blacksmiths to demonstrate old-fashioned skills and crafts. They teach everything from soap making to fireplace cooking.

What's Nearby Brandon

Brandon started as a farming community, but over the years it has transformed into a popular business and shopping district. The Brandon Town Center claims to be one of the country's largest shopping malls. If you enjoy ice skating, don't miss the new Ice Sports Forum, which has two skating rinks. The Tampa Bay Lightning regularly practice there.

Verona House B&B Best Buy

201 South Main Street
Brooksville, Florida 34601
(352) 796-4001 or (800) 355-6717

E-MAIL: veronabb@gate.net

WEB SITE: bbhost.com/veronabb

INNKEEPERS: Jan and Bob Boyd

ROOMS: 4 rooms and 1 cottage; all with private bath, phone, ceiling fan, clock radio. 1 room is wheelchair accessible; 1 room is set up with desk, two phone lines, data port, power bar, and surge protector

ON THE GROUNDS: Full-length front veranda, outdoor hot tub

RATES: $55 to $80 single or double, including breakfast, newspaper, and early coffee

CREDIT CARDS ACCEPTED? Yes

OPEN: Year-round

HOW TO GET THERE: From I-75, take exit 61, FL 50, west to Brooksville. At the town square, turn left onto South Main Street. The inn is on your left

Once upon a time the great catalog purveyor Sears Roebuck offered complete home-construction kits for as little as $645. Now, we're not talking about a set of plans—we're talking about all the materials necessary to construct a six- or seven-room house. You paid extra only for the land and the labor. Sears even offered financing with no money down. In the years between 1908 and 1937, around 100,000 home kits in nearly a hundred designs were sold, many of which survive today and are listed on the National Register of Historic Places. One such dwelling houses the Verona House B&B.

Built in 1925, this charming seven-room Dutch Colonial design, to which a full-length front veranda was added, was one of the more expensive Sears models at $2,461. Although added at a much later date, ornately carved panels topped by whimsical cherubs flank the front door. They are believed to have come from Europe. Over the intervening years the house has variously served as a private residence, an antiques store, and now a bed and breakfast. Huge, sprawling live oaks surround the structure, adding to its southern charm. The two largest trees are more than a hundred years old and are registered with the Louisiana Live Oak Society. In the early 1990s a previous owner wanted to cut them down to provide space for off-street parking; after a legal wrangle they were saved and now provide attractive shade for today's appreciative visitors.

Since 1995 Jan and Bob Boyd have been offering generous helpings of gracious Southern hospitality. The Boyds want guests to feel at home, and to feel as if they're slipping back in time to yesteryear. The bywords here are *comfort* and *informality*. In the tradition of homes of the period, Jan and Bob have furnished Verona House with simple antiques, quilts, collectibles, and memorabilia from a simpler time—many pieces of which are for sale.

Several of the compact, simply furnished and decorated guests rooms feature old iron beds, but all are queen size; one offers an additional twin daybed. Each has a private bath, although one requires that you go out in the hall to reach it. Baths have tubs or showers. One is quite eccentric. A former owner surrounded an authentic claw-foot tub in an elaborate tile enclosure—very 1950s looking.

Guests are encouraged to gather in the formal downstairs sitting room or the informal one upstairs, which is equipped with a television, radio, and small refrigerator. Coffee, tea, and hot chocolate are always available here.

The Boyds will fix you any type of breakfast you want. They say that most businesspeople prefer a simple breakfast, and weekend guests often prefer a full one, but just speak up and let them know what you want. They aim to please.

What's Nearby Brooksville

It's Christmas every day except December 25 at Roger's Christmas House and Village, which closes its doors on Christmas. If you need to do some Christmas shopping six months or six days in advance, Roger's is the place to visit. The village sells holiday gifts, wreaths, trees, and the widest selection of ornaments in the country. The holiday spirit may inspire you to shop 'til you drop, which may take you to Brooksville's antiques shops, crafts and gift shops.

Cypress House Bed and Breakfast Inn

5175 Southwest 90th Boulevard
Bushnell, Florida 33513
(352) 568-0909 or (888) 568-1666

WEB SITE: www.bbonline.com/fl/cypresshouse/

INNKEEPER: Jan Fessler

ROOMS: 5; 3 with private bath, 2 share; all with ceiling fan, TV

ON THE GROUNDS: Verandas, horseback riding, screened lap pool, extensive grounds

RATES: $60 to $80 double, including full breakfast buffet; horseback riding $10 to $15 per hour

CREDIT CARDS ACCEPTED? Yes

OPEN: Year-round

HOW TO GET THERE: Take I–75 to exit 62, County Road 476B. Go west for about 2 miles to Southwest 90th Boulevard and turn right. The B&B is about 1 mile ahead at the end of the road.

We knew we were in the real Florida of the old days the minute we turned off the county road onto the sandy double track that brought us to Cypress House. Don't be fooled by the seemingly urban address—this property is pure country. As we shimmied along the uneven track, we were glad to be driving a rental pickup truck rather than our low-slung classic Cadillac. We passed open meadows with the occasional horse raising its head from grazing to see who was disturbing the silence, small stands of pines, and a couple of houses before entering the gates of the B&B. A small sign indicated that family and deliveries were to take one driveway, guests another. Then the rambling cypress farmhouse—known as the Big House—wrapped with verandas came into view. The setting was so peaceful and beautiful, the trees so old and stately, it was hard to believe that the house hadn't stood here for generations. It's new, however—built to accommodate both a family and B&B guests. We were welcomed by a friendly old dog and a cat or two before Jan, a retired teacher, came out to greet us.

Because Cypress House was specifically designed as a bed and breakfast, Jan and her mother are able to have a private wing with its own porch while guests are treated to the run of another extensive wing with a large dining room, small sitting room, three guest rooms, and a rocker-filled veranda. Additional accommodations are located in the pasture wing—a guest room and a suite (whose separate sitting room can sleep several children) located upstairs over the open-air horse stalls.

Antique farm furniture, quilts, and other country accents give each public and guest room a comfortable, casual ambience. We particularly enjoyed the old family photographs and collection of folk art in the dining room, which impressed us as the heart of the house. Of the guest rooms in the Big House, one is quite spacious and includes a sitting area with a television and a private bath. The other two rooms (one has a double bed, the other twins) share a bath. If these are not rented together to a family or two couples traveling together, Jan only rents one so that you'll have a private bath.

Breakfast is a generous buffet of entrees, breads, pastries, cereals, juices, seasonal fruits, and hot and cold beverages. Fixings for hot beverages are always available, and dessert is served each evening.

Cypress House is located on ten acres, so guests come here for peace and quiet and for outdoor activities. A simple walk around the property may afford sightings of deer, sandhill cranes, bobcats, eagles, or wild turkeys. Badminton or croquet can be set up under the towering oaks, and you might enjoy a splash in the lap pool. The most popular activity is riding through the farm's trails or in the nearby Withlacoochee Forest on one of the farm's nine horses, which are suitable for experienced and inexperienced riders. Riders are asked to view a safety and handling video and to wear protective helmets. During the hot summer months, rides are made in the morning or the evening for the protection of the horses, but even when they aren't being ridden, the equine members of the farm family are available for petting and feeding.

What's Nearby Bushnell

You don't have to flee far from Bushnell to find something interesting to do. Check out Webster Flea Market and visit more than 1,700 outdoor vendors. Be sure to wear good walking shoes, though, if you plan to survey all forty acres of stands.

Veranda House Bed and Breakfast

Best Buy

202 West Noble Avenue
Bushnell, Florida 33513
(352) 793-3579

WEB SITE: www.bbonline.com/fl/
veranda/

INNKEEPERS: Barbara and Bill Pownall

ROOMS: 2; 1 bath (unless rented to a
family or two couples traveling together,
only one room is rented so guests will have a private bath)

ON THE GROUNDS: Upstairs and downstairs verandas, guest sitting room,
garden, gazebo, tearoom, antiques shop

RATES: $68 double, including early-morning coffee, expanded continental
or full breakfast, and afternoon refreshments

CREDIT CARDS ACCEPTED? Yes

OPEN: Year-round in theory, but check ahead

HOW TO GET THERE: From I-75, take exit 63 to County Road 48 East. At the
first traffic light, turn right. At the next traffic light, turn right again. Go
2 blocks and look on the right side of the street for the two-story yellow
house surrounded by a white picket fence.

Blood, sweat, and tears—that's what we imagine Barbara and Bill Pownall
must have expended over the four years it took them to rehabilitate this
wonderful old house. The Pownalls are mum about the blood and tears,
but they'll readily admit that they spent more than 10,000 hours of sweat
equity on the renovations—commuting from Tampa where Bill was working as a firefighter (he's retired now). And they're still always finding more
things that need to be done. From our standpoint, their efforts have been
well worth it: They've created a gracious haven for themselves as well as for
their guests. Built in 1888, the beautiful cross-gabled Queen Anne Victorian
was originally used as a boardinghouse, so it's only appropriate that it has
returned to its hospitality function. Majestic live oaks, camphor trees, magnolias, azaleas, and a water tupelo envelope the house in shade.

The first thing we noticed about the Veranda House was the white
picket fence inviting us to step through into another time. (The fence itself
has a story to tell: The original ornate cast-iron one was removed in the
1940s and contributed to the World War II effort.) Next we were captivated

by the many-columned wraparound verandas on both the first and second floors. These porches, from which the bed and breakfast takes its name, give the house the festive air of an old-fashioned riverboat. Cooled by ceiling fans and filled with wicker and lush plants, both these verandas will be the site of many happy hours rocking away with a drink, a good book, or good conversation. Locals report that in the old days, the verandas were a popular place for courting.

Inside, we admired the spaciousness created by the 11½-foot ceilings downstairs and the 9½-foot ceilings upstairs, as well as the heart pine used throughout for floors, walls, and ceilings. Most of the walls and ceilings are constructed of narrow tongue-and-groove beaded paneling—some stained, some painted. We could almost imagine Teddy Roosevelt holding forth on one of his adventures in the guest sitting room, which has a turn-of-the-century safari- or hunting-lodge look. Dark paneling and hardwood floors, heavy Victorian furniture, a profusion of collectibles, and faux animal hide rugs, seat covers, and furniture throws fill the room to overflowing, yet merely serve as a backdrop for the dozens of mounted animals and animal heads—raccoon, fox, otter, armadillo, bobcat, deer, turtle, and more. (Don't worry about political incorrectness—Barbara assures us they were all roadkills given another life by one of Bill's fellow firefighters, who does taxidermy as a hobby.) Breakfast, which can be as heavy or light as you like, is served in the cozy dining room. On nice days Barbara will throw open the French doors, which overlook a modern deck, a landscaped garden, and a large Victorian gazebo.

Upstairs, two comfy-cozy guest rooms each boast gas-log fireplaces. Antique furnishings, ornate bed coverings and window treatments, and diverse collections of bric-a-brac give each room a distinctive personality. The room with the king-size bed looks into what Barbara calls her playroom—a narrow room filled with antique toys. The other room's twin beds can accommodate two adults traveling together, or be pushed together to make a king for a couple.

Because Barbara is German, the Pownalls go to Europe sometime during the year and close down the bed and breakfast for a few weeks, so don't just show up. Be sure to have an advance reservation.

What's Nearby Bushnell

See page 91 for what's nearby Bushnell.

The Cottage at Shadowbright Best Buy

8140 South Shadowbright Place
Floral City, Florida 34436
(352) 341-0546

E-MAIL: shadowbright@juno.com

WEB SITE: www.bbonline.com/fl/
shadowbright

INNKEEPERS: Cathy Ayers and Barry
Pendry

ROOMS: 1 cottage with kitchen, bedroom, private bath, telephone, TV; no
smoking, including on the screened porch

ON THE GROUNDS: Patio, terrace, two acres of grounds

RATES: $60 single or double ($5 is donated to the Floral City Heritage
Council), including continental breakfast; ask about special-occasion
packages

CREDIT CARDS ACCEPTED? Yes

OPEN: Year-round

HOW TO GET THERE: From I-75, take exit 63, Bushnell, and go west 12 miles
to Daniels Road, which is 2.8 miles past the bridge over the Withlacoochee River and just around the bend from the Department of Transportation maintenance site. Turn left onto Daniels. The first drive to
your right is Shadowbright Place. From US 41, go east on FL 48 at the
light in Floral City. Go 1 mile to Daniels Road and follow the above
directions.

From the moment we turned off Daniels Drive, we knew we'd entered a
fairy-tale world. A mere track ran through heavy woods and a line of
orange trees. Once through the gates, we came out into a parklike setting
along a canal. Ancient live oaks created towering canopies over lush beds of
ferns and other flora, with pieces of Oriental statuary scattered about the
grounds. This idyllic scene was created in the 1930s by Dr. Edward
Porter-St. John, a renowned theologian and botanist. It was he who named
his beloved hideaway Shadowbright. (Some of his writings are published in
a book called *Shadowbright Poems and Prose*.) Dr. Porter-St. John built a small
house and a separate garage, to which he attached a study. A subsequent
owner converted this humble structure into a cottage. Today Cathy and
Barry live in the house and guests are treated to a very secluded and private
stay in the vine-covered stone cottage.

Furnished with simple antiques and artwork and equipped with heat and air-conditioning, the cozy cottage features a comfortable living room with a television and VCR, a small fully equipped kitchen, a bedroom with a double bed and stone fireplace, a bathroom with shower, and a screened front porch. Breakfast is brought to the porch at a prearranged time, so you can dine at your leisure in any number of places: the porch, kitchen, terrace, or even in bed. We imagine that we'd spend endless hours reading and walking the grounds.

Whether you're looking for a romantic getaway, a personal retreat, or a base from which to explore the Nature Coast, you'll find privacy, comfort, convenience, and a delightful place to stay at Shadowbright. Former guests describe the cottage as "a little piece of heaven," "truly enchanted," "tranquil"; you will, too.

What's Nearby Floral City

Floral City offers plenty of nature activities, water sports, and antiquing. Bring your bike and try the Rails-to-Trails bicycle trail. If you enjoy boating, check out the Withlacoochee, Rainbow, Homossassa, Chassobowitzda, and Crystal Rivers.

The Magnolia Plantation

309 Southeast Seventh Street
Gainesville, Florida 32601
(352) 375-6653 or (800) 201-2379;
fax (352) 338-0303

E-MAIL: info@magnoliabnb.com

WEB SITE: www.magnoliabnb.com

INNKEEPERS: Joe and Cindy Montalto

ROOMS: 5 rooms and 1 corporate cottage; all with private bath, some with gas-log fireplace; telephone and TV available; cottage and Garden House have office with fax, answering machine, desk

ON THE GROUNDS: Gift shop, garden with waterfall, tandem bicycle

RATES: $85 to $150 single or double, including full breakfast and refreshments; inquire about weekday and extended-stay rates

CREDIT CARDS ACCEPTED? Yes

 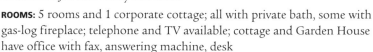

OPEN: Year-round

HOW TO GET THERE: From I-75, take FL 26, which becomes University Avenue in Gainesville. Continue on University Avenue past Main Street until you come to Southeast Seventh Street. Turn right onto Southeast Seventh and go through one intersection. The inn is on your left.

The Montaltos didn't have to buy much to furnish this inn. When their families, friends, and even neighbors saw what they were doing with this huge old Second Empire Victorian house, everyone started contributing antiques, china, and other treasures, as well as labor. Joe's father, a landscape architect, designed and helped plant the gardens. Cindy's aunt contributed family heirlooms that had belonged to Cindy's grandparents. Cindy's mother, who lives in the carriage house on the property, keeps the garden in shape and helps manage the inn. Joe's aunt and uncle donated the German lace curtains that grace some of the guest rooms. A priest from St. Augustine donated an old melodeon. A descendant of a woman who had once lived in the house brought a tea set. Everywhere you look you see pictures and mementos that have a story.

From your point of view, this matters for two reasons. First, it makes an interesting place to stay. Second, it tells you a lot about these innkeepers—their devotion to restoring the 1885 building authentically and their personal charm.

They're just nutty enough (Cindy has a small butterfly tattoo on her arm) to be fun, and caring enough to make people enjoy helping them.

When you enter the inn, you'll be glad they're honoring its original design intact; you first see an 8-foot-wide central hallway with a grand mahogany staircase. Then you go into the gentleman's parlor and library next to it. Here there will be fires in two of the inn's ten fireplaces if the weather is nippy.

You see the Montaltos' generosity in the dining room, where a refrigerator holds snacks, soda, wine, and beer, available any time you want them.

Cindy's breakfasts give you another insight into her nature. She says she serves "nothing you would get at home." Instead, you may get an elaborate baked French toast or, if you prefer, something more healthful. "Sometimes you gotta have yogurt, nuts, and twigs," Cindy says. After all, you may have worked up quite an appetite lounging in your bath in a claw-foot tub in your room!

To sum it up, the whole experience of staying at the Magnolia Plantation is nothing you would get at home!

What's Nearby Gainesville

If you have a taste for something different, visit the Wine and Cheese Gallery in Gainesville. Inside the gallery you'll see a gourmet food and wine shop. Outside, take a seat at one of the umbrellaed tables in the gallery's courtyard. After lunch, spend the afternoon at Gainesville's Florida Museum of Natural History and see a replica of a Mayan palace and a reconstructed Florida cave. Located in the University of Florida campus, the museum has one of the largest natural history collections in the country. Another fun attraction is the alligator-populated Lake Alice Wildlife Preserve, which is just down the street from the museum. See ya later, Alligator!

Sweetwater Branch Inn Bed and Breakfast

625 East University Avenue
Gainesville, Florida 32601
(352) 373-6760 or (800) 595-7760; fax (352) 371-3771

E-MAIL: reserve@sweetwaterinn.com

WEB SITE: www.sweetwaterinn.com

INNKEEPER: Cornelia Holbrook

ROOMS: 12 rooms, honeymoon cottage, and carriage house; all with private bath, claw-foot tub and shower, queen-size bed (except Blue Moon Room), telephone, sitting area and desk; TV on request; 4 accommodations with private sitting rooms; some with whirlpool bath; fax machine and other office services, meeting rooms, banquet facilities

ON THE GROUNDS: Porches, extensive grounds

RATES: $72 to $120 for a single or double room, $85 to $125 for a suite, $105 to $150 for the Honeymoon cottage; ask about rates for the carriage house; $20 for each additional person; all rates include full breakfast and afternoon refreshments

CREDIT CARDS ACCEPTED? Yes

OPEN: Year-round

HOW TO GET THERE: From I-75, take exit 76, FL 26, and follow it until it becomes University Avenue. The inn is on your right.

Nestled in a historic district of downtown Gainesville, Sweetwater Branch is really in a little world all to itself. Housed in two mansions and two cottages surrounded by lush tropical gardens with seven unique fountains, the inn offers gracious guest accommodations and special-events facilities.

Newly restored, the elegant Victorian home that contains the guests quarters was built in 1885. Inside, well-proportioned rooms, hardwood floors, antique furnishings, and period wall coverings and fabrics combine to create a soothing atmosphere of comfort and sophistication.

The day we arrived a glamorous wedding was under way in the secluded garden, but the inn's able staff was quite able to greet us, direct guests to the wedding, instruct the caterer, and make everyone feel completely at home. Of course, the cookies fresh out of the oven did their part as well!

Furnished to reflect the Victorian era of the mansion, elegant guest rooms feature pencil-post, sleigh, or canopied beds—all queen size but one. Bathrooms feature claw-foot tubs and showers. Among the most popular rooms because of its additional amenities, the Tiffany Room, which is the master suite, features an extra-large bathroom and a columned fireplace. Its second room can sleep an additional person. A whirlpool tub for two and a fireplace attract the romantic to the Tea Rose Room, our personal favorite. The Piccadilly Room features a sunroom/sitting room, which can sleep two additional people. Also built in 1885, the romantic Honeymoon Cottage boasts a living room with a large whirlpool tub and fireplace, as well as a fireplace in the bedroom, and a kitchen. More suited for a family or group of friends, the Carriage House sleeps five. Since we visited in 1998, five additional guest rooms have been created in the upstairs of McKenzie Hall next door, where the meeting rooms and banquet facilities are. These rooms are similarly furnished with Victorian reproductions and feature queen-size beds.

Although you'll luxuriate in your guest room, you'll also want to spend some time in the formal parlor, or relax outdoors on the porch or patio or while strolling through the gardens.

Awaken in the morning to the tantalizing aroma of the inn's own special blend of Costa Rican coffee. Enjoy a morning newspaper, then follow your nose to the formal dining room, where a delicious breakfast awaits. Among the favorite breakfast offerings are the inn's famous crepes and quiches. No matter what the entree, breakfast is always accompanied by fresh fruits and juices and hot beverages. If it's a special occasion, request breakfast in bed.

The Lake House Bed and Breakfast

8604 East Gospel Island Road
Inverness, Florida 34450
(352) 344-3586

E-MAIL: lakehouse@hitter.net

WEB SITE: www.bbchannel/usa/florida

INNKEEPER: Caroline Jenkins

ROOMS: 5; all with private bath, ceiling fan, TV

ON THE GROUNDS: Terrace, lakeshore

RATES: $60 to $100 single or double, including an expanded continental breakfast

CREDIT CARDS ACCEPTED? Yes

OPEN: Year-round

HOW TO GET THERE: From I–75, take exit 66, Wildwood and FL 44 and go west 12 miles to County Road 470. Turn right and continue for 2 miles. The Lake House is on your left and is identified by a sign.

A 1930s fishing lodge meets a Roman villa here on the shores of Lake Henderson. Really it's not as strange as it may sound—in fact, the overall look is quite appealing. Here's what happened. The modest fishing lodge was expanded at least five times by previous owners over the years, and fancified with pink stucco, temple pediments, and white columns. Two wings wrap around a pleasant formal courtyard centered on a fish pond filled with koi. The formal walkway down to the lake is lined with tall hedges and punctuated by pedestals topped with urn planters. Pairs of reclining lions guard the front entrance and the foot of the lake pathway. The Roman look ends at the entry hall, however. Inside, Caroline has created an upscale country-casual ambience in the guest rooms and public areas.

It's not surprising that Caroline would take on this unusual rambling house to operate as a bed and breakfast—after all, she's descended from generations of hoteliers. Her grandparents and parents had hotels in Wales, but like many young people, when Caroline became an adult, she swore she wouldn't have anything to do with the family business. Then fate intervened. Her parents came to Inverness to buy and operate the venerable Crown Hotel. They begged Caroline, who was working at an architecture firm in London at the time, to come over and help them—just for a year, they promised. She grudgingly agreed, completed her year, and was just ready to go back to England when she met Blake, who was to become her husband. The couple decided to open a bed and breakfast. They searched Florida, Georgia, and other areas before they found just what they wanted right in their own backyard in Inverness.

Once structural renovations were complete and the public spaces decorated, Caroline devised a clever scheme to decorate each of the five guest rooms. She took one room herself and assigned the remaining four to four other females in her family. Each woman was given a budget, but then allowed to let her own creativity take over. The results are striking. Each room, which is named for its creator—Caroline, Claire, Jill, Bonnie, and Dawn—is completely different, but they all complement each other. A lot of subdued blues are used, but in plaids, florals, and solids. Beds, most of which are queens, boast pencil posts, ornate posters, cannonball posters, or wicker headboards. To accommodate different kinds of travelers, one room has twin beds, and another boasts a twin-size daybed in addition to the queen bed. Several beds invite you to snuggle under down comforters. Bathrooms sport everything from the traditional tub/shower combo, to a shower tucked under the eaves, to a huge garden soaking tub.

There are plenty of places besides your room to be alone if that's what you want, or to mingle with other guests for breakfast or a glass of wine: the huge great room with its cathedral ceiling, enormous stone fireplace, and big-screen television; the library/game room; the dining room; several terraces; or the big side yard shaded by ancient live oaks dripping with Spanish moss.

What's Nearby Inverness

Inverness is nestled on the shore of Tomales Bay, and is a popular spot for swimming and boating. The Inverness Yacht Club holds weekly sailboat races in the summer and fall. The small downtown area is close to Chicken Ranch Beach. More beaches await in Tomales Bay State Park, such as Shell Beaches I and II and Heart's Desire Beach.

Magnolia Glen Bed and Breakfast

Best Buy

7702 East Allen Drive
Inverness, Florida 34450
(352) 726-1832 or (800) 881-4366

E-MAIL: bonbon@citrus.infi.net
WEB SITE: www.magnoliaglen.com
INNKEEPER: Bonnie Kuntz
ROOMS: 3; 1 with private bath, 2 share;
all with clock and ceiling fan, Greenleaf toiletries
ON THE GROUNDS: Brick courtyard with umbrella table and chairs, lawn
leading to lakeshore, canoe, small sailboat
RATES: $65 single or double, including full breakfast; two nights or more
midweek $100; weekend special $120
CREDIT CARDS ACCEPTED? Yes
OPEN: Year-round
HOW TO GET THERE: From I-75, take exit 66, Wildwood and FL 44. Go west
12 miles to County Road 470. Go right. Turn left onto East Allen Drive
just before you see a sign for the Bel Air neighborhood. Follow East Allen
until you see the sign for Magnolia Glen on your right.

Bonnie is a petite, effervescent woman whom we could easily believe is a
former interior designer. What we were amazed to learn is that she is
also a champion sailboat racer. Her love of the sea led her to theme her
B&B around Lord Admiral Horatio Nelson; you'll see several models of sailing ships in prominent places, including the mantel over the fireplace in the
cathedral-ceilinged great room.

But first, the house and property. After we drove through a neighborhood of modest one-story bungalows, the stately Tudor residence came as a
surprise. The manor, built in 1984, sits back from the street amid old live
oaks draped in swaying Spanish moss as well as mature magnolias and azaleas. In the rear the lawn slopes gently to the lakeshore.

Inside, Bonnie has let her creativity run riot in decorating the guest
rooms and public spaces. The walls in several of the rooms are embellished
with very unusual faux finishes, and you'll see many other dramatic accents.
The dressy Trafalgar Room is a favorite with romantics because of its
Jacuzzi tub. The Lake Room and Savannah Room, which share the nautical
Admiral's Head bathroom, couldn't be more different. Oversize twin beds
with headboards, footboards, and canopy frames created from small stag-

gerwood and hickory saplings dominate the rustic Lake Room. Southern floral freshness is created with one burgundy wall and ample use of pink and burgundy floral prints in the Savannah Room. The queen-size bed in this room has an unusual headboard created from an antique mirror, originally from a buffet.

On chilly nights guests will want to gather around a crackling fire in the great room, but since Florida doesn't have many of these, you're more likely to relax in the Florida room, at the umbrella table out on the patio, or on Adirondack chairs in the rear yard to watch the sun set over the lake. Breakfast is an elegant meal consisting of a fruit course and an egg entree served on antique china.

What's Nearby Inverness

See page 100 for what's nearby Inverness.

Running Deer Lodge

3405 East Stagecoach Trail
Inverness, Florida 34452
(352) 860-1791 or (800) 830-7012

E-MAIL: rundeer@citrus.infi.net

WEB SITE: www.bbonline.com/fl/ runningdeer

INNKEEPERS: Betty Schilling and Susanne Hill

ROOMS: 2; both with private bath, robes, fireplace, TV, ceiling fan, chocolates, bottled water

ON THE GROUNDS: Porches, nature trails, lawn games, barbecue grill, double swing, double hammock

RATES: $95 to $110 double for the first night, $80 to $95 for additional nights; weekend specials Friday afternoon through late Sunday $195 to $225; two-night minimum stay on weekends

CREDIT CARDS ACCEPTED? Yes

OPEN: Year-round

HOW TO GET THERE: From I-75, take exit 63, Bushnell. Go west 12 miles on FL 48 to Floral City. Turn left at the light onto US 41 and go approximately 1 mile to County Road 480, Stagecoach Trail. Turn right and go

4 miles to County Road 581. Turn left, then make an immediate right back onto County Road 480. Go 1 mile and look for the small running deer on top of the mailbox; there's also a BED AND BREAKFAST sign. Follow the paved driveway to the house.

When Sue was looking for a house in which to open a bed and breakfast, she found to her sorrow that many older homes needed too much work to be financially feasible. Then she found this contemporary home, primarily paneled in knotty pine and hidden away on ten acres of heavily wooded property. She knew right away it was tailor-made to be a B&B for nature lovers or those who just want to get away from all the chaos of daily life to seek some peace and tranquillity. This is a place where you can walk in the woods, play a leisurely game of croquet or horseshoes, nap in a hammock, or just gaze at the stars.

Two lovely guest rooms, named the Fawn and the Yearling, are spacious and romantically furnished. Each has a private bath, king-size bed, television (your challenge is to find the cleverly hidden one in the Fawn Room), and sitting area with an electric fireplace for any chilly evenings or simply for the ambience. These fireplaces re-create not only the flickering glow of a real fire but the crackling sounds as well. In the Yearling Room the huge shower is not only large enough for two but could be considered a play-room. The Fawn Room, a favorite with honeymooners and others celebrating a romantic occasion, boasts an enormous whirlpool tub and a private balcony.

Although with such sumptuous bedchambers, you're likely to spend a lot of time in the privacy of your room, you might want to venture out to socialize with your hosts or fellow guests. The spectacular great room boasts a 25-foot cathedral ceiling, television, VCR, stereo system, and piano. This is also the setting for welcome refreshments, English-style tea or wine and cheese in the late afternoon, and a hearty full breakfast, although you may choose to eat out on one of the porches. In addition, there's a pool table in the game room in a separate building; a patio area located away from the house includes a firepit where you can roast marshmallows, old-fashioned swings, grill, and a picnic table. Benches are scattered throughout the grounds as well.

What's Nearby Inverness

See page 100 for what's nearby Inverness.

House on Cherry Street

Best Buy

1844 Cherry Street
Jacksonville, Florida 32205
(904) 384–1999; fax (904) 384–5013

E-MAIL: houseoncherry@
compuserve.com

WEB SITE: www.1bbweb.com/cherry

INNKEEPER: Carol Anderson

ROOMS: 4; all with private bath; TV and telephone available.

ON THE GROUNDS: Bicycles, canoe, kayak, fishing from inn dock; located in Historic Riverside neighborhood

RATES: $80 to $110 double, including continental breakfast and wine and hors d'oeuvres at 6:00 P.M. each evening

CREDIT CARDS ACCEPTED? Yes

OPEN: Year-round

HOW TO GET THERE: From I–95 South, take exit 113, the Stockton Street exit. Go 12 blocks to Riverside; turn right onto Riverside, and go 4 more blocks. Turn left onto Cherry Street and continue 1½ blocks to the river. The inn is the last house on your right.

Expect to be greeted by Chardonnay, a yellow Lab you just have to love. And then expect to love this B&B within your first ten minutes here. The house, a three-story Colonial, is furnished with period antiques, Oriental rugs, and such interesting touches as a large collection of duck decoys. Many of the objects you see belong to personal collections of Carol or her late husband, Merrill. Among the most appealing are the old car vases on the walls; Carol usually keeps them filled with fresh flowers.

In addition to using the downstairs public rooms (including a good-size dining room next to the screened porch), you have the option of hiding away in an upstairs sitting room, where you can count on being able to read or knit or just sit and think without interruption.

Most of the guest rooms, which have canopied beds and comfortable sitting areas, overlook the St. Johns River and a broad expanse of well-manicured lawn.

The house is in a residential area, but because of its proximity to the river and the way the house is landscaped, once you're inside you feel as though you're alone with the greenery and the river. And, of course, with the innkeeper.

Carol used to be a guidance counselor, and although she's not offering to solve your problems, she has the easy communication style of one who has enjoyed getting to know lots of people.

When you try one of her continental breakfasts, you may decide that she can talk or not—whatever pleases her—as long as she keeps cooking. You get fresh juice and fresh fruit along with fresh-baked breads, coffee, and cereal.

What's Nearby Jacksonville

You'll never be bored in Jacksonville. Just visit the city's refurbished boardwalk, named the Riverwalk, and you'll be surrounded by restaurants overlooking the St. John's River. The Riverwalk is a short walk away from the Museum of Science and History, which displays a 28-foot dinosaur skeleton. If all the walking makes you hungry for dessert, visit the Peterbrooke Chocolatier. The store's specialty is truffles, but you can also buy chocolate-covered Oreos, popcorn, and strawberries.

Center Court Historic Inn and Cottages

916 Center Street
Key West, Florida 33040
(305) 296-9292 or (800) 797-8787;
fax (305) 294-4104

E-MAIL: centerct@aol.com

WEB SITE: www.centercourtkw.com

INNKEEPER: Naomi Van Steelandt

ROOMS: 7 rooms and suites available for bed and breakfast (other units available with no breakfast); all with private bath, hair dryer, cable TV, telephone, alarm clock, ceiling fan, in-room safe, beach towels and bags; fax, e-mail, and phone line for computer available; pets welcome in some cottages

ON THE GROUNDS: Pool, exercise equipment

RATES: $88 to $298 double, including expanded continental breakfast, concierge service; additional person $15; weekly rates available

CREDIT CARDS ACCEPTED? Yes

OPEN: Year-round

HOW TO GET THERE: Entering Key West on US 1, bear right. When US 1 narrows to two lanes, turn right after the fifth traffic light onto Center Street, which is between Simonton and Duval. Center Court is on your left, midway down the first block.

You've heard of Southern hospitality. Well, at Center Court—at the very tip of the continental United States—they offer "southernmost" hospitality. True to its name, this bed and breakfast is located on Center Street in one of Key West's oldest and most charming neighborhoods. Just ½ block from the celebrated sights and sounds of the island's famous Duval Street, the B&B is located in four historic cottages: the Main Guest House, Cistern House, Cottage, and Family House.

Naomi supervised the renovation, design, and decoration of the late-nineteenth-century properties, for which she was rewarded with a 1994 Award of Excellence from the Key West Historical Preservation Society. She lavished the same attention to detail on the landscaping, with lush tropical trees laden with exotic foliage—palm, frangipani, Barbados cherry, gumbo, limbo, and Key lime trees, along with fragrant flowering plants. A fish and lily pond adds to the tropical ambience.

Island history and unique architectural styles are well represented within the compound. Built in 1873 by a sea captain, the two-story Main Guest House captures the style of early settlers, who built their homes to look much like their ships. Two identical 1880s cottages built by cigar makers have been redesigned to exhibit distinct personalities. The Cistern House completes the varied accommodations.

Each of the guest chambers is as diverse as the cottages themselves, even though they're all done in bright, colorful Florida/Caribbean style. Four bed-and-breakfast rooms are offered in the main house and the suite that takes up the entire Cistern House. With an efficiency kitchen, this house is preferred by honeymooners. Breakfast fixings are left in these houses so you can enjoy the meal whenever you want it, and either indoors or on the covered veranda. The Cottage, which can sleep four, and the Family House, which can sleep six, do not include breakfast.

Awaken refreshed and begin another day in paradise with an expanded continental breakfast that features gourmet coffees and herbal teas, bagels, English muffins, and cereals. Amenities generally reserved for resorts are readily available at Center Court: a heated pool, hot tub, European-style sundeck, and exercise pavilion with treadmill, power glider, free weights, and water weights.

What's Nearby Key West

What could be more inspiring than a beautiful sunset? Just ask Key West residents, and they'll tell you to join them at Mallory Docks about half an hour before sundown. The date at Mallory Docks is actually a daily ritual. But there's more to watch than the sun setting—there's the Cookie Lady on a bicycle selling cookies and brownies, pet parrots and iguanas on display, and local artists juggling, dancing, singing, and swallowing flaming swords. What a bunch of characters! Ernest Hemingway wrote several novels while living at home in Key West, and you can visit the Ernest Hemingway Home and Museum. Remember—the sun also rises, and there is still lots more to see and do at Key West!

The Curry Mansion Inn

511 Caroline Street
Key West, Florida 33040
(305) 294-5349 or (800) 253-3466;
fax (305) 294-4093

E-MAIL: frontdesk@currymansion.com

WEB SITE: www.currymansion.com

INNKEEPERS: Edith and Al Amsterdam

ROOMS: 4 in main house (24 in modern addition); all with private bath, telephone, cable TV, ceiling fan, refrigerator; ask about small pets; no wheelchair access in the mansion

ON THE GROUNDS: Swimming pool, hot tub

RATES: $125 to $275 double, including European breakfast buffet and afternoon cocktail party; two-night minimum stay on weekends; special rates and minimum stays on holidays and special events

CREDIT CARDS ACCEPTED? Yes

OPEN: Year-round

HOW TO GET THERE: When arriving in Key West via US 1, bear right, following US 1 South about 3 miles to Duval Street. Turn right. Go 10 blocks to Caroline Street and turn right again. The Curry Mansion is ¼ block up on your left.

unky Key West is mainly a place of small turn-of-the-century cottages. An exception is the palatial three-story, multigabled Curry Mansion, a Classical Revival home completed in 1899. William Curry, a Bahamian immigrant who earned his fortune as a salvager—one of those scurrilous fellows who preyed on shipwrecked travelers in Florida's pirate-infested waters—is believed to have been Key West's first millionaire.

Curry began building his home in 1855. Architectural details he incorporated into his opulent mansion are common to wreckers and several ports of call: a New England widow's walk, New Orleans ornate trellises and balustrades, and the columns, colonnades, and verandas of the Deep South. Curry didn't get to see the construction to its completion, however. His son Milton finished the house in 1899 and furnished it with eighteenth- and nineteenth-century antiques that still grace the parlor today.

How did Edith and Al Amsterdam, the successful proprietors of upstate New York's Casa Blanca, end up owning and operating an inn in Key West? In 1975 the Amsterdams brought their yacht into Key West's harbor and were going for a stroll when Edith spied the wedding-cake mansion. As luck would have it, it was for sale. The rest, as they say, is history. The bed and breakfast they created has been named the best in Key West six out of nine years and one of the nation's top ten by INNovations National Network Services.

We toured the mansion several years ago on a trip to Key West and marveled at the bird's-eye maple paneling, hand-wrought spindles on the porch railings and stairways, Tiffany glass sliding doors, magnificent fireplaces, and exquisite antiques, including an 1853 Chickering piano reputedly from Henry James's Newport home.

The four antiques-filled bedchambers in the mansion were created from the original master suite, the children's room, and the nanny's room. (A contemporary addition provides two dozen more rooms, which are similarly furnished and decorated; they just lack the architectural detailing of the main house.)

Lucky guests in the opulent two-room Master Suite enjoy a king-size bed and a whirlpool tub. This is the perfect luxurious hideaway for honeymooners and other romantics. The long-ago children and their nanny surely didn't have it anywhere near as good as you will staying in their former rooms, one of which now boasts a queen-size brass bed, the other a queen-size canopy bed.

Haviland china and faux replicas of the Curry family's solid-gold Tiffany flatware create the backdrop for an elegant breakfast buffet of the freshly baked bagels, muffins, and pastries for which the Curry Mansion is known;

you'll also find three different cream cheeses, including their famous salmon cream cheese, as well as fresh tropical fruit, cereals, and at least one hot specialty item. Every afternoon the Curry Mansion sponsors a complimentary cocktail party for it's guests. This is sure to be a big hit before you go down to Mallory Square to see the sunset. Another note: It is claimed that Key lime pie was created in the mansion's kitchen at the turn of the century by the Currys' cook, Aunt Sally.

Although most guests like to hang out by the pool and hot tub, you might want to take advantage of the mansion's many public rooms—a music room, a library loaded with Hemingway memorabilia, and a third-floor billiards room. Early in the morning or late in the afternoon is a good time to go up to the widow's walk for unparalleled views of Key West.

For those not fortunate enough to stay at the Curry Mansion, tours are offered 10:00 A.M. to 5:00 P.M.

What's Nearby Key West

See page 107 for what's nearby Key West.

Herlong Mansion

402 Cholokka Boulevard
(mailing address: P.O. 667)
Micanopy, Florida 32667
(352) 466-3322 or
(800) 437-5664;
fax is the same

INNKEEPER: H. C. (Sonny) Howard Jr.

ROOMS: 5 rooms and 4 suites in main house and 2 restored cottages; all with private bath, some with whirlpool bath, some with fireplace, some with wheelchair access

ON THE GROUNDS: Wraparound veranda, gift shop, studio, ice cream parlor

RATES: $65 to $175, double, Friday, Saturday, and holidays; $55 to $165 other nights; single $5 less; including full breakfast; $20 each additional person; inquire about corporate and government rates

CREDIT CARDS ACCEPTED? Yes

OPEN: Year-round

HOW TO GET THERE: From I-75, take exit 73 and go east 0.5 mile. At the HISTORIC MICANOPY sign, turn right. The road ends in less than a mile in downtown Micanopy. Turn left. The inn is 1½ blocks farther on your left.

This building absolutely knocks your eyes out. The building you see today has a wide front veranda with four two-story Roman Corinthian columns carved from wood. Imposing.

The original two-story Victorian house with a detached kitchen was built about 1845. In 1910 the owners built a brick Classical Revival imitation of a Southern colonial design (that's hard to follow!) all the way around it—sort of a house within a house.

Inside, all the guest rooms and public areas, which have 12-foot ceilings, are exceptionally spacious. You can prowl through the place and inspect leaded-glass windows, ten (count 'em) fireplaces, inlaid floors of oak and maple, and glorious floor-to-ceiling windows in the dining room.

On a more personal level, Sonny's walking stick collection, 300 sticks and growing as guests send him more, is fun to study, too.

The guest rooms variously have canopy beds, private porches, claw-foot tubs, white wicker furniture, and gas-log fireplaces, depending on the room. They're all tasteful and pretty. Sonny has stayed in bed and breakfasts all over the world, so he knows how to create appealing rooms.

Then we have Inez. This resident ghost has become a topic of much interest. Over blueberry waffle breakfasts, Sonny and guests discuss the peculiar and inexplicable little episodes that keep happening in one of the guest rooms. Could Inez also have something to do with strange noises coming from a room with a hidden outside entrance under the house? Nobody knows what the room was for. Bootleg liquor? Hiding runaway slaves? Insane aunts? Well, Inez has been busy enough that now you can even pick up a T-shirt at Herlong Mansion that says, I SAW INEZ.

What's Nearby Micanopy

Roam like the buffalo and visit Payne's Prairie State Preserve in Micanopy, where archaeologists discovered Indian artifacts dating back to 7000 B.C. The preserve began as a large Spanish cattle ranch, and now the visitor center displays exhibits on the history of the preserve. The park borders Lake Wauberg, which is a popular boating and fishing spot. Other outdoor options include camping, bird-watching, and horseback riding.

Shady Oak Bed and Breakfast

203 Cholokka Boulevard
Micanopy, Florida 32667
(352) 466-3476

E-MAIL: Via Web site

WEB SITE: www.shadyoak.com

INNKEEPER: Frank James

ROOMS: 7 rooms and suites; all with private bath and cable TV; most have queen-size beds, though one has a king-size water bed and another a double bed; 2 new downstairs rooms will be wheelchair accessible

ON THE GROUNDS: Wraparound veranda, porches, Southern Expressions gift shop, Shady Oak Studio, ice cream parlor

RATES: $75 to $150 double, including full breakfast; deduct $10 for single; add $20 for each additional guest

CREDIT CARDS ACCEPTED? Yes

OPEN: Year-round

HOW TO GET THERE: From I-75, take exit 73 and turn east; in 0.25 mile you'll reach the historic Micanopy Monument. Turn right onto Seminary Street. The Shady Oak Bed and Breakfast is straight ahead at the next stop sign on Cholokka Boulevard.

Among the many things that make us like a particular bed and breakfast or inn is a sense of humor, and owner Frank James has given Shady Oak that aplenty. Just check out his playful purple velvet bordello theme in Victoria's Suite, or his stained-glass renditions of Mae West in her bath and a nineteenth-century dance hall girl. You'll find Frank's stained-glass windows and panels everywhere; in fact, you can participate in a stained-glass workshop while staying at the inn, because Frank runs his Shady Oak Studio downstairs. (See the sidebar.)

Frank is the kind of guy whom you feel you've known for years just minutes after you've met him. He made us feel we were old friends visiting after a long separation as he showed us around his bed and breakfast. Located in a nineteenth-century commercial building with full-length verandas on the first and second floors, the inn is situated on the second and third floors over the studio and several stores. Once we climbed the stairs to the elegant second-floor lobby, we were in for many surprises. First was a clubby room where breakfast is served and light refreshments are available during the day.

Then we stepped through the common room and exited onto a fabulous screened porch known as the Florida Room, well equipped with hammocks,

Make Your Own Stained-Glass Masterpiece

Whether you're a neophyte who's always dreamed of learning stained-glass techniques or an intermediate or advanced artisan who'd like to hone your skills, there's a personalized seminar for you at the Shady Oak Studio connected with the Shady Oak Bed and Breakfast. In fact, what better arrangement could there be than to work under the tutelage of owner/innkeeper Frank James and have your accommodations and a full breakfast provided each day? Workshops—limited to three students, so each can benefit from one-on-one instruction—are conducted Monday through Friday, with arrival at the B&B on Sunday. Each student receives extensive training in glass design, pattern making, glass cutting, and soldering techniques, producing a window or panel project of approximately 4 to 6 square feet. Frank James began his career in glass crafting in 1968, studying techniques used by old-time masters in North Carolina. Vickie McQuinney has ten years' experience as studio manager and works individually with every student. Tuition for the workshop is $325, materials cost $25 per square foot of the finished project. A special rate for accommodations at the inn for the five nights is $275 for a single or $350 for a double, including breakfast.

comfortable chairs, settees, and rockers. The newest addition is a twin-bed-size swing that's obviously very popular with couples. We spent a lot of time in the Florida Room, although the widow's walk at the very tiptop of the structure is perfect for sunbathing, stargazing, people-watching, and enjoying the spectacular view of downtown.

Among the guest accommodations, several deserve special mention. The Master Suite, our personal favorite for romance, is extremely fanciful with its canopied king-size water bed. The suite also features a ceiling fan, sitting room with sleeper sofa, private balcony, and bathroom with stained-glass shower windows. Victoria's Suite, our favorite on the humorous front, is the one playfully decorated in an 1890s bordello theme with purple velvet and floral draperies, stained-glass windows—one depicts a dance hall girl—a fainting couch, and a private whirlpool bath surrounded by a wall of mirrors and another stained-glass window. This suite opens onto the Florida Room. Melody's Suite features a four-poster pencil-post bed with lanterns atop each post and a mirrored headboard. French doors lead to a private rooftop balcony with a commanding view of Main Street. Mae's Room is named after (you guessed it) Mae West, and is decorated in an 1880s theme. The redwood cedar bathroom features a stained-glass panel depicting Mae in her bath; the spacious lover's shower is always a hit with romantic couples. Alice's Room and the Heron's Nest are tucked up under the eaves and therefore have lower ceilings, mostly sloped but with good views of downtown. As we speak, two more rooms are under construction downstairs in a space formerly occupied by a store. These will be wheelchair accessible.

Gourmet meals can be provided with advance notice and for an additional fee by contacting Custom Catering (352-466-0307); you can also arrange for on-site services from a licensed massage therapist.

What's Nearby Micanopy

See page 110 for what's nearby Micanopy.

Inn by the Sea

287 11th Avenue South
Naples, Florida 34102
(941) 649-4124 or
(800) 584-1268;
fax (941) 434-2842

INNKEEPER: Tara Jones

ROOMS: 5; all with private bath

ON THE GROUNDS: Beach cruiser bicycles

RATES: $94 to $189, single or double, including tropical continental breakfast; $15 per extra person

CREDIT CARDS ACCEPTED? Yes

OPEN: Year-round

HOW TO GET THERE: From I-75, take exit 16. Bear right to Goodlette Road. Turn left and follow Goodlette Road 4 miles to its end. Turn right onto Highway 41. Continue toward the beach to Fifth Avenue South. Turn left onto Third Street South to 11th Avenue South. The inn is on the corner.

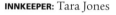

nn by the Sea is a beach house for vacationers and sometimes a lodging place for travelers who come to Naples on business. It's hard to see how they could remain in a business frame of mind staying here, though. The building of wooden cove siding is surrounded by tropical plants—coconut palms, bougainvillea, an orange tree, and luxuriant specimens of many plants we barely keep alive in pots on the windowsill farther north. Inside, the casual decor, which includes wicker and cheerful floral-print fabrics, complements the heart-pine floors and cypress and pine ceilings and feels light and cool.

Ceiling fans turn lazily, making the air-conditioning more effective and adding to the tropical atmosphere. On cooler days you can open windows in the guest rooms and enjoy a great cross-breeze. The Captiva Room looks especially refreshing with green and white striped walls and drapes against white eyelet bedclothes. When it is cool outside, keep the windows open and drop off to sleep feeling the breeze and listening to the night sounds of summer peepers.

In the morning, spend time looking at the inn's art—seascapes, beach scenes, birds—mostly done by local artists, much of it for sale to guests.

The "tropical" breakfast emphasized all the local fruits that simply never seem to taste as good outside southern Florida; everyone at our table had seconds.

Part of the importance of this house is that it preserves another of Naples's old homes. (Each guest room is named for a local island.) Although there are new condominiums on one corner, the neighborhood ambience is still that of Old Naples.

What's Nearby Naples

If you decide to go shopping in Naples, you just may go off the deep end. The 1,000-foot fishing pier is a very popular shopping center. Then visit the Old Marine Market Place, an old-fashioned shopping bazaar, and swing by the upscale shops and emporiums on Third Street and Fifth Avenue. If you'd rather dip into the water than your wallet, retreat to the 7-mile stretch of sandy public beach right in Naples.

Seven Sisters Inn

820 Southeast Fort King Street
Ocala, Florida 34471
(352) 867-1170 or (800) 250-3496;
fax (352) 867-5266

E-MAIL: sistersinn@aol.com

WEB SITE: www.7sistersinn.com

INNKEEPERS: Bonnie Morehardt and Ken Oden

ROOMS: 8; all with private bath; 3 with fireplace; 1 with private phone and computer setup; 1 on first floor with wheelchair access and equipped for handicapped

ON THE GROUNDS: Smoking porches, bicycles

RATES: $115 to $185, depending on season, single or double, including full breakfast and tea (4:00 to 6:00 P.M.); five-course gourmet dinner by reservation for an additional fee; inquire about senior, corporate, and military rates

CREDIT CARDS ACCEPTED? Yes

OPEN: Year-round

HOW TO GET THERE: From I-75, take exit 69 onto FL 40, which becomes Silver Springs Boulevard downtown. Turn right at Southeast Ninth Avenue and right again in the next block at Southeast King Fort Street.

"Being an innkeeper is like having 1,800 of your best friends visit you each year," Ken said. His comment sets the tone here. Ken is an airline pilot and accustomed to meeting lots of people.

"It's a great way to stay in the hospitality business," his wife, Bonnie, said. Well, she's a pilot, too, and for a while decided that the innkeeping business was more stable than flying, so she put all her energy into the inn in what Ken calls a "damn the torpedos" mode. Practically everything pretty you see is a project of Bonnie's, from the lacy, yellow, Monet-like breakfast room to the beautifully conceived and executed decor of the guest rooms. However, the air is a temptress that cannot be denied, and Bonnie is now flying again.

The Seven Sisters Inn started as a family home in 1888. The rooms on the upper two floors are named for the seven sisters of the woman who renovated the building in 1985. The decor of each room reflects the interests of each of the sisters, and you'll find a picture of each sister somewhere in her room. The downstairs room that is equipped for handicap access really works, because a member of the family who lived here was handicapped.

More of Bonnie's formidable energy and creativity go into special weekends, ranging from slick murder mysteries to scavenger hunts and chocolate extravaganzas. The inn often has wine-tasting weekends, cooking classes, Friday-night bistros, and theater packages, too.

Bonnie is proud of her special breakfasts. She likes to serve unusual juices such as pear nectar, followed by fresh fruit and cream and specialties such as blueberry French toast. Bonnie started as a flight attendant and worked to earn her pilot's license because, as she put it, "I decided I'd rather drink coffee than serve it." Come to think of it, the day we visited, Ken was pouring the coffee.

When it first opened, Seven Sisters Inn occasionally served candlelight dinners for small groups and dinner buffets for some of the special weekends. However, bowing to demand, they are now deep into the dinner trade.

Apparently things were too calm around the inn so Bonnie and Ken bought the house next door and are now in the process of adding six more rooms. Each represents one of their favorite destinations: Argentina, Egypt, India, Paris, China, Bali. All the furniture is hand-carved in Bali. The accent pieces and fabrics come from their respective countries—silk from India, leather from Argentina. The rooms have hydro showers, fireplaces, whirlpool tubs, and so much more that we don't have room to describe it all.

What's Nearby Ocala

If you enjoy the outdoors, Ocala is the ideal place to visit. Go canoeing, swimming, camping, hiking, and hunting at the Ocala National Forest, which offers more than 300,000 acres of springs, streams, and lakes. Canoers and swimmers will also enjoy Alexander Springs, Juniper Springs, and Salt Springs Recreation Area. Silver Glens Springs and Silver Springs are not to be missed. Silver Springs may look familiar—many filmmakers have captured the springs in movies and television shows. It's just picture perfect.

Casa de la Paz

22 Avenida Menendez
St. Augustine, Florida 32084
(904) 829-2915 or (800) 929-2915

INNKEEPERS: Bob and Dana Marriott

ROOMS: 4 rooms and 2 suites; all with private bath, TV, and telephone; on-site parking for all guests

RATES: $115 to $215, single or double, including full breakfast and afternoon refreshments; two-night minimum stay on weekends

CREDIT CARDS ACCEPTED? Yes

OPEN: Year-round

HOW TO GET THERE: From I-95, take FL 16 to A1A into the city, where A1A becomes Avenida Menendez. The inn is just past Hypolita Street.

This is a beautiful inn in a fine old building—the only remaining example in St. Augustine of pure Mediterranean Revival architecture from the turn of the century, complete with barrel-tile roofing. The house overlooks Matanzas Bay.

Inside, the sunporch with huge arched windows, black and white tile flooring, white walls, and white wicker furniture feels so airy and spacious that you scarcely distinguish between the outside and the inside.

Elsewhere, English antiques and Oriental rugs suggest older, elegant times. The Venetian chandelier of Strauss crystal draws special attention from guests who admire fine old things.

In the guest rooms, king- and queen-size beds with orthopedic mattresses are dressed in custom-made spreads, shams, and tons of coordinating pillows. The beds are made up with all-cotton sheets and lots of feather pillows.

In the dining room you eat your elaborate, full breakfast from 8:45 to 9:30 A.M. at a mahogany table graced with a sterling silver serving set. Served buffet-style, breakfast here goes well beyond the usual bacon and eggs routine. For instance, you might have blueberry soufflé, raspberry stuffed French toast, or turkey crepes topped with cheddar cheese and toasted almonds. There's always a coffee or tea cake, buns, and fruits, as well as the Marriotts' own specially blended and roasted coffee.

Thus fortified, you take off for a day of sight-seeing in St. Augustine's historic district. When you get back, probably warm and tired, you'll appreciate the complimentary wine, beer, and soda offered before dinner. The good news about dinner is that there are several nice little restaurants right in the area. You can walk to them, and some will even pick you up. The Casa de la Paz staff keeps menus on hand to help you choose your restaurant and, after you decide, will make the reservation for you.

This is a nice way to learn your history: Stay in a historic building while sleeping on a thoroughly contemporary and comfortable mattress; tour the old sites; and dine well at a nearby restaurant.

What's Nearby St. Augustine

St. Augustine will make you feel like a kid again. Visit the Fountain of Youth Park, which is dedicated to Spanish explorer Ponce de Leon. In 1513, Ponce de Leon claimed he discovered the Fountain of Youth here in St. Augustine. Spain occupied St. Augustine until 1565. Learn about the region's rich Spanish history by visiting an ancient fort called Castillo de San Marcos National Monument. Step back in time and see the Spanish Quarter, where costumed guides re-create the lives of soldiers and settlers.

Bayboro House

1719 Beach Drive Southeast
St. Petersburg, Florida 33701
(727) 823-4955; fax is the same

E-MAIL: bayborohouse@juno.com

INNKEEPERS: Gordon and Antonia
Powers

ROOMS: 4; all with private bath,
TV, and VCR with complimentary movies

ON THE GROUNDS: Beach chairs and
towels

RATES: $95 to $165, single or double, including continental-plus breakfast
and wine/beverages in afternoon and evening; inquire about weekly and
monthly rates

CREDIT CARDS ACCEPTED? Yes

OPEN: Year-round

HOW TO GET THERE: From I-275, take exit 9. Go south on Fourth Street
South to 22nd Avenue South; turn left and go 5 blocks to Tampa Bay,
then left onto Beach Drive Southeast.

Bayboro House generates stories that tell you as much about staying here
as a room-by-room description. Seems relatives of the man who used to
own the house held a reunion here. Gordon and Antonia were excited
because they thought it would be a sentimental occasion and also an opportunity for them to learn more about the house and family. The old owner
was C. A. Harvey. The family knew that he had died in 1913, but no one
knew what his name was. "C. A." was it.

The family had included C. A.'s very old family servant, Olivia, in the
party. She hobbled in leaning on a black and gold cane, repeating, "Thank
you, Lord. Lord, thank you for letting me come into this house one more
time." But she didn't remember anything about how the house used to be.

All the Powerses learned was that the original light fixtures are still in
the house.

Then there's the story about Herb Hiller, a respected travel writer who
specializes in Florida. He was at Bayboro House, moving from room to
room, sitting on one antique chair after another, taking notes furiously. He
sat on the red fainting couch, and then finally he moved to the porch and
sat on the swing. His eyes seemed suddenly unfocused and wide with
amazement. He said, "Why, this could be Florida a hundred years ago."

Yet another story is about guests who checked into Bayboro House and left their kids with neighbors—not neighbors from back home, but neighbors of the Bayboro House. "The neighborhood has been good to us," Gordon said.

What it all comes down to is a nice old Victorian house built shortly after 1900, filled with the antiques and odds and ends that Gordon and Antonia have collected over the years: the fainting couch that Hiller made famous, marble-topped tables, quilts, the inevitable player piano, and all the doilies, dollies, and dishes that used to catch the Victorian fancy. The inn is run by friendly, accommodating people in a friendly, visually unremarkable neighborhood. It's directly across the street from a beautiful part of Tampa Bay, close enough to walk barefoot to the beach in the kind of area that usually gives way to whatever waterfront high-rise project comes along first.

"It's amazing that the house is still there. Who knows how long we'll be here?" Gordon said.

In fact, the odds look better than they used to. The building has been designated a historical landmark by the city of St. Petersburg, and the inn has been getting great ratings from "those other" guidebooks, now that they've found it.

What's Nearby St. Petersburg

St. Petersburg is home to the world's largest art collection by surrealist Salvador Dali. It's so real, too—oil paintings, watercolors, drawings, graphics, and sculptures. The $35 million collection is exhibited at the Salvador Dali Museum. After visiting the museum, spend the rest of the day at Fort DeSoto Park's 900 acres and 7 miles of waterfront. Ponce de Leon also visited St. Petersburg back in 1513. What a discovery!

Other Recommended B&Bs in St. Petersburg

The Inn on the Beach, a beachfront inn, offers rooms and suites with cable TV and fully equipped kitchen; 1401 Gulf Way, St. Petersburg Beach, FL 33706; (727) 360-8844. *Island's End Resort* features cottages with fully equipped kitchens on a small private beach; 1 cottage with private pool; 1 Pass-A-Grille Way, St. Petersburg Beach, FL 33706; (727) 360-5023.

Bay Gables Bed and Breakfast, Garden, and Tea Room

340 Rowland Court

St. Petersburg, Florida 33701

(727) 822-8855 or (800) 822-8803

E-MAIL: solomio@msn.com

WEB SITE: www.baygablesbb.
citysearch.com

INNKEEPER: David Lee

ROOMS: 9 rooms and suites; all with private bath, ceiling fan, air-conditioning, telephone with data port, cable TV, clock radio; fax and small computer center with Internet access available; one room wheelchair accessible

ON THE GROUNDS: Verandas, garden, gazebo, adjacent restaurant

RATES: $85 to $150, including breakfast and afternoon refreshments; children under eight are free

CREDIT CARDS ACCEPTED? Yes

OPEN: Year-round

HOW TO GET THERE: From I-275, take exit 10, I-375, which becomes Fourth Avenue North. You'll see the restaurant on your right in the 100 block. The B&B and gift shop are behind it.

Bay Gables is truly a hidden treasure, situated as it is behind the Bay Gables Restaurant between Third and Fourth Avenues. Locate the cheerful, many-gabled pink Victorian cottage with a wraparound veranda that houses the Tea Room, then stroll through the tranquil, shady, secret garden to the three-story Key West–style structure that serves as the bed and breakfast. In the best tradition of the Victorian era, porches wrap around each floor of the inn, providing attractive spots to sit and gaze over the garden—which may be empty and quiet or the scene of a wedding or other special event—or, from the third floor, to the busy downtown waterfront. Every room opens directly onto a veranda.

Nine simple but tastefully furnished period guest rooms and suites, given English names such as Windsor Rose, Wellington, Staffordshire, and Yorkshire, offer a variety of accommodations. Although each bedchamber is outfitted with antiques and an old-fashioned claw-foot tub, each also boasts all the modern amenities to ensure your comfort. Double beds, many of them brass or iron, grace the guest rooms, while suites feature queen-size beds and a twin-size daybed. Popular with romantics of all ages is the Camelot Suite. Secluded on the third floor, this romantically decorated hideaway features a double canopy bed and an extra-large bathroom with a whirlpool bath, double shower, and bidet. Especially appropriate for those who want some extra room to spread out, those traveling with an additional person, or those making a longer stay, all the suites offer a separate sitting room. Several also have kitchenette facilities: sink, refrigerator, microwave, and coffeemaker.

In the morning you can get your day off to a leisurely start with an expanded continental breakfast of fresh fruits, juices, baked goods, and other delicious offerings in the breakfast room, on the verandas, in the garden, or in your room. If you're staying over a Saturday night, treat yourself to brunch in the restaurant.

What's Nearby St. Petersburg

See page 119 for what's nearby St. Petersburg.

Mansion House Bed and Breakfast

105 Fifth Avenue, Northeast
St. Petersburg, Florida 33701
(727) 821-9391 or (800) 274-7520

E-MAIL: mansion1@ix.netcom.com

WEB SITE: www.mansionbandb.com

INNKEEPERS: Rose Marie and Rob Ray

ROOMS: 12; all with private bath (1 down the hall), air-conditioning, cable TV, telephone with data port, and clock radio

ON THE GROUNDS: Courtyard, heated pool, hot tub; bikes and beach chairs available

RATES: $90 to $165 single or double, including breakfast and complimentary snacks and refreshments; some periods require a minimum stay

CREDIT CARDS ACCEPTED? Yes

OPEN: Year-round

HOW TO GET THERE: From I-275 South, take exit 10, I-375 East. This is the exit to the Pier. Go to exit 2, Fourth Avenue North. Continue to the fifth traffic light at First Street North and turn left. Go 1 block and cross Fifth Avenue North. The B&B is on the corner.

From a B&B called the Mansion House, we weren't sure what to expect. Just to let you know, we're not talking a Greek Revival white-columned villa here, but rather two simple, but spacious turn-of-the-century homes built next door to each other in the historic Old Northeast District in 1904 and 1912. While neither is a pure example of any one architectural style, both stucco homes display attributes of the craftsman and mission styles. Together with a carriage house, they provide a variety of attractive, comfortable bed-and-breakfast accommodations. Separated by an attractive brick-paved courtyard fenced in for privacy, the houses boast a lovely backyard swimming pool and hot tub. Although the convenient location makes it easy for you to walk to the Pier, to the historic Vinoy Hotel for casual and fine dining, as well as to the waterfront, parks, museums, restaurants, galleries, arts and entertainment, and boutiques, you'll want to leave lots of time in your schedule to do nothing but soak up some sun around the pool.

Although these houses have many elegant architectural details not found in contemporary homes, they're still on the casual side—not at all stiff or formal. Exposed beams, gleaming hardwood floors and paneling, and stately fireplaces in the living rooms set the backdrop. Energetic Rob, a building contractor and boat captain, showed us around with obvious pride at what he and Rosie have accomplished in just a few years. First they took over the existing bed and breakfast in the main house; then they added the house next door, as well as creating a suite upstairs in the carriage house.

The previous owners, who were Welsh, had named the guest rooms for castles in their homeland, and the Rays retained these intriguing names for the bedchambers in the main house. For the house next door, they chose names of places that were important to them: Marblehead, Simione, and Sydney, to name a few. The main house is decorated with contemporary pieces left over from the previous owners as well as with the Rays' own antiques, eclectic artwork, and decorative accents. To perk up the bland contemporary furnishings, they hired local artist Marva Simpson to paint Florida scenes and florals on the headboards and armoires. Pat Berry created a variety of bed coverings, from comforters to quilts and bedspreads, as well as matching or coordinating window treatments. Beds, which are primarily queen size, run the gamut from simple headboards to brass, four-poster, and canopy in style. These appealing features, combined with abundant use of floral wallpapers and borders, give every room a distinctive personality. (You need to see the unique bed in the Pembroke Suite even if you aren't fortunate enough to stay there.) In addition to all the modern amenities we'd expect in a guest room, the Rays supply robes and lots of extra pillows—a plus for us when we read in bed.

At the casual, friendly Mansion House, you can be as private or as sociable as you like. Each house offers a formal living room as well as an informal upstairs sitting room amply supplied with a television, books, magazines, games, snacks, wine, and soft drinks. In addition to the pool area, a screened porch beckons guests out-of-doors. We've heard that the orange French toast, blueberry pancakes, and other breakfast items served in the two dining rooms of the main house are to die for.

Rose Marie, Rob, and their friendly pets will make your visit to their home as comfortable and enjoyable as a visit to favorite relatives or friends. Only we'll bet your friends or family can't take you on a personally guided cruise aboard their sport cruiser, the *Aussie Spirit*.

What's Nearby St. Petersburg

See page 119 for what's nearby St. Petersburg.

Sunset Bay Bed and Breakfast

635 Bay Street Northeast
St. Petersburg, Florida 33701
(727) 896–6701 or (800) 794–5133

E-MAIL: wrbcom@aol.com

WEB SITE: www.sunsetbayinn.com

INNKEEPERS: Bob and Martha Bruce

ROOMS: 8; all with private bath (all but one with whirlpool bath), TV, telephone and two data ports, clock radio, ceiling fan, desk, hair dryer, iron and ironing board

ON THE GROUNDS: Verandas

RATES: $150 to $220 double, including an expanded continental breakfast buffet on weekdays and a full breakfast on weekends; snacks are available in the kitchen twenty-four hours a day

CREDIT CARDS ACCEPTED? Yes

OPEN: Year round

HOW TO GET THERE: From the Tampa International Airport, take I–275 south to St. Petersburg. Take exit 10, I–375. Off I–375, take exit 2, which runs into Fourth Avenue North. Continue east for 6 blocks and turn left onto Bay Street. Go 2 blocks. The inn is on the northeastern corner.

As a child Martha lived in this imposing 1911 three-story Colonial Revival home, which her parents ran from 1947 to 1967 as the Boyce Guest House. A couple of years ago, she and husband Bob were visiting in St. Pete and drove by the old home place. As fate would have it, it was for sale.

Bob retired from his career in Atlanta and Martha moved her business to St. Pete so they could set to work renovating the house, which Martha described as being in a state of total disrepair. Their efforts have been well rewarded with a four-diamond rating from AAA and the 1999 Preservation Award of Commercial Rehabilitation and Restoration from the American Institute of Architects, Tampa Bay Chapter, St. Petersburg Preservation, Inc.

The public rooms on the main floor have been revitalized. Hardwood floors gleam. Tiles around the fireplace and on the hearth now match the Cuban tiles on the floor in the adjoining sunroom—created by enclosing a porch. We loved its cheerful airiness, created by windows on three sides. This comfortable room features upholstered pieces covered in an ivy print, as well as a television and an ample supply of books, magazines, and games. Although the sun-filled formal dining room is the perfect spot for breakfast, on a particularly nice day you might want to take your meal out on the adjoining porch.

Each guest room is decorated with its own distinct personality around a theme that's meaningful to the Bruces. For example, you'll find deep greens and brilliant azalea colors in the Augusta Room; tropical prints with birds, flowers, and beach accents in the Kihei. We stayed up under the eaves in the Sapphire Room where we enjoyed the cathedral ceiling and skylights. Martha's childhood room, called Marthasville, is also on the third floor and features its original claw-foot tub. For special occasions or just because you deserve it, the Sunset Bay Suite has a dramatic midnight and roses theme, with a king-size canopy bed, a double-size whirlpool tub, and a separate shower.

The Bruces are masters at exquisite little touches. Fresh flowers adorn your room; a small Whitman's sampler awaits on your pillow. There's a hair dryer in the bathroom, along with Caldwell-Massey and Crabtree and Evelyn amenities. Early-morning coffee and tea and newspapers are set out in the second-floor hall.

As delightful as hosts Martha and Bob are, the most important member of the household is Cher, the resident standard-size poodle, who considers herself a poodle person (and if you don't believe us, just ask her). Friendly and easygoing, she is the recipient of the most mail from departed guests; they even send her gifts.

Despite all Martha and Bob have accomplished, they're not ones to rest on their laurels. Current renovations of the adjoining carriage house will provide a small conference room on its first floor and two suites upstairs. The area between the house and carriage house will be transformed into a brick-paved courtyard with a hot tub. We can't wait to visit again to see the results.

What's Nearby St. Petersburg

See page 119 for what's nearby St. Petersburg.

Pasa Tiempo Bed and Breakfast Inn

7141 Bay Street
St. Petersburg Beach, Florida 33706
(727) 367-9907

E-MAIL: info@pasa-tiempo.com

WEB SITE: www.pasa-tiempo.com

INNKEEPERS: Pat Bishop and Sally McGuiness

ROOMS: 8; all with private bath, air-conditioning, ceiling fan, two telephones (with data port and voice mail), electric kettle; most with two TVs

ON THE GROUNDS: Courtyard, docks, bay frontage

RATES: $100 to $150, including expanded continental breakfast and afternoon wine and refreshments

CREDIT CARDS ACCEPTED? Yes

OPEN: Year-round

HOW TO GET THERE: From I–275 South, take exit 4, Pinellas Bayway (this is a toll road). Cross the bay to St. Pete Beach. When the Bayway dead-ends into Gulf Boulevard, turn right, go north to 72nd Avenue, and turn right again. Look for the sign for the inn on your right.

The translation may not be exactly grammatical, but Pasa Tiempo is a perfect place to pass some time—some quality time. As sisters Pat Bishop and Sally McGuiness say, "Kick off your shoes, put on your shorts, hide the beeper, pour a generous glass of wine. Now it's time for you."

When we pulled up to the tasteful brick facade and high stucco wall—the only clues this bed and breakfast present to the world—we were little prepared for the delights that awaited once we stepped through the ornate iron gate. The large brick-paved courtyard filled with lush tropical plantings immediately reminded us of the hidden gardens so typical of Savannah, Charleston, New Orleans, and the Caribbean. Little hidden nooks provide places to be alone if that's what you want. At the end of this earthly paradise we found a private dock filled with comfortable chairs and lounges overlooking Boca Ciega Bay. Heavenly. But, we wondered, could the interior live up to the gorgeous natural surroundings? In a word, yes.

Located in a quiet, almost residential neighborhood, the two-story inn was once an apartment building. We arrived just in time for the late-afternoon wine and cheese hour, so we not only got to nibble on some goodies but had a chance for a lively chat with many of the guests—several of whom were visitors to the United States from far-flung spots around the globe. Everyone sang the praises of their accommodations, the facilities, the food, and their hostesses. We knew we were in the right place.

Situated so that it has a view of the bay, the common room—with its tile floor, corner fireplace, and comfortable seating—opens onto the enclosed porch where breakfast is served. Everywhere are vases lavishly filled with fragrant flowers. Books, magazines, and games provide diversions if you need them, and complimentary snacks and beverages are always available.

Luxurious accommodations are offered in beautifully appointed suites, one of which boasts its own private balcony overlooking the bay. Bright and airy, the suites exude Florida charm. Tile floors and carpeting, bright colors, floral prints, and king-size beds combine with all the modern conveniences to create a home away from home.

This is a place to get away from it all—to drop a fishing line off the pier, to soak up some sun while absorbing the peace and quiet, to recharge your batteries, to enjoy life's simple pleasures. Come and take a well-deserved breather.

What's Nearby St. Petersburg Beach

See page 119 for what's nearby St. Petersburg.

McLeran House Bed and Breakfast

Best Buy

12408 County Road 137
Wellborn, Florida 32094
(904) 963-4603

INNKEEPERS: Robert and Mary Ryals

ROOMS: 2; both with private bath, cable TV, VCR, video- and audiotapes, ceiling fan, mini refrigerator stocked with soft drinks, juices, and mineral water

ON THE GROUNDS: Porch, gazebo, garden, extensive lawns, antiques shop

RATES: $75 single or double, including full breakfast and beverages; additional person $35

CREDIT CARDS ACCEPTED? Yes

OPEN: Year-round

HOW TO GET THERE: From I–10, take exit 41, County Road 137. Proceed south 4.5 miles directly to the B&B. From I–75, take exit 82 and go west on US 90 to County Road 137. Turn north and go 0.3 mile to the B&B.

The house is charming, the accommodations comfortable, the owners warm and hospitable, and there's even an antiques shop on the premises, but we think the main attraction here is the five and a half acres of manicured grounds. Well-kept lawns stretch out in every direction, shaded by ancient trees. A cedar gazebo makes a pleasant place to retire with a good book or just commune with nature. The lush garden contains a goldfish pond, fountain, arbor, brick walkways, an open well, lots of bird feeders, and comfortable seating on a deck. In good weather we know we'd spend every waking moment out here fanned by cool breezes and entertained by hummingbirds, bluebirds, cardinals, and other winged beauties. The wraparound porch is a great place to while away some time if the weather is drizzly. Bob's mother made the hammock in the 1940s from surplus parachute rip cord.

The ambience is so peaceful we could easily believe we'd returned to the quiet days when the house was built. It was constructed in 1909, the same year Mary's mother was born in Wellborn, by E. B. McLeran, a wealthy banker-businessman, as a country manor house, not a grand mansion. Distinguishing features of the dusky gray house include a small temple pediment supported by four columns leading onto the wraparound front porch, and a smaller upstairs porch.

McLeran House Peach Custard

2 cups frozen peaches, thawed, drained, and sliced

1 tablespoon lemon juice

1 tablespoon powdered sugar

¼ cup (½ stick) margarine, softened

1 cup skim milk

3 egg whites (or ½ cup cholesterol-free egg product)

¾ cup granulated sugar

1 cup Bisquick reduced-fat baking mix

1 tablespoon vanilla extract

1 tablespoon almond extract

Preheat the oven to 350 to 375 degrees F. Grease an 8- by 8-inch-square pan. Place peaches in the pan. Sprinkle with lemon juice and powdered sugar. Set aside. Mix the remaining ingredients in a separate bowl until well blended. Pour the mixture over the peaches. Bake for 40 to 50 minutes or until the edges are light brown and a toothpick inserted in the center comes out clean. Serve warm with powdered sugar sprinkled on top. Serves 6 to 8.

Inside are 10½-foot ceilings, six original fireplaces—each with a different style of mantel—a grand staircase lined with Mary's collection of Raggedy Anns and Andys and bears, and elegant woodwork. Furnishings and accessories are a tasteful blend of old and new. Of particular note are a pump organ, Mary's great-grandmother's quilts, and Bob's collection of clocks, one of which was from a barbershop and can only be read in a mirror; there are many other interesting knickknacks and pieces of Florida memorabilia, however. The immense china cabinet in the dining room was salvaged from a local drugstore. Be sure to admire Mary's kitchen. Cypress cabinets were built in place by a local artisan; Mary hand-punched their copper panels. Ancient heart-pine logs retrieved from river bottoms by divers from the nearby Goodwin Heart Pine Company and restored by its artisans were used for the floors.

Two guest accommodations are offered, both with private bath. Downstairs is a large, lavishly decorated room furnished with a queen-size iron bed. One of the attractions of this room is its private entrance from the wraparound porch. Sunlight streams in from stained-glass-accented windows. The private bath sports a claw-foot tub. Southern art, embroidered homilies, and old Florida souvenirs provide the lighthearted personality.

The upstairs room features an iron double bed, a wicker fainting couch, wicker dressers, and an art deco pine armoire.

Breakfast is a three-course meal featuring freshly ground coffee, a parfait of tropical fruits of the season, egg soufflé, and baked pears in cream if you're lucky.

Located to the rear of the property in a quaint barn is the Collectibles Shoppe, the repository of a vast array of records, radios, books, old fishing tackle, old cameras, old tools, lunch boxes, Southern folk pottery, dolls, baskets, bears, and more. We could spend hours poking through all the fun stuff.

What's Nearby Wellborn

Wellborn is best described as a small town in the countryside. The closest city is Lake City, which offers a host of interesting activities. The Stephen Foster State Folk Culture Center is dedicated to the composer of Suwanee River fame who wrote "Oh Susannah" and Florida's official state song, "Old Folks at Home." If you're down here in May, check out the Florida Folk Festival and hear live folk music. Or take a day trip to Suwanee River State Park and bring your picnic basket.

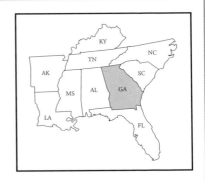

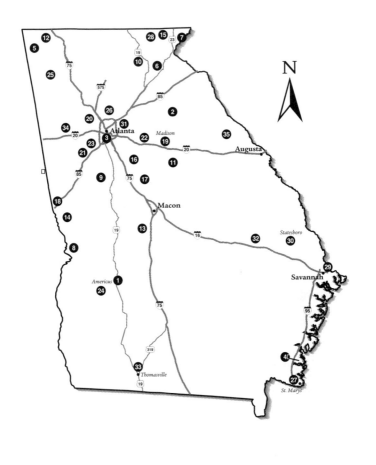

Georgia

Numbers on map refer to towns numbered below.

Guerry House, 1833/Springhill Plantation

723 McGarrah Street
Americus, Georgia 31709
(912) 924–1009

E-MAIL: guerryhouse@hotmail.com

INNKEEPERS: Pamela and Walter Stapleton

ROOMS: 8; all with private bath; Honeymoon Suite with whirlpool tub

ON THE GROUNDS: Verandas, 26 acres, gardens, 3 ponds

RATES: $75 to $125, including full breakfast and access to a nearby fitness center; ask about golf package

CREDIT CARDS ACCEPTED? Yes

OPEN: Year-round

HOW TO GET THERE: McGarrah Street branches east off US 19, north of downtown. The B&B is the first house on your left.

The elegant old lady of Americus—that's how Sumter County's oldest antebellum plantation is fondly known. An unusual style for southwestern Georgia, the Guerry House is a perfect example of Louisiana raised-cottage construction. Built entirely by slaves, it was begun in 1833 and finished in 1836 for Representative James P. Guerry. The two-story house is assembled from hand-hewn yellow pine with mortise and tenon construction. A veranda with front and back staircases completely encircles the house. In fact, there is no interior staircase and there never has been—perhaps to keep the servants from having easy access to the living quarters of the original owners. Other architectural features of note include hand-blown glass, six fireplaces, and a cypress-shingled roof.

Restoration took Pam and Walter ten years. They restored the lower level first as their living quarters, where they maintain a Confederate library and Civil War artifacts. Recording artists, the Stapletons are also active in Civil War reenactments. They want their guests to know that at Springhill Plantation, Southern hospitality is never "gone with the wind."

Guest rooms, which feature private baths, are in the main house and several historic outbuildings that have been moved from other locations in Georgia. Furnishings are primitive heart-pine pieces and other antiques that reflect another period while at the same time provide modern comforts. Custom-made wrought-iron details such as chandeliers, door hinges, and latches enhance the decor. We stayed in a spacious guest room at one end of the kitchen house, where the paneled walls, beamed ceiling, quilts, and other country memorabilia created a warm, cozy feeling. Having the entire building to ourselves all night gave us a delicious, romantic tryst. The next morning we simply had to step into the large country kitchen to enjoy juice and coffee while we chatted with Pam, who was busy preparing a big plantation-style breakfast with eggs, breakfast meats, and, of course, grits. (Since 1985 the Stapletons have also provided gourmet dining for luncheons and dinners by reservation only at an additional fee.) After breakfast, Pam obligingly donned one of her antebellum-style gowns to do a photo session with us.

Once located far from town, the property has been encroached upon by Americus. With twenty-six acres, however, the bed and breakfast still manages to retain a rural feeling. In fact, Civil War reenactments are held here periodically. The landscaped grounds and gardens, which overlook three ponds and feature the original carriage house and well, make a wonderful place for a relaxing stroll.

What's Nearby Americus

Americus is right next door to Plains, the hometown of our thirty-ninth president Jimmy Carter. Learn all about his life at the Jimmy Carter National Historic Site. Take a guided tour with B.J.'s Tours, which departs from Plains Peanuts on Main Street. You'll stop at the Plains High School, Welcome Center and Museum, Carter's family farm and boyhood home, and his present-day ranch home.

1906 Pathway Inn

501 South Lee Street
Americus, Georgia 31709
(912) 928-2078 or (800) 889-1466;
fax is the same

E-MAIL: pathway@sowega.net
WEB SITE: www.bbonline.com/
ga/pathway/

INNKEEPERS: Angela and Chuck Nolan

ROOMS: 5; all with private bath; 3 with one-person whirlpool tub; two with shower, ceiling fan, robes, telephone, clock radio, down comforter; some have TV as well; pets accepted with prior approval; limited wheelchair access

ON THE GROUNDS: Verandas

RATES: $75 to $125, including breakfast and afternoon refreshments

CREDIT CARDS ACCEPTED? Yes

OPEN: Year-round

HOW TO GET THERE: From I-75, take US 280 to Americus. As you reach the historic commercial district, US 280 becomes one way going west on Forsyth Street. Turn left (south) onto South Lee Street. The inn is located at the corner of South Lee Street and College, and is clearly identified by a sign. Guest parking is in the rear.

With so many striking attributes, where shall we begin? First of all, how about the architecture? The two porticos of this 1906 Neoclassical Revival mansion are among the most unusual and stunning we've ever seen. An immense two-story square portico supported by four columns towers over and shelters a one-story round portico supported by smaller columns. We've never seen this portico-within-a-portico arrangement before. A wraparound veranda has still more columns and an ornate porch railing. Even though their home is centrally located in a historic district brimming with numerous splendid examples of turn-of-the-century opulence, the Nolans' residence is extraordinary.

The bed and breakfast is named to honor not only the year it was built but also the state-designated Presidential Pathways tourism region in which it is located. This region honors Franklin D. Roosevelt, whose Little White House getaway was in Warm Springs, and Jimmy Carter, who still makes his home in Plains. The inn has been named the best B&B in the Presidential Pathways region by *Georgia Journal*.

Considerable talents and excellent taste worked together to create gracious retreats out of the palatial public rooms—among them two elegant parlors, a formal dining room, and an informal sitting room—all exquisitely furnished. Sumptuous guest rooms, which feature king- or queen-size beds as well as luxury mattresses and linens, are named for the two former presidents; another is called Rosalynn, to honor Mrs. Carter; still another is named Lindbergh, for the famous aviator who made his first solo flight and bought his first plane in Americus; and the new Bell Room is named for the builder and first owner. Although not every room boasts every feature, among the outstanding amenities are private porches, fireplaces, and whirlpool tubs.

Old-fashioned swings, wicker pieces, and lots of rockers—all with cheerful floral cushions—grace the vast front porch. Antique wicker, painted pink, invites guests to unwind on the small back porch. Chaise longues in the formal gardens and around the fish pond beckon you to work on your tan or take a nap. Even more sybaritic, an outdoor hot tub is planned as well.

The Nolans make every effort to attract and please discriminating guests. It is a rare B&B that allows children of any age, but this one welcomes them. It is even more uncommon that a B&B permits pets, but you may be in luck at the Pathway Inn: With prior approval, the Nolans permit small, easily controlled pets. You must check ahead, however, because they allow only one at a time for the comfort of other guests. Because you deserve the best, a sumptuous four-course sit-down breakfast is served by candlelight using china, silver, crystal, and crisp linens. Assorted beverages, cheese, cookies, and candy are always available for guests in the downstairs ·hall, and afternoon tea and a wine and cheese reception take place each day. For honeymooners, room service is available. The Nolans say, "Come to the 1906 Pathway Inn to rekindle relationships and make new memories."

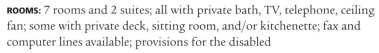

What's Nearby Americus

See page 133 for what's nearby Americus.

The Nicholson House  (Best Buy)

6295 Jefferson Road
Athens, Georgia 30607
(706) 353-2200;
fax (706) 353-7799

E-MAIL: SJKELLEY@Bellsouth.net

WEB SITE: www.bbonline.com/ga/ nicholson/

INNKEEPER: Stu Kelley

ROOMS: 7 rooms and 2 suites; all with private bath, TV, telephone, ceiling fan; some with private deck, sitting room, and/or kitchenette; fax and computer lines available; provisions for the disabled

ON THE GROUNDS: Verandas, patio, beautiful lawns, woods, natural springs

RATES: $75 to $85 single or double, including continental-plus breakfast (higher on event weekends); reservations required

CREDIT CARDS ACCEPTED? Yes

OPEN: Year-round

HOW TO GET THERE: From Atlanta, take I-85 North to exit 50. At the top of the ramp, turn right onto US 129. Follow 129 through the town of Jefferson. When you have traveled 17.5 miles from exit 50, you will see a sign directing you to the Nicholson House on your right directly across from the medical clinic

For casual elegance in classic Athens, we suggest the tranquil haven of the Nicholson House. We loved the setting the minute we started down the long, winding drive through open meadows that led us not only to the historic house, but back to another time. Although the original part of the house was built in 1820, the property dates from 1779 when William Few, a signer of the U.S. Constitution, was granted the land. Ransom Nichols bought it from Few and built a four-room, two-story, hand-hewn log home. His property became known as Gum Springs, because a hollow gum tree was used to cap off a spring, enabling it to spout in different directions like a fountain. The old Federal Highway wove its way in front of the property; cotton farmers often camped out and watered their horses here on the way to and from Athens. In 1947 J. P. Nicholson bought the farm and built a Classical Revival home around the existing log structure. Today, although the estate has been reduced to six wooded acres, they are beautiful rolling hills dotted with magnolias and wild azaleas. With its tradition of hospitality, it seems only natural that the Nicholson House has returned to a lodging function.

A cozy feeling of casual elegance permeates the inn. Guests often gather around the fireplace in the formal parlor with its comfortable overstuffed furniture, or curl up next to the woodstove in the library, where they can browse through materials about the history of the house and property.

Six of the beautifully appointed guest rooms are in the main house, two in the converted carriage house, and one in a newly constructed carriage house. Although each room has its own decor and personality and is furnished with antiques and reproductions, all feature modern amenities and such luxuries as feather and down pillows. Many boast a carved four-poster king- or queen-size bed, private deck or balcony, and decorative fireplace as well. Some have the added convenience of a private entrance. Each suite in the carriage house offers a small sitting room as well. A second one-bedroom carriage house offers a kitchenette and a sitting room with a queen-size sofa bed perfect for families or friends traveling together.

Stu serves his guests a generous continental-plus breakfast of freshly baked muffins, English muffins, bagels, cereal, yogurt, a fruit plate, juices, and hot beverages. In good weather, why not take it out on the veranda, where you can relax in a rocking chair and watch the deer at play? Then if you're feeling the slightest bit energetic, take a stroll around the sweeping lawns or through the woods to see the natural springs.

Located within minutes of the University of Georgia, the Nicholson House is an excellent place to stay whether you're a visiting parent, businessperson connected with the university, or football fan attending a game. Athens has many historic attractions, and it's a good base from which to explore the mountains to the north or the Antebellum Trail to the south.

What's Nearby Athens

Athens is home to 30,000 students from the University of Georgia. The college campus is known for its classical Greek Revival architecture, inspired by the city's namesake. The State Botanical Garden, located a few miles from the campus, is filled with ferns, orchids, birds of paradise, and other lush plants.

Another Recommended B&B in Athens

Magnolia Terrace, a 1912 Classical Revival home in the historic district, offers rooms with private baths, 1 with whirlpool tub, and continental-plus breakfast; 277 Hill Street, Athens, GA 30601; (706) 548-3860 or (800) 891-1912.

Gaslight Inn

1001 St. Charles Avenue
Atlanta, Georgia 30306
(404) 875-1001; fax (404) 876-1001

E-MAIL: innkeeper@gaslightinn.com

WEB SITE: www.gaslightinn.com

INNKEEPER: Jim Moss

ROOMS: 6; all with private bath; two with whirlpool tub; one with steam shower and cable TV; 3 with fireplace; 4 with deck, balcony, or porch; 2 with wheelchair access

ON THE GROUNDS: Enclosed gardens

RATES: $85 to $195 including continental-plus breakfast; reservations required

CREDIT CARDS ACCEPTED? Yes

OPEN: Year-round

how to get there: From I-75/85 in downtown Atlanta, take the Freedom Parkway east to Ponce de Leon Avenue. Turn right and go to North Highland Avenue. Turn left there, then left again at St. Charles Avenue.

The Gaslight Inn is on your left midway down the block. Parking for check-in is on the street; overnight parking is behind Jim's house across the street.

You know how it is when something's practically in your own backyard. You keep saying you're going to take advantage of it one of these days, but you almost never do. After seeing the very swanky bed and breakfast called the Gaslight Inn, that's the way it's been with us: We keep saying we're going to go spend our anniversary or some other special occasion there, but we're so often on the road doing research or on a trip of another sort (a guilt trip about always being behind schedule) that we haven't gotten around to spending a night yet. We will, though.

But we did stop by for a tour. The original granite carriage step at curbside was our first clue that we were about to see a unique and historic inn. A flickering gas lantern outside drew us up the steps to the inviting front porch of the 1913 Craftsman-style bungalow. We stepped inside to the elegance and sophistication of the public rooms and guest accommodations, where the dining room chandelier is still gas operated and five working fireplaces throughout the house add to the cozy ambience. One of the most outstanding bed and breakfasts in Atlanta, the Gaslight Inn has been profiled in regional and national magazines, as well as having been featured several times on travel segments aired by CNN.

Coolly elegant twin parlors make a pleasant, though formal, gathering place for guests. The parlors flow into the formal dining room, where breakfast is served by glimmering gaslight, and continue into the marvelous informal sunroom addition, which contains a grand piano, comfortable overstuffed seating, and a generous supply of books and magazines. This lovely room opens into a walled garden—a quiet oasis of abundant flowers, a lush grass carpet, a fish pond, and a tinkling fountain. This garden, which has been showcased on several garden tours, is a serene place to sit under giant crape myrtles. More than 2,000 flower bulbs bring this area alive in the spring. Both public rooms and guest rooms are furnished in antiques and reproductions and embellished with sumptuous fabrics and dramatic window treatments—all created by the prestigious firm Pineapple House Interior Design.

A variety of lavish accommodations in the main house and the converted carriage house are offered in exquisite rooms and luxurious suites. Each room displays its own personality and features some special attribute, such as original antique light fixtures or a stained-glass window. As an added attraction, the Garden Room opens onto a private secret garden. The

English Suite features a fireplace, a sitting room with sofabed, a large bathroom with a two-person whirlpool tub as well as a steam shower, and a private deck overlooking the rear garden. The opulent St. Charles Suite features a private veranda, a living room, a working fireplace and wet bar, and a two-person whirlpool tub. Ivy Cottage, a suite of rooms in the carriage house, is decorated in Nantucket style and boasts a bedroom, a living room, a kitchen, and laundry facilities. The only stress we could possibly envision when staying in this B&B is choosing among the rooms and suites.

Located in the trendy Virginia-Highland neighborhood, the Gaslight Inn is within walking distance of thirty-five fine restaurants, as well as shops, theaters, and art galleries. All the sophisticated attractions of downtown Atlanta are only a five-minute drive away.

What's Nearby Atlanta

There's no shortage of things to do in Atlanta. The problem is choosing where to go. If you're looking for someplace peaceful, visit Piedmont Park and the Atlanta Botanical Garden. If you're in the mood to shop, explore the Virginia-Highland neighborhood, Little Five Points, and East Atlanta Village. If you're the outdoorsy type, go to the Chattahoochee River National Recreation Area for rafting, canoeing, and kayaking. Don't forget tomorrow is another day, and you may have time to visit the Margaret Mitchell collection at the Atlanta Public Library, which is just across the street from the theater where *Gone with the Wind* made its 1939 world premiere.

Other Recommended B&Bs in Atlanta

Atlanta's Woodruff Bed and Breakfast Inn offers 12 rooms, most with private baths, in a turn of-the-century home; 223 Ponce de Leon Avenue, Atlanta, GA 30302; (404) 875-9449 or (800) 473-9449; fax (404) 875-2882. *Heartfield Manor*, a 1903 English Tudor-style cottage in historic district, offers rooms with cable TV, microwave, and refrigerator; 182 Elizabeth Street Northeast, Atlanta, GA 30307; (404) 523-8633. *Lismore House*, a Tudor-style home built in 1917 in Midtown, offers rooms with private baths; 855 Penn Avenue, Atlanta, GA 30308; (404) 817-9640. *Shellmont Bed & Breakfast Lodge* features rooms in a lovely turn-of-the-century federalist Greek Revival home; 821 Piedmont Avenue Northeast, Atlanta, GA 30308; (404) 872-9290.

King-Keith House Bed & Breakfast

Best Buy

889 Edgewood Avenue Northeast
Atlanta, Georgia 30307
(404) 688-7330

INNKEEPERS: Jan and Windell Keith

ROOMS: 3 rooms and 1 suite; all with private bath

ON THE GROUNDS: Veranda

RATES: $60 to $95, including full breakfast; reservations required

CREDIT CARDS ACCEPTED? Yes

OPEN: Year-round

HOW TO GET THERE: From I-75/85, take the Edgewood Avenue exit and go east approximately 2 miles. The house is on your right. Parking is on the street.

One of the oldest houses in Inman Park, Atlanta's first planned suburb (now on the National Register of Historic Places), this opulent Victorian mansion was named for its first occupant, George E. King, the founder of King Hardware. The construction date, 1890, is inscribed on an ornate brick panel outside one of the chimneys. With the exception of a circular gazebo with a fanciful curved roofline at the corner of the wraparound porch, the architecture of the house is that of highly articulated masses and very angular wood ornaments, reflecting the Eastlake style. A triangular pediment over the front entrance echoes the gable above it. As a further embellishment, the exterior of the entire house is ornamented with delicate lacework. The house has been restored to a warm peach color, with trimwork accented in four to five bright hues—typical of the turn of the century.

In complete contrast to the traditional gaily colored and often whimsical exteriors of Victorian houses, the interiors of these homes typically displayed a dark, elegant ambience. The King-Keith House is no exception. The house retains its high ceilings, original hardwood floors, ornate moldings, and massive pocket doors. Only the fifth owners of the house, the Keiths have furnished their home with a magnificent collection of heavy Victorian pieces and opulent accents, which they have acquired over many years. Be sure to take notice of the old prints, ornate frames, and colorful pieces of majolica.

Guest rooms are furnished in period antiques as well. The downstairs suite features an immense bedroom with a seating area, a bathroom, and kitchen and laundry facilities, all of which make it appealing for a long-term stay. Two of the ornate upstairs bedrooms share a hall bath with a claw-foot tub and shower. The Master Bedroom features a stained-glass window and a big bathroom, which also offers a claw-foot tub and shower. Each bedroom is adorned by a decorative fireplace. Opening off the upstairs hall is a balcony with several rocking chairs, which provides a place to relax and get a bird's-eye view of Edgewood Avenue.

In the morning coffee service is available in the upstairs hall for early risers or those who need their jolt of caffeine before venturing out into civilized company. Then a full breakfast is served in the formal dining room.

Inman Park is a vibrant neighborhood, which is undergoing an exciting renaissance. You can spend hours just strolling the tree-lined streets and admiring the varied architecture. Only a short walk away is funky Little Five Points, a commercial area where you'll find New Age stores, tattoo and body-piercing parlors, cafes, and alternative entertainment. It is one of the best places in Atlanta for people-watching. Bus and rail transportation can zoom you into downtown Atlanta and outlying neighborhoods.

What's Nearby Atlanta

See page 139 for what's nearby Atlanta.

Brunswick Manor/ Major Downing House

Best Buy

825 Egmont Street
Brunswick, Georgia 31520
(912) 265–6889

INNKEEPERS: Claudia and Harry Tzucanow

ROOMS: 5 rooms, 2 suites, and 2 cottages; all with private bath, TV, VCR; some with kitchenettes

ON THE GROUNDS: Verandas, courtyard, gardens, hot tub on patio

RATES: $65 to $90, including full breakfast, complimentary beverages, tray of fruit and cheese in each room, early coffee, afternoon refreshments; ask about corporate rates or discounts for multinight stays

CREDIT CARDS ACCEPTED? Yes

OPEN: Year-round

HOW TO GET THERE: From I-95, take exit 7, US 341, about 7 miles south to Brunswick, where it turns left onto Prince Street. Stay on Prince to Egmont. The B&B is on the corner of Prince and Egmont.

We kidded Harry, who was always a perfect host, for several years that either Claudia never existed or he had done away with her, because despite several visits and innumerable phone calls, we never saw or talked to her. Of course, the real reason for her absence was that even after they purchased and renovated the houses and opened as a bed and breakfast, she remained up north during the school year completing her tenure as a teacher, so she could retire. Now that she's joined Harry at Brunswick Manor full time, we've finally met her in person!

Facing Halifax Square in Old Town Brunswick, the stately redbrick Major Downing House (built in 1886) and the simpler house next door (1890) together serve as a bed and breakfast. Between the two houses is a garden with a pleasant courtyard, fish pond, fountain, and greenhouse—a great place to hang out. A majestic upper-class manor, the main house has a wraparound first-floor veranda supported by columns, a porte cochere, numerous gables, high ceilings, hardwood floors, and lovely moldings and other woodwork. Its original carved oak staircase rises grandly to the second floor, and stained-glass "eyebrow" windows admit jewel-toned sunbeams. The middle-class 1890 house lacks the grandiose size and ornamentation of its sister, but nevertheless has spacious, well-proportioned rooms.

The bedchambers in both houses are decorated in opulent turn-of-the-century style. Those in the main house are more formal and feature private baths; the ones in the smaller house are more casual and share. Regardless of which house you're in, each guest room offers a king- or queen-size bed, designer linens, bathrobes, and all the modern conveniences. Exquisite little pampering touches such as fresh flowers, fruit, and sherry make each chamber a restful, romantic haven.

A full gourmet breakfast featuring local specialties is served by candlelight each morning in the formal dining room. Harry makes a mean French toast served with all the traditional Southern accompaniments. In the afternoon, when you're tired from a day of sight-seeing, enjoy tea and goodies in the parlor. Whether you're looking for a casual meal or a fine dining experience, your hosts can give you lots of great recommendations for places to go for dinner.

Harry's a train buff, so be sure to ask him about his collection. In addition, the Tzucanows own two oceangoing boats and operate fishing charters, so a stay at Brunswick Manor can be an all-in-one vacation.

What's Nearby Brunswick

Brunswick is the center of Georgia's shrimping and fishing industry. On that note, a fun activity for your own shrimps is a visit to the Mary Miller Doll Museum. There are 4,000 dolls on display, including hundreds of dresses and accessories. The dolls represent about ninety different countries around the world.

Another Recommended B&B in Brunswick

Rose Manor Guest House offers rooms in an 1890 Queen Anne Victorian bungalow with veranda overlooking gardens; 1108 Richmond Street, Brunswick, GA 31520; (912) 267-6369.

Gordon-Lee Mansion

217 Cove Road
Chickamauga, Georgia 30707
(706) 375-4728 or (800) 487-4728;
fax (706) 375-9499

E-MAIL: GLMBB1@aol.com

WEB SITE: www.fhc.org/gordon-lee

INNKEEPERS: Frank Green, owner;
Richard Barclift, innkeeper

ROOMS: 3 rooms and 1 suite (also log house, but breakfast is not included); all with private bath, cable TV

ON THE GROUNDS: Veranda, gazebo, chapel, old plantation structures

RATES: $75 to $125 double, including full breakfast and afternoon refreshments; two-night minimum stay on weekends and holidays; ask about corporate rates

CREDIT CARDS ACCEPTED? Yes

OPEN: Year-round

HOW TO GET THERE: To get to Chickamauga, at exit 141, turn west off I–75 onto GA 2 to Fort Oglethorpe, and then turn south onto US 27. Proceed all the way through the national park. At the first traffic light after exiting the park, turn right. Follow that road to the next traffic light. Turn left, continue until you reach the traffic light in downtown Chickamauga, and turn left again. The mansion is the fourth building on your right. Enter the driveway indicated by the sign.

Looking at this majestic Greek Revival mansion and the serene grounds surrounding it, we'd have never guessed the dark period in its distant past. The elegant Gordon-Lee Mansion, which sits well back from the street, is just visible through a tree-lined avenue of ancient oaks and maples. Built in 1847, it is the only structure left standing from the fierce Battle of Chickamauga—the bloodiest two days of the Civil War, a battle in which the South achieved one of its major victories. Constructed as the centerpiece of a 2,500-acre plantation by wealthy mill owner James Gordon, the mansion was commandeered as a headquarters for Union general William Rosecrans, who used the parlor to plot his strategy with his staff, among them the future president James Garfield. The beautiful downstairs library served a grim function as an operating room. Both the beauty of the structure and its historical significance qualified the house to be listed on the National Register of Historic Places.

Lovingly restored and exquisitely furnished with Oriental rugs, crystal and brass chandeliers, and federal, Empire, and early-Victorian antiques, the Gordon-Lee Mansion today serves as a bed and breakfast. The library is of great interest, of course, although you won't find bloody reminders of its once dark purpose. Today, it's an elegant and peaceful place to read a good book or engage in interesting conversation.

Superb accommodations are offered in three luxurious bedrooms and one suite, all with decorative fireplace and private bath. We felt like royalty in the Gold Room with its massive full-tester bed, but the other rooms are equally sumptuous. In Louisiana they have a word for unexpected pleasures: *lagniappe*. Well, *lagniappe* isn't limited to that state: An unexpected pleasure at the Gordon-Lee Mansion is the upstairs bedroom that has been converted into a display of Civil War memorabilia, which guests can peruse at any time. Accommodations are also offered in the two-story log house with two bedrooms, a bath, and a fireplace, but breakfast is not included.

Although the vast amount of the plantation acreage is gone, the extensive grounds still encourage strolling to see the old plantation structures, including a smokehouse, old slave quarters, and a log cabin. Or you can tarry in the gazebo for some quiet reflection. Since our last visit there have been big doings at the Gordon-Lee Mansion. A wedding chapel has been built and an attractive pavilion refurbished, so now there are often weddings and other special events. What a perfect place! You could have a romantic ceremony, followed by an elegant reception, and then spend your honeymoon in luxurious surroundings in the suite.

Burns-Sutton House

855 Washington Street
Clarkesville, Georgia 30523
(706) 754-5565; fax (706) 754-9698

WEB SITE: www.georgiamagazine.com/burns-sutton/

INNKEEPER: Jaime Huffman

ROOMS: 7 (4 of them suites); most with private bath and gas-log fireplace

ON THE GROUNDS: Verandas, English gardens, croquet lawn

RATES: $65 to $125, including full breakfast

CREDIT CARDS ACCEPTED? Yes

OPEN: Year-round

HOW TO GET THERE: From Atlanta, take I–85 to I–985 and follow it until it becomes US 365. Stay on it heading north to GA 197. Turn left onto GA 197 North and go 4.1 miles. Washington Street is both GA 197 and Historic US 441. From Greenville, South Carolina, take US 123 south to GA 17 West. Follow it to US 441. From Chattanooga, Tennessee, take I–75 to Dalton, Georgia. Go east on GA 76 and turn south onto GA 197 into Clarkesville. The inn is on the western side of the street several blocks south of the town square.

This stately asymmetrical, three-story Queen Anne Victorian mansion, which was built in 1901 for the Dr. John K. Burns family, stands majestically on a large tree-shaded lot along Clarkesville's main thoroughfare. Constructed entirely of heart pine, the house rises from a pierced-brick foundation and features large, wicker-filled, wraparound verandas—perfect places to retreat with a frosty glass of iced tea and a good book on a warm summer day.

Listed on the National Register of Historic Places, the graceful mansion features a formal interior that shows off high ceilings and varnished hardwood floors as well as original architectural gems such as brilliant jewel-toned stained-glass windows, delicate cutwork in the balustrades, picture molding, and ornate mantels. Guests are encouraged to relax in the formal downstairs parlor, which is well supplied with diversions such as a television, books, and magazines.

Each spacious, romantic guest room is individually decorated with impressive antiques. Many feature stained-glass windows, canopy beds, and decorative or gas-log fireplaces. Although the suites have private baths, the guest rooms share, so be sure to ask if that's important to you. Among the suites, the Homer's Suite's queen-size canopy bed, gas-log fireplace, and stained-glass window overlooking the two-person whirlpool tub make it the most popular. The focal point of the Victorian is the 1890s Gothic bedroom suite. The Presley Suite is dominated by an iron half-tester bed. Additional guests can be accommodated on daybeds in the Victorian, Presley, and Wicker Suites.

Jaime says that at the Burns-Sutton House, "We don't dance the continental." Instead, a full breakfast is served in the dining room at your convenience. Always homemade, the morning meal features fresh seasonal fruit, juice, tea and coffee, and specialties of the house such as stuffed omelettes, fruited waffles, or meat, eggs, grits, and homemade biscuits. When we talked to Jaime recently, she said she was opening a restaurant in the B&B as well.

What's Nearby Clarksville

When you're not hanging out in the parlors or on the verandas, there are English gardens in which to stroll, and a croquet lawn awaits a challenging match or two. Clarkesville was once the summer home of many prominent families from coastal Georgia, who escaped to the Blue Ridge Mountains to enjoy the cool fresh air and beautiful lakes and rivers. Today, the area has many more permanent residents and visitors, not just in the summer but throughout the year as well. The charming turn-of-the-century town offers many antiques and crafts shops and makes an excellent base from which to explore the northeastern Georgia mountains.

Beechwood Inn

7 Beechwood Drive
Clayton, Georgia 30525
(706) 782-5485

INNKEEPER: Marty Lott

ROOMS: 6 rooms and 1 suite; all
with private bath

ON THE GROUNDS: Porches, patio, gift
shop, lawn games

RATES: $85 to $125, including full breakfast

CREDIT CARDS ACCEPTED? Yes

OPEN: May through November

HOW TO GET THERE: From the junction of US 441/123 and GA 76, turn east
and go 0.1 mile. Turn left onto Beechwood Drive, which is the first road
to your left. At the stop sign, turn right. Follow the signs up the steep
winding road and into the inn's driveway. Parking is to the side.

Poised on a steep hillside overlooking Clayton, this weathered frame and
fieldstone inn faces Black Rock Mountain, which you can see in the distance through a break in the trees. Built as a one-room cottage in 1922
by the Bucholz family, the mountain getaway offered an escape from the
sweltering summer heat of lower elevations in Georgia. Early on, the family
had a separate log-construction summer kitchen (already on the property)
attached to the cottage. More additions over the years resulted in the rustic,
rambling inn you see today. The largest of the current common rooms was
the one-room cottage; you can still see the log walls of the cabin where it
was incorporated into the building.

Surrounded by huge, ancient pines and hardwoods, the inn is usually
cooled by north breezes. Apparently, when the Bucholzes bought the property there were beech trees on it, but the name of the inn actually comes from
their last name, which means "grove of beech trees." Time was unkind to the
beeches, however. Still, a frequent guest recently presented Marty with a
beech sapling so that she would have at least one beech on the property.

The wraparound flagstone porch creates a popular gathering place for
today's guests, just as it has for more than seventy years. From the porch,
the terrain drops steeply to a small, level lawn that's perfect for playing croquet and other lawn games. The high position of the inn and the bounty of
trees make you feel secluded and far removed from today's stresses,

although you are only a minute from the center of town. In fact, we felt as if we were in an oversize tree house.

Care has been taken to retain the hardwood floors, some exposed plank walls, and numerous fireplaces. Each public and guest room is enhanced by simple, casual antique pieces, period reproductions, and country accents. High-back sofas and chairs are drawn up around the stone fireplace in the largest common room, while a television and comfortable overstuffed sofas and chairs furnish a smaller public room.

Each of the spacious guest rooms and suites features a private bath as well as a fireplace, and radiates charm with collections of family treasures, folk art, and antiques. Each is air-conditioned, but whenever possible Marty opens all the windows so the ceiling fans can distribute the natural breezes. Most chambers offer romantic canopy or four-poster beds; several boast a sitting area and/or a private balcony, screened-in porch, or patio. Longer-term accommodations are available in a suite that boasts a private fully equipped kitchen. Among the bathrooms, one sports an enclosed antique copper tub with a European shower, another has a claw-foot tub with a European shower, and the remainder feature step-in stall showers. Beds are standard double size, with the exception of one room that features twin beds.

What's Nearby Clayton

Visit the picturesque Tallulah Gorge Park and Terrora Park and Campground. You'll definitely fall for the beautiful Tallulah Falls and Tallulah River. If you're in the market for mountain handicrafts, stop by the Tallulah Gallery and Lofty Branch Art and Craft Village. Shop for paintings, pottery, weaving, woodwork, leather, and glass.

Rothschild-Pound House Bed and Breakfast

201 Seventh Street
Columbus, Georgia 31901
(706) 322–4075 or
(800) 585–4075;
fax (706) 322–3772

E-MAIL: mpound@webtv.net

WEB SITE: www.awts.com/poundhouse

INNKEEPERS: Mamie and Garry Pound

ROOMS: 8 rooms and 5 suites; all with private bath, cable TV, telephone, and in-room coffeemaker; provisions for the disabled

ON THE GROUNDS: Verandas, landscaped lawns and gardens

RATES: $97 to $165, including full breakfast, afternoon refreshments, complimentary use of nearby health club

CREDIT CARDS ACCEPTED? Yes

OPEN: Year-round

HOW TO GET THERE: From I-185, take the exit to Phenix City and downtown. Turn left onto Second Avenue. The inn is at the corner of Second Avenue and Seventh Street.

W hy did we love this bed and breakfast? Let us count the ways. First of all, vivacious, energetic Mamie and Garry (he's a noted artist and portraitist) are gregarious hosts whose goal is to pamper their guests. They certainly succeeded with us. Second, we loved the architecture—Second Empire Victorian is our favorite. Third, we were intrigued by the story of the house; more about that in a minute. Last but not least, the food is fabulous.

Built in the 1870s, this magnificent mansion was the home of several civic and industrial leaders over the years, but over time the grand old dowager suffered ill use and disrepair. Learning that the house was on the verge of destruction, Garry and Mamie saved it from the wrecking ball by spearheading a concerted community effort to move it and several other threatened homes to the protection of the historic district. In fact, all four of the houses on this block were moved to the site during that project or another. Be sure to ask to see the fascinating video Garry and the historic preservation committee produced to chronicle the massive undertaking.

The Pounds have made a mission of saving old houses. Their original intent in moving the Rothschild House was not to own it themselves, but through a series of unforeseen events, that's what happened. Completely renovated in 1994, the gracious residence boasts 14-foot ceilings, fireplaces in every room, immense pocket doors, a carved mahogany staircase, and heart-pine floors. In addition, Garry and Mamie renovated the modified shotgun house next door, which they've dubbed the Painter's Cottage and use for guest accommodations as well. Both houses are furnished in toto with antiques. Original art—Garry's and his mother's—hangs everywhere. Both houses boast rocker-filled porches.

Every guest room is designed with comfort and convenience in mind, but the pampering only starts there. Nightly turndown service with chocolates and a liqueur, fresh flowers from Mamie's garden in season, and 100 percent cotton sheets are standard. Some guest chambers feature a period bath with a claw-foot tub, while others boast a whirlpool tub, a stocked mini refrigerator, or a wet bar. One opens into a private kitchen. The rooms that don't have a mini refrigerator of their own have access to a communal one in the hall, and each house has a goodie basket filled with cookies, chips, and other munchies.

Each evening at the Rothschild-Pound House begins with wine and hors d'oeuvres in one of the parlors. In nice weather you may prefer to take your drink outside for a stroll in the English garden with its lily pond and fountain.

Mamie creates a big Southern breakfast with imagination and a sense of fun. Served according to your schedule, the meal might consist of gourmet grits, specialty pancakes, homemade breads, quiches, and preserves.

You'll experience the hospitality and warmth of old Columbus at the Rothschild-Pound House, which Air France's in-flight publication has called "one of the top five places to stay in Georgia." Several statewide publications have called it "the number one place to stay in Columbus."

What's Nearby Columbus

Columbus is the third largest city in Georgia. It offers quite an assortment of activities. The Columbus Riverwalk is a good place to start. Walk ¼ mile along the Chattahoochee and visit the Riverwalk's Coca-Cola Space Science Center. Catch a show at the restored Springer Opera House, which dates to 1871. Some famous performers who graced the stage included Oscar Wilde, Will Rogers, and Edwin Booth.

Inn Scarlett's Footsteps

40 Old Flat Shoals Road
Concord, Georgia 30206
(800) 886-7355;
fax (770) 884-9012
E-MAIL: gwtw@gwtw.com
WEB SITE: www.gwtw.com/
INNKEEPERS: K. C. and
Vern Bassham

ROOMS: 5 rooms and 5 cottages; all with private bath; some with fireplace, whirlpool tub, and porch

ON THE GROUNDS: Veranda, screened porch, extensive grounds, gift shop

RATES: $89 to $125, including full Southern breakfast

CREDIT CARDS ACCEPTED? Yes

OPEN: Year-round

HOW TO GET THERE: Drive south from Atlanta on I-75. At Griffin, go south on US 19/41 to Zebulon. In Zebulon, turn right (west) at the traffic light onto GA 18 and follow it through Concord 0.4 mile past the R. F. Strickland Building. The bed and breakfast is on your right and is identified by a sign. From I-85 South, take I-185 South to GA 18 and go east. Look for the bed and breakfast just at the edge of town.

When it comes to *Gone with the Wind* obsession, few folks can hold a candle to K. C. Bassham, proprietress of Inn Scarlett's Footsteps, a bed and breakfast in the Old South tradition. K. C. tells us that when she was six years old, she saw *the* movie for the first time with her grandfather, and told him right then that she was going to live in a house like that someday. Since then, she says, she has seen the movie at least 700 times, all the while dressing up in hoop skirts any chance she gets, and looking for her antebellum dream. She found it in a small town south of Atlanta—a magnificent redbrick, white-columned, 8,000-square-foot mansion that she has turned into her own *Gone with the Wind* world, complete with rooms named after the characters and a place to display her astounding collection of memorabilia. Soon after they opened she and Vern began offering costume balls and barbecues that were so successful, the couple bought another property to use as a special-events facility.

Visitors to Atlanta from as far away as the Orient search in vain for Tara, which never really existed outside Margaret Mitchell's imagination, but they can find something like Ashley's Twelve Oaks at Inn Scarlett's Footsteps south of Atlanta. When we drove up the sweeping circular drive through magnolia-dotted grounds surrounded by acres of horse farms, K. C. met us by saying, "We're living our dream. . . . We sell fantasy." She readily admits that the inn's not for everyone, but she adds, "It's just right for someone who wants to be Scarlett for a day."

The manor house, built in 1905, features inlaid hardwood floors, 12-foot ceilings, and original chandeliers and ceiling medallions. Commodious rooms are furnished with antiques and reproductions. One downstairs parlor is devoted to K. C.'s collection—one of the largest in the world. If you're covetous of the items, you can assuage your desires by picking up some collectibles in Miss Margaret's Carriage House gift shop.

Guest rooms are found in the main house and four newly constructed cottages. Boldest of the bedchambers—in deference to its namesake—is Scarlett's Room. A portrait of our heroine in her barbecue dress hangs over the mantel, where several collector plates are displayed. Don't be disconcerted by the full-size mannequin of Scarlett dressed to kill. Vibrant colors, a queen-size four-poster bed, and a claw-foot tub help create just the right mood. Rhett's Room, in contrast, is more masculine. English antiques reflect his European travel and sophistication. The room showcases movie stills and a top hat tossed rakishly on one of the two high beds. Melanie's Room, which features a dainty iron bed, is pretty and pastel to reflect her gentle spirit. Ashley's Suite, which depicts his military experience with an authentic uniform and portraits of favorite generals, has the added comfort of a sitting room with an additional daybed. Mr. Gerald's Room is decorated around an equestrian theme reminiscent of his love of horses and jumping; it overlooks the horse pastures.

More Fun at Inn Scarlett's Footsteps

If you're a died-in-the-wool *Gone with the Wind* fan, who knows what otherwordly experience you might have at Inn Scarlett's Footsteps? K. C. reports that characters from the story have appeared to some guests. Some claim to have seen ladies and gentlemen in antebellum apparel floating down the grand staircase. One lady reported that Rhett, cigar in hand, appeared and kissed her on the cheek. Another group of ladies had a slumber party in Rhett's Room and sipped white Russians while waiting for him to appear.

News flash: We've just learned that K. C. and Vern have bought Whitehall, a magnificent plantation house in Covington, Georgia, east of Atlanta. In 1939 Margaret Mitchell wrote a letter to Wilbur Kurtz at David O. Selznick's studios suggesting Whitehall as her preference for the prototype for Twelve Oaks. After some restoration of the mansion, the Basshams will open it for tours. K. C. quotes Prissy as saying "We sho' is gonna have fun now."

New since we visited are four guest cottages: Aunt Pitty's Parlor, Mammy's Retreat, Miss Ellen's Chamber, and Dr. Mead's Quarters, each with a queen-size bed, whirlpool tub, television, and porch. Miss Ellen's is subdued in decor, in deference to her refined background and personality. Aunt Pitty's features pastels, lace, and wicker. Mammy's is decorated with that famous red petticoat in mind. Of course, Mammy never had it so good, with an iron bed and rocking chairs in addition to the other luxuries here. Completely over the top is Wedding Belle's Cottage, a popular honeymoon suite. This 1890s three-room cottage is as flamboyant as Belle Watling, with a gas-log fireplace beside the four-poster bed and another fireplace beside the red heart-shaped whirlpool tub.

What's Nearby Concord

Concord is located in the pine-covered rolling hills of Pike County. A quiet, small town just south of Atlanta, Concord is a perfect escape from the chaos of the city. But if you begin to miss the attractions of a big city, drive to nearby Atlanta. Then you can begin to appreciate the best of both worlds.

Worley Homestead Best Buy

410 West Main Street
Dahlonega, Georgia 30533
(706) 864–7002

WEB SITE: www.bbonline.com/ga/worley/

INNKEEPERS: Frances Stumphf, owner; Christine Summerville, manager

ROOMS: 7; all with private bath and cable TV; 3 with decorative fireplace

ON THE GROUNDS: Verandas, gardens, two courtyards, gazebo

RATES: $85 to $95 single or double, including full breakfast

CREDIT CARDS ACCEPTED? Yes

OPEN: Year-round

HOW TO GET THERE: From the center of Dahlonega, take GA 52 West. Because traffic flows one way around the square, depending on the direction from which you're approaching, you may have to go left all the way around the square to make a right turn. The B&B is located on your right about 4 blocks from the square and across from one of the college entrances.

We had a preconceived idea of what an old stagecoach inn should look like, and the historic Worley Homestead met our expectations in every way. The simple clapboard two-story structure has massive chimneys at each end, and porches run full length across both stories. What is now the circular driveway in front of the structure was once the road to Atlanta, so many stagecoaches would have stopped here on the long, rough journey.

If the old girl could talk, what stories she would tell! The old place, built in 1842, was still new and proud in 1846 when volunteers from Dahlonega marched off to Texas and Mexico to fight in the Mexican War. In 1849 Mathew F. Stephenson, the assayer at Dahlonega's U.S. mint, begged local gold miners not to desert the area for newly found gold in California. His speech trying to convince them that there was still plenty of gold to extract is reputed to be the origin of the saying, "There's gold in them thar hills." In 1864 local men and boys joined Confederate forces in their unsuccessful attempt to keep the Union from destroying Atlanta. One of those men was William J. Worley, who was elected captain of Company D of the First Georgia State Line Regiment. Later, mule-drawn wagons left Dahlonega laden with gold to be used to gild the State Capitol in Atlanta. In the early 1900s the structure housed cadets from North Georgia College.

After a hard life, with her timbers sagging badly and water damage having taken its inexorable toll, the venerable old girl was about to pass into history when Mick and Mitzi Francis bought the property in 1983. Mitzi, the great-granddaughter of Captain Worley, couldn't bear to see the historic home fall down. Although they later sold the house, their prodigious restoration efforts saved a valuable piece of Dahlonega history and permitted visitors to enjoy romantic overnights at the mint-condition property.

Today, the atmosphere of the Worley Homestead is that of a very upscale stagecoach stop. Without the high ceilings so typical of the period, the house has a very cozy feel. Furnishings are exquisite antiques—some reminiscent of farm trappings, others more formal, such as those in the parlor. Old photographs adorn the walls and tell Dahlonega's historic story.

Guest rooms, named for long-ago family members such as Maude, LeeAnn, and Capt. Worley, are individually decorated with antiques. We were fascinated by the still-working antique toilet with a tin-lined water reservoir in one of the baths. Some guest rooms boast decorative fireplaces.

A hearty full breakfast consisting of juice, fruit, meat, grits, breads, and a choice from two main dishes—which run the gamut from quiche to blueberry crepes or omelettes—is served in the dining room.

Rockers and benches on the downstairs and upstairs front porches beg visitors to slow down and sit a spell, as do the flagstone patio and the gazebo in the sunken backyard. When you're sufficiently rested, stroll the couple of blocks to the town square to visit the gold museum, shop for antiques and mountain crafts, stop in at the fudge or ice cream shops, or enjoy a gargantuan family-style lunch or dinner at the renowned Smith House.

Worley Homestead is very popular with college parents and ideal for honeymoons and anniversaries. The whole house can be rented for reunions or small corporate meetings.

The Crockett House Best Buy

671 Madison Road
Eatonton, Georgia 31024
(706) 485-2248

WEB SITE: www.bbonline.com/ga/crocketthouse

INNKEEPERS: Christa and Peter Crockett

ROOMS: 6; 4 with private bath; 5 with working fireplace, all with hair dryer

ON THE GROUNDS: Veranda, extensive grounds

RATES: $65 with shared bath, $85 to $95 with private bath, including full breakfast and afternoon refreshments

CREDIT CARDS ACCEPTED? Yes

OPEN: Year-round

HOW TO GET THERE: Approach Eatonton via US 441 from the north or south, or by way of GA 16 from the east or west. They intersect at the courthouse square. From the square, go north on US 441, which is also North Jefferson Avenue. As you leave town, it becomes Madison Road. The Crockett House is on your left and is clearly identified by a large sign. If you get to the railroad crossing, you've gone too far.

The Crockett House, a stately and gracious Victorian mansion built by the wealthy Jones sisters, celebrated its one hundredth birthday in 1995. Both sisters, who were educated in Europe, were talented in art and music. Surprisingly for two such refined ladies, when modern conveniences came along, they didn't add them to their home. They continued to live here without electricity or plumbing until 1971, when the last one died at age ninety-four. During their long years of residence, the reclusive sisters were rarely seen by townsfolk; occasionally at night, their lanterns could be glimpsed moving from room to room. They did, however, maintain exquisite camellia gardens well known to camellia fanciers.

Today the home has been exquisitely restored and modernized in unobtrusive ways by Christa and Peter to serve as both their home and a traditional bed and breakfast. Spacious rooms are embellished by 12- to 14-foot ceilings, eleven working fireplaces (several with marble mantels), and large windows. Burnished woods are evident in the ornamental moldings, heart-pine hardwood floors, pocket doors, and twenty-three-step staircase. These antiques-filled rooms are further adorned with tapestries, Oriental and needlepoint carpets, and family memorabilia. The formal sitting room is well appointed with television, VCR, guest telephone, games, and reading material.

Finely appointed guest rooms are named for flowers or flowering trees—Rhododendron, Rose, Dogwood, Camellia, and Magnolia—and you'll find each room's namesake in tasteful touches in the fabrics or accent pieces. Beds range from doubles to kings, and from brass to iron and four-poster. The Rose Room shares a bath with the Dogwood Room, but every other room boasts a private bath. Both the Magnolia and Camellia Rooms sport claw-foot tubs prominently situated within the bedroom beside a working fireplace, instead of in the bathroom. Romantics also favor the two-headed shower in the Azalea Room.

More important than the physical beauty of the property and the elegance of the house, the public rooms, and the guest rooms is the outlook of the owners. Between them, the Crocketts have more than twenty-five years in the hospitality industry, so they know what guests want and they aim to deliver. Christa and Peter want you to feel as if you are family or honored guests. While we were visiting, a frequent guest told us "Coming here definitely feels like coming home—it's very familiar." In fact, this guest told us that she comes so often, she has her own key.

When you arrive, the Crocketts will greet you with refreshments—iced tea or hot beverages (depending on the weather), fruit, and what they like to call "sweet creations." After you unwind, they'll be happy to give you suggestions about where to eat dinner. In fact, if you'd rather eat in, with prior arrangements and at an additional cost they'll prepare you a romantic candlelight dinner at the inn. The Crocketts provide a plenitude of books, magazines, and games for their guests' leisure pursuits, but if you don't want to do anything except veg out, that's okay, too.

Guests are treated to other luxuries and indulgences: private-label bubble bath, soaps, and lotions, luxurious bedding, down comforters, fluffy bathrobes, breakfast in bed for special occasions, to name just a few. They'll even pack you a picnic and send you off with a quilt to sit on for a day's outing. They'll get your morning off to a great start with a candlelight breakfast using china, crystal, and silver. This morning feast might showcase such gourmet dishes as butter pecan pancakes with rum raisin sauce, three-cheese- and berry-stuffed French toast, or egg and vegetable soufflés along with fresh or baked fruit, homemade breads, and sweets. What we liked even better than the scrumptious food was the easy camaraderie and humor shared by both guests and hosts.

What's Nearby Eatonton

Br'er Rabbit, Br'er Fox, Br'er Bear, and Tar Baby are some of the unusual characters you'll meet in Eatonton. Joel Chandler Harris, the author of the *Uncle Remus Tales,* was born in Eatonton in 1848. Now you can visit The Uncle Remus Museum and view original illustrations and first editions of the book.

Rosewood Bed and Breakfast

Best Buy

301 North Madison Avenue
Eatonton, Georgia 31024
(706) 485–9009;
fax (706) 485–3277

INNKEEPERS: Lynda and Ken Ramage

ROOMS: 4; 2 with private bath, 2 share

ON THE GROUNDS: Verandas, rose gardens

RATES: $75 to $95, including breakfast and refreshments; ask about corporate rates

CREDIT CARDS ACCEPTED? No

OPEN: Year-round

HOW TO GET THERE: Approach Eatonton by way of US 441 from the north or south, or via GA 16 from the east or west. They intersect at the courthouse square. Church Street parallels US 441 just 1 block west of the square. Rosewood is on your left 3 blocks north of the square, and is easily identified by its gaily painted mailbox and a large sign.

When Ken took an early retirement several years ago, he wanted easily accessible golf, tennis, and fishing. Lynda actually wanted her grandmother's house in Gaffney, South Carolina, but its current owners didn't want to sell. Happily, all their desires could be fulfilled in Eatonton—a treasure trove of magnificent homes from the last century. Ken can play golf and tennis and fish to his heart's content on Lake Oconee. And although Lynda didn't get her grandmother's house, she found one very similar to it.

Built in 1888 by the Davis family, the house was partially damaged by fire in 1898, after which it was remodeled to its present Classical Revival style. The interior boasts some of the most beautifully carved woodwork in the state. In fact, it was the serendipitous discovery that the Cherokee rose, Georgia's state flower, is carved into the mantel, stairways, and other moldings and displayed in the stained-glass of the front doors that prompted Lynda to name the house Rosewood. Roses are Lynda's favorite flower, and she firmly believes that everyone should "stop and smell the roses." Toward that end she has planted a formal rose garden and fills the house with its fragrant blossoms whenever they're in season.

Rather than opening into a large central hall, the front doors lead into a large, intricately paneled reception room off which the formal parlor and dining rooms open. Original heart-pine floors, seven mantels, and beaded wainscoting are featured throughout. The lovely staircase is a sight to behold. Antiques, collectibles, family pictures, and other memorabilia make you truly feel that you are in someone's home rather than a museum or a hotel.

Spacious guest rooms boast 11-foot ceilings, handsome moldings, and decorative fireplaces—some working. Although the rooms do not ordinarily contain televisions or phones, they can be requested. Downstairs, Scarlett's Room features (naturally enough) pictures, plates, and other memorabilia from the famous Georgia book. A mural depicting scenes from the story is painted all the way around the room above the picture rail, starting with the picnic at Twelve Oaks and ending when Rhett walks out on Scarlett. Ken points out with some amusement that the Civil War begins directly over the intricately carved bed. This room also boasts a decorative raised-brick fireplace and a bathroom with a claw-foot tub.

Upstairs, the Color Purple Room, named for the book written by the famous former local resident Alice Walker, features a private bath. The Rose Room features a queen-size bed. Across the hall is the Cherub Room, which has an angel motif. These two share the Joel Chandler Harris Bath, where Lynda has painted characters from the Uncle Remus stories on the cabinets to honor the author, who also was born in Eatonton.

Special touches that make every guest feel pampered include a welcoming beverage, fresh flowers and a candy basket in the guest rooms, nightly turndown service with a mint on your pillow, and bath amenities. Sherry is available in the parlor.

Although Rosewood has many, many pleasant areas in which to relax, the best place of all is the vast wraparound porch with rounded gazebolike sections at both ends from which you can admire all the other outstanding neighborhood architecture. If you want a bird's-eye view, take advantage of the small upstairs porch. And by all means wander through the rose gardens.

Nearby Eatonton

See page 157 for what's nearby Eatonton.

Captain's Quarters Bed and Breakfast Inn

13 Barnhardt Circle
Fort Oglethorpe, Georgia 30742
(706) 858-0624; fax (706) 861-4053

E-MAIL: innkeeper@captains-qtrs-inn.com

WEB SITE: www.captains-qtrs-inn.com

INNKEEPERS: Betty and Daniel McKenzie

ROOMS: 9; all with private bath, cable TV, ceiling fan, clock radio, iron and ironing board; 4 with working fireplace; hair dryer available on request; telephones available for computer use

ON THE GROUNDS: Verandas with swings, hot tub

RATES: $89 to $129

CREDIT CARDS ACCEPTED? Yes

OPEN: Year-round

HOW TO GET THERE: Turn west off I-75 onto GA 2A. Turn left at US 27, which is also known as LaFayette Road. Turn right at Harker Road and left again into Barnhardt Circle. You'll also be following the signs to the Chickamauga Battlefield, so you shouldn't have any trouble finding the B&B.

The U.S. Army Post of Fort Oglethorpe was established in 1902 and the Third, Seventh, Tenth, Eleventh, and Twelfth Cavalries had their headquarters here. Once the Sixth Cavalry arrived in 1919, this was considered to be an elite posting known far and wide for the polo matches held on its parade grounds, as well as for its fox hunts. From the beginning Barnhardt Circle was the location of posh homes built for married officers. These were monumental duplex houses in the classic Renaissance Revival style. Tuscan architecture was found not only in the homes and military buildings but also in the bandstand, the barracks, and even the stables.

When the fort closed in 1946, all the buildings were sold at public auction, and over the years the survivors have served in various capacities. Yet this is still a gracious street of stately residences. And now both sides of one of these duplexes have been put into creative use as a bed and breakfast where you can relive the glory days of the fort.

The B&B is elegantly furnished and decorated down to the most minute detail. Spacious common rooms display the family antiques and personal collectibles of the innkeepers. Most of the beautiful guest rooms are appointed with a king-size bed—many of them four-posters. All guest chambers offer private baths—two with claw-foot tubs, the remainder with marble showers. Four especially romantic rooms feature working fireplaces—a perfect place to curl up beside with your loved one on a chilly evening. In good weather the ample porches are furnished with swings and wicker; flowers burst from planters in season.

After a hard day's sight-seeing, hiking, or shopping, or if your idea of a good time is doing as little as possible, just soak in the new hot tub. You bring the swimsuit; Betty and Daniel provide the towels and the robes.

Daniel loves to cook, and you'll enjoy the fruits of his labors at a full three-course, sit-down gourmet breakfast. It begins with a specialty beverage such as orange Julie and homemade muffins, and proceeds to a fruit course—perhaps a pear-apple compote with whipped cream and nutmeg. The entree might be as simple as eggs and meat, but could be Hawaiian French toast or a wild rice and mushroom quiche. We'll bet your mouths are watering by now. Ours are. This feast is served in both dining rooms using china and silver. We hear it on good authority that the meal is a delight for the eye as well as the palate.

What's Nearby Fort Oglethorpe

The Sixth Cavalry Museum is on the parade grounds, and the Chickamauga National Battlefield—the site of one of the Confederacy's greatest victories during the Civil War—is located directly across the street. Fort Oglethorpe makes an excellent base from which to explore northwestern Georgia, northeastern Alabama, Chattanooga, and Middle Tennessee. You can find just about any indoor or outdoor activity that strikes your fancy. In addition, the town is only 6 miles from I-75 and many of the attractions of the northwestern Georgia mountains. Chattanooga, Tennessee, is only ten minutes away.

The Evans-Cantrell House

Best Buy

300 College Street
Fort Valley, Georgia 31030
(912) 825-0611; fax (912) 822-9925

WEB SITE: www.bbonline.com/ga/evanscantrell/

INNKEEPERS: Cyriline and Norman Cantrell

ROOMS: 5; all with private bath (well supplied with toiletries), telephone, TV, robes

ON THE GROUNDS: Porch

RATES: $65 single, $65 to $95 double, including full breakfast, refreshments, and turndown service; ask about corporate rates

CREDIT CARDS ACCEPTED? Yes

OPEN: Year-round

HOW TO GET THERE: From I-75 take Exit 44, Fort Valley, onto GA 96. As you enter town, turn left onto South Camellia Boulevard, then right onto College Street. The house is at the far right corner of College and Miller.

We've only stayed at the delightful Evans-Cantrell House once, but we've had dozens of lively phone conversations with Cyriline over the years. No matter how long it's been between calls, it's as if we're old friends who talked only yesterday. Cyriline always wants to know when we're coming back to stay. Oh if only we had more time, we'd dearly love to return to some of our favorite B&Bs. This one is near the top of the list for its elegant, comfortable surroundings, fine food, and loquacious owners.

A. J. Evans was known as the Peach King in both Georgia and South Carolina. The tycoon and philanthropist built his home—an Italianate Renaissance Revival mansion—in 1916 in what is now designated as the Everett Square Historic District of Fort Valley. Features that were high-tech in 1916 remain today—an electric bell system that could be activated from any room in the house to summon the servants, lighted closets with an automatic switch in the doorjamb casing, a central vacuum system, and a shower in the master bedroom that sprays water both vertically and horizontally.

The Cantrells—only the second owners of the 6,100-square-foot mansion—have done a masterful job of renovating and updating without changing the elegant interior or the honey-colored brick exterior. Plentiful windows and French doors keep the house cheerful and airy. The only room updated to the 1990s is the immense kitchen; two baths have been added as well.

Downstairs, the house features a cavernous greeting room, parlor, library, formal dining room, and breakfast room as well as the kitchen and butler's pantry. High ceilings soar above hardwood floors, lots of mahogany paneling, and original chandeliers and wall sconces. The dining room features the furniture built specifically for the room. Be sure to admire the ornately carved marble fireplace in the parlor; it's similar to one found in England's Windsor Castle. Then take the graceful staircase to the second floor, where the individually decorated guest rooms are located.

Spacious bedchambers are named for the Evans children—Ruth, Christine, Mary, Charles, and Albert. For the most part these rooms feature queen-size beds, although Albert's Room has the convenience of two doubles for families or friends traveling together. Some are more formal than others. We stayed in the informal Mary's Room, once the sleeping porch, which is furnished in wicker. All guest rooms offer a desk, making them popular with business travelers.

Cyriline serves a full breakfast in the sunny, informal breakfast room. The morning repast might include fruit, juice, muffins, an egg dish, and breakfast meat. A feature particularly popular with guests is the butler's pantry, which can be reached by a set of back stairs. Coffee and soft drinks are always available there and guests can use the refrigerator for their personal items. Strategically placed candy dishes are always full. Nightly turndown service includes a chocolate-covered or praline pecan treat.

The vast public rooms and 1,000-square-foot porch make the house ideal for small corporate meetings, weddings, luncheons, and other functions.

What's Nearby Fort Valley

Feeling peachy? Then visit the Georgia Peach Festival in Fort Valley. The weeklong event is held in mid-June. The festival kicks off with parades, dancing in the streets, peach pie cookoffs, peach-eating contests, and culminates in the crowning of Georgia's Peach King and Queen.

Magnolia Hall Bed and Breakfast

Best Buy

127 Barnes Mill Road
Hamilton, Georgia 31811
(706) 628–4566

WEB SITE: www.bbonline.com/ga/
magnoliahall/

INNKEEPERS: Dale and Centric
(Ken) Smith

ROOMS: 3 rooms and 2 suites; all with private bath, hair dryer, iron; TV
and VCR in most rooms; telephone lines for computers; fully wheelchair
accessible

ON THE GROUNDS: Veranda, terrace

RATES: $95 to $105, including full breakfast and evening desserts

CREDIT CARDS ACCEPTED? No

OPEN: Year-round

HOW TO GET THERE: Hamilton is located at the intersection of GA 354 and
GA 116 just 9 miles east of I–185. The signage directing you to Magnolia
Hall is excellent.

Built in 1890 and recently restored, Magnolia Hall is a magnificent Victorian cottage with multiple chimneys, numerous gabled dormers, and decorative ironwork at the roof's peak. Wraparound porches adorned with intricate scrollwork encircle the dark green house. Lushly hung with trailing ferns, the rocker-filled porch invites guests to relax outside.

Located just around the corner from the courthouse in the center of Hamilton, this bed and breakfast is situated on a luxuriantly landscaped acre highlighted by hundred-year-old hollies and a magnificent old magnolia. In addition, there is a formal garden with a brick courtyard in the rear of the house. A ramp from the ample side parking lot and a downstairs guest room with a wheelchair-accessible shower make the inn fully accessible to the disabled.

Inside, antiques, patterned carpets, and opulent window treatments enhance the generously proportioned rooms with their heart-pine floors, soaring ceilings, original fireplaces, floor-to-ceiling shuttered bay windows, and burnished woodwork. Elegant twin parlors offer diversions to suit any guest.

Each of the finely appointed and individually decorated guest rooms and suites is furnished with antiques and/or reproductions, as well as

embellished with rich fabrics and striking wallpapers. Furnished with pieces that belonged to Ken's father, the spacious Walton Room is an elegant chamber on the first floor. Upstairs, the two suites have a more intimate ambience because of their lower, slanted ceilings and the delightful alcoves these create. The recesses provide private space for a sitting room and a nook for a daybed.

A welcoming beverage, a plate of freshly baked cookies in your room, coffee and tea set out for early risers, evening turndown service, and a guest refrigerator with soft drinks and juices are among the amenities offered at Magnolia Hall.

Dale and Ken love bringing old houses back to life. This is their third restoration, and they say it will be their last. But, we say, seeing is believing. Dale, who's a former librarian, loves books as much as you'd expect, and you'll see them everywhere. She even reads cookbooks for entertainment. Guests are the beneficiaries of that hobby. Ken, who's the mayor of Hamilton, is a financial planner; all you have to do is look around to see how successful he is at it. Both Smiths are musical and love gardening.

What's Nearby Hamilton

Hamilton is a picturesque, little town with lots of charming antiques shops. Some popular outdoor activities include hiking and horseback riding. Other possible activities include visits to Callaway Gardens, Franklin D. Roosevelt State Park, and Pine Mountain Wild Animal Safari. Columbus is just a short ride away.

Mountain Memories Inn of Hiawassee

385 Chancey Drive
Hiawassee, Georgia 30546
(706) 896-VIEW or (800) 335-VIEW

E-MAIL: mtnmem@stc.net

WEB SITE: www.mountain-memories-inn.com

INNKEEPERS: Yolanda and David Keating and Allen Scherer

ROOMS: 6 rooms and 1 suite; all with private bath and whirlpool tub; telephone available for computer use; ask about pets; provisions for wheelchair access

ON THE GROUNDS: Decks and patios, views

RATES: $100 to $125, including full breakfast, evening dessert buffet, and other refreshments

CREDIT CARDS ACCEPTED? Yes

OPEN: Year-round

HOW TO GET THERE: From 1 block west of the traffic light in the center of town, take Bell Street north. You'll see a sign indicating where you need to turn right. Continue up the incredibly steep hill to the inn at the summit. It is identified by a sign, and there is plenty of parking.

Some inns are outstanding because of their hosts, some because of an exceptional house or furnishings, some because of their locations, others because of their amenities. This inn is exceptional for all of the above. First are the views—we can attest that they're among the best in the state. The contemporary inn is poised high on a hilltop overlooking the town of Hiawassee and the glistening waters of Lake Chatuge. As if this particular view weren't enough, from other directions you can see Brasstown Bald— the highest point in Georgia—and the mountains of three states: Georgia, North Carolina, and Tennessee.

The hosts identified themselves to us as hopeless romantics, and they've created a place where you can indulge in your fantasies. Each spacious, individually decorated guest room features a king- or queen-size bed, private outside entrance, private bath, cable television, and VCR. The pièce de résistance in each room, however, is a two-person whirlpool tub at your bedside. Some rooms also boast a two-person shower, and one sports a fireplace. Each bedchamber is romantically decorated and supplied with plush robes, candles, bubble bath, bath salts, and a whimsical rubber ducky for your bath.

If you can tear yourselves out of your room, among the public spaces are an informal downstairs gameroom with a fireplace, television, VCR, videos, Nintendo games, pinball machine, books, and magazines. Another option is a small, more formal upstairs sitting room with a fireplace and television. Decks, patios, and a gazebo encircle both levels of the rambling house and entice guests to enjoy the great outdoors and spectacular views.

The owners have a pontoon boat aboard which they provide sunset cruises during warm weather. What a romantic way to set the stage for your evening! Some kind of special event is planned for Thanksgiving, Christmas, New Year's, and the Fourth of July. If you're celebrating a special occasion, let your hosts know ahead of time and they can fulfill a romantic dream of yours—or create one for you. For an additional charge they can provide flowers, champagne or wine, cakes, candlelight dinners, candy, decorations, and/or picnic baskets. Your imagination is the only limitation.

One of the most generous breakfast buffets we've ever seen at a B&B is served in the large, cathedral-ceilinged dining room, where you can admire the views from three sides. Breakfast is served using china, silver, crystal, and linens. In addition, guests are treated to an evening dessert buffet to die for—it will probably consist of six rich sinful goodies. Sodas, hot beverages, and cookies are available all the time.

What's Nearby Hiawassee

Hiawassee is the home of Lake Chatuge and of Young Harris College where *The Reach of Song,* the state historical play, is performed each summer. Hiawassee is also the home of the annual summer Georgia Mountain Fair. Numerous outdoor activities can be found nearby, as well as antiques and gift shops.

Another Recommended B&B in Hiawassee

Swan Lake Bed and Breakfast, a Cape Cod–style home overlooking a private lake, offers rooms with private baths; 2500 Hickorynut Cove, Hiawassee, GA 30546; (706) 896–1582.

The Carmichael House

149 McDonough Road
Jackson, Georgia 30233
(770) 775–0578; fax (770) 775–0578/
pin 21

E-MAIL: info@carmichaelhouse.com

WEB SITE: www.carmichaelhouse.com

INNKEEPERS: Linda Sullivan and John Herdina

ROOMS: 6 rooms and 1 suite; all with private bath (some with claw-foot tub), cable TV, private telephone; cottage rooms have coffeemakers, microwave, refrigerator; 3 telephone lines for computer use; traveling dogs can share a fenced-in area with house pets

ON THE GROUNDS: Verandas, patio, gazebo, extensive gardens

rates: $95 to $125 double; $10 less for single; third person in the Rose Suite $10 extra, fourth person $15 extra. All rates include breakfast. Ask about corporate rates

CREDIT CARDS ACCEPTED? Yes

OPEN: Year-round

HOW TO GET THERE: From I-75, take GA 16 East. Turn left onto McDonough Road. The inn is on your left and is identified by a sign. Parking is to the side and rear.

Probably the finest example of the Queen Anne Victorian style in Georgia, the Carmichael mansion perfectly reflects the opulent era at the end of the nineteenth century. In 1898 wealthy J. R. Carmichael, who had made a fortune as a manufacturer of horse-drawn carriages, used $16,000 to build this magnificent mansion, which was positioned at the head of the main street so that he could look straight downtown to his businesses.

Boasting 9,000 square feet, the classic home is embellished by a whimsical turret, twelve commodious rooms, five soaring chimneys, six spacious porches, ten graceful fireplaces—each with a different mantelpiece—eleven stunning stained-glass windows, a two-story entry rotunda, a picture rail burnished with gold leaf, lighting fixtures that were created for either gas or electricity, vertical wood paneling, intricate fretwork, carved newel posts, and the original call box used to summon the servants. The focal point of the kitchen is an operable wood- and coal-burning cookstove installed in the early 1900s. Seventy-seven windows retain their original shutters. The music room is graced with an original piano that belonged to the Carmichael family and portraits of Mr. and Mrs. Carmichael that have hung there for nearly one hundred years.

Reflecting their immense wealth, the Carmichaels had the house designed for running water and even for electricity ten years before the newfangled invention came to Butts County. Power was originally supplied by a gas-powered generator. The exterior of the mansion was adorned with shingles, plaster garlands, and a slate-tiled roof, and every effort has been made to retain or reproduce these ornaments.

The Carmichaels needed this immense house because they had eleven children. Although Mr. Carmichael died only ten years after the family occupied the house, Mrs. Carmichael continued to live here until her death in 1953. During the depression, she subdivided the house to include two apartments upstairs. After her death the house went into a decline, but J. R. Jr. executed a loving restoration in the 1960s and succeeded in having it placed on the National Register of Historic Places. He lived here until 1992, when Linda and John bought it complete with many of its original contents.

Imposing public rooms include opulent twin parlors and the elegant dining room. Upstairs, the large central hall serves as an informal guest sitting room. Guest accommodations are in four tastefully appointed bedrooms and a suite. The downstairs Rose Suite, which can accommodate four, features a master bedroom with a king-size bed and a fireplace; an adjoining study with a sofa bed, fireplace, and desk; a claw-foot tub and shower in the private bath; and a private entrance. The four upstairs bedrooms—Ivy, Magnolia, Morning Glory, and Iris—feature private baths and antique furnishings including four-poster, high-back, or brass beds. The turret alcove in the Morning Glory Room provides enough additional space for two full-size brass beds. In addition, this special room has a fireplace and a private balcony. The charming carriage house has been converted into two guest accommodations—Dogwood Cottage North and South.

You can choose items from a menu for the full breakfast served in the cheery tearoom, which was created by enclosing a rear porch. You'll be drawn outside during good weather to unwind on one of the porches, in the brick-paved rear courtyard with its gay cast-iron umbrella tables, in the gazebo, or anywhere on the extensive, garden-filled property. When we visited, the impressive annual art show was being held on the grounds.

What's Nearby Jackson

Visit Indian Springs State Park, which is one of the country's oldest state parks. A long time ago, Indians believed that the waters from the sulfur springs possessed magical healing powers. Centuries later, visitors still gather at the sulfur springs and bottle the "magical" water.

The Jarrell 1920 House

715 Jarrell Plantation Road
Juliette, Georgia 31046
(912) 986–3972; fax (912) 742–5334

E-MAIL: jarrellhouse@yahoo.com

WEB SITE: www.jarrellhouse.com

INNKEEPERS: Amelia and Philip Jarrell Haynes

ROOMS: 2; both with private bath, gas-log fireplace, TV, ceiling fan; no alcohol

ON THE GROUNDS: Veranda, Jarrell Plantation State Historic Site

RATES: $95 to $150, including full breakfast and tour of the house and plantation; two-night minimum stay on weekends

CREDIT CARDS ACCEPTED? Yes

OPEN: Year-round

HOW TO GET THERE: From I–75 in Forsyth, take exit 60 (the Gray exit) and go east. Follow the signs to Jarrell Plantation, a drive of about 18 miles.

The Jarrell 1920 House shares a driveway with the Jarrell Plantation State Historic Site. Follow the road past the private drive sign to the house. Parking is to the side.

Having previously visited the Jarrell Plantation State Historic Site, we were intrigued to learn that bed-and-breakfast accommodations were offered at the one remaining Jarrell family home, so we went to visit with great anticipation. We got a fascinating history lesson as well as a tour of the unusual Jarrell 1920 House, Phil's ancestral home, which is adjacent to the historic site.

Phil's family started the farm before the Civil War; it gradually became a simple, self-sufficient plantation with several homes, farm buildings, a sawmill, cotton gin, carpentry shop, and blacksmith shop. This was not Tara by any means, but a collection of rough houses and farm buildings. Listed on the National Register of Historic Places, the entire plantation (with the exception of the 1920 house) as well as its contents and all the farm equipment were donated to the state in 1974 to be operated as a state park. Considered to contain one of the most complete collections in Georgia of original family artifacts of 1847 to 1945, the plantation buildings contain looms, spinning wheels, cradles, a cobbler's bench, and many other pieces, implements, and utensils constructed and used by family members. The Jarrell family, however, retained the big house.

To construct the 1920 house, which was begun in 1916, Phil's grandfather Dick Jarrell and other family members felled 200-year-old pines on the plantation, sawed them to size on the site, and assembled them to create a 5,000-square-foot house that emulates mid-nineteenth-century style with upstairs and downstairs porches, tall windows, and ten fireplaces. Ten years later indoor plumbing was added when a pumping system and tower allowed water to be gravity-fed into the house. Preserved in its original condition, the house features interior walls, floors, and ceilings of beautiful heart pine that have never been plastered, painted, or papered. Most of the simple, practical, and functional nineteenth- and early-twentieth-century furnishings, dishes, needlework, and other contents are original to the family.

Guest accommodations feature double or queen-size beds and gas-log fireplaces. Dick and Mamie's Room is named for Phil's grandparents and served as their bedroom for thirty-seven years. They were married in 1891 and died within a month of each other in 1958. Their room contains their furniture and some of their prized possessions; its private bath features a claw-foot tub. The other downstairs guest room features a private bath, although it is located down the hall.

Breakfast is a treat not to be missed. Generally we don't recommend B&Bs whose morning meal isn't served on the premises, but in this case we're making an exception because the country breakfast is served at the Whistle Stop Cafe, where the movie *Fried Green Tomatoes* was filmed. The cafe remains exactly as you fondly remember it from the movie.

For those not staying at the Jarrell 1920 House, tours are offered on Sunday afternoons from 1:00 to 5:30 P.M. (6:00 P.M. April through October).

What's Nearby Juliette

You've probably heard of fried green tomatoes, but have you ever tasted them? Well, here's your chance. The Whistle Stop Cafe serves fried green tomatoes, like the fare made famous in the 1991 film *Fried Green Tomatoes*. Enjoy old-fashioned Southern cooking, including barbecue and fried chicken. After your meal, stop by the row of antiques and gift shops down the road from the cafe.

Thyme Away Best Buy

508 Greenville Street
LaGrange, Georgia 30240
(706) 885–9625; fax (706) 845–8824

INNKEEPER: Karen Wilson

ROOMS: 5; all with private bath, whirlpool tub, ceiling fan, desk or work-table with a computer jack, TV, telephone, alarm clock, small refrigerator, flashlight

ON THE GROUNDS: Porches, gardens

RATES: $75 single, $85 double, including full breakfast

CREDIT CARDS ACCEPTED? Yes

OPEN: Year-round

HOW TO GET THERE: Thyme Away is located just five minutes from I-85. Take exit 4, which is Lafayette Parkway. Turn right onto Horace King Street and go 1 block. Turn left onto Greenville Street. The house is the last one on your left in the first block and is identified by a sign.

It should come as no surprise—what with the hint given in the inn's name—that Karen is into herbs. As a matter of fact, bunches of herbs are stenciled onto the walls downstairs, and herbs from her garden are featured in many of her culinary specialties. The theme is carried even into the names of the guest chambers—Rosemary, Chamomile, Lavender, Caraway, and Bay Laurel.

Built in 1840, the commodious Classical Revival home, which dominates a quaint residential neighborhood of much smaller houses, has been lovingly restored and warmly furnished to offer a charming, genteel lodging alternative. The appealing inn has become very popular with traveling businesspeople as well as with vacationers.

Karen, a pharmacist who worked in the pharmaceutical industry for a long time, decided several years ago to get out of the rat race and start a bed and breakfast, so she left Texas and moved to LaGrange to be near her family. She's not sure she's working any less hard, but she does know that she's enjoying it a whole lot more. Karen knew from experience what she looked for in lodgings when she was on the road, and she has tried to provide those comforts and amenities for her guests.

Each individually decorated, antiques-filled guest room features a private bath with a whirlpool tub to ease those aching muscles at the end of a long day. The rooms also have closets, which is quite unusual in an old house. Fresh flowers from Karen's garden scent the air of your bedchamber in season.

Light pours into the public rooms and glints off the hardwood floors, making these rooms inviting places to be. Guests may want to gather around the fireplace in the sunny parlor to read, play games, or even tinkle the piano keys. The informal sitting room in the upstairs hall is well stocked with books and magazines. Front and side porches are furnished with comfortable wicker for lounging.

If you're a Type-A personality or fitness enthusiast, Karen can arrange health club privileges for you. If you're in town on business or just have to check in with the office, she also offers modem and fax capabilities.

What's Nearby LaGrange

Tour the Bellevue Mansion, a grand Greek Revival home. Visit the Lamar Dodd Art Center's permanent collection of American Indian Art. Also, check out the Chattahoochee Valley Art Museum. If watersports float your boat, visit West Point Lake, a popular destination for fishing, boating, swimming, and waterskiing.

Burnett Place Best Buy

317 Old Post Road
Madison, Georgia 30650
(706) 342-4034

INNKEEPERS: Ruth and Leonard
Wallace

ROOMS: 3; all with private bath,
TV, fluffy bathrobes, coffeemaker,
fixings for hot beverages; ask about
pets; smoking permitted

ON THE GROUNDS: Porch

RATES: $60 to $75 single or double, including full breakfast and afternoon refreshments

CREDIT CARDS ACCEPTED? Yes

OPEN: Year-round

HOW TO GET THERE: From I-20, take exit 51 onto US 441/129. After you
pass the Madison-Morgan Cultural Center, look for a Baptist church on
your right and its parking lot on your left. Turn left immediately onto
Central Avenue. The inn is on the next corner, at Old Post Road and
Central.

Located in Madison's historic district, Burnett Place is just 1 block off
Main Street on the Old Post Road—the old stagecoach route between
Charleston and New Orleans. In fact, at one time Madison was known as
the most beautiful and cultured town between those two cosmopolitan
cities. Today, although Madison is little more than a sleepy footnote to history, it is still a wonderful place to visit, especially during its renowned theater festival. When you're here, what better place to stay than Burnett Place?

Slave built, this circa-1830 house is a two-story federal-style dwelling
typical of the Piedmont region. It was enlarged in the 1840s, and the present
owners have added more without disturbing the historical integrity. Before
restoring the house, the Wallaces did extensive research and Leonard, an
interior designer, worked closely with the Madison Historic Preservation
Commission. The Wallaces have re-created the original bright yellow of the
entry hall and the sitting room trim—a hue that was originally created from
mullein. The remainder of the woodwork throughout the house reflects the
original colors and/or finishes. A glass panel on one landing allows guests
to examine the original methods used in the construction of the house.

The decor is a stunning mix of traditional antiques and reproductions accented with contemporary pieces—especially in the artwork chosen to accent the rooms. Guest rooms are individually decorated, but all offer a double bed and private bath. Two feature working fireplaces. Children are welcome; the Wallaces can even supply a baby bed.

The full breakfast—served in the dining room—begins with a fresh fruit plate containing five seasonal fruits. The remainder of the meal includes French toast, eggs or a breakfast casserole, a breakfast meat, cheese grits, juice, and hot beverages. The menu is varied for guests who stay several nights. High tea is served in the living room in the afternoon, and evening cordials are offered in the den. Nightly turndown service includes a treat on your pillow.

What's Nearby Madison

Madison is known for its lovely antebellum architecture. Take a scenic walking tour around Madison's town square. Pick up walking tour maps and even take in a show at the Madison-Morgan County Cultural Center. Stroll through the Madison National Historic District and see more stunning architecture, including Greek Revival, Neoclassical, and Victorian homes.

Whitlock Inn

57 Whitlock Avenue
Marietta, Georgia 30064
(770) 428-1495

E-MAIL: Alexis@whitlockinn.com

WEB SITE: www.whitlockinn.com

INNKEEPER: Alexis Edwards

ROOMS: 5; all with private bath, cable TV, working fireplace, telephone, desk, ceiling fan, luggage rack; fax and copier available

ON THE GROUNDS: Veranda, gardens, and roof garden

RATES: $100 to $125, including continental-plus breakfast and afternoon refreshments

CREDIT CARDS ACCEPTED? Yes

OPEN: Year-round

HOW TO GET THERE: From I–75 or US 41, take GA 120 West past the town square. The bed and breakfast is the first house on your left in the second block after you pass the square.

As the Edwardses explain, "Here in Marietta we hold on to anything that's old: our houses, our furniture, our recipes, and our accents." The Whitlock Inn, a white Neoclassical mansion built just at the turn of the century, is a perfect case in point. The molded swags and panels on the exterior resemble a delicately iced wedding cake.

Once upon a time in the last century the M. G. Whitlock House, a famous 150-room resort, stood on this spot. The popular showplace drew visitors from hot, humid coastal Georgia to the cooler foothills of the northern Georgia mountains. Unfortunately, the magnificent pleasure palace burned to the ground. In 1900 a portion of the land from the old hotel was purchased by Herbert and Annie Dobbs, who built this stately home for their family of eight. From before 1920 to 1977, the Dosser family lived there. Mrs. Dosser was remembered for giving piano lessons and for elaborately decorated Christmas parties. After that the city of Marietta bought the venerable old building and used it for a while as a senior citizen center, but then put it up for sale.

The Edwards family, who live nearby, had watched with concern as the wonderful home deteriorated; they finally decided to purchase and restore it for use as a bed and breakfast to be operated by their daughter Alexis. Opened in 1994, the Whitlock Inn is once again in the hospitality business, welcoming tourists, business travelers, weddings, parties, and corporate functions.

The newly restored interior showcases high ceilings, hardwood floors, elaborate moldings, and ornate mantels. To this backdrop the Edwardses added exquisite antiques and reproductions, Oriental carpets, brass chandeliers, and dramatic window and bed treatments. A floral theme recurs frequently in the wallpapers and fabrics.

Each of the striking bedchambers has a distinctive personality, although each boasts all the modern comforts and conveniences. We particularly admired the crocheted canopy on the full-tester bed in the predominantly red and green Magnolia Room, but the four-poster in the Bridal Room runs a close second. We also liked the white carved twin beds in the Pink Room, which can be converted into a king-size bed, and the sleigh bed in the Marietta Room. Televisions are discreetly disguised in beautiful armoires.

Picture a candlelight breakfast of juice, fruit, quiche, muffins, breads, and hot beverages beneath a crystal chandelier in the formal dining room. After a day of sight-seeing or shopping, relax with a cool beverage on the wraparound veranda or on the roof garden enjoying an afternoon snack. Drift up to the prettiest town square in Georgia for a quiet dinner and an evening of theater, then back to the Whitlock Inn for a perfect night's sleep.

The Old Garden Inn

1 Temple Avenue
Newnan, Georgia 30263
(770) 304–0594

E-MAIL: oldgarden@webtv.net

WEB SITE: www.communitynow.com/old garden

INNKEEPERS: Patty and Ron Gironda

ROOMS: 4; all with private bath, TV, clock radio

ON THE GROUNDS: Verandas with Adirondack furniture, flower and herb gardens

RATES: $79 to $119, including breakfast, beverages, and refreshments; holidays require two-night minimum stay

CREDIT CARDS ACCEPTED? Yes

OPEN: Year-round

HOW TO GET THERE: From I–85, take exit 9, GA 34, toward Newnan. As you near town, it becomes Bullsboro Drive. Turn right onto Clark Street, left onto Jackson Street, then right onto Temple Avenue. The inn is at the corner of Temple and Dent Street and is identified by a sign. Parking is in the rear.

Yes, this bed and breakfast is located in a beautifully decorated, stately, white-columned home, but when we visited we realized right off that the physical surroundings weren't the focus here. Pampering, respite and renewal, new friendships, and fantastic food are the specialties.

Located in a neighborhood of tidy Victorian cottages, this turn-of-the-century, two-story, redbrick Greek Revival is a standout among its neighbors. Although the exterior—with its hip roof, seven soaring columns, and broad veranda—is in the stereotypical Southern style, the interior is full of surprises. Rather than the dark, heavy, ornate woodwork, window treatments, and furnishings so typical of the era, both the appearance and ambience are of a romantic English cottage. The decor is enhanced by pastel floral chintzes, overstuffed sofas, and gently swirling fans.

Instead of a large foyer flanked by twin parlors, typical of Greek Revival houses, you enter a grand hall made light and airy by the sun filtering through the 132 beveled windowpanes on three sides of the room. This arrangement came about in the 1960s when dancer and local resident Bettina Carroll established a dance school in her new home. She removed the walls between the foyer and parlors to create one big studio around which she placed the mirrors and barres that her pupils needed. Now that the dance-school equipment is gone, this beautiful room, with paneled walls and coffered ceilings, features separate seating and dining areas. In cold weather guests like to gather around the corner fireplace.

There's an informal sitting room in the upstairs hall and a sunroom/television room on an enclosed balcony. One of the most popular gathering places is the massive veranda, comfortably furnished in Adirondack furniture with deep cushions.

Your hosts at the Old Garden Inn welcome guests with a hospitality normally reserved for family and very good friends. In fact, Patty, who loves to garden and cook, says she wants you to feel as if "you have a friend who has a getaway house." The emphasis is on food and spontaneous conversation and entertainment. We were greeted by our choice of Black Sangria or Iced Raspberry Herb Tea. Both were delicious and refreshing. Other ways the Girondas pamper their guests include a wide selection of books, videos, and musical selections; a stocked refrigerator with a choice of wines and soft drinks; and hazelnut cappuccino, available at the push of a button.

Guest rooms are cozy and feature king- or queen-size beds, along with private baths with showers or claw-foot tubs, English toiletries, robes, and wall-mounted hair dryers. Beds boast egg-carton mattress pads, pillow-top mattresses, and high-quality 250- to 300-count linens. Depending on the season, beds are covered with down comforters or summer quilts. Each room has a fireplace.

An unassuming cottage built in the 1940s provides very private accommodations often requested by honeymooners and other romantics celebrating an anniversary or special event. The cottage contains a sitting room with a television, and a bathroom with a claw-foot tub.

Mornings are an important part of any visit. Begin with great coffee and orange juice with fruited ice cubes, then sample a crystal champagne glass filled with strawberries, bananas, and red grapes topped with Black Currant Creme Sauce. More taste-tempting surprises might include banana dumplings with banana yogurt and raspberry sauce or a Georgia peach breakfast taco. Hearty hot dishes such as tomato, mushroom, and goat cheese frittata with home fries and bacon are sure to bring a smile. Patty got her love for good food naturally from her Louisiana-born mother and her world travels.

What's Nearby Newnan

Newnan is an interesting historic town, located forty minutes southwest of Atlanta. You can take a driving tour through five historic districts of beautiful old mansions that survived the Civil War. Besides home tours, Newnan is also noted for its unique bookstores, art and design studios, restaurants, malls, and antiques shopping. If you're interested in spending time in the outdoors, Newnan offers golf, horseback riding, tennis, and fishing.

The Hopkins House

1111 Wesley Street
Oxford, Georgia 30267
(770) 784–1010; fax (770) 786–3684

E-MAIL: hopkinshouse@
hotmail.com

WEB SITE: www.bbonline/ga/
hopkins

INNKEEPERS: Nancy and Ralph Brian

ROOMS: 4 rooms and 1 suite, all with private bath, cable TV with HBO, telephone, computer outlet, desk

ON THE GROUNDS: Flagstone-paved front veranda, screened-in sunporch, garden, swimming pool

RATES: $90 to $160, including continental-plus or full breakfast, afternoon refreshments, and nightly turndown service; ask about corporate rates

CREDIT CARDS ACCEPTED? Yes

OPEN: Year-round

HOW TO GET THERE: From I-20, take GA 81 north through Covington to Oxford. At the traffic light at Soule Street, turn left onto Soule. Go 2 blocks to Wesley. The Hopkins House is located on the far left corner and is identified by a sign.

Located in the heart of the historic district of Oxford—birthplace of both Emory University and the Georgia Institute of Technology—the Hopkins House occupies a graceful one-story 1847 Greek Revival cottage poised on a three-acre wooded and landscaped lot. The inn is named for Isaac Stiles Hopkins, who served from 1884 to 1888 as Emory College's ninth president. Hopkins was responsible for the establishment of a technical department at the college after the Civil War. That department eventually evolved into the Georgia School of Technology—today's renowned Georgia Tech, now headquartered in Atlanta. The new school's first classes were held in a building that serves today as the pool house of the Hopkins House, and Hopkins himself became Georgia Tech's first president. Although Emory University has moved to Atlanta as well, Oxford College—a division of the university—remains in Oxford.

Tastefully furnished in a delightful blend of antique and contemporary furniture, the Hopkins House provides guests with the romance of the Old South at the same time that it ensures the comforts of the present. A variety of appealing indoor and outdoor spaces provides the opportunity to visit with others or enjoy your privacy. Nancy's family lives in another house on the property, so the entire inn is available for guests' use—formal and informal parlors with fireplaces, a formal dining room, kitchen, flagstone-paved front veranda, screened-in sunporch, garden, and swimming pool—making it an excellent choice for families, small family reunions, special events, and small corporate meetings.

Cheerfully decorated guest rooms, each with a private bath, generally follow a floral theme: Rose, Green, Violet, and Peach. Because the baths for the Rose and Violet Rooms are reached by way of the hall, plush robes are provided for guests there. The Green and Rose Rooms can be combined by way of French doors into a two-bedroom suite with two baths. A see-through gas-log fireplace separates the spacious sleeping area from the library alcove in the Red Room.

During the week, guests enjoy an extended continental breakfast. On the weekend, however, guests are invited to indulge in the luxury of sleeping late and then lingering over a full Southern breakfast. And it's not just at breakfast that ebullient Nancy aims to pamper her guests: When you arrive, she'll welcome you with coffee, tea, or a cold beverage and a tour of the house. What she advertises as Afternoon Tea and Treats is actually a sumptuous feast consisting of cakes, cookies, muffins, and flavored coffees and teas. In addition, no matter what the time of day, a selection of cakes and cookies is set out for guests' enjoyment.

What could be better on a hot afternoon than a refreshing dip in the pool or relaxing on the screened porch sipping a glass of lemonade and munching on Nancy's renowned chocolate chip cookies from the "bottomless" cookie jar?

What's Nearby Oxford

Oxford is the birthplace of Emory University and Georgia Tech, and home to Oxford College. You can go fishing, play some golf at one of Oxford's PGA golf courses, or browse the antiques shops. You can also taste wine at family-owned Fox Vineyards in nearby Social Circle.

Serenbe

10950 Hutcheson Ferry Road
Palmetto, Georgia 30268
(770) 463-2610;
fax (770) 463-4472

WEB SITE: www.serenbe.com

INNKEEPERS: Maria and Steve Nygren

ROOMS: 3 rooms and 1 cottage; all with private bath; 1 with a whirlpool tub

ON THE GROUNDS: Outdoor recreation area, croquet lawn, farm, swimming pool, hot tub, lake for fishing and canoeing, streams, waterfalls, trails, woods

RATES: $140 to $175, including full breakfast, afternoon refreshments

CREDIT CARDS ACCEPTED? Yes

OPEN: Year-round except between Christmas and New Year's

HOW TO GET THERE: From Atlanta, take I–85 south. Just past Atlanta-Hartsfield International Airport, take exit 16 and follow the signs to Spur 14, which becomes South Fulton Parkway. Go 13 miles. At the third traffic light, turn left onto GA 154. Continue 3.5 miles and turn right onto Carlton Road. In 1.5 miles Carlton dead-ends at Hutcheson Ferry Road. Turn right and go 3.5 miles. The property is located on your left and is identified both by a sign and the black barns. From the south, take exit 11 off I–85 and turn left. Take the first right onto Collingsworth Road, which becomes Fayetteville Road. Drive under the railroad tracks and through the traffic light at GA 29, after which the road becomes Toombs. At the flashing light, turn right onto Hutcheson Ferry. Go about 4.5 miles and follow the directions above.

*S*uch a farm you've never seen! Although operated by two former city folks, televisions's falling-down *Green Acres* it ain't. This cozy haven is a refined retreat for the overworked and underloved—a place for strung-out couples to kick back to a simpler way of life that includes feeding the animals or gathering eggs or doing nothing, all the while staying in the lap of luxury and feasting on gastronomic delights created by one of Atlanta's leading culinary couples.

Serenbe—a serene place to be—is an idyllic 284 acres of verdant pastures, pecan trees, woods, streams, and a lake, all enchantingly unencumbered by modern distractions. Accommodations are found in a converted horse barn and a cottage. One of the many highlights at Serenbe is the Nygrens' vast collection of whimsical folk art, which fills the airy breakfast room as well as the other public rooms, guest rooms, and many outdoor spaces.

Steve and Maria have cleverly converted a 1930 horse barn into public areas and three guest accommodations. A flagstone floor, massive stone fireplace, and exposed plank walls and ceiling characterize the cozy, infor-mal common room. Filled with casual, comfortable furniture, this room is a delightful place for guests to gather. Each guest accommodation is simply furnished with antiques and hand-painted pieces, bathed with natural light, and accented with whimsical pieces of folk art, bright colors, knotty-pine floors, scatter rugs, patchwork quilts, cheerful pillows, and botanical prints. Fresh flowers and potted plants complete the homey ambience. The upper-floor bedroom features a king-size bed. Although the downstairs bedroom has only a double bed, it boasts a Jacuzzi tub and a private porch overlooking the flower garden. Because the third bedroom has three double beds, it is perfect for a family. Completing the horse barn is an enticing out-door breezeway area equipped with a game table, comfortable seating, and a swing big enough to take a nap on—all overlooking the pool and hot tub on one side and formal vegetable and flower gardens on the other side. Additional accommodations are available in an old cottage, which features a sitting room, a kitchen, two and a half bedrooms, a bath, an open porch, and a screened-in porch.

Classic Atlanta Couples: Maria and Steve Nygren

Maria remembers meeting Steve when she was about twelve. Since he was already an adult, he made a much bigger impression on her than she did on him, but because Steve was a friend of Maria's mother, fellow restaurateur Margaret Lupo of Mary Mac's Tea Room, the two continued to be thrown together over the ensuing years. Maria reports with appropriate modesty that Steve began noticing her when she turned eighteen. They started dating and a year later were married—much to the surprise (some say shock) of the Atlanta restaurant community, because Steve had often declared that he planned to remain a confirmed bachelor for the rest of his life. A year after that the first of their daughters arrived, followed by two more over the next few years. After fifteen years of wedded bliss, the rest, as they say, is history.

There is literally little or nothing to do here—that's the charm and allure of the farm. More than one hundred animals live at the farm, and most allow guests to get up close and personal with them. Especially popular with children are the miniature goats and pigs, but there are horses, cattle, chickens, turkeys, geese and ducks, dogs, cats, and more. Guests of all ages can hand-feed the animals or help gather eggs for breakfast. We asked Steve if any of the animals ended up on the dining room table. He said, "Every animal has a name, and you can't eat something you've named."

Outdoor enthusiasts will enjoy the lake, where they can fish with poles (provided) or use one of the canoes. Perhaps you'd prefer to hike along one of the three streams and linger beside the two waterfalls. Sometimes there are hayrides and marshmallow roasts; new this year is a croquet lawn.

What's Nearby Palmetto

Palmetto has been called a "Mayberry" small town. Twenty-five minutes from downtown Atlanta, Palmetto offers a number of activities. There's golfing, antiquing, and hiking. Spend an afternoon at the waterfalls, and treat yourself to dinner at one of Palmetto's downtown restaurants. If your plans are really up in the air, consider taking an airplane sightseeing and leisure tour.

The Plains Bed and Breakfast Inn

100 West Church Street
Plains, Georgia 31780
(912) 824–7252; fax (912) 824–5265

INNKEEPER: Janet Nixon

ROOMS: 4; all with private bath; ask about pets; smoking permitted

ON THE GROUNDS: Verandas

RATES: $70 double, including tax and full breakfast; additional person $20; ask about extended-stay and corporate rates

CREDIT CARDS ACCEPTED? Yes

OPEN: Year-round

HOW TO GET THERE: When you arrive in town by US 280 from Americus, the B&B is on your right across from the police department and is identified by a sign.

Who ever heard of Plains, Georgia, before Jimmy Carter became president of the United States back in 1977? Now who hasn't heard of it? The former president and international statesman and his wife still live in their modest home in Plains, and Mr. Carter teaches Sunday school when he's in town. You might even see the dynamic duo riding their bicycles around town—trailed by their Secret Service contingent. Yet despite all this world attention, Plains remains a small quaint turn-of-the-century railroad and agricultural town filled with historic Victorian homes.

Just one of these attractive homes is now the Plains Bed and Breakfast Inn. Painted a soft rose pink, the 1910 Classical Revival mansion has been carefully restored to preserve the gracious charm of the Old South. Conveniently located in the heart of town, the house overlooks a park and the Carter Welcome Center in the old depot where Carter had his first campaign headquarters. The inn was once a boardinghouse where Miss Lillian—Carter's mother—lived in her single and early married days, until just before Jimmy was born.

You can watch the unhurried world go by and perhaps catch a glimpse of the Carters from the old-fashioned swing or the wicker rockers on the beautiful wraparound front porch of the B&B. Inside the foyer, you can't help but admire the two gorgeously carved staircases and intricate ceilings. Guests are invited to gather in the downstairs parlor, where there is a television. Upstairs, in addition to the guest rooms, are a wicker-filled parlor and a substantial library. The whole aim of the bed and breakfast is to provide a comfortable atmosphere that will make you feel right at home.

Bedrooms—all with private baths—are named Miss Lillian's Room, the Honeymoon Suite, and the Front Room, which has its own upstairs porch. Bedrooms are individually furnished with antiques and feature decorative fireplaces and queen-size beds.

Guests enjoy a full Southern breakfast that includes grits, eggs, sausage or bacon, a selection of breads, and homemade jellies served in the formal dining room.

What's Nearby Plains

See "What's Nearby Americus," page 133.

Claremont House Bed and Breakfast

Best Buy

906 East Second Avenue
Rome, Georgia 30161
(706) 291-0900 or
(800) 254-4797;
fax (706) 232-9865

E-MAIL: clarinrome@aol.com

WEB SITE: www.bbonline.com/ga/claremont

INNKEEPERS: Gwen and George Kastarias

ROOMS: 4 rooms and 1 cottage; all with private bath, cable TV, ceiling fan, desk, telephone

ON THE GROUNDS: Verandas, patio

RATES: $80 to $125, including full breakfast

CREDIT CARDS ACCEPTED? Yes

OPEN: Year-round

HOW TO GET THERE: From I-75, take US 411 West toward Rome, then turn north onto US 27. Exit at Second Avenue and turn left. Turn left again almost immediately onto 10th Street. Although the Claremont House faces Second Avenue and is identified by a sign on that street, the easier of the two driveways is on the 10th Street side. Parking is in the rear, and you can enter the B&B through the back door.

The exuberant Second Empire Victorian style of architecture is our favorite, so you can imagine our pleasure when we beheld this magnificent example of the style sitting majestically on a hill amid oaks and magnolias in one of Rome's historic districts. In 1880 Colonel Hamilton Yancey bought the hillside property on Second Avenue and built a compact two-story Gothic Revival Victorian house at the back of the lot to provide interim housing for his family during the two years it took to construct his grand Second Empire mansion. The small house was not removed when the big house was finished and was used for various purposes over the years; now it provides suite accommodations.

Colonel Yancey spared no expense in building his manor, and it is truly imposing—surely one of the most photogenic houses of its style in Georgia. Inside, it boasts some of the most opulent woodwork we've ever seen. Massive carved cornices tower over jib windows, doorways, archways, and built-in cabinets. The hardwood floors in several rooms have inlaid patterns created from different types of wood. Original ornate brass hinges and some etched-leather wallpaper remain, as do eleven fireplaces. The colonel installed a massive safe, which survives, into the wall in the foyer because he didn't trust banks and because he entertained a great deal of overnight company and wanted a place where guests would feel comfortable leaving their valuables. Still, perhaps the best reflection of his ego is the silver urinal that he had installed in the downstairs powder room. (Just look at it, don't test it—it's no longer functional.) With an ego of this size, you'd think the colonel would have named the house for himself. However, he honored his daughter Clare instead.

Lavish twin parlors filled with Victorian antiques invite guests to gather and relax, as do the wicker-filled front porch and the brick-paved rear patio. Luxurious accommodations are offered in both Yancey houses—spacious guest rooms in the main house and suites in the smaller house. Each room displays its own personality in decor and furnishings, but all feature a private bath and decorative fireplace. Three of the nostalgic period bathrooms boast claw-foot tubs and showers. All in all, the Claremont House provides an irresistible getaway from modern-day stresses and strains.

Rome is blessed with several historic neighborhoods and other attractions of historic significance. It is an excellent base from which to explore the small towns and off-the-beaten-track sights in the northwestern Georgia mountains, or to indulge in myriad outdoor activities.

Ten-Fifty Canton Street

1050 Canton Street
Roswell, Georgia 30075
(770) 998–1050

E-MAIL: canton1050@aol.com

INNKEEPERS: Susie and Andy Kalifeh

ROOMS: 3; all with private bath, clock radio

ON THE GROUNDS: Porch

RATES: $89 to $125 single or double, including continental-plus breakfast and turndown service

CREDIT CARDS ACCEPTED? Yes

OPEN: Year-round

HOW TO GET THERE: From I–285, Atlanta's perimeter highway, take exit 19, GA 400 North. From there, take exit 6, Northridge Road. Go right at the end of the ramp, turn right immediately onto Dunwoody Place, and take it until it dead-ends into Roswell Road; turn right. After you cross a bridge, the road changes names, to South Atlanta Street. When you come to a Y in the road, take the left fork onto Canton Street. The inn is in the first long block on your left and is well marked by a sign and flags.

We drive by the cheerily waving flags on the front of this bed and breakfast located in the historic district of our fair city almost every day and we always see visitors' cars out front, so we know the B&B has been discovered. The small, late-nineteenth-century cottage was originally the home of a millworker in Roswell's textile heyday. Although the exterior lacks interesting architectural details, a large porch well equipped with inviting rockers and an old-fashioned swing stretches across the nicely landscaped, postage-stamp front garden.

Like many such cottages, this one is surprisingly large once you get inside; high ceilings enhance the spaciousness. The Kalifehs have done such a superb job of renovating the house that the Roswell Historical Society presented them with an Award of Excellence when the restoration was complete. The attractive, tree-shaded district has recently had a face-lift of its own, with new sidewalks, brick crosswalks, period-style streetlights, and old-fashioned benches placed at intervals along the street.

Guests are welcome to relax in either the formal sitting room or the wicker-filled informal sunroom. Bedchambers are individually decorated with country charm and furnished with simple antiques, including beds piled high with fluffy comforters and pillows. Decorative fireplaces add to the feeling of elegance and romance.

Although the house sits close to a street busily traveled during the day, traffic eases in the evening, and the bedrooms are in the back of the house away from any street noise. There's plenty of off-street parking both in front of and behind the B&B.

Breakfast, which is served in the formal dining room, is an ample continental-plus meal of fresh fruits and juices, cereal, and muffins. Soft drinks, coffee, and tea, as well as something salty and something sweet can always be found in the butler's pantry just off the kitchen.

What's Nearby Roswell

Because Roswell is one of the few areas around Atlanta that escaped major destruction during the Civil War, there is much to see—and most of the attractions, as well as shops and restaurants, are within easy walking distance of this B&B. Stroll past several antebellum homes on Mimosa Boulevard on your way to tour Bulloch Hall—home of Teddy Roosevelt's mother, Mittie Bulloch. Several days a week you can find demonstrations of open-hearth cooking in the kitchen as well as ladies practicing period crafts such as basket and quilt making. Just below Roswell Mill you can hike along the creek to the dam and waterfall that once powered the mill. They're now part of the Chattahoochee River National Recreation Area, through which you can meander along 11 miles of trails.

Goodbread House

209 Osborne Street
St. Marys, Georgia 31558
(912) 882–7490 or (888) 236–6482

INNKEEPERS: Gaila and Jerry Brandon, owners; Michele Becnel, manager

ROOMS: 5; all with private bath, decorative fireplace, ceiling fan

ON THE GROUNDS: Veranda

RATES: $75 to $85 single or double, including full breakfast and afternoon refreshments

CREDIT CARDS ACCEPTED? Yes

OPEN: Year-round

HOW TO GET THERE: From I-95 or US 17, take GA 40 East. As you enter town, it becomes Osborne Street. The inn is past Orange Hall on your right.

Gaila and Jerry own the venerable Riverview Hotel, a long-standing fixture in St. Marys. They've recently bought the Goodbread House as well, in order to offer both more rooms and slightly different accommodations for guests who like a more intimate, homey atmosphere. But they're not the first to do so. The Sandiford-Goodbread House was built in 1870 by Samuel Burns, then sold to Ralph Sandiford, who in turn sold it to steamboat captain Walton Goodbread. In 1918 Kate Brandon Bagwell and her sisters Sallie, Semora, and Ethel bought the house to handle the overflow from the hotel; later, they also purchased the hotel. During its long life the house has served as a boardinghouse with a restaurant popular with locals, as an apartment house, as a private home, and as a bed and breakfast. Now it's back in the Brandon family: Jerry is the great-nephew of the Brandon sisters, who started the tradition. In addition to operating the hotel, Jerry's also the mayor of St. Marys. Gaila's sister Michele serves as hostess at the Goodbread House.

Located on the main street of St. Marys's small but charming historic district, the Goodbread House sits in a small landscaped yard behind a neat picket fence. It just has the look of a bed and breakfast. In fact, when previous owners moved into the house in 1988, one night a perfect stranger knocked on their door and asked if the house was a B&B. Although they hadn't ever even thought of opening a bed and breakfast, the idea took root, and the Goodbread House has been a B&B ever since.

The exterior of the house is enhanced by full-length porches both upstairs and down. From these porches you can see the town pier on the Intracoastal Waterway and the famous Cumberland Island ferry. The antiques-filled interior is embellished with high ceilings, wide-pine floors, seven fireplaces, and intricate moldings. Each of the spacious guest rooms is individually decorated to showcase its unique personality. A variety of bedding options from twins to kings should fill the needs of any traveler.

Michele serves an elegant full breakfast in the formal dining room using china and silver. At night you can unwind with complimentary beverages.

What's Nearby St. Marys

You'll wish we all lived in a yellow submarine when you visit St. Marys Submarine Museum. You'll see authentic diving equipment, uniforms, and a re-created submarine interior. Plus, learn about submarine life at Kings Bay Submarine Base. It's hardly a sub-stitute for the real thing.

Royal Windsor Bed and Breakfast

4490 Highway 356
Sautee, Georgia 30571
(706) 878–1322; fax is the same

INNKEEPER: Don Dixon

ROOMS: 4; all with private bath, balcony, or deck; can make arrangements for pets

ON THE GROUNDS: Porches and decks, acreage, trails

RATES: $95 to $145, including full breakfast and refreshments

CREDIT CARDS ACCEPTED? No; checks accepted only by prior arrangement

OPEN: Year-round

HOW TO GET THERE: From GA 75 at the northern edge of Helen, take GA 356 East past the entrance to Unicoi State Park. You'll find the Royal Windsor on your right by looking for the full-size suit of armor holding a sign identifying the B&B. Enter the formal gates topped with welcoming pineapples and drive up the curving driveway. Parking is to the side. If you already know which accommodations you'll be sleeping in, the parking spaces are identified by the name of the room.

lthough we'd caught Don Dixon's British accent when we called to make arrangements for a visit, the first thing that alerted us to the fact that we were in for a unique experience here was the full-size suit of armor identifying the driveway we were to turn into. We followed the winding lane through a thick stand of trees and came out into a clearing to see a Union Jack flapping merrily on the flagpole. A dapper white-haired gentleman bustled out and introduced himself as the proprietor. We knew we were in for a little touch of England in the mountains of northern Georgia.

Named for the royal family in Don's native England—he's from Harrow in northwestern London—this is a homey but elegant bed-and-breakfast with impeccable service that you'll want to visit again and again. Although the exterior of the twenty-five-year-old cottage is rustic contemporary in style, inside you'll find the floral patterns and other elegant touches that you'd expect from a stately English country house. Still, what sets this bed and breakfast apart is Don's bubbly personality, sparkling eyes, quick wit, and ever-ready smile. He's a former entertainer and shop owner who has lived in this country for more than twenty years; the B&B is the project of his retirement years. With boundless energy he'll regale you with stories about his life, tinkle the ivories on the piano in the lounge (great room), or dazzle you with card tricks.

The cathedral ceiling of the lounge is proof of the contemporary origins of the house. In this comfortable room you'll find the television, VCR, telephone, and a supply of English magazines, newspapers, and videos, as well as a piano. Many of the furnishings throughout the bed and breakfast are English, because Don's trying to make this retreat as reminiscent of his homeland as he can. A loft towering above one end of the lounge and reached by way of a spiral stairway provides a private place to read or watch television. Its small step-out balcony affords the best views of the mountains.

Each of the four tasteful guest accommodations, named for a member of past or present English royalty—Queen Elizabeth, Prince Charles, King George, and Prince Albert—is decorated in floral prints and features a private bath, a queen-size bed, and a private balcony or deck. Several boast romantic four-poster beds.

One of the highlights of any visit to the Royal Windsor is the opportunity to have English tea and biscuits (cookies). Don will fix a pot of tea from his selection of flavors using his fantastic old-fashioned kitchen stove, instructing you on how to pour in the milk first, then the tea. Soft drinks, bottled water, teas, hot chocolate, snacks, and candy are available to guests at all times in case an attack of the munchies strikes.

Another highlight is Don's candlelit full English breakfast, which consists of juices, scones, clotted cream, strawberry jam and English marmalade, crumpets, scrambled eggs, and smoked bacon with tomato slices. The morning repast is served on English bone china in the formal dining room next to the fireplace, which will have a crackling fire going in cool weather.

Situated on twenty-two acres of unspoiled mountaintop, the B&B is adjacent to Chattahoochee National Forest and Unicoi State Park outside Helen, a knockoff Bavarian town. The heavily wooded property provides stunning mountain views and several trails to explore. Deer, rabbits, and other wildlife often browse in the yard in the evening.

What's Nearby Sautee

Sautee is a popular cultural center. The Sautee-Nacoochee Arts & Community Center is a great spot for entertainment. Enjoy the center's concerts, gallery, and museum. Sautee is also a lively outdoors community. You can go fishing or rafting in the Chattahoochee River and try hiking at Unicoi State Park and the Appalachian Trail. If shopping is in order, browse the antiques and crafts shops. You can also try shopping in alpine Helen, which is right next door to Sautee.

The Azalea Inn

217 East Huntingdon Street
Savannah, Georgia 31401
(912) 236-2707 or (800) 582-3823;
fax (912) 236-0126

E-MAIL: info@azaleainn.com

WEB SITE: www.azaleainn.com

INNKEEPERS: Jessie Balentine and John McAvoy

ROOMS: 8; all with private bath, TV, radio; some with whirlpool tub, some with private porch

ON THE GROUNDS: Veranda, off-street parking, garden with pond

rates: $149 to $189 double, including continental-plus breakfast

CREDIT CARDS ACCEPTED? Yes

OPEN: Year-round

HOW TO GET THERE: Where I–16 ends, it merges with Montgomery Street at the Civic Center. At the traffic light on the near side of the Civic Center, turn east onto West Liberty Street. After you cross Bull Street, the street becomes East Liberty. Turn right (south) onto Habersham. You will go around Troup and Whitfield Squares. Turn right (west) onto East Huntingdon. The inn is on your left.

We always appreciate a good sense of humor, so we were intrigued when we saw the Azalea Inn's advertised claim that you can breakfast with Sherman, Lee, and Juliette. When we checked it out for ourselves, we weren't disappointed: A mural depicting important events in Savannah's history is painted all the way around the walls above the chair rail in the seven-sided dining room. Panels show General James Oglethorpe, who founded Savannah; Sergeant Jasper, a Revolutionary War hero; the heyday of the Cotton Exchange; Civil War generals Grant and Sherman; the founder of the Girl Scouts, Juliette Gordon Lowe; the Old City Market; and the Savannah River in 1885. Although the topics are serious, look closely and you'll find touches of whimsy. The peripheral characters include Ted Kennedy, current sports figures, movie stars, and Savannah notables. The painting serves as a topic of lively conversation among guests around the breakfast table. Needless to say, the atmosphere at this inn is casual and comfortable, not stuffy or pretentious.

Unusual in Savannah, where the norm is attached town houses, the Azalea Inn is located in a Victorian detached house near Forsyth Park. Constructed in 1889, it was the home of the then prominent sea captain and member of the Cotton Exchange Walter Coney. This fascinating gentleman was turned down by the Confederate Army, so he spent the Civil War serving aboard a blockade runner. He was stranded for a while in Cuba, but eventually made his way to Nova Scotia and from there *walked* back to Savannah, where he became a successful businessman after the war.

In keeping with its Victorian architecture and ornate woodwork, the house is embellished with floral wall coverings, jewel tones, rich fabrics, and heavy, opulent furniture throughout, creating the busy, overblown decor so typical of the turn of the century. Each of the uniquely decorated guest rooms has its own personality and features a private bath, king- or queen-size bed, period furnishings, beautiful decorative fireplace, and cable television. Several rooms boast two-person whirlpool tubs. Some also have a private entrance onto the front or rear second-story porches. Since our visit, a two-bedroom suite has been created in the carriage house.

If you're interested in renting an entire historic house, Trompe l'Oeil Manor, which is accented with several trompe l'oeil paintings throughout, is available. *Tromp-l'oeil* (pronounced *trump loy*) is French for "deception or illusion of the eye," and here includes realistic paintings of doorways, windows, fireplaces, bookshelves, books, vases, or other accents where you would expect the real items to be.

What's Nearby Savannah

A good place to begin your exploration of Savannah is the Savannah National Historic District, which will give you a feel of the city's rich history. Then stop at the Savannah Visitor Center to receive free brochures, walking tour maps, and other kinds of information. The Savannah History Museum is connected to the center, and the museum will give you a complete orientation to the city as well as a historic background. Take a guided tour aboard a minibus and enjoy the view. Don't forget to stop at River Street and Bull Street. And if you get a chance, drop by City Market and enjoy artist studios and outdoor dining and entertainment.

Other Recommended B&Bs in Savannah

Catherine Ward House Inn, an 1886 Italianate town house near Forsyth Park, offers 10 rooms with courtyard and veranda; 118 East Waldburg Street, Savannah, GA 31401; (912) 234-8564 or (800) 327-4270. *The Grande Toots Inn*, a mansion built in 1890, features rooms with private baths; 212 West Hall Street, Savannah, GA 31401; (912) 236-2911 or (800) 835-6831. *Gaston Gallery* offers rooms in an elegant nineteenth-century duplex with verandas, galleries, and a courtyard; 211 East Gaston Street, Savannah, GA 31401; (912) 238-3294 or (800) 671-0716. *Joan's on Jones*, another Italianate town house built in 1883, offers rooms with private baths and kitchen or kitchenette; 17 West Jones Street, Savannah, GA 31401; (912) 234-3863.

Broughton Street Bed and Breakfast

511 East Broughton Street
Savannah, Georgia 31401
(912) 232-6633; fax (912) 231-1111

E-MAIL: SAVANB@aol.com
WEB SITE: www.broughtonst.com
INNKEEPERS: Tonya Snow-Saleeby
ROOMS: 7; all with private bath

 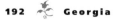

ON THE GROUNDS: courtyard

RATES: $125 to $225, including full breakfast, afternoon refreshments, and evening turndown service; $50 additional person

CREDIT CARDS ACCEPTED? Yes

OPEN: Year-round

HOW TO GET THERE: I-16 ends on Montgomery Street in Savannah. Continue several more blocks on Montgomery, past the traffic lights at West Liberty and West Oglethorpe, and turn east onto West Broughton Street. As you cross Bull Street, it becomes East Broughton. You will drive through the commercial district and emerge once again into a residential neighborhood. The inn is on the right side of the street in the middle of the block, and is identified by a sign. Park on the street. After you check in, Tonya will direct you around back to the inn's off-street parking.

An exquisite miniature version of Savannah's opulent town houses, this inn—which was built in 1883 for Daniel O'Connor, the uncle of Flannery O'Connor—has three intimate, perfectly proportioned public rooms and two flawless guest chambers in the main house, all of which reflect a more gracious way of life. Since we last visited, four more guest chambers have been created in the annex, an adjacent town house, and a nearby town house. Impeccably restored, the inn showcases gleaming hardwood floors, intricate moldings, some exposed brick walls, and decorative mantelpieces. To these original features the young owners Tonya Snow-Saleeby and her husband, physician J. P. Saleeby, have added stained-glass transoms, elegant antiques, other period furnishings, and some contemporary pieces, as well as rich fabrics and numerous collectibles. If you fall in love with a particular piece, ask about it. Many of the antiques are for sale.

Guests can gather in the finely appointed formal parlor or gravitate to the cozy, comfortable library, which is enhanced by green-plaid wall coverings and warm moldings, a gas-log fireplace, a leather sofa and chairs, an entertainment center with a television, VCR, and CD player, as well as many books about Savannah. Be sure to examine the fascinating collection of masks hung over the fireplace, along with the family trees and other personal memorabilia. Although the library is an interior room with no windows, it's brightened by a large skylight.

Sumptuous guest rooms feature private baths supplied with thick towels and fluffy robes. The luxurious Daniel O'Connor Room is a pleasurable retreat for the romantic or hedonistic. A king-size, four-poster, heavily carved rice bed dominates the room and faces a gas-log fireplace. The large, thoroughly modern bathroom—some might call it the playroom—reveals marble floors as well as a marble wall behind the magnificent two-person Jacuzzi with its gold-toned fixtures and built-in circular shower. In addition to all these luxuries, guests in the Daniel O'Connor Room can request that breakfast be served in their room. The John E. Tanner Room, which overlooks the courtyard, features a queen-size sleigh bed and a stall shower in its private bath.

Located in the annex, the Palmer and Andrew Rooms are decorated with antiques and fine art. In the Andrew Room be sure to notice the nineteenth-century Chinese armoire and the 1640 oak Bible desk, which was used by Virginia's Royal Governor Alexander Spotswood. These two rooms have private toilet facilities but share a shower/tub, so they are best rented by families or friends traveling together. Located in the town house next door, the C. H. Medlock and Eugene Switzer Rooms share a parlor and dining room. The Medlock Room boasts a king-size four-poster bed and a working fireplace, while the Switzer Room's special feature is a private balcony overlooking the courtyard. A fully equipped apartment, the Dr. Alfred Simmons Suite is located two doors away from the main inn. Created with longer-term stays in mind, the suite—which can sleep three adults or two adults and two small children—comes with use of all facilities and amenities at the main inn, as well as a living room with a television, VCR, fireplace, fully equipped kitchen, dining area, and laundry facilities.

Get to know your fellow guests during the full gourmet breakfast served each morning in the formal dining room. Afternoon refreshments are served, offering an excellent opportunity to examine the works of local and out-of-town artists—which are featured in the downstairs rooms and rotated every two months—as well as J. P.'s collection of antique medical equipment. Beds are turned down at night and a cordial and a sweet such as baklava are left in your room. Tonya and J. P. are happy to make recommendations for sight-seeing and meals. Although the owners don't live on the property, they have a helper who stays overnight to assist if you need anything.

What's Nearby Savannah

See page 192 for what's nearby Savannah.

The Manor House

201 West Liberty Street
Savannah, Georgia 31401
(912) 233–9597 or (800) 462–3595;
fax (912) 236–9419

INNKEEPERS: Richard F. Carlson and
Timothy C. Hargus

ROOMS: 5 suites; all with private bath,
sitting room, gas-log fireplace; some
with whirlpool tub, kitchenette, laundry
facilities; ask about pets; provisions are
made for the disabled; smoking allowed

ON THE GROUNDS: Verandas

RATES: $185 to $225 weekends, holidays, and March through May (lower
out of season), double, including continental breakfast

CREDIT CARDS ACCEPTED? Yes

OPEN: Year-round

HOW TO GET THERE: Where I–16 ends, it merges into Montgomery Street at
the Civic Center. At the first traffic light, which is at the near corner of
the Civic Center, turn right (east) onto West Liberty Street. The inn is on
your right in the next block, and is identified by a sign. Private off-street
parking is provided in the rear. You can enter the inn from the front or
rear on the second level to register.

If we wanted to retreat from the real world for a luxurious and romantic
tryst, this would be our idea of leisured elegance. We'd indulge ourselves
at the Manor House, the smaller and more intimate sister to the esteemed
Ballastone Inn (see our *Recommended Country Inns: The South*). This all-suite
bed and breakfast, also located in Savannah's historic district, is a perfect
setting for a fantasy getaway.

Although the majority of the elegant homes in Savannah's historic district are town houses, the Manor House occupies a large single-family
dwelling that was built for the Lester Byrd family in the 1830s. It is considered the oldest building south of Liberty Street. As the Civil War wound
down, General Sherman captured Savannah—just in time to present it to
Lincoln as a Christmas gift in December 1864. Fortunately, though, he
spared both the city and this house from the torch; in fact, Union officers
commandeered the Manor House for use as their headquarters.

The architectural integrity of the structure has been carefully preserved.
Public rooms and guest suites retain many original features such as high

ceilings, ornamental fireplaces, elaborate moldings, pocket doors, and heart-pine floors. Sophisticated double parlors, where guests often gather to enjoy the honor bar, boast cozy gas-log fireplaces, American and European antiques, dramatic window treatments, and highly polished floors covered with vivid Oriental carpets.

Guest suites, similarly decorated, are appointed with the comforts of a luxury hotel. Each consists of a master bedroom with a private bath separated by pocket doors from a comfortable sitting room. Either the sitting room or the bedroom features a gas-log fireplace. With one exception, the beds are queen- or king-size. In addition, each suite has an interior entrance as well as a private entrance from a porch or patio. The Twelve Oaks, Eastern Influence, and Robert E. Lee Suites each boast a sophisticated two-person whirlpool tub on a raised dias, and a separate stall shower enclosed in glass brick. The Tara and Magnolia Suites contain kitchens and washer/dryers, which make them ideal for travelers on an extended stay in Savannah. The Twelve Oaks and Robert E. Lee Suites also have queen-size sofa beds, which makes them desirable for two couples or a family.

A few of the extra-special luxury touches include fresh flowers, specially milled soaps and fragrant bath salts, high-quality bed linens, extra down pillows for comfortable reading in bed, and nightly turndown service with chocolates and brandy. The staff will be glad to work with you to arrange long-stemmed roses, champagne, or any other amenities that make a special occasion more memorable (at an added fee, of course).

Conveniently located across the street from the Civic Center, the Manor House is within easy walking distance of Bull Street, the riverfront, and many restaurants and nightspots.

What's Nearby Savannah

See page 192 for what's nearby Savannah.

Georgia's Bed and Breakfast Best Buy

122 South Zetterower Avenue
Statesboro, Georgia 30458
(912) 489-6330

INNKEEPER: Helen Cannon

ROOMS: 4; all with private bath, TV, telephone, clock radio, ceiling fan; ask about pets

ON THE GROUNDS: Small backyard

RATES: $45 to $75, including full breakfast

CREDIT CARDS ACCEPTED? Yes

OPEN: Year-round

HOW TO GET THERE: Take GA 15 South to Wrightsville, then US 80 East to Statesboro. Once you've gotten into town, look for a Dairy Queen on the corner, then turn right at the next light onto Zetterower Avenue. As you proceed on Zetterower, you will go through a four-way stop; the second light beyond this is at Grady Street. The B&B is on the near right corner at Zetterower and Grady. If you arrive via US 301 North, turn south onto Zetterower Avenue and go to the intersection with Grady. Parking is behind the house off Grady. You can enter the inn through the back door.

A beautiful home, comfortable accommodations, a gourmet breakfast, a cordial innkeeper, and extremely reasonable prices—for any Georgia Southern University parent, these factors create an ideal place to stay when visiting a child at the university. Business and leisure travelers will enjoy this bed and breakfast as well.

Although we didn't guess it from the redbrick federal-style exterior, this house was actually built as a frame Victorian-style home around 1890. It was in 1948 that the wraparound porches were removed and the brick facade added, which completely changed the look of the house.

One of the early owners was Jack Averitt, who was the owner of a local sawmill. He created beautiful hardwood floors that are different in each of the downstairs rooms—one is cherry, another oak, the third pine, and the foyer is patterned with each of the three woods. Mr. Averitt also salvaged a black Italian marble fireplace surround from the First Federal Bank Building and used it in one of the parlors. Another unique architectural feature is the paneling he placed in the dining room. When Mr. Averitt's son was studying architecture at Georgia Tech in Atlanta, the son wrote to his father about using paneling in conjunction with a chair rail. However, he didn't make it clear that the paneling was to be *below* the chair rail. As a surprise, Mr. Averitt had the paneling installed—above the chair rail. His son never had the heart to tell him that his father had installed it upside down. Helen has added her own unique touch to the decor—splashy representations of dogwoods, hydrangeas, roses, and magnolias painted above the four doorways in the foyer.

Guests have many pleasant places in which to gather or retreat on their own. Two sunny, airy formal parlors are painted a cheery yellow and feature coffered ceilings, huge bay windows, fireplaces, and elegant traditional furnishings. In contrast, the enclosed sunporch is a cozy, casual room featuring warm paneling, tile floors, and exposed brick. A Florida room, which serves as an informal den, television room, and breakfast room, features a parquet floor, wicker, soft colors, and comfortable overstuffed sofas. Family collectibles throughout the house create a homey atmosphere.

Appealing guest rooms, which are named for the states that border Georgia, express their own personalities through eclectic mixtures of antique and contemporary furnishings. Two offer private baths, and two share a bath.

What's Nearby Statesboro

Georgia Southern University is located in Statesboro. The University Museum is a fun stop to make, especially if you're interested in dinosaur fossils. The Center for Wildlife Education and the Lamar Q. Ball Jr. Raptor Center have popular nature trails complete with bald eagles, falcons, and owls. Or you might visit the Botanical Gardens, which is very close to the campus.

The Village Inn Bed and Breakfast

992 Ridge Avenue
Stone Mountain, Georgia 30083
(770) 469–3459 or (800) 214–8385

E-MAIL: villageinn@mindspring.com

WEB SITE: www. villageinnbb.com

INNKEEPERS: Christy and Earl Collins

ROOMS: 5 rooms and 1 suite; all with private bath, telephone with voice mail, coffeemaker, TV, VCR, ceiling fan; 5 rooms with two-person whirlpool tub; 1 room is wheelchair accessible

ON THE GROUNDS: Verandas, gardens, gazebo

RATES: $115 to $160 double, including full breakfast and refreshments; additional person $20

CREDIT CARDS ACCEPTED? Yes

OPEN: Year-round

HOW TO GET THERE: From I–285, take exit 30B to US 78 East. Exit at Stone Mountain Village/Memorial Drive and stay in the right lane. Exit again at East Ponce de Leon Avenue. At the stop sign, turn left onto Ponce de Leon Avenue. As you enter town, it becomes Main Street. At the second traffic light, turn right onto West Mountain Street. Go 1 block and turn left onto Ridge Avenue. The bed and breakfast is the first building on the right corner and is identified by a sign.

Christy and Earl hit the nail on the head when they said, "Treats shared with new friends are always the sweetest." They may have been referring to sitting down and enjoying an icy-cold lemonade or a steaming cup of coffee or tea and a snack with their guests, but we think this truism applies to your entire stay at the Village Inn. Your hosts go out of their way to provide each guest with personal attention and that's what counts. Still, the bed and breakfast and its accommodations are outstanding as well. And it attracts congenial guests who may go home as friends.

Built in 1850 as a hotel, the venerable building has now returned to its original function after many years. During the Civil War it was commandeered for use as a Confederate hospital. After the war it became the private residence of the Reverend Jacob Stillwell, pastor of the First Baptist Church, because the structure was the only building in town large enough to house his family of eleven. It remained in the Stillwell family for more than one hundred years and is still referred to around town as the Stillwell House. The structure was restored in 1995 and opened as a bed and breakfast.

Of simple clapboard construction on the exterior with full-length verandas both upstairs and down, the house features heart-pine walls and floors. A simple parlor is dominated by a fireplace and furnished in Victorian style. This comfortable gathering place offers a television, VCR, books, and magazines. In nice weather you might prefer to unwind on the front or back verandas, in the garden, or in the gazebo.

Guest rooms, which exude Southern charm, are warmly decorated in period antiques. These elegant bedchambers feature queen-size beds—many of them romantic four-posters—and private baths. Most of these love nests boast two-person whirlpool tubs and gas-log fireplaces. Two of the rooms are named for Scarlett and Rhett. Of particular interest in Scarlett's Room, aside from her portrait above the fireplace, are the armoire, which was collapsible to travel by wagon, and the fainting couch, which was necessary for young ladies laced so tight it took their breath away. Rhett's retreat, done in rich, deep colors, is more gentlemanly. The two-room suite, converted from the former third-floor ballroom—also used as a nursery and schoolroom—has a bedroom and a separate sitting room with a daybed and a trundle bed, as well as a refrigerator and microwave, plus televisions and VCRs in both rooms. The Angel, Blue, and Yellow Rooms each have their own special attractions.

Mornings begin with the aromas of breakfast drawing you inexorably out of bed, no matter how much you may want to snuggle under your quilt or down comforter. This scrumptious Southern meal might revolve around raspberry-cheesecake-stuffed French toast complemented by bacon, cheese grits, spiced peaches, juice, and hot beverages. If an attack of the munchies strikes during the day or evening, a goodie basket is always available in the kitchen with an assortment of coffees, teas, and hot chocolate mixes. A brimming cookie jar can be found on the counter, and a supply of soft drinks and lemonade is in the refrigerator.

What's Nearby Stone Mountain

Don't miss Stone Mountain Park, which attracts six million visitors each year. Then visit Stone Mountain Village, a restored nineteenth-century Main Street. The village shops sell lots of interesting vintage books, arts and crafts, and antiques. You'll enjoy the old-fashioned shopping and quaint village ambience.

Another Recommended B&B in Stone Mountain

Silver Hill Manor, a newly constructed traditional Southern white-columned inn, offers rooms with private baths, some with whirlpool tub; 1037 Main Street, Stone Mountain, GA 30083; (770) 879-6800.

Coleman House

323 North Main Street
Swainsboro, Georgia 30401
(912) 237-9100; fax (912) 237-8586

INNKEEPERS: Connie and David Thurman

ROOMS: 10; all with private bath, cable TV, ceiling fan, telephone; ask about pets

ON THE GROUNDS: Verandas and porches

RATES: $55 single, including full breakfast and refreshments; each additional person $10

CREDIT CARDS ACCEPTED? Yes

OPEN: Year-round

HOW TO GET THERE: Take I–16 to exit 21. Turn north onto US 1 and go approximately 14 miles to Swainsboro. Go straight through to where US 1 and US 80 cross. Stay on US 1 for 2½ blocks. The inn is on your right.

"We're going to like this one," we said to each other as we pulled up in front of the magnificent Queen Anne Victorian mansion, which sits well back from the street on an immense three-acre lot. And we weren't a bit disappointed.

Anyone who has ever seen the "painted ladies" in San Francisco in person or in photographs will appreciate both the architecture and the paint job of the Coleman House. Built between 1901 and 1904, it is one of the best examples of the Queen Anne style in the state. Painted in the traditional manner associated with the style, this majestic three-story residence uses cream as its predominant color, with subdued rust, blue, and brown trim accentuating the moldings, eaves, columns, and porch railings.

Previous owners did such a magnificent job of restoring the thirty-two-room house—listed on the National Register of Historic Places—that they received an award from the Georgia Trust for Historic Preservation.

Inside we found the anticipated 12-foot ceilings and intricate moldings, as well as eleven fireplaces. One of the architectural elements that make this house so special, however, is its burl-pine floors. In fact, this is one of only three surviving houses in Georgia with such floors. We also noted with appreciation the traditional Bradbury & Bradbury wallpaper.

But let's put first things first. What caught our immediate attention when we stepped inside was the central hall, which is 55 feet long. As you can imagine, this magnificent space is often the scene of weddings and other special functions. Just to give you an idea of the immensity of the mansion, it covers 10,000 square feet.

All of the ten bedrooms feature private baths with a claw-foot tub, decorative fireplace, and period antiques and accessories. Because the beds are antiques, most of them are double size, but several rooms have queens or twins. There is an eleventh sleeping room without its own bathroom that can be rented in conjunction with the adjoining room, in essence making it a two-bedroom suite. This arrangement is ideal for a family or friends traveling together. An immense wraparound porch with polygonal gazebolike turrets complete with conical roofs and finials, as well as several upstairs porches, offer guests places to socialize or enjoy some solitude. The grounds themselves invite you for a leisurely stroll.

Since we last visited, most of the downstairs rooms and part of the veranda have been incorporated into a restaurant, which serves lunch Monday through Friday and a popular brunch on Sunday. You can enjoy your full breakfast, which might include bacon and eggs, waffles, or pancakes, in the breakfast room or out on the veranda. Dinner can be prepared for overnight guests on request at an additional fee.

What's Nearby Swainsboro

Swainsboro, home of East Georgia College, is located between Macon and Savannah. Macon is a notable musical city. Some Macon hometown acts include Little Richard, Otis Redding, and the Allman Brothers. Macon's rich musical heritage inspired the 1996 opening of the Georgia Musical Hall of Fame. The three-story, 42,000-square-foot museum features exhibits on country, gospel, symphony, blues, big band, and Southern rock. For more culture, head into Savannah. (See page 192.)

1884 Paxton House Inn

445 Remington Avenue
Thomasville, Georgia 31792
(912) 226-5197

E-MAIL: 1884@rose.net

WEB SITE: www.1884paxtonhouseinn.com

INNKEEPER: Susie Sherrod

ROOMS: 9 rooms and suites; all with private bath, cable TV, private telephone with data port, ceiling fan, iron and ironing board, clock radio, hair dryer, robes, full-length mirror

ON THE GROUNDS: Verandas, indoor swimming pool and hot tub

rates: $99 to $250 double, including full breakfast and refreshments; ask about honeymoon and anniversary packages and corporate rates

CREDIT CARDS ACCEPTED? Yes

OPEN: Year-round

HOW TO GET THERE: From US 319, which becomes Jackson Street, turn right onto Hansell Street. The mansion is located on the corner of Remington and Hansell and is clearly identified with a sign.

"Our aim is to pamper," says Susie Sherrod, owner of this gorgeous bed and breakfast housed in an exquisitely restored and furnished—almost museumlike—Gothic Victorian mansion built in 1884. Her philosophy is to provide European-style service combined with Southern hospitality, and in this she succeeds admirably.

When Thomasville was a fashionable winter retreat for wealthy Northerners, Colonel Paxton built one of the first seasonal "cottages." To the original mansion, a massive neoclassical wraparound porch was added in 1905. Today this porch invites guests to relax in the numerous rockers and swings.

This lovely home is graced with twelve fireplaces, a circular staircase, 12-to 13-foot ceilings, heart-pine floors, original light fixtures, beveled glass, plaster moldings, and unique transom windows. After restoring the house, Susie added custom decorating, antiques, high-quality reproductions, homemade quilts, and the prominent displays of her collectibles from around the world. For her efforts she's been rewarded with several local and state preservation awards.

Each guest suite is individually decorated using designer fabrics and features a ornamental fireplace and private bath. Luxuries include Egyptian bath towels and goose-down pillows. In the main house the first-floor Grand Suite is filled with vintage details to create a sense of nostalgia. This room boasts a queen-size rice bed, his and her bathrooms, a sitting room, and fabrics from the Henry Ford Museum collection. Comprised of two bedrooms, the Blue Suite spotlights the allure of oak furniture. The centerpiece of the Eighteenth-Century Suite is a queen-size canopy bed. The spacious Peach Suite boasts one bedroom with a king-size canopy bed and another with a queen-size canopy bed, along with a sitting room and a bath that has a claw-foot tub.

Additional accommodations are located in a Victorian cottage that has been moved to the property, and in the pool house. Naturally enough, most of these rooms are named for flowers: English Rose, Magnolia, and Rose of Sharon. All showcase four-poster beds. A fourth bedroom in the garden cottage is the Quilt Room, where, as you'd expect, a quilt covers the Jenny Lind bed. A king-size plantation bed, Victorian furnishings, a whirlpool tub, and direct access to the pool and hot tub make the Pool House Suite a surefire hit.

Early risers might want to savor a beverage while they watch the sunrise and listen to the birds from the gazebo or veranda. Susie serves an elegant gourmet breakfast in the garden room using one of her several sets of fine china, crystal, and silver. Breakfast might consist of stuffed orange French toast, Belgian waffles, eggs Benedict, egg and cheese strata, or crepes accompanied by homemade breads, apricot jam, fresh fruits, and juices.

Fresh flowers from Susie's garden fill the house. Guests are treated to bedside chocolates, turndown service, and refreshments in the butler's pantry. Honeymooners can expect extra pampering.

Although the house is filled with several gracious common areas where guests can get to know each other or retreat in solitude with a good book, some of the most sought-out areas are outside. There's the wraparound veranda, of course, but also the gardens, where you can swing under the trees, linger under the arbor, or tarry in the gazebo. But this bed and breakfast is just full of surprises, so there's more—a lap pool. Indeed, there's so much to keep you content here that it will be hard to tear yourselves away to explore enchanting Thomasville and the surrounding area.

What's Nearby Thomasville

Take time to smell the roses at Thomasville's annual Rose Festival in April. Enjoy the weeklong parades, pageants, and rose contests. The Thomasville Rose Garden is not to be missed. Among Thomasville's lavish mansions, the Pebble Hill Plantation is a recommended destination. Tour the twenty-eight room Georgian and Greek Revival house. Inside, you'll enjoy the collection of original John James Audubon bird prints decorating the walls.

Serendipity Cottage Best Buy

339 East Jefferson Street
Thomasville, Georgia 31792
(912) 226-8111 or (800) 383-7377;
fax (912) 226-2656

E-MAIL: GOODNITE@rose.net

WEB SITE: www.bbhost.com/serendipity

INNKEEPERS: Kathy and Ed Middleton

ROOMS: 4; all with private bath, TV or VCR, robes, ceiling fan, clock radio, telephone

ON THE GROUNDS: Veranda

RATES: $85 to $110 double, including full or continental breakfast, refreshments, and turndown service; ask about golf package, corporate rates; two-night minimum stay on some weekends

CREDIT CARDS ACCEPTED? Yes

OPEN: Year-round

HOW TO GET THERE: From the north, take I-75 to Tifton, then US 319 South into Thomasville. It becomes East Jackson Street as you enter town. Take it to the traffic light at Hansell Street and turn right. Proceed 1 block to Jefferson Street and turn left. Serendipity Cottage is 1 block away on your right, at the corner of Jefferson and Love. If you are coming from the south, take US 319 into town, where it becomes West Jackson Street. Proceed to the traffic light at Madison Street and turn left. Go 1 block to the traffic light at Jefferson Street and turn right. Serendipity Cottage is 4 blocks ahead on your left.

Kathy and Ed enjoyed running a bed and breakfast in Virginia, so when they decided to move south, it was only natural that they would search for a house in which they could continue to offer B&B accommodations. They found what they were looking for in the Mack House, a traditional four-square house (four rooms over four rooms) built by Elmer Mack in 1906. So pleased were the Middletons with their serendipitous discovery that they named their B&B Serendipity Cottage.

Mack was a wealthy lumberman from the North who relocated to Thomasville. Not only did he purchase the first automobile in Thomasville, but he also owned a prizewinning bull that he transported all over the country in a private railroad car. Mack handpicked all the lumber for the house, and many of the original architectural details he created remain. Ornate paneling, above which is a plate rail that Mack created to display the trophies his bull won, graces the dining room.

Hardwood floors gleam throughout, and original leaded-glass windows allow light to flood into the downstairs rooms. Large oak decorative columns separate the reception hall from the formal parlor, and beautiful oak pocket doors separate several other rooms.

To these features, the Middletons have added their own personal touches—antiques and reproductions, tasteful window treatments, and beautiful fabrics. Both Middletons enjoy counted cross-stitch, and you'll find many examples of their work throughout the house.

Serendipity Cottage has so many enticing public spaces that you'll have a hard time deciding whether to unwind in solitude or to mix with your genial hosts and fellow guests. In addition to the formal and informal parlors, there's a delightful enclosed sunroom, which features deeply cushioned rattan seating and binoculars for bird-watching. In nice weather you'll want to take advantage of the rocker-filled front veranda.

Guest accommodations are found in four individually decorated rooms. For a touch of yesterday, the Victorian Rose Room is a romantic choice with its queen-size bed, rose wallpaper, framed LOVE needlework over the fireplace, and cherubs in the bathroom. A crocheted bedspread and pillow covers enhance the carved four-poster, queen-size canopy bed in Kate's Room. You do have to step out into the hall to reach this room's private bath. The most casual is the Country Garden Room, with a queen-size brass bed, antique trunks, teddy bears, and pine furniture. Sara's Room is furnished entirely with Victorian-era antiques.

The Middletons outdo themselves in providing luxuries for their guests. A basketful of every bath amenity imaginable is found in each bathroom. Hair dryers, clock radios, telephones, and sherry in the rooms are standard as well. A small stocked hall refrigerator provides soft drinks. Nightly turn-down service includes a chocolate treat as well as a surprise for the ladies on their first night. Coffee or other hot beverages are delivered to your room in the morning, and then breakfast is served in the dining room or on the sun-porch.

What's Nearby Thomasville

See page 204 for what's nearby Thomasville.

Twin Oaks Cottages Bed and Breakfast

9565 East Liberty Road
Villa Rica, Georgia 30180
(770) 459–4374 or (770) 459–5156

E-MAIL: ecturner@bellsouth.net

WEB SITE: www.bbonline.com/ga/twinoaks

INNKEEPERS: Carol and Earl Turner

ROOMS: 3 cottages and 1 two-bedroom suite; all with private bath, queen-size bed, TV, VCR, radio, CD player, microwave, coffeemaker, sink, refrigerator, and toaster; all but 1 with fireplace or woodstove; decks and patios; some with access for wheelchairs

ON THE GROUNDS: Swimming pool, twenty-three acres, gardens, trails, animals

RATES: $100 to $155, including full or continental breakfast; weekly rate on efficiency; corporate rates

CREDIT CARDS ACCEPTED? No

OPEN: Year-round

HOW TO GET THERE: From I–20, take exit 6 to Villa Rica. Turn left. At the first paved road, turn left onto East Liberty. There is a small sign that says twin oaks at the intersection. The B&B is the second driveway on your right and is identified by a sign. Proceed to the parking area, then walk across the footbridge to register.

We've been captivated by the swanky cottages and suites at Twin Oaks, the lush and peaceful rural surroundings, and the congenial owners ever since we visited to see its first cottage—probably close to ten years ago—and whenever we've gone back to see the new additions. Carol keeps inviting us to stay, but we've never had time. More's the pity, because this upscale farm is just the type of R&R getaway we so desperately need.

Those who want a serene, private atmosphere can find just what they're dreaming of at Twin Oaks. Three exquisite guest houses and a two-bedroom suite connected to the main house sit on a twenty-three-acre farm five minutes off I-20 west of Atlanta. The Turners built two of the elegant cottages well away from their house to ensure privacy, making them ideal for a honeymoon, anniversary, or other special occasion.

The cottages—each is actually one large, airy room plus a bath—aren't country cute, as you might expect, but sleek and sophisticated. Although two of them are named for those famous Southern characters Scarlett and Rhett, you won't find them filled with kitschy memorabilia. In Scarlett's Cottage, which is contemporary in style and boasts Palladian windows across the front, the sense of size is accentuated by the sun streaming through the large windows and the reflections bouncing off an entire wall of floor-to-ceiling mirrors. This one features 12-foot ceilings, ceiling fans, a carpeted bedroom area with a queen-size bed, a kitchen and dining area, and a sitting room area with a woodstove and a sofabed to accommodate other guests. An attached sunroom furnished with rattan invites guests to enjoy the view. Outside on a covered deck is a private hot tub in which to soak away your cares and woes.

Rhett's Cottage belies the elegance within. Sitting behind a white picket fence, its exterior is traditional country with a full-length front porch amply furnished with bent-willow furniture and interesting country antiques. Inside, the decor is more what we'd expect in a posh city penthouse. The sexy black marble bathroom is the star here, with its two-person whirlpool tub.

Next, the Turners added a two-bedroom suite with a sunroom and a fireplace to their house. Traditionally furnished, the bedrooms boast four-poster rice beds. The latest addition to the accommodations is the Pool House Cottage, a log house overlooking the pool and with a view of the gardens.

Guests are invited to use the Turners' swimming pool, hot tub, and three-tier garden with water ponds and a waterfall on each level. In addition, the top level has a gazebo, patio furniture, and grills; the middle level has brick and rock walls, furniture, and grills; and the bottom level has a shade garden and park benches. City folks will particularly enjoy the Turners' menagerie of koi and goldfish in the pond, white mute swans, black Australian swans, Canada geese, guineas, dogs, cats, and Elmer Leroy, the pot-bellied pig. You can enjoy a peaceful walk on the nature trails, taking time to stop at some of the more than one hundred bluebird houses. Horseback riding and airplane rides are offered at an additional fee.

Food is an important part of any visit to Twin Oaks. Homemade pound cake is served on your arrival, and evening tea is served under the arbor. Depending on whether you want to be alone or be sociable, you can choose to have your breakfast brought to the cottage, or enjoy it in the Turners' cheery kitchen or in the garden. Breakfast might include biscuits, grape jelly, grits, eggs, bacon, and sausage. Carol will vary the menu if you stay several nights. Dinners for guests or roses in the room can be arranged on advance notice and at an additional fee.

What's Nearby Villa Rica

Villa Rica is another great town for antiques collectors, who will certainly enjoy Villa Rica's charming antiques stores. There is also a local antiques auction once a month. If you're looking for family fun, Villa Rica is twenty minutes away from Six Flags over Georgia amusement park. Other possible day trips include downtown Atlanta and Historic Sweetwater Battle Ground, just thirty minutes and twenty minutes away respectively.

Hill and Hollow Farm

Best Buy

2090 Thomson Road (US 78)
Washington, Georgia 30673
(706) 678-4439

INNKEEPER: Elizabeth (Bunny) Boyd

ROOMS: 4; 2 with private bath, 2 share a bath; ask about pets

ON THE GROUNDS: Stable, trail rides, lake, paddleboat

RATES: $70, including continental-plus breakfast

CREDIT CARDS ACCEPTED? No

OPEN: Year-round

HOW TO GET THERE: From I-20, take US 78 North toward Washington for approximately 16 miles. After you pass Aonia Road to your right, look for the number 2090 on Bunny's mailbox to your left. There is no sign, but she usually has a welcome flag flying from a tree. If Bunny isn't in the house, she's probably in the barn, the riding ring, or the garden—all of which are close to the house

If you want your children to experience an authentic country weekend that they'll remember all their lives, Hill and Hollow Farm makes a splendid setting. In fact, your hostess Bunny describes her farm as the "perfect family playground." Whether you are traveling with children or not, Bunny invites you to swap urban stress for the sweet sounds and peaceful sights of country living.

Conveniently located between Washington and Thomson and not far from Augusta and Athens, the one-hundred-acre farm unfolds with rolling pastures surrounded by woods as far as the eye can see. In addition, there's a ten-acre lake equipped with a paddleboat and fishing boat. Bring your own poles or use the ones Bunny provides. You may simply want to watch the Canada geese and their goslings, which often stop over at the lake, or the deer that venture out of the woods for a cool drink. There are two wonderful golden retrievers. In season you can help Bunny pick blueberries or vegetables from the garden. Kids (and kids-at-heart) can get up close and personal with farm animals, but what's even more exciting is that Bunny has riding horses. An experienced rider and teacher, she supervises lessons and trail rides for adults and children. Kids have the opportunity to participate in grooming and saddling up their favorite horses. Hard hats and all tack are provided. (There is an additional charge for trail rides and lessons.)

Bunny's father bought this farm when she was in college, and she later decided to settle here permanently. Unfortunately, the old farmhouse was beyond redemption, so she had to have it torn down. The present house was built in 1985. Bunny was able to salvage a lot of heart pine from the old house, though, which she used for her kitchen cabinets and built-in bookshelves. The current house is a lengthy one-and-a-half-story brick with front and back porches on which to relax.

A spacious great room and an enticing sunporch are popular public rooms. Guest accommodations are provided in four small but comfortable rooms. Downstairs there are two guest chambers with queen-size beds and private baths—one of which even boasts a Jacuzzi tub. The two bedrooms upstairs share a connecting bath, so they are better suited for a family or two couples traveling together.

Holly Ridge Country Inn (Best Buy)

2221 Sandtown Road
Washington, Georgia 30673
(706) 285-2594

E-MAIL: hollyridge@g-net.net

INNKEEPERS: Vivien and Roger Walker

ROOMS: 10 (1 is a suite); all with private bath; 2 with gas-log fireplace; ask about pets

ON THE GROUNDS: Verandas, deck, water gardens, pond, hiking and biking trails

RATES: $85 to $105, including continental or full breakfast

CREDIT CARDS ACCEPTED? Yes

OPEN: Year-round

HOW TO GET THERE: Take GA 44 East out of Washington. Go 8 miles to Sandtown Road and turn right. The inn is 0.5 mile farther on your left.

One of the most unusual bed and breakfasts we've run across is the Holly Ridge Country Inn located on one hundred acres near Washington, Georgia. The brainchild of Vivien and Roger Walker, the B&B is actually two completely dissimilar houses that Vivien wanted to save from the wrecking ball. Not only did she save and refurbish them, but she moved them to her property and stuck them together.

Although now connected, the houses aren't side by side. Fronting the country road is a stately red Queen Anne Victorian house with quaint towers and generous verandas. Behind this house and attached to it at right angles is an ancient farmhouse once lived in by Vivien's great-grandparents.

The ambience in each house is entirely different, so be sure to state your preference for formal or informal. The interior decor and furnishings of the

Victorian are formal, befitting the exterior, while the interior of the farmhouse is rustic and its furniture is unadorned country style. The newer house has a wraparound porch with lots of wicker and swings; the older has a small porch with rockers. Both houses are air-conditioned and have ceiling fans. Each guest room is unique in color scheme and furnishings.

The Victorian house features high ceilings, beautiful moldings, a huge central hall, parlor, and a dining room so astounding that it will seat forty-five people and often serves as the scene of weddings, receptions, luncheons, showers, and parties. A large upstairs hall in this house serves as an informal sitting room for guests if a major activity is in progress downstairs. The older house is much more rustic: Ceilings are lower, rooms smaller, and the floors, walls, and ceilings are constructed of exposed heart-pine boards.

Breakfast, which can be continental or a full meal, depending on the guests' desires, is generally served in the inviting sunroom of the Victorian house, although in particularly pleasing weather it might be served on either of the expansive porches.

If you can bestir yourselves from one of the sitting rooms or verandas, the acreage includes English water gardens, a pond, and trails for biking and hiking. Those who want to roam can explore the barn and the remains of an old country store. Grounds near the house are equipped with plenty of lawn furniture for the guests' relaxation.

Vivacious Vivien has lots more plans, so we expect this B&B to expand.

What's Nearby Washington

See page 210 for what's nearby Washington.

Maynard's Manor

219 East Robert Toombs Avenue
Washington, Georgia 30673
(706) 678-4303

WEB SITE: www. kudcom.com/
maynard/

INNKEEPERS: Louise and Ross
Maynard

ROOMS: 6; all with private bath, decorative fireplace, ceiling fan

ON THE GROUNDS: Porches, gardens

RATES: $85 to $125, including full breakfast, evening refreshments, beverages in rooms

CREDIT CARDS ACCEPTED? Yes

OPEN: Year-round

HOW TO GET THERE: From I-20, take US 78 North to Washington. Turn right onto North Alexander Avenue and go 2 blocks. The B&B is on your left at the corner of North Alexander and Sims. Park on either street. If you are approaching on US 78 South from Athens, at the second traffic light after the town square, turn left onto North Alexander. Continue 2 blocks to North Alexander and Sims.

Built in 1820, the stately Greek Revival mansion that houses Maynard's Manor provides a grand introduction to the opulence of the Old South. This regal two-story home has been lovingly restored by Louise and Ross, and is exquisitely and formally furnished to reflect the time when it was in its first heyday. Don't get the idea, however, that this is one of those museumlike places that's so perfect, you're afraid to sit down. Everything is done with the intent of making guests feel comfortable, and the Maynards' sense of humor is evident here and there. For example, when you first enter the front foyer, in addition to being greeted by one or both of your hosts, you will also make the acquaintance of Hannah and Horace—two mannequins dressed in turn-of-the-century garb that changes with the season—and Hannibal the Pig (not live, of course). Instead of a real household of cats, the Maynards have several of those mechanical toys that move their heads and tails and say *meow* whenever they detect motion.

High ceilings, hardwood floors, ornamental moldings, elaborate mantelpieces, stained-glass windows, and fancy chandeliers combine with elaborate window treatments, rich fabrics, and fine Victorian antiques to delight the eye. You'll want to spend some time examining the architectural details and perfect accent pieces in every room—the formal parlor, the decorous dining room, and the stately library. The parlor and library are ideal places to curl up with a book by the fire or engage in lively conversation with your hosts or fellow guests. You'll want to spend some time on any one of four verandas, which are amply supplied with wicker furniture and rocking chairs. Finely appointed guest accommodations feature queen-size beds and modern private baths with showers. Decorative fireplaces add special enhancement to this graceful style of living.

The Maynards didn't rest when they finished creating a perfect physical setting. They next set about providing their guests with all manner of pampering. Complimentary light refreshments such as iced tea and fruit are available upon your arrival, and you'll find fresh fruit to nibble on in your room. Wine and hors d'oeuvres are served in the library each evening before

It's All So Taxing

As we all know only too well, present-day property tax is based on the appraised value of your property, including the house and lot. In early America this was not the case. Taxes were often based on all kinds of seemingly whimsical dictates—for instance, the number of rooms, or even the numbers of windows. Closets were actually counted as rooms, which explains why so many otherwise castlelike homes of the very wealthy had no closets. (Of course, it was a boon for armoire makers.) Where taxes were determined by the number of windows, ingenious homeowners used French doors and jib windows, which doubled as doors. For the uninitiated, the way a jib window works is this: The tall window is pushed all the way up, and the area between the bottom of the window and the floor swings open. The combination of the two actions creates a space tall enough to step through. As long as the gap created had a threshold, it was classified as a door instead of a window and was therefore not taxable. In many old mansions jib windows provided easy access to first- and second-story verandas.

you go off to dinner. While you're out, the Maynards will turn down your bed and leave a chocolate on your pillow and sherry by your bedside. Save room for dessert, which the Maynards serve in the evening. Fresh flowers in your room are standard in season from the lovely gardens that surround the house. Your morning begins with hot beverages available in the main hall as early as 7:00 A.M. A full gourmet breakfast is served in one of the morning rooms from 7:30 A.M.

Washington was once the temporary capital of Georgia, by the way. It's also known as the place Dixie died, because the fleeing Jefferson Davis disbanded his cabinet here before being captured in nearby Irwinton.

What's Nearby Washington

See page 210 for what's nearby Washington.

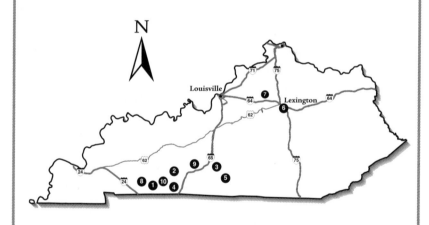

Kentucky

Numbers on map refer to towns numbered below.

1. Auburn, Federal Grove Bed and Breakfast, 216

2. Bowling Green,
   Alpine Lodge Bed and Breakfast, 218
   1869 Homestead Bed and Breakfast, 219

3. Cave City,
   Rose Manor Bed and Breakfast, 221
   The Wayfarer Bed and Breakfast, 223

4. Franklin, College Street Inn, 224

5. Glasgow, Hall Place, 226

6. Lexington, The Brand House at Rose Hill, 228

7. Midway, Scottwood, 230

8. Russellville,
   The Log House, 231
   Washington House Bed and Breakfast, 233

9. Smiths Grove, Victorian House Bed and Breakfast, 235

10. South Union, The Shaker Tavern, 237

Federal Grove Bed and Breakfast

475 East Main Street
Auburn, Kentucky 42206
(270) 542-6106 for the inn or
(270) 542-6687 for the antiques
shop; fax (270) 542-7439

WEB SITE: www.bbonline.com/
ky/fedgrove/

INNKEEPERS: Terry and Wayne
Blythe

ROOMS: 4; all with private bath,
queen-size bed, ceiling fan, clock
radio; ask about pets

ON THE GROUNDS: Patio, veranda, stable, extensive grounds

RATES: $65 single, $75 double, including full breakfast; additional
person $10

CREDIT CARDS ACCEPTED? Yes

OPEN: Year-round

HOW TO GET THERE: From the south (Nashville), take I-65 to exit 2, US 31
West. Go north to Franklin, then north on KY 73 to US 68. Travel west
on US 68 and take the first Auburn exit. The B&B is the first house on
your left. From the north (Louisville), take I-65 to William Natcher
Parkway. Take it north to exit 5, US 68. Travel east on US 68 and take
the first exit into Auburn. Go through Auburn; the B&B is the first
house on your right just past the city limits.

It was a perfect spring day when we arrived: The sun was shining, the sky
was a clear blue, a gentle breeze ruffled the trees. Terry was out on the rear
patio of the stately Greek Revival mansion with her small granddaughter
Shelby. A pair of cats tumbled at their feet. Four Halflingers (small draft
horses) and a miniature horse strolled along the fence in the adjacent pasture. "Is this idyllic or what?" we asked each other. It got better.

We settled in on the patio, scratched the cats behind the ears, and let
Terry tell us about the house before we went inside. It was built in 1886 on
a 1,200-acre land grant, although the acreage dwindled over the years. The
lucky Blythes were able to purchase the house and fifteen acres at auction
in 1991.

They've done a marvelous job renovating and putting their own stamp on the property. Both public and private rooms are furnished with antiques. If you see something you like, ask about it—it might be for sale. Because the Blythes do so many special events, all the downstairs rooms are devoted to dining. Be sure to admire Terry's extensive collection of Flo Blue china displayed in one of the former parlors.

Follow the central staircase up to the guest quarters. An informal sitting room is equipped with a television, coffeemaker, small refrigerator, and lots of magazines. The guest chamber that's the most fun is the American Christmas Room. Although this unusual room sports a large poplar bed specially made from wood rescued from an old school, the Christmas decorations are the focal point. A large throw rug with the likeness of Santa on it covers the floor, a large cutout wooden Santa stands guard by the fireplace, a small decorated tree stands in the corner . . . you probably think you're getting the idea. But wait, there's more. Accent pieces such as quilts and pillows are decked out in red, white, and blue stars and stripes. Terry says that guests who have booked some other rooms on their first visit usually request the Christmas Room on future visits. Still, don't bypass the others—each has its own special appeal. The Oak Room features a pencil-post queen-size bed and an additional twin bed as well as a desk. This room's special accent is a spinning wheel. The softly romantic Victorian Room boasts a four-poster rice bed so high you need steps to climb into it, a sitting area, and a television. Although small, the Sun Porch is a favorite because it's so light and cheerful.

Wayne enjoys swapping stories with guests at breakfast, which might consist of Terry's homemade pastries, sour cream coffee cake, buttermilk biscuits, locally cured ham, country-fried potatoes, or blueberry pancakes with all the trimmings, including their own blend of freshly squeezed orange juice. Breakfast can be served in one of the downstairs dining rooms or in the upstairs sitting room overlooking the balcony. For a complete Federal Grove experience, romantic evening dinners can be arranged with advance notice at an additional fee.

Horses are treated just as well as two-legged guests at Federal Grove. In addition to four guest accommodations for humans, there are four stalls for equine visitors, as well as pasturage for others.

What's Nearby Auburn

See "What's Nearby South Union," page 239.

Alpine Lodge Bed and Breakfast

Best Buy

5310 Morgantown Road
Bowling Green, Kentucky 42101
(270) 843–4846 (9:00 A.M.
to 9:00 P.M.);
fax (270) 843–4833

WEB SITE: www.bbonline.com
/ky/alpinelodge/

INNKEEPERS: Joyce and Davis Livingston

ROOMS: 3 rooms and 1 two-bedroom suite; 3 private baths, 2 shared baths; dogs accepted

ON THE GROUNDS: Deck, gazebo, swimming pool, hot tub, lawns

RATES: $38.50 to $90, including full breakfast

CREDIT CARDS ACCEPTED? Yes

OPEN: Year-round

HOW TO GET THERE: From I–65, take exit 20 and go west. After you cross US 68/80, take William Natcher Parkway to exit 7. Turn left. The bed and breakfast is on your right.

There's nothing fancy here, just comfortable accommodations in a Swiss-chalet-style contemporary home built in 1982 and located on eleven and a half scenic acres. This is a good place for a family reunion that won't break the bank.

Not only are your hosts retired music teachers, but they were the first two music teachers at Franklin County High School. Dr. Livingston wrote the school song. After winning many previous awards, he's recently been honored by having a new building at the school named after him. Perhaps while you're visiting, you can talk one of the Livingstons into a melody on the baby grand piano.

Their home is furnished with an eclectic mix of antiques and reproductions from various periods, and crammed with lots of mementos. Gathering places include a formal living room, a great room with a cathedral ceiling and a brick fireplace, an enclosed sunporch, and outdoor recreational facilities.

Guest rooms offer a variety of accommodations. Downstairs, two more formal rooms share a bath. Upstairs, the Honeymoon Suite features a four-poster canopy bed with Mombasa mosquito netting, a love seat in front of the electric fireplace, a television, a small refrigerator, and a private bath, so a romantic couple can stay holed up here in their love nest almost indefinitely. The Family Suite consists of a bathroom and two large bedrooms—one has a double bed, and the other a double and a twin. The upstairs sitting room has two sofa beds. This room can be combined with either of the suites to accommodate additional guests. There are even baby beds and high chairs for small children.

It's the out-of-doors, however, that draws many visitors to Alpine Lodge. Sweeping lawns provide endless opportunities to stroll. An aboveground pool and hot tub surrounded by a deck create hours of relaxation.

You won't go hungry with a Southern breakfast of eggs, sausage or ham, biscuits and gravy, hash browns, fried apples, grits, juice, and hot beverages served in the cheery enclosed sunporch or, in good weather, in the gazebo.

What's Nearby Bowling Green

Every Corvette made in the United States is produced right here in Bowling Green. If you'd like to watch the car-making process, take a tour of the General Motors Corvette Assembly Plant. Prefer theater to cars? Visit the Capitol Arts center and check out a local show. This community arts center, which used to be the Old Capitol Theatre building, is located in the historic downtown area. The center offers two art galleries and a 840-seat theater, which hosts local and touring stage productions. The focus of Bowling Green's downtown is Fountain Square Park, a lovely landscaped public park. You'll enjoy the park's statues, fountain, and benches.

Another Recommended B&B in Bowling Green

Bowling Green B&B, a traditional six-year-old house in a subdivision, is furnished in antiques, reproductions, and mementos from world travels; 3313 Savannah Drive, Bowling Green, KY 42104; (270) 781-3861.

1869 Homestead Bed and Breakfast Best Buy

212 Mizpah Road
Bowling Green, Kentucky 42101
(270) 842-0510

E-MAIL: wendell@wku.campus.mci.net
WEB SITE: www.bbonline.com/ky/bbak/ members/1869homestead.html

INNKEEPERS: Jan and Wendell Strode

ROOMS: 2 rooms and 1 suite; all with private bath, queen-size bed, cable TV, clock; some with ceiling fan, fireplace

ON THE GROUNDS: Extensive lawns, pond, covered parking

RATES: $69 to $89 double, including expanded continental breakfast and in-room snacks

CREDIT CARDS ACCEPTED? Yes

OPEN: Year-round

HOW TO GET THERE: From I-65, take exit 28 (Corvette Museum). Go west a short distance to US 31 West and turn right (north). Follow US 31 West about 5 miles. You'll pass a high school and middle school on your left; about a mile past this, watch on your right for Mizpah Road and a sign for the 1869 Homestead. After making the turn, bear left into the driveway.

As we followed a stacked split-rail fence along a winding gravel lane, we indeed felt as if we were going back in time to an upscale mid-nineteenth-century farmhome. Newly planted fields of corn stretched out in all directions. The two-story, federal-style, redbrick house with a red tin roof sits regally on a small knoll, framed by ancient trees blowing in a gentle breeze. Two friendly pooches ran out to meet us, quickly followed by Jan.

As Jan began our tour, she explained that Andrew James Wardlaw purchased 600 acres of land in 1818 and built the first house on the property for his wife and three children. Unfortunately, that house burned in 1868, so Wardlaw's grandson James III began rebuilding; he completed the existing home in 1869. Wardlaw heirs continued to live on the farm until 1956—a stretch of 138 years. Emit Strode bought the property in 1958. Currently Emit's son Wendell and his wife, Jan, reside here, the second generation of only the second family in the house. Wendell and Jan restored the house in 1997, sprucing it up and adding five bathrooms so they could offer bed-and-breakfast accommodations. To avoid taking space out of the guest chambers for the bathrooms, several of them have been cleverly tucked into closets—the toilet and sink in one, the shower in another.

Jan pointed out the three-layer-thick interior and exterior walls, 11-foot ceilings, grand curving cantilever walnut staircase, six fireplaces—several converted to gas-log use—and original poplar flooring. Each room is painted a bold color accented with gleaming white woodwork. Beautiful antiques and reproductions of the Civil War era adorn the historic residence. Downstairs are a graceful parlor and a formal dining room.

At the top of the stairway, white wicker with cheerful floral cushions creates an informal sitting area. Three spacious, well-appointed guest chambers await you. A four-poster bed dominates the Andrew James Wardlaw Room, named for the original owner. The Benjamin Starr Room, named for a Union soldier, has a massive bed and a beautiful gilt mirror over the mantel. A queen-size bed in one room and a twin bed in the other create sleeping space for three in the two-room suite. All the guest rooms feature private baths and all the modern comforts and amenities. Depending on which side of the house your bedroom is in, you can enjoy a spectacular sunrise or sunset.

Either way, you'll awaken in the morning to the sun streaming through your windows. Downstairs a tasty expanded continental breakfast awaits. This welcome meal might include homemade muffins, waffles, cereal, fruit, juices, and hot beverages. Afterward, spend hours strolling down the lane, wandering over the grounds, wandering down to the pond, or viewing the historical Wardlaw family, slave, and church cemeteries.

What's Nearby Bowling Green

See page 219 for what's nearby Bowling Green.

Rose Manor Bed and Breakfast

Best Buy

204 Duke Street
Cave City, Kentucky 42127
(270) 773-4402 or
(888) 806-ROSE (7673)

WEB SITE: www.mammoth cave.com/rose.htm

INNKEEPERS: Mona and John Bjorkman

ROOMS: 5; all with private bath (2 with two-person whirlpool and robes), clock, ceiling fan; CD player, TV on request; ask about pets

ON THE GROUNDS: Porch

RATES: $85 to $95 double, including full breakfast, beverages and refreshments, turndown service

CREDIT CARDS ACCEPTED? Yes

OPEN: Year-round

HOW TO GET THERE: From I-65, take exit 53 and turn right. Immediately get into the left-turn lane to turn left. Continue about 1.5 miles until you cross railroad tracks. Turn left onto First Street and go 1 block. Turn right onto Duke. The bed and breakfast is on the right side of the street.

When we first pulled up beside the sturdy, sensible-looking, dark brick prairie- and Craftsman-style house, we had little idea what romantic enticements lay within. John told us that the place had been built in the 1920s by a local hotel family, who used it for overflow housing when the hotel was full. He and Mona bought the house in 1995 and took a year to renovate it for use as a bed and breakfast. They thought it only appropriate that a structure that was built for hospitality should return to that function again.

Everything about the interior is geared toward romance. Hardwood floors, oak woodwork, high ceilings, and crystal chandeliers evoke another era. Deep, rich jewel tones are used throughout. Burgundy love seats, wing chairs, and fringed lamps dominate the formal parlor. The five guest rooms are named Sapphire, Amethyst, Amber, Emerald, and Pearl, with the appropriate color featured in each. Several of these rooms are located in former sleeping porches with windows on at least two sides, so they're incredibly light and cheerful.

Satin bedspreads, candles, aromatherapy, and soft music accentuate the mood and allow the two of you to be king and queen for as long as you stay. The Bjorkmans can even arrange a horse-drawn carriage ride. Book early to get the Sapphire Room with its king-size bed, or the Amethyst Room with its queen-size iron and brass bed. Both these royal chambers boast large, triangular two-person whirlpool tubs. We particularly liked the Amethyst Room's bath—there are two walls of windows and a chaise longue covered in a white fabric scattered with bunches of violets. Guests in the Emerald Room enjoy an old-fashioned radio/tape player with a collection of old-time radio shows. Twin beds in the Pearl Room can be reconfigured as a king. Although this room's bathroom is across the hall, a screen blocks off that end of the hall to make your short journey a private one.

If couples ever wish to come out of their rooms, popular places to gather are the deeply shaded front porch, the formal parlor, and the cozy den, which is well stocked with a television, a VCR, a large selection of nostalgic and contemporary videos, and CDs. Mona and John will even pop up a batch of popcorn so you can settle in for an evening's entertainment. If you're looking for things to enjoy in the privacy of your room, the upstairs hall is loaded with soft drinks, games, puzzles, and brochures to study for tomorrow's outing.

The Bjorkmans say, "If you get up from the table with an inch in your tummy . . . we've failed our goal!" After gorging on a Southern country breakfast of eggs, pancakes with cooked apples and whipped cream, or a four-cheese omelette accompanied by ham and biscuits, you're sure to leave the table full, satisfied, and with your taste buds feeling good all over.

What's Nearby Cave City

Visit Kentucky's number one tourist attraction, Mammoth Cave National Park. Nearly 2.5 million visitors enter the world's longest cave each year. Or you can visit Crystal Onyx Cave and Campground and Onyx Cave, which are both located right in Cave City. Besides touring caves, you can take advantage of Cave City's horseback riding, miniature golf, and local museums—such as the Wildlife Museum—or enjoy the area's flowers, trees, birds, deer, and hiking trails. The Kentucky Action Park Alpine Slide is also a possible afternoon adventure.

The Wayfarer Bed and Breakfast

1240 Old Mammoth Cave Road
Cave City, Kentucky 42127
(270) 773-3366

E-MAIL: thewayfarer@ivprog.com

WEB SITE: www.bbonline.com/ky/wayfarer

INNKEEPERS: Becky and Larry Bull

ROOMS: 5; all with private bath, ceiling fan, in-wall sound system, clock

ON THE GROUNDS: Gift shop, museum

RATES: $65 single, $75 double, including full breakfast and admission to the museum; additional person $20

CREDIT CARDS ACCEPTED? Yes

OPEN: Year-round

HOW TO GET THERE: From I-65, take exit 53 and go west on Highway 70 for about 5 miles. The bed and breakfast is on your right just before Mammoth Cave National Park.

The way Larry tells it, when Becky came home one day and told him the venerable old Mammoth Cave Souvenir Shop was going to be auctioned off and she wanted to bid on it, he thought she was crazy. But when auction day came, he tagged along and decided purchasing it wouldn't be such a bad idea after all. The rest, as they say, is history.

The shop had been built in 1933 at the boundary line of Mammoth Cave National Park; at the time it was the largest souvenir shop in the South, perhaps in the nation. After spending well over $100,000 on the renovations, Becky and Larry reopened the structure as a bed and breakfast, gift shop, and museum.

In one wing a cozy paneled sitting room filled with overstuffed furniture and appointed with a television, VCR, books, magazines, puzzles, and games invites you to settle in for good conversation, down-home recreational pursuits, or just propping your feet up. Breakfast in the sunny farm-style dining room is an event featuring award-winning Broadbent secret-cured country ham, eggs, cheese grits, fried apples, and biscuits.

Located upstairs, the five cozy guest rooms are comfortable, tastefully decorated with country charm, and furnished with a combination of old and new. Beds, which are double or queen size, are antique wood or brass. Some seating is provided in each room.

More than just a bed and breakfast, the Wayfarer offers an excellent gift shop that carries quality handmade Kentucky crafts, antiques, country hams, and a selection of Kentucky candles, jams, and jellies. There's a museum dedicated to the memory of Floyd Collins, the first person to explore Sand Cave. He became trapped in 1925 when a rock fell on his foot; the ensuing eighteen-day rescue attempt received nationwide media coverage. Unfortunately, Collins did not survive. In addition, the Bulls offer canoe and kayak rentals, and Larry provides guided trips on the Green River inside the park.

What's Nearby Cave City

See page 223 for what's nearby Cave City.

College Street Inn Best Buy

223 South College Street
Franklin, Kentucky 42134
(270) 586-9352 or (800) 686-9352

INNKEEPERS: Donna and
Mike Houston
ROOMS: 4; 2 with private bath,
2 with shared bath; all have TV
with remote, clock radio,
ceiling fan, robes; 1 room has telephone and computer access
ON THE GROUNDS: Porch, gazebo, gardens, off-street parking

RATES: $45 to $65 single, including early coffee, full breakfast, afternoon refreshments; second person $10; ask about corporate rates

CREDIT CARDS ACCEPTED? Yes

OPEN: Year-round

HOW TO GET THERE: From I-65 traveling south, take exit 6, Highway 100. Travel west about 3 miles through the second traffic light in Franklin. Go 1 more block to the stop sign and turn right onto College Street. The bed and breakfast is the fourth house on your right. Traveling north, take exit 2, Highway 31 West. Turn left and go to the second traffic light, then turn left again and go to the first stop sign. Turn right; the B&B is the fourth house on your right.

Donna and Mike's motto is, "Our goal is to exceed your expectations." Little did they know what a challenge we would be. Although we weren't lucky enough to be able to spend the night, we had a lovely visit touring their home and chatting with the Houstons about everything from B&Bs to teaching—they're both teachers as both of us were in former lives. When it came time to leave, though, we found we'd locked our keys in the car. Being from the big city of Atlanta, we had visions of waiting hours for a locksmith and paying big bucks—not to mention how far behind we'd grow in our travel schedule. But Donna calmly called the local police, and Mike offered us a glass of wine while we waited. An officer showed up shortly thereafter and had our car open in no time. This is just one example of the pleasures of small-town life and the unflappability of the Houstons.

The pleasant 112-year-old Queen Anne Victorian house, although not a mansion in the strictest sense of the word, is nevertheless roomy and filled with the superb architectural details that were common in even middle-class homes at the turn of the century. For many years it was inhabited by a brother and sister, neither of whom ever married. When Mike's parents bought it in the 1960s, while he was in high school, it was crammed to the gills with their furniture and possessions. Some of these wonderful old pieces remain in the house today.

In 1992 the Houstons began to convert the family home into a bed and breakfast—the first in Franklin. A delightful alternative to conventional accommodations, it features inviting common rooms and four comfortable guest rooms. Be sure to admire the poplar and oak woodwork, built-in cabinets, and ornate overmantels downstairs.

Cozy guest rooms, most named for their predominant color, feature double or queen-size mattresses topped with featherbeds, antique iron or carved high-back beds, antique furnishings including marble-topped dressers, and comfortable seating. As appealing as the Green Room is, it's the bathroom that gets the most raves. Located under a skylight created in the space where a chimney was removed, the focal point of this large room is a raised whirlpool tub mounted in a frame. A separate shower and double sinks complete this special playroom. The Red Room features two beds, a private bath, and television. The Blue and Round Rooms share a bath.

A plentiful and delicious Southern gourmet breakfast might include an entree such as eggs Rachel, layered omelettes, or pecan waffles, as well as popovers or Donna's famous banana bread, fruit, juice, and hot beverages. Eat in the dining room where you can chat with your hosts and fellow guests, or ask to dine in your room for those special occasions.

In good weather, the outdoors beckons. From the front porch you can watch slow-paced life in Franklin. We particularly loved the old-fashioned wicker swing in the backyard gazebo, from which you can admire the herb and flower gardens. The Houstons also have a great dog who'd love to chase any tennis balls you throw.

What's Nearby Franklin

Franklin was named to honor the great Benjamin Franklin. Here you'll find antiques shops and antique car shows. Stroll through the Historical Society Archives and Old Jail, and Gallery on the Square. You're also a short ride away from the Corvette Museum, Shakertown, and Dueling Grounds Race Track.

Hall Place

313 South Green Street
Glasgow, Kentucky 42141
(270) 651-3176

INNKEEPER: Caroline Royse

ROOMS: 2 rooms and 1 two-bedroom suite; all with private bath, telephone, clock, luggage rack

ON THE GROUNDS: Off-street parking

RATES: $50 single, $55 double, $75 for the suite, including full breakfast

CREDIT CARDS ACCEPTED? Yes

OPEN: Year-round

NOTE: Transitional neighborhood

HOW TO GET THERE: From I-65, take KY 90 or the Cumberland Tollway toward Glasgow. Follow US 31 East to downtown. Hall Place is 1 block off the square on South Green.

Tucked away as it is on a postage-stamp lot between a parking lot and a large house converted to medical offices, we almost missed historic Hall Place, an Italianate villa built in 1852 by Dr. James Hall. Spry, energetic Caroline, a proper Southern lady in her seventies, told us that when she and her late husband bought the house it was uninhabitable, but they saw its potential. They worked wonders restoring it in only seven months for their own home, and now Caroline shares it with B&B guests and as a special-events facility. She's made good use of her small lot to create English-garden-like borders of flowers and plants alongside the house.

She pointed out with justifiable pride the original floors, 13-foot ceilings, 14-inch-thick walls, plain and ornate fireplaces, and several funeral doors. (In a day when the deceased were laid out at home before burial, some doors had to be wide enough to accommodate a casket.)

A formal parlor with a grand piano and gas-log fireplace is joined (by a large double doorway) to a library, which also has a gas-log fireplace, a television, and a game table. Painted a deep red, accented by white trim, furnished with antiques, and attractively accessorized, together they make one very spacious and appealing place for guests to gather. We especially liked the rolling ladder that offers access to the library shelves. All we had to do was close our eyes to envision the fabulous parties that must've been held in these handsome rooms.

If you want to be more casual, there's an informal sitting room upstairs appointed with comfortable seating a game table, television, coffeemaker, telephone, and a big supply of magazines.

The prize guest room features Caroline's grandfather's carved high-back bed, an impressive armoire, and a lovely fainting couch as well as modern comforts and conveniences. Another simple room has an iron bed. The two-bedroom suite, which is not as fancy, has a high-back bed and a desk in one bedroom, a bed and sofa in the other. This arrangement works well for family members or friends traveling together who don't mind sharing a bath.

Caroline serves an ample breakfast in the dining room that might consist of mouthwatering specialties such as scrambled eggs and ham served with strawberries and cream, melon, hash browns, biscuits, and peach jam. Be sure to note the jaunty pair of foxes dressed in hunting togs sitting on the mantel, and the Civil War musket attached to the front of the fireplace.

Glasgow, named for the city in Scotland, is a historic district with interesting shopping and restaurants. Glasgow is close to Horse Cave, home of Kentucky's state theater, the Horse Cave Theatre. This popular playhouse features all kinds of productions, including much loved older and newer classics by Shakespeare, Arthur Miller, and Tennessee Williams. Glasgow is also close to Mammoth Cave and the Barren River Reservoir.

The Brand House at Rose Hill

461 North Limestone Street
Lexington, Kentucky 40508
(606) 226-9464 or (800) 366-4942; fax (606) 252-7940

E-MAIL: info@brandhouselex.com

WEB SITE: www.brandhouselex.com

INNKEEPERS: Pam and Logan Leet

ROOMS: 5; all with private bath, whirlpool tub, telephone, TV with movie channels, ceiling fan; 3 with fireplace; some telephones have data port

ON THE GROUNDS: Courtyard with fountain, lawns

RATES: $99 to $229, single or double, including full breakfast, desserts, and beverages; additional person $25; two-night minimum stay weekends in April and October; four-week cancellation policy in April and October

CREDIT CARDS ACCEPTED? Yes

OPEN: Year-round

HOW TO GET THERE: From I-75/64, take exit 113 and turn right onto North Broadway. Continue south about 2.7 miles and turn left onto Third Street. Go 2 blocks and turn left onto North Limestone Street. The Brand House is 2 blocks ahead on your left at the southwestern corner of Fifth Street. Turn left at Fifth and left again into the parking lot. From the Bluegrass Parkway, follow US 60 East (Versailles Road) until it turns into Maxwell, a one-way street. Turn left at the fourth traffic light onto South Limestone. Continue north through downtown and turn left at Fifth, then left again into the parking lot.

Pam says, "We want to be your B&B cruise ship." There are some similarities. Like a cruise ship, Brand House is a destination in itself. Elegant yet comfortable, it strives to provide every amenity. You can spend most of your time here, going off for occasional excursions.

Lauded by such publications as *Southern Living*, *National Geographic Traveler*, and *Country Inns* magazines, the Brand House at Rose Hill is the only four-diamond bed and breakfast in Kentucky. One of the most significant examples of federal-style architecture in the state, the 1812 home, which is listed on the National Register of Historic Places, features a Greek temple portico to welcome travelers. Although the bed and breakfast is located in town, it sits on nearly one and a half acres in the heart of bluegrass country.

John Brand may have left Scotland as a failure, but in Lexington he and his partner, John Wesley Hunt, became very successful as the first producers of hemp bagging in this country. Brand built Rose Hill as a testament to his newfound prosperity. Beautifully restored to its original glory, the Brand House is decorated with casual elegance in mind, without being overdone. It also offers all the modern comforts and conveniences.

Create your own little haven in one of the romantic guest rooms, which are furnished with antiques and reproductions and feature canopy beds and whirlpool tubs. Three boast gas-log fireplaces as well to snuggle down next to on a chilly evening while you watch a movie on one of the movie channels.

Pam says the billiards room has been extremely popular. She laughs and tells us that some husbands whose wives drag them off kicking and screaming to a B&B for a romantic weekend decide that maybe it's okay after all when they see the billiard table. In nice weather the tinkling of the fountain on the brick terrace is a pleasant accompaniment to a cool drink and some good conversation with the hosts and fellow guests.

Your bountiful full gourmet breakfast may feature such delicacies as Grand Marnier French toast, crème brûlée French toast, blueberry or cantaloupe mousse, country ham soufflé, freshly baked breads and pastries, and whatever is fresh and in season. For the convenience of guests, a service bar stocked with beverages is available twenty-four hours a day. Desserts are served in the afternoon.

We love Lexington and all its horsey attractions. We can't think of a better place to stay while visiting bluegrass country than at the Brand House.

What's Nearby Lexington

Saddle up! Lexington abounds with history and horses. Horsey must-see attractions include the Kentucky Horse Park, American Saddle Horse Museum, Kentucky Horse, Thoroughbred Park, and the Keeneland and Red Mile Racetracks. Other important attractions include Mary Todd Lincoln's House, the Kentucky Gallery of Fine Crafts and Art, Hunt-Morgan House, Loudoun House, and the Henry Clay Estate.

Scottwood

2004 East Leestown Pike
(mailing address: P.O. Box 4370)
Midway, Kentucky 40347
(606) 846-5037; fax (606) 846-4887

INNKEEPERS: Tim and Annette Grahl

ROOMS: 3, plus guest cottage; all with
private bath, TV, and VCR; 2 with
fireplace, robes

ON THE GROUNDS: Formal rose garden, nature path, bird-watching

RATES: $85 to $125, single or double, including full breakfast

CREDIT CARDS ACCEPTED? Yes

OPEN: Year-round

HOW TO GET THERE: From I-64, take the Midway exit. The inn is 1½ miles
east of I-64.

Scottwood is an early (about 1795) federal-style Kentucky brick house set
among green fields, near a creek, across from a horse farm. Tim and
Annette want guests to think of it as a place to which they can escape for
periods of retreat and rest.

Just being inside takes you from your ordinary life. A fanciful mural of
local houses and farms (in the Rufus Porter style) sweeps up the stairwell
and into the hall. It serves as a lighthearted introduction to outstanding
antiques throughout the house. The Grahls have been collecting antiques
for twenty years and came to the B&B business well prepared to furnish
their rooms.

The common room, done in period antiques, reminds you of a New England keeping room. The ash floors in this room are painted like a red and
beige checkerboard, "the way it *should* be in New England."

In the living room the focal point is a large red American architectural
cupboard that houses an outstanding china collection.

For those of us who prefer the creature comforts to antiques, the guest
cottage has been renovated to include French doors, a new deck, working
wood fireplace, queen-size bed, and whirlpool tub.

In addition to whatever time you spend here admiring the antiques collections, reading, and walking outside, consider experimenting with photography. The flowers, the nature trail, the creek, and the nearby horses
represent enough possible subjects to keep a photographer busy for a life-
time. We understand some guests come for just that.

Since you're staying in a Kentucky house, you can reasonably expect a Kentucky breakfast. Annette's the cook. She prepares varied menus, trying to include some healthful choices and, she says, "something not so healthful" every day. Traditional favorites include country ham, spoon bread, fruits, and pancakes.

Tim and Annette also love their Williamsburg-style gardens and grounds. Their expeditious use of pruning shears and the addition of new roses have really spruced up the property.

What's Nearby Midway

Tired of the same old daily grind? Then visit the Weisenberger Mill. It is the oldest continuously operating mill in the state, and it is still run by the same family. The mill grinds tons of grain daily, but the process is now entirely water-powered. Midway, which is located midway between Franfort and Lexington, offers antique shopping, too.

The Log House (Best Buy)

2139 Franklin Road
Russellville, Kentucky 42276
(270) 726-8483;
fax (270) 726-4610

E-MAIL: hossom@logantele.com

WEB SITE: www.bbonline.com/ky/bbak/ members/loghouse.html or www.bbchannel.com/ky

INNKEEPERS: Sam and Mike Hossom

ROOMS: 4; all with private bath, robes and slippers, coffeemaker, clock radio; 2 with fireplace

ON THE GROUNDS: Fiber studio, solarium with hot tub, deck, acreage, and hiking trails

RATES: $95 double, including full breakfast

CREDIT CARDS ACCEPTED? Yes

OPEN: Year-round

HOW TO GET THERE: Head east from Russellville on KY 100. The B&B is the second driveway on your right after the 2-mile marker. There's a discreet sign just inside the driveway entrance.

It was pitch dark. Our headlights picked up the soft, green new growth on the pine trees that crowded in along the long, winding driveway. Suddenly the rustic log house appeared in a clearing. As soon as we shut the motor off, a deep, peaceful silence enveloped us—broken only by the call of a bird singing, "Chuck Will's widow."

Our genial hosts "Sam" (her given name is Margaret) and Mike greeted us warmly, as did their friendly dog and cat. We shared some refreshments and great conversation before touring their house—a perfect example of not being able to tell a book by its cover. We were wowed. When we'd first made arrangements to visit, we envisioned a smallish log cabin, not this rambling 8,000-square-foot structure with thirteen-plus rooms and seven bathrooms. We'd have sworn the house was 200 or more years old, rather than having been built in 1976. Huge hand-hewn logs were recovered from several old cabins and barns around the area; the doors and nearly foot-wide floorboards came from a school, and the bricks used to lay the kitchen floor were from an old sewing factory.

Furnished in eclectic formal and informal Early American style, both the public and guest rooms feature antiques, auction finds, and folk art and mementos from around the world. Among the public rooms are a formal living room with two crystal chandeliers (a surprisingly appealing juxtaposition of styles) and a stone fireplace; a dining room; an informal music room with a pump organ, upright piano, banjo, and guitar; a den/TV room with a fireplace decorated in a cowboy theme; and an upstairs sitting room with stained-glass windows salvaged from an old hotel in Atlantic City, a kimono wall hanging Sam purchased in Taiwan, and some Oriental paintings of her own.

Guest rooms are large and well appointed. Our palatial abode for the night was the Noah's Ark Room, a spacious chamber with a camelback love seat drawn up in front of the fireplace and direct access onto the upstairs screened porch, where we spent some pleasant time in the old-fashioned swing before retiring. Then we went to bed with the door to the porch open so we could hear the birds and enjoy the fresh air. Extra little touches in our room included fresh flowers, a plate of cookies, and a dish of candy. The other guest rooms—called the Cat Room, Toy Room, and Rabbit Room—are each furnished with antiques and accented in pieces appropriate to the name. A fireplace and access to the screened porch are special features of the Rabbit Room. Every guest room has a private bath, although two are across the hall.

Besides being terrific hosts, Sam and Mike are fascinating people. Both are accomplished spinners and weavers who have participated in many

Sheep-to-Shawl contests at the Indiana State Fair. They've both won many prizes at the county and state level, and provide demonstrations for local schools and the Shakertown Museum. They operate Hollow Tree Fibers Studio at the Log House, although Mike also holds a day job as director of engineering at a nearby engineering firm. They hand-card, dye, and spin their own yarns. In addition, Sam is an accomplished knitter. They'll be more than happy to show you their various spinning wheels and looms, and even demonstrate some skills for you. Some of the finished one-of-a-kind products such as shawls, place mats, throws, coverlets, and sweaters are for sale. As if all this isn't enough, they're both active in the Episcopal Church, Sam as an organist and Mike a senior warden.

We only wished we'd been able to stay long enough to enjoy the screened porch more, spend some time sunning ourselves on the deck, hike through the fifteen acres of heavy woods, and end the day by soaking in the hot tub in the solarium.

We wrote in the Hossoms' guest book that we wanted them to adopt us so we could stay here forever. We've never said that about a B&B before.

What's Nearby Russellville

Russellville has the largest historic district in the state for a community of its size. The history of the town will steal your heart away. For instance, visit the Southern Bank of Kentucky at Sixth and Main, which is the site of Jesse James' first bank robbery. If you're staying here in October, check out the annual reenactment of the famous robbery during the Logan County Tobacco Festival. Stop by the town's visitors center to pick up walking tour brochures and information on local antiques shopping.

Washington House Bed and Breakfast

Best Buy

283 West Ninth Street/
Highway 79 South
Russellville, Kentucky 42276
days (270) 726-7608 or nights
(270) 726-3093 or (270) 726-2266

INNKEEPER: Roy Gill

ROOMS: 3 rooms and 1 suite (only the rooms are bed and breakfast); all with private bath

ON THE GROUNDS: Sunporch

RATES: $65 single, $70 double, including full breakfast; $10 less without breakfast; additional person $10

CREDIT CARDS ACCEPTED? Yes

OPEN: Year-round

HOW TO GET THERE: From I-65, take US 31 West to Franklin. From there, take KY 100 for about 20 miles to the outskirts of Russellville, where it dead-ends at a stop sign. There are BP and Phillips 66 gas stations on the corners. Turn left and immediately get into the left-turn lane to make another left turn onto Ninth Street, US 79. Continue up a big hill, then down past the historic Russellville stadium. After the blinking caution light, the B&B is on the near left at the next corner and is identified by a sign. Turn the corner to enter the driveway from the back.

This lovely federal-style house located on a tree-shaded corner lot in a historic district of Russellville was built in 1824 by John Whiting Washington, a third cousin of George Washington. We could envision gentlemen in knee britches and ladies in flowing gowns congregating in its gracious public rooms. Today the beautifully restored home is entirely devoted to accommodations, because Roy lives in the house next door. One suite is devoted to long-term stays, and three handsome guest rooms are available for bed-and-breakfast stays.

Roy is in the antiques business and owns a florist shop as well, so you know that his taste is exquisite in both the decor and the furnishings he's chosen. He uses bold colors and historically authentic patterns to create dramatic backdrops in each room. In the sitting room, for instance, the use of three navy walls focuses all your attention on the white-paneled fireplace wall, with its lovely mantel and built-in bookcases. Guests love to gather here to watch television or play the baby grand piano.

The sophisticated decor of the dining room provides an outstanding background for your morning meal. Navy blue below the chair rail sets off the blue and gold wallpaper above it. Blue upholstery and blue and white china are perfect complements to a full meal that might consist of bacon and eggs, a ham and cheese omelette, or a sausage casserole, accompanied by hash browns and cheese grits.

Located on the first floor, the Blue Room showcases a double-size, carved high-back bed, a highboy, and a beautiful pier mirror. On the way up the graceful staircase, be sure to admire the grandfather clock and the pretty mirror on the landing. The focal point of the Rose Room is the full-tester bed covered with a quilt that has a cross-stitched floral design. For folks traveling together who don't want to share the same bed, the Green Room offers two double beds with spindle head- and footboards. Although each bedchamber has a private bath, the one in the Green Room is the most modern.

What's Nearby Russellville

See page 233 for what's nearby Russellville.

Victorian House
Bed and Breakfast

130 North Main
(mailing address: P.O. Box 104)
Smiths Grove, Kentucky 42171
(502) 563–9403

WEB SITE: www.bbonline.com/ky/victorian/

INNKEEPER: Velma Crist

ROOMS: 4; all with private bath, decorative fireplace, cable TV, ceiling fan, individual air conditioner

ON THE GROUNDS: Veranda, gardens, lawn

RATES: $85 double, including early-morning wake-up coffee, full breakfast, evening desserts, turndown service; additional person $20; honeymoon/anniversary package

CREDIT CARDS ACCEPTED? Yes

OPEN: Year-round

HOW TO GET THERE: From I–65, take exit 38, Smiths Grove, and go north into town. Victorian House is located on your right in the center of town.

Antiquers will love staying at this antiques-filled bed and breakfast, which is just across the street from several antiques shops. So will fans of *Gone with the Wind* and those who love to be pampered. We knew we were in for a pleasant experience the minute we pulled up in front of the redbrick mansion pleasantly shaded by statuesque old trees. We quickly noted the extensive garden-filled grounds and the inviting wraparound porch with its intricate rails and fretwork.

Velma welcomed us warmly as we stepped inside. The first thing that caught our eye was a large print of the famous picture of Scarlett wearing her blue velvet gown. Black and white stills from the movie and commemorative plates are prominently displayed as well throughout the house, so we weren't a bit surprised to learn that the guest chambers are named for Scarlett, Rhett, Melanie, and Ashley.

Since the house and its decor are the epitome of Southern style, we were surprised to learn that Velma isn't a born-and-bred Southerner at all. In fact, she hails from Oregon. She told us that four years ago she was visiting her daughter, who lives nearby, and fell in love with the area, the town, and this house. She packed up lock, stock, and barrel and moved here in March 1995, after which she spent eight and a half months renovating the house. She opened her doors as a bed and breakfast in November 1995. Fortunately, the house was in fairly good shape, and she's even been able to retain a lot of its Victorian wallpaper.

Built in 1875, the immense house has 5,000 square feet, of which Velma is using only 4,000. Like many of its contemporaries, it features high ceilings, spacious rooms, hardwood floors, huge pocket doors, intricate moldings and woodwork, eight fireplaces, beautiful mantels, and original chandeliers—each one of them different. As was typical of the era, the rooms are filled with heavy Victorian furniture and accented with floral wallpapers, velvet draperies, Oriental carpets, gilt-framed mirrors, and fringed lamps. Two large formal parlors and a casual upstairs sitting room, as well as the veranda and grounds, make perfect places to relax.

Although the bedchambers could have come right out of the pages of *Gone with the Wind*, Velma has made some concessions to modern comforts and conveniences. Each room has a private bath and a gas-log fireplace as well as a television. Three of the rooms have reproduction beds so she can provide king-size mattresses; Rhett's Room has an antique queen-size bed. A high-back king-size bed and a fainting couch characterize Melanie's Room. Ashley's has an iron and brass king-size bed and a twin sofabed. The fanciest, of course, is Scarlett's, which boasts a king-size four-poster bed carved with acanthus leaves. The corner shower and a sink mounted in an antique dresser are incorporated on a raised dias in the room, while the toilet is hidden in a former closet. Scarlett's and Melanie's Rooms can be connected to form a two-bedroom suite.

Perfect little touches pamper guests to the fullest. An early-morning silver tray is brought to your room with coffee, juice, and fresh flowers. Italian chocolates are left at your bedside with evening turndown service.

Although some B&Bs provide robes, Velma goes a step farther and provides slippers as well.

Breakfast is an elegant meal served in the formal dining room using china, crystal, and silver. We've heard that the oven-baked orange French toast is out of this world, but whatever the breakfast entree is, it will probably be accompanied by a hash brown casserole and specialty muffins.

In her spare time, and we can't figure out when that is unless it's between 2:00 and 4:00 in the morning, Velma creates quilts and fringed Victorian lamp shades, many of which appear in the guest rooms. She always has a quilt in progress on a frame set up in one of the parlors. She invites you to sit down and add a few stitches of your own. Quilts, oak or maple quilting frames, lamp shades, gift baskets, and antiques are for sale.

What's Nearby Smiths Grove

Smiths Grove is big on antiques. Lots of antiques shops fill the downtown area, and the town holds spring and fall antiques festivals. Smiths Grove is just a short ride away from Mammoth Cave, Cave City, and Bowling Green.

Another Recommended B&B in Smiths Grove

Cave Spring Farm Bed and Breakfast, an antebellum home on a seventeen-acre estate, offers rooms with private baths and free Cave Springs Cavern tour; P.O. Box 365, Smiths Grove, KY 42171; (502) 563-6941; www.bbonline.com/ky/cavespring/.

The Shaker Tavern **Best Buy**

KY 73
South Union, Kentucky 42283
(502) 542-6801; fax (502) 542-7558

WEB SITE: www.logantele.com/
~shakmus/

INNKEEPER: Jo Ann Moody

ROOMS: 6; 3 with private bath, ceiling fan

ON THE GROUNDS: Veranda

RATES: $65 with shared bath, $75 with private bath, $120 for two adjoining rooms with bath; all include full breakfast and free admission to the

Shaker Museum; children age six to ten are $5, children younger than six free; dinner on request for an additional fee

CREDIT CARDS ACCEPTED? Yes

OPEN: Year-round

HOW TO GET THERE: From I-65, take exit 20, William Natcher Parkway (formerly Green River Parkway), to exit 5 (US 68/80). Turn left and follow US 68/80 to KY 73. Turn south and follow the signs approximately 10 miles to South Union.

Many people are familiar with the simple, clean lines of Shaker-style furniture while knowing nothing about its origins. The Shakers were a religious organization that flourished during the nineteenth century. Their charismatic founder, Mother Ann Lee, established a theology that promoted simplicity and perfection, celibacy, communal ownership of property, public confession of sin, and withdrawal from worldly society. A dancelike ritual performed as part of their worship service gained them the title Shakers. The Shakers created twenty-four villages (mostly in the East), acquired and worked farmland, constructed buildings, and maintained industries such as selling garden seeds and fruit preserves, as well as making furniture, brooms, hats, bonnets, baskets, rugs, and linen and silk fabrics—all of which gained them a national reputation. Unfortunately, celibacy and a marked decrease in new converts eventually diminished the population of Shakers to nearly nothing. Only one active Shaker Village still exists, in Maine. Several former villages are open to the public as museums, however, and some offer accommodations and meals.

One of the Shakers villages was at South Union from 1807 to 1922. The community here acquired and worked 6,000 acres of farmland, constructed more than 200 buildings, and developed and maintained several industries. In the commercial district of the village, just across the street from the newly constructed Louisville and Nashville Railroad, they built, in 1869, a hotel with a grand columned facade, intricate brickwork, and an ornate staircase. The Shakers then leased it to an outside interest for $100 a month—a purely moneymaking project, since management of the hotel was left to the worldly people. For more than forty years, the hotel catered to railroad travelers. When the village was closed in 1922, the tavern became a private residence, but was reopened as a bed and breakfast in 1992 and is operated by the Shaker Museum today.

What would be more natural if you're visiting the Shaker Museum than to stay at the Shaker Tavern Inn? In fact, a stay at the inn includes free admission to the museum. The attractive high-ceilinged downstairs rooms are occupied by innkeeper Jo Ann Moody's quarters and dining rooms used for special events. Upstairs, a guest common room with a television and six bedrooms are furnished with Victorian-era antiques. Although simple, these pieces are all more opulent than the Shakers would have ever used for themselves. Most of the beds are queen size and boast carved, high-back headboards. Many of the carved dressers have marble tops. Several rooms feature decorative fireplaces, and most have private baths (some down the hall).

The Shakers started their strenuous day with a substantial meal. Guests here can do the same even if they're going to do nothing more physical than wander through the museum. Breakfasts vary but might consist of an entree such as German pancakes, an egg casserole, or sausage and eggs accompanied by hash browns and biscuits. Evening meals are available for guests at an additional fee.

Given the hotel's proximity to the railroad tracks, we had some concern about noise, but Jo Ann assured us that trains only come through at 8:30 A.M. and 2:30 P.M.; indeed, guests actually enjoy their passing. At all other times of the day, you can gaze endlessly across the tracks into the beautiful country setting.

What's Nearby South Union

South Union offers an important museum dedicated to the former Shaker village that existed here from 1807 to 1922. You can see the nation's largest collection of Shaker furniture and visit the last Shaker post office in the country, where you can still mail a letter with the South Union Shaker Village postmark. Throughout the year are special events: Shaker Farm Day, South Union Seminar, November Shaker Breakfast, Southern Furniture Symposium, and Christmas at Shaker-town—although be aware that the town's major attraction, the Shaker Museum, is only open March 1 through December 1.

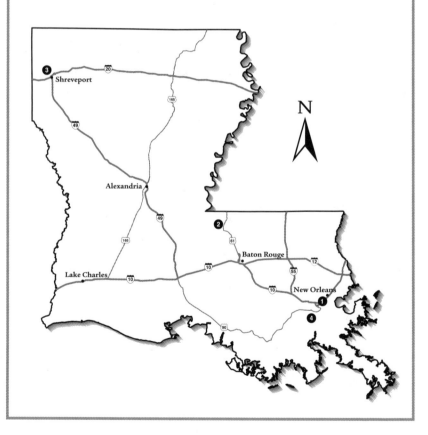

Louisiana

Numbers on map refer to towns numbered below.

The Melrose Mansion

937 Esplanade Avenue
New Orleans, Louisiana 70116
(504) 944–2255 or (800) 650–3323;
fax (504) 945–1794

E-MAIL: melrosemansion@worldnet.att.net

WEB SITE: www.melrosemansion.com

INNKEEPER: Sidney Torres

ROOMS: 8 rooms and suites; all with
private bath, robes, telephone, cable TV; 4 with whirlpool tub; some with
ceiling fan, deck or balcony, wet bar; wheelchair access

ON THE GROUNDS: Courtyard, patio, swimming pool

RATES: $250 to $425 single or double, including Creole breakfast and
afternoon refreshments; parking is an additional $12 per day; three-
night minimum stay on weekends; minimum stays and full prepayment
for special events such as Mardi Gras, Jazz Festival, New Year's Eve

CREDIT CARDS ACCEPTED? Yes

OPEN: Year-round

HOW TO GET THERE: Exit from I–10 onto Esplanade and follow it to the corner of Burgundy. Melrose Mansion is on your left.

The winner of dozens of accolades from national magazines and hotel rating services, sumptuous Melrose Mansion is a charming Victorian built
in 1884 at the edge of the French Quarter. Its flamboyant architecture
shows evidence of Queen Anne, Second Empire, and Victorian Gothic influences. In contrast to the Quarter's stucco construction and ornate iron balconies, Melrose showcases stately white-columned first- and second-story
verandas and a quirky three-story square corner tower with a peaked roof.
Restored to perfection and offering all the amenities of a grand hotel, this
little gem of a guest house provides the intimacy of a fine New Orleans
home. Fine old architectural details such as original mantels, hardwood
floors, ceiling medallions, and stained-glass windows characterize the public rooms and guest rooms. Although the ambience is formal, the mood is
relaxed and friendly.

One of the most magnificent accommodations in the city, the
Donecio Suite is the honeymoon suite to end all honeymoon suites. One
writer described it as taking romance to new heights. Light pours in

through the tall windows to brighten the high-ceilinged rooms and spotlight the king-size four-poster rice bed and beautiful antiques. Step out onto your own balcony to get a bird's-eye view of Esplanade Avenue and the French Quarter. But it's this suite's ivory marble bathroom that's the real showstopper. Located in the square tower, it boasts a step-in whirlpool tub, separate shower, vanity, and wet bar as well as views of the French Quarter's rooftops.

A chronicle of the Donecio Suite's attractions isn't meant to denigrate any of the other superb accommodations, each of which is exceptional in its own way. Resplendent with an eclectic sampling of styles, they all feature rice, carved, sleigh, or iron beds, Victorian antiques, armoires, seating areas, wet bars, and lavishly appointed bathrooms. There are luxurious little touches: fresh flowers in the rooms, Caswell-Massey toiletries, plush robes, and down pillows. Miss Kitty's Room and the Prince Edward Suite share a balcony. Each of the four suites boasts a whirlpool bath. The only room separate from the mansion is the Parc Henry Suite, which is found above the original carriage house and features a view of the pool and the French Quarter skyline.

Melrose guests arise each morning to an expanded Creole breakfast of hot butter muffins, quiche, yogurt, bagels, fruit salad medley, juice, and tea or freshly ground coffee flavored with hazelnut cream. You may join your fellow guests in the parlor or request room service the night before. Cocktails and hors d'oeuvres are served in the parlor—a formal room with tall French windows that overlook the lushly landscaped grounds—in the late afternoon or early evening. The Melrose also offers an honor bar, a wine cellar, mixers, and ice for your convenience. A twenty-four-hour concierge can help you with other requests.

All guests have the use of the Sol Owens Suite, a fitness and health area with a life cycle, treadmill, Stairmaster, and weight machine along with a television, workout videos, and a comfortable lounge area. A variety of massages, manicures, and pedicures is offered here with twenty-four-hour reservations. Adjacent to it, the third-floor turret has a sitting area perfect for reading a good book. Located on stately Esplanade Avenue, the bed and breakfast is an easy stroll from the attractions of the French Quarter. When you're exhausted from all the shopping, eating, and partying in the Big Easy, imagine languid afternoons sipping cool drinks on the tropical patio or splashing in the heated pool, both of which provide year-round relaxation.

Visit the famous French Quarter and browse its antiques shops, art galleries, and boutiques. Then visit Aquarium of the Americas. If you desire to travel by streetcar, take the St. Charles Streetcar from Canal Street and pass through the Garden District's lovely villas and mansions. Visit Audubon Zoo and Audubon Park. At the park you can enjoy a nice picnic or a game of tennis or golf. If you're looking for great shopping and food, visit Magazine Street's stretch of shops, galleries, and restaurants.

Sully Mansion

2631 Prytania Street
New Orleans, Louisiana 70130
(504) 891-0457; fax (504) 899-7237

E-MAIL: sully-mansion@travelbase.com

WEB SITE: www.sullymansion.com

INNKEEPER: Maralee Prigmore

ROOMS: 5 rooms and 2 suites; all with private bath, telephone, TV, decorative fireplace; some with ceiling fan

ON THE GROUNDS: Veranda

RATES: $89 to $275 single or double, including continental-plus breakfast and complimentary beverages

CREDIT CARDS ACCEPTED? Yes

OPEN: Year-round

HOW TO GET THERE: Take I-10 into downtown New Orleans, and US Business 90 off the ramp. Follow US Business 90 to the St. Charles exit and turn south onto St. Charles. Follow it to First Street in the Garden District. Turn left onto First. Go 1 block and turn left onto Prytania. The B&B is on your right.

About the Sully Mansion, the *Houston Chronicle* wrote, "This is New Orleans the way it should be." We couldn't agree more. A beautiful house, a quiet neighborhood slightly away from the hubbub of the French Quarter but within easy access of it, and superb service—what more could you ask for a visit to the Big Easy?

Maralee has very high expectations of her staff and has been known to fire them all if her standards—such as making sure the pillows are fluffed and the bathrooms absolutely spotless—aren't being met. You can only benefit from her philosophy that guests deserve nothing but the best. She's been offering bed-and-breakfast accommodations since 1984 and Sully Mansion is the only true B&B (as opposed to an inn) in New Orleans's beautiful Garden District.

The magnificent Queen Anne–style house itself was designed by renowned architect Thomas Sully in 1890, and in fact is the best preserved of the few surviving Sullys in New Orleans. You know you're in for something special as soon as you start up the graceful front steps leading to the imposing wraparound porch. Inside, among the outstanding architectural features restored to their original splendor are a grand staircase, stained-glass windows, ornate ceiling medallions, heart-pine floors, 14-foot ceilings, and marble vanities in the bathroom or dressing room. In addition to the elegant backdrop of the mansion, to which she has added exquisite antiques and art, Maralee's done things like putting in a fifty-five-gallon water heater for every two rooms to assure that her guests always have plenty of hot water.

Beautiful guest rooms, named for colors, are naturally enough decorated in hues of their namesakes. The formality of each is enhanced by a four-poster bed, a brass or crystal chandelier, elegant bed coverings, dramatic window treatments, and, something we especially like, good reading light—not only on both sides of the bed, but on the desk or by the comfortable chairs as well.

Awaken after a divine night's sleep to a bountiful continental-plus breakfast served using silver, china, and crystal. Just about every B&B brags about its fresh-baked breakfast products, but not many go as far as Maralee to provide quality baked goods. She has a French Quarter bakery deliver right-from-the-oven croissants each morning. In addition, there's a hot entree such as angel fluff from a Greenbriar recipe or omelettes as well as cereal, fresh fruit and juice, and hot beverages.

The Sully Mansion's ideal location in the heart of New Orleans's historic Garden District is within easy walking distance of the historic St. Charles Streetcar, which will whisk you to all the city's attractions.

What's Nearby New Orleans

See page 244 for what's nearby New Orleans.

Butler Greenwood Plantation

8345 US 61

St. Francisville, Louisiana 70775

(225) 635-6312; fax (225) 635-6370

WEB SITE: www.butlergreenwood.com

INNKEEPER: Anne Butler

ROOMS: 6 cottages; all with private bath with double whirlpool tub, full or partial kitchen, cable TV, porch or deck, telephone jacks; 3 with wood-burning fireplace; ask about pets

ON THE GROUNDS: Formal and sunken gardens, nature walk, pool, gift shop, hot-air balloon rides by reservation

RATES: $100 to $110 double, including continental breakfast and tour of home

CREDIT CARDS ACCEPTED? Yes

OPEN: Year-round

HOW TO GET THERE: From New Orleans, take I–10 toward Baton Rouge, then I–110 north to the end, where it becomes US 61. Follow it through St. Francisville; 2.5 miles north of town is the plantation.

A delightfully different bed and breakfast, Butler Greenwood Plantation, which is located on the fabled Great River Road along the Mississippi River, offers six cute, private, self-sufficient cottages scattered across the peaceful landscaped grounds. The main house was built (beginning in the 1790s) for the climate: It features lots of shade trees, good cross-ventilation, and broad wraparound galleries. Filled with fine antiques collected by eight generations of the same family, it is notable for one of the finest original formal Victorian parlors in the South. Its twelve-piece set of rosewood furniture boasts its original scarlet upholstery. Setting the backdrop are original scarlet lambrequins gracing floor-to-ceiling windows. French pier mirrors, a marble mantel, Sevres vases and lamps, floral Belgian carpets, and family portraits are well-preserved relics of a bygone era. Throughout the house are priceless antiques, including a rare 1855 French Pleyel concert piano and several Prudent Mallard four-poster beds. Don't leave without taking a tour.

Guest accommodations are found in historic and recently constructed outbuildings. The brick Old Kitchen was built in 1796. Amazingly, it served as the main kitchen for the plantation until 1962. For generations food was

cooked on an open hearth, then on a woodstove. Today the history-filled building still has exposed beams, but skylights make it light and airy. The nineteenth-century Cook's Cottage, where the plantation's cook lived, features a working fireplace, a full kitchen, and a full bath with a whirlpool tub. You'll want to while away some time on the old-fashioned swing on the pint-size front porch.

The Gazebo is a six-sided enclosed building with 9-foot-tall, arched, antique stained-glass church windows on three sides. Surrounded by a deck, the cottage overlooks the pond, where you might see ducks, geese, and herons. Inside, a king-size bed, whirlpool tub, and kitchenette make this a romantic hideaway. You'll head right for the hammock on the gingerbread-trimmed porch of the Pond House. You guessed it—it overlooks a pond, too. A large deck on the other side of the cottage overlooks a meadow where deer browse in the early morning and late evening.

A whole wall of glass looking into the forest and a wonderful three-level deck at the edge of a steep wooded ravine characterize the Treehouse, a kind of garden-shed-like building with a steeply pitched roof. A king-size four-poster bed with hand-turned posts made from old cypress beams is the showpiece of the interior, but the working fireplace, full kitchen, and whirlpool tub make this another popular choice.

The most requested accommodation, however, is the Dovecote, a three-story shingled windmill with a big deck overlooking a wooded ravine. It has two bedrooms—one with a king-size mahogany four-poster bed and two baths, the other with a whirlpool tub, a working fireplace, and a full kitchen.

No matter which cottage you choose, the ingredients of a continental breakfast are already on hand so you can enjoy your meal on your own schedule. Fifty acres of landscaped grounds surround the main house and cottages. When conditions are just right, shafts of sunlight stream through the trees and Spanish moss, creating an otherwordly ambience. Antebellum formal and sunken gardens bloom with ancient camellias and azaleas, hydrangeas, sweet olives, and magnolias. Interspersed among the boxwood parterres and old-fashioned garden plants are a whimsical Victorian gazebo, urns, and benches. Birdhouses attract brightly colored feathered friends. Thousands more wild acres permit frequent sightings of wildlife.

What's Nearby St. Francisville

If you think small towns are for the birds, then you may be on to something. John James Audubon conducted many of his famous bird studies while working in this area as a tutor. Now you can visit the Audubon

State Commemmorative Area and stop in the Oakley House, a restored museum which houses several first-edition Audubon prints. The Oakley House is surrounded by gardens, nature trails, and a wildlife sanctuary. If you're visiting in May, find out about the Audubon Pilgrimage, which leads guided tours of plantation homes and gardens, all in St. Francisville.

Another Recommended B&B in St. Francisville

Greenwood Plantation B&B, a new bed and breakfast on the grounds near the Greek Revival mansion, offers 12 rooms; P.O. Box 1800, St. Francisville, LA 70775; (225) 655–3850.

Myrtles Plantation

7747 US 61
St. Francisville, Louisiana 70775
(225) 635-6277 or (800) 809-0565;
fax (225) 635-5837

INNKEEPERS: John and Teeta Moss

ROOMS: 10; all with private bath, claw-foot tub

ON THE GROUNDS: Verandas, lawn, restaurant

RATES: $95 to $195, including continental breakfast and a historical tour of the house; $7 for ghost tour given Friday and Saturday nights after dark

CREDIT CARDS ACCEPTED? Yes

OPEN: Year-round

HOW TO GET THERE: The Myrtles is on US 61, 1 mile north of its intersection with LA 10.

It was thickening twilight and the heavy rain had stopped, but trickles of water still ran off the Spanish moss dripping from the ancient live oaks that surrounded the darkened old French-style plantation house. Suddenly an eerie, flickering light appeared inside the house. "What's you want?" a husky female voice inquired. "Dis ain't no place to be at night. Too many people died here."

This was our introduction to the Myrtles, reputed to be haunted by so many ghosts that it has been named America's Most Haunted House by the

Smithsonian Institution and the *Wall Street Journal*, as well as being featured on several television programs. (Scientists measured, among other things, magnetic fields and temperature and pressure gradients before reaching this conclusion.) We had arrived for a ghost tour, to be followed by an overnight stay if we were brave enough.

Originally built in 1796, the house has a history of elegance and intrigue. Ten murders have occurred here, and a well on the property is said to hold the bodies of hundreds of slaves. Of the five bedrooms in the house, deaths have occurred in four. The fifth was the master suite of an owner who made it only to the top of the stairs before dying of a gunshot wound.

Innocent enough looking, the 12,000-square-foot antebellum cottage (considered small in an era when houses of up to 55,000 square feet were being built nearby) sits on a hill well back from the road in deep shadows created by immense magnolias and live oaks. The exterior is characterized by magnificent double dormers and lacy iron grillwork on the 120-foot-long veranda. Flickering wraithlike shadows cast by tendrils of Spanish moss drifting in the breeze intensify the eerie mood. Behind the house, a vast lawn stretches back to the gloom of a dark pond and deep woods.

Our raconteur guide took us on a tour of the darkened house by the light of one candle while recounting spine-tingling details of all the gory deaths. With quivering apprehension, we agreed to stay for the night. Once the lights were flicked on, the house was bathed in soft, friendly light. All the goblins disappeared until another night, and the house was transformed into an intimate inn with elaborate plaster friezework and faux bois as well as lovely antique furnishings and art treasures—many of French influence.

The members of our group retired to the front and back rocker-lined verandas with mint juleps to share our own mystical experiences with each other, and we all went to bed that night hoping for some sign from beyond—just not one that was too scary. Much to our disappointment, nothing untoward happened beyond the pranks of one group member, who delighted in jumping out from behind doors or putting things in people's beds. Because everyone yearned to be spooked, the jokes were taken in good humor.

In addition to the elegant guest rooms in the main house, there's a garden cottage that contains several more rooms and a cozy restaurant. Nothing unusual has ever been reported to have happened in the garden cottage, so if you're a little squeamish about the possibility of ghosts, perhaps you'd be more comfortable in one of those rooms. Kean's Carriage House Restaurant serves lunch and dinner Wednesday through Saturday, along with Sunday brunch. The cuisine is traditional Louisiana, with choices such as gumbo, étouffée, and wild duck.

Assuming that you've had an uneventful night, you'll awaken refreshed and ready for a breakfast of muffins, pecan spins, fresh biscuits, fresh fruit and juices, and hot beverages.

What's Nearby St. Francisville

See page 247 for what's nearby St. Francisville.

Rosedown Plantation B&B

12501 LA 10
St. Francisville, Louisiana 70775
(225) 635-3332

INNKEEPERS: Staff

ROOMS: 13; all with private bath

ON THE GROUNDS: 28 acres of gardens, swimming pool, tennis court

RATES: $95 to $145 double, including continental breakfast

CREDIT CARDS ACCEPTED? Yes

OPEN: Year-round

HOW TO GET THERE: The plantation is located at the intersection of US 61 North and LA 10.

We went to Rosedown Plantation to see its world-famous gardens—considered among the five most important historic gardens in the nation—but fell in love with the mansion and B&B accommodations. A monument to the splendor of the Old South, Rosedown was built by the Turnbulls in 1835 and named for a play they had seen on their European honeymoon. The majestic, many-columned house sits at the end of an alley of ancient oaks; twenty-eight acres of gardens stretch out around it, with 2,000 untamed acres beyond. This is the epitome of the Southern way of life long past.

Modeled after the gardens of seventeenth-century Versailles, Rosedown's formal gardens feature statuary, gazebos, and other garden ornaments. The Turnbulls were among the first Southerners to import azaleas, camellias, and other Oriental flora. Mrs. Turnbull tended the gardens herself and kept a meticulous journal from which the restoration was made. Naturally, a portion of the gardens is devoted to roses.

The family's wealth was so vast that they owned a racetrack and their own steamboat, with enough space on it for horses and packs of hunting dogs. As with many Old South families, their fortunes declined after the Civil War, although family members lived in the house until the last descendant died in the 1950s. The mansion had never been modernized with electricity and by that time it and the gardens were decaying badly, but the original family furniture was still intact. Then Catherine Fondren Underwood bought the property and restored the house and gardens, opening them to the public.

The most convenient way to see the gardens and the plantation house at your leisure is to stay right on the property, where bed-and-breakfast rooms are located in the 1950s house built for the Underwood family to live in during the renovations. Guest rooms, which are decorated in the manner of the bedrooms in the main house, feature private baths and queen-size beds—some of them romantic canopy beds. Although the guest house has no telephones or television, guests enjoy the swimming pool and tennis court. A minimal continental breakfast of muffins, hot beverages, and juice is offered in the morning. This is definitely an inn where the property itself far outshines the accommodations.

What's Nearby St. Francisville.

See page 247 for what's nearby St. Francisville.

Fairfield Place Bed and Breakfast Inn

2221 Fairfield Avenue
Shreveport, Louisiana 71104
(318) 222-0048; fax (318) 226-0631

E-MAIL: Via Web site

WEB SITE: www.fairfieldbandb.com

INNKEEPER: Jane Lipscomb

ROOMS: 11; all with private bath, telephone with data port, TV, clock radio, ceiling fan, hair dryer, robes, refrigerator, cold drinks, fruit; some rooms have whirlpool bath

ON THE GROUNDS: Verandas, courtyard, terraced and walled gardens

RATES: $112 to $250 double, including full breakfast and afternoon tea; $14 for each additional person in the room

CREDIT CARDS ACCEPTED? Yes

OPEN: Year-round

HOW TO GET THERE: From I-20 West, take the Fairfield Avenue exit and turn left onto Fairfield Avenue. The inn is about 11 blocks on your left. From I-20 East, take the Line Avenue exit and turn right onto Jordan Street, then left onto Fairfield. The inn is about 7 blocks ahead on your left.

We met Janie about ten years ago at her turn-of-the-century Victorian bed and breakfast. She was up to her elbows in wallpaper paste—papering the outside of a claw-foot tub with Victorian-vintage wallpaper to match the adjoining room. What a neat idea! We've seen it copied since, but Janie was the first. This little project is just one of many that this dynamo of artistic and business acumen dives into.

Since we first met her, Janie has acquired the house next door, another great 1890s Victorian home—this one Greek Revival—from its ninety-nine-year-old owner, who finally decided that he needed a smaller place. "The property was covered with thornbushes—a little like Sleeping Beauty's castle—and while the house was wonderful, I don't think they ever threw anything out. We found empty canned-ham cans from what must have been a weekly tradition of Sunday dinners that dated back forty-plus years. Luckily, they had all been washed out."

It took four months simply to get the yard and gardens cut back and the house emptied out; only then could Janie start the process of refurbishing and redecorating the fine old home to provide additional guest rooms as well as meeting and banquet space. Now the house and enlarged grounds are an integral part of this great property, which includes a full commercial kitchen where the internationally known classical/Cajun/Creole chef John Foles performed his magic last year while taping an episode of his PBS program at Fairfield Place.

Janie was also the first B&B owner to point out to us the tremendous potential there is for matching up business travelers—particularly businesswomen—with B&Bs. Any vacationer will be enthralled by Janie's Victorian rooms and luxury suites in the two spacious, casually elegant, turn-of-the-century homes in the historic Fairfield-Highland district, but she also encourages business travelers to stay by providing an elegant, relaxing alternative to standard lodging.

Unlike anonymous, standard-issue, cookie-cutter hotels where you keep to your room and reluctantly awaken in confusion about where you are, at Fairfield Place you're a valued individual.

Mingle with other guests in the library, which is well stocked with books by Louisiana writers; in the richly decorated parlor with its baby grand piano; on the first- and second-story verandas; in the New Orleans–style courtyard; or in the acre and a half of terraced and walled gardens.

Sleep as if on a cloud on a hypoallergenic feather bed, then awaken eagerly knowing that you're cared about and pampered as an individual. King- or queen-size beds—some of them romantic four-posters—European and American antiques, paintings by Louisiana artists, Bradbury & Bradbury wallpapers, and writing desks characterize the bedchambers. Modern creature comforts include telephone, television, clock radio, ceiling fan, hair dryer, thick robes, and refrigerator, as well as cold drinks, fruit, books, and magazines. Some suites boast whirlpool baths and towel warmers.

A full gourmet breakfast is served in the dining room and might include Cajun coffee, fresh fruits and juices, a breakfast casserole, muffins, and pastries.

It's hard to guess what Janie will take on as her next project, but rumor has it that one of her associates is in London attending a Cordon Bleu cooking school.

What's Nearby Shreveport

Shreveport is a big city with big entertainment. Because of its gambling casinos and live music and shows, Shreveport has been compared to Las Vegas. Shreveport also has its share of history. Visit the historical Highland-Fairfield area's grand mansions. Stop by the Louisiana State Fairgrounds and Louisiana State Exhibit Museum. Switch gears and look into the future at Shreveport's Sci-Port Discovery Center, located on the Riverfront. Then travel back into the past at the Spring Street Historical Museum. Finally, after you're done painting the town red, visit the R. W. Norton Art Gallery and see some of the largest collections of American western paintings.

Oak Alley Plantation, Restaurant and Inn

3645 Highway 18 (Great River Road)
Vacherie, Louisiana 70090
(225) 265-2151 or (800) 44-ALLEY;
fax (225) 265-2626

E-MAIL: oakalleyplantation@worldnet.att.net
WEB SITE: www.oakalleyplantation.com
INNKEEPER: Zeb Mayhew Jr., owner

ROOMS: 4 cottages, 5 units; all with private bath, clock radio, ceiling fan; only the restaurant and the first floor of the mansion are wheelchair accessible

ON THE GROUNDS: Mansion, lawns, restaurant, gift shop

RATES: $95 to $125 double, including full breakfast; each additional person $15; children younger than twelve stay free; the tour of the house is an additional $8 for adults

CREDIT CARDS ACCEPTED? Yes

OPEN: Year-round, although the mansion is closed Thanksgiving, Christmas, and New Year's Days as well as Mardi Gras, and breakfast is not served in the restaurant on those days (continental breakfast is left in the cottages)

HOW TO GET THERE: From Baton Rouge, take I-10 east to exit 194, Lutcher/Mississippi River Bridge. Turn right onto LA 641 South, which becomes County Road 3213. Continue over the Veterans Memorial Bridge (also known as the Gramercy/Wallace Bridge) and turn left onto LA 18. Go 7.5 miles to Oak Alley Plantation. From New Orleans, take I-10 West to exit 194, Gramercy. Turn left onto LA 641 and follow the previous directions.

Oak Alley Plantation is known as the Grande Dame of the Great River Road because of the spectacular ¼-mile canopy of giant 300-year-old live oak trees over an avenue leading up to the magnificent white-columned Greek Revival mansion. In the early 1700s a French settler planted the twenty-eight trees in two rows of fourteen each 80 feet apart leading from the river. By 1722, when Capuchin priests arrived in the area to establish a settlement, the young trees had already achieved impressive stature.

It wasn't until 1837 that a wealthy French Creole sugar planter from New Orleans began construction on a house at the head of the alley of trees. When it was completed in 1839, its most notable feature was the stately parade of twenty-eight columns surrounding the house. Although Celine Roman, the first mistress of the house, called it Bon Sejour (pleasant sojourns), what stuck was the popularly used name given to it by locals, Oak Alley.

We were initially disappointed to learn that the bed-and-breakfast accommodations are offered not in the main house but in six plain turn-of-the-century Creole cottages scattered about the grounds. We were reassured once we saw the romantic interiors, though. Four-poster or iron beds, other antiques, floral fabrics used for the bed coverings and window treatments, and appropriate art and accessories imbue the guest rooms with an upscale nineteenth-century flavor. Cottage 3 boasts a claw-foot tub, and its bed is romantically draped with mosquito netting. Surely none of the plantation

Oak Alley Plantation's Famous Pralines

3 cans evaporated milk
1 cup (2 sticks) butter
8 cups sugar
8 cups shelled pecans
⅓ cup vanilla extract

Combine milk, butter, and sugar in a saucepan. Add the vanilla. Cook over high heat to a rolling boil. Lower the temperature to medium and continue to boil for 20 minutes, stirring constantly. Remove from heat. Add the pecans and stir until mixture thickens. Quickly drop onto greased foil. Let cool.

workers who once inhabited these cottages ever lived this well! Most of the cottages feature one or more bedrooms, a sitting room with a sofabed, a kitchen, a deck or screened porch, and one bathroom, so they are best shared by families or groups of friends traveling together.

A full country breakfast of Southern favorites such as beignets, grits, eggs, bacon and ham, fresh fruit, and hot beverages is served in the Oak Alley Restaurant, which is also open for lunch daily. Located in another Creole cottage, the restaurant serves a wide selection of traditional Cajun and Creole dishes. Stop in the restaurant's gift shop for a wide variety of Louisiana and Oak Alley souvenirs, handmade collectibles, cookbooks, regional photography, and books on the architecture, history, and culture of the region.

While you're staying at Oak Alley, you'll want to take a tour of the plantation house (additional cost). These are given by costumed docents and last about forty minutes. Be sure to try one of the famous mint juleps at the souvenir table at the back door of the mansion. You can also take a leisurely stroll of the grounds or along the Mississippi River levee and relax on your deck or screened-in porch.

What's Nearby Vacherie

Visit local gardens and plantations in the area. Or take a day trip to St. Francisville and New Orleans. See "What's Nearby St. Francisville" and "What's Nearby New Orleans."

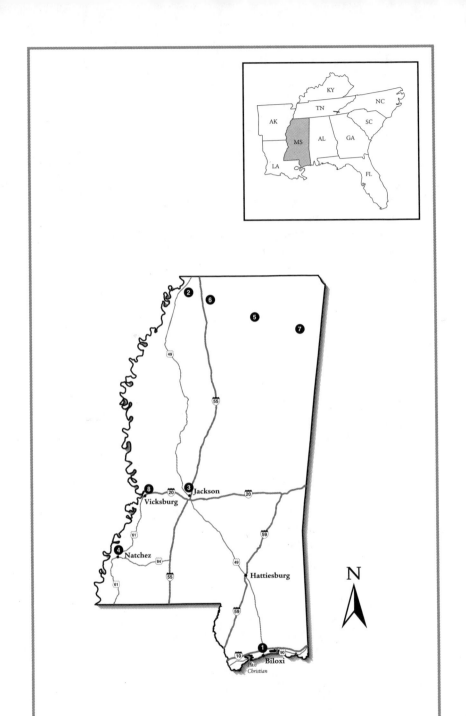

Mississippi

Numbers on map refer to towns numbered below.

Green Oaks B&B

580 Beach Boulevard
Biloxi, Mississippi 39530
(228) 436–6257 or (888) 436–6257; fax (228) 436–6255

E-MAIL: greenoaks4@aol.com

WEB SITE: www.gcww.com

INNKEEPERS: Oliver and Jennifer Diaz

ROOMS: 8; all with private bath, cable TV, telephone with data port

ON THE GROUNDS: Veranda, landscaped lawns, beach, casino shuttle bus that stops at the door

RATES: $88 to $155, including breakfast, afternoon tea, mint juleps, and snacks; $15 for each additional person in the room

CREDIT CARDS ACCEPTED? Yes

OPEN: Year-round

HOW TO GET THERE: Green Oaks is centrally located in Biloxi between New Orleans and Mobile. Take I–10 to I–110 South. Turn east onto US 90 (Beach Boulevard). The inn is located 1 mile east between Bellman Avenue and Lee Street. Approaching from the west on Beach Boulevard, the inn is 2 miles east of the Biloxi Lighthouse.

Considered Biloxi's finest example of period architecture, this circa-1826 home is the oldest remaining beachfront residence and is listed on the National Register of Historic Places. Elegantly appointed with an impressive collection of fine period furnishings, including many family heirlooms, the house and historic outbuildings provide eight guest rooms and suites. Each is named for a member of Judge Diaz's family—which dates back to 1700, when his first ancestor arrived on the Mississippi Gulf Coast with Pierre Le Moyne, Sieur d'Iberville, on his second voyage to the area.

The luxurious guest chambers are appointed with massive four-poster, full-tester, and heavily carved beds. The most popular room is the Carquot, with French doors that afford a breathtaking view of the Gulf of Mexico and provide access to the south gallery. In addition, this room boasts 14-foot ceilings, a spectacular mahogany full-tester bed carved by Clee, a bath with a full-body shower, and a fireplace, but every room has its own specialty. In the main house the Bosarge Room features a fireplace; the Ladner Room its original chandelier and a claw-foot tub; the Fountain room brick walls and an antique brass and wrought-iron bed. In the guest cottage the Fayard Room has screened doors onto the front porch and a claw-foot tub;

the Ryan Room boasts hand-stenciled walls while the Moran Room is actually a three-room suite.

Take a leisurely, romantic stroll around the two acres of landscaped grounds with twenty-eight live oaks overlooking the beach and Gulf of Mexico, or relax on the veranda with its unparalleled views.

Breakfast is an event. Gourmet selections are served using china, crystal, and silver in the dining room overlooking the Gulf. There are always two to three courses—perhaps eggs Diane, grits Jeff Davis, Cajun sausage, or poached eggs topped with hollandaise sauce and lump crabmeat and accompanied by steamed asparagus, all topped off with something like baked pears with caramel sauce or bananas Foster. All the delicious breads are home baked.

In the late afternoon after a day of activity or inactivity, a traditional English tea is served with at least two sweet and two savory selections.

What's Nearby Biloxi

Forget about those Biloxi blues. Your spirits will be flying high, because there's simply so much to see and do here. Biloxi is considered a resort town, probably because of its many beaches and gambling casinos. Another tourist attraction is the 65-foot Biloxi lighthouse, which was built in 1848. To learn more about Biloxi's history, visit a very beautiful waterfront estate, Beauvoir, which was once home to Confederate President Jefferson Davis.

Magnolia Grove Bed and Breakfast

140 East Commerce Street
Hernando, Mississippi 38632
(601) 429-2626; fax (601) 429-1585

E-MAIL: bobwolfe@worldnet.att.net

WEB SITE: www.magnoliagrove.com

INNKEEPERS: Phyllis and Bob Wolfe

ROOMS: 4; all with private bath, cable TV, clock; 3 with gas-log fireplace; one with hookup for computer

ON THE GROUNDS: Verandas, landscaped lawns

RATES: $85 to $100 double, including full breakfast and refreshments

CREDIT CARDS ACCEPTED? Yes

OPEN: Year-round

NOTE: Commercial neighborhood

HOW TO GET THERE: From I-55, take exit 280, Hernando, and go 0.6 mile west (toward town) on Commerce Street. Magnolia Grove is on your right.

This three-acre estate is an oasis of privacy in an area that has gradually turned commercial with its proximity to I-55. Just turn into Magnolia Grove's drive and you'll leave the hustle-bustle world far behind for the charm of the turn of the century when life moved at a much more leisurely pace. Ancient magnolias and an abundance of other trees shield guests from the twentieth century. The Greek Revival mansion is everything you'd expect from the Old South. Four soaring pillars support a temple-pedimented portico, under which are a graceful second-story balcony and an inviting front door framed by a fan light and sidelights. Inside 12-foot ceilings, hardwood floors, pocket doors, transoms, a graceful staircase, beautiful fireplaces, and stained-glass have been retained without sacrificing any of today's modern comforts. Most of the wallpapers are original.

When current owners Phyllis and Bob—who are, by the way, only the third owners—were poking around in the attic, they found a virtual treasure trove of material about the house. It was built in 1900 by the Williams family, one of whose daughters was named Ladye Eugenia Williams. Love letters the Wolfes discovered reveal that in 1916, Ladye was in love with a young man of whom her parents didn't approve. They refused to let her marry him; as a result, she never married and became a recluse. When she died in 1982 at the age of ninety-two, she willed the property to the Methodist Church, which eventually sold it to the Wolfes in 1997. You can see Miss Ladye's calling cards on a silver tray in the foyer. One of the rooms is named in her honor.

Each of the four generously proportioned guest rooms has a private bath—two sport claw-foot tubs. Beautifully furnished in antiques, each bedchamber has its own personality. Among the special features in the Rose Room are a ruby cut-glass chandelier, a pair of Miss Ladye's tiny boots, a gas-log fireplace, and an additional daybed. An iron canopy bed, a corner gas-log fireplace, and a porcelain chandelier identify the Ladye Magnolia. Cole's Cottage features a gas-log fireplace and a private porch as well as Bob's grandmother's bedroom suite and his mother's prom dress. Guests like to gather in the two formal parlors or outdoors on one of the porches. Right now the fourth room is called Golfer's Haven and sports golf prints and antique clubs, but Phyllis says she's going to redecorate, so stay tuned.

Early risers may want to slip into the butler's pantry to get some coffee, which they can enjoy in the formal parlor, the informal upstairs sitting room, or the cheery little porch off the dining room. Afterward they can enjoy a sumptuous meal in the elegant formal dining room. Phyllis, who loves to cook and has her own cookbook, might serve such specialties as hot crab casserole or apricot French toast with generous accompaniments. With prior arrangements and at an additional fee, she'll prepare romantic private candlelight dinners for two including such entrees as catfish Lafitte, chicken breast, and pork tenderloin. Massage therapy can also be arranged on request.

What's Nearby Hernando

Hernando has been described as a quaint, friendly town. It is known for its abundance of antiques shops and lovely antebellum homes. With all that charm, Hernando is just ten minutes away from the city of Memphis. This means you have an opportunity to explore Graceland, the Pyramid, and all the other great Memphis attractions.

Sassafras Inn Bed and Breakfast

785 Highway 51 South
Hernando, Mississippi 38632
(601) 429-5864 or (800) 882-1897

E-MAIL: From Web site

WEB SITE: www.memphis.to/ guest.html

INNKEEPERS: Francee' and Dennis McClanahan

ROOMS: 3 rooms and 1 cottage; all with private bath, TV with remote, clock radio, sound machine, soft drinks, and crackers; wheelchair access only in cottage; no unmarried couples or public consumption of alcohol

ON THE GROUNDS: Pool, hot tub, courtyard

RATES: $65 single, $95 to $110 double in the main house; cottage $165 to $225; all include full breakfast and treats in rooms. Additional person $20

CREDIT CARDS ACCEPTED? Yes

OPEN: Year-round

HOW TO GET THERE: Going south out of Memphis, take the Nesbit exit. Turn right at the stop sign and go 1 block to Highway 51. Turn left; the B&B is 2.5 miles on your right.

This is not your stereotypical bed and breakfast in a historic house or even a rustic lodge. Instead it's located in an English Tudor–style home built in 1985. Attractive as this may be, it's usually not our cup of tea, but this B&B deserves a more in-depth look. What makes it really special is the enclosed swimming pool and the honeymoon cottage.

Heart's Content is an apt name for the honeymoon hideaway. Located off by itself at the back of the property, it's reached across a small arched bridge outlined in tiny lights for an extra touch of romance. The octagonal building with its cupola, cathedral ceiling, and stained-glass is outfitted for a night of fantasy. A queen-size canopy rice bed opulently draped in lace dominates the bedroom, which has an entertainment center with a television, VCR, and CD player. The focal point of the bathroom is the two-person whirlpool tub. A refrigerator, microwave, and a selection of snacks means you lovebirds can create your own little cocoon and hardly ever have to venture outside unless you want to. More than likely, however, you'll want to enjoy the indoor pool.

The large free-form swimming pool is enclosed in a bright, airy Florida room, with a cathedral ceiling accented by stained-glass skylights. Pictures of playful whales and other aquatic creatures painted on the sides of the pool beckon you to join them. An eight-person hot tub can contain all the B&B guests at once, but more than likely you'll only have to share it with each other. For more playtime, the rec room is outfitted with a pool table, Ping-Pong table, jukebox, treadmill, and other fitness equipment.

Three cozy, tastefully decorated guests rooms in the main house offer a variety of accommodations. Each features a queen-size bed and a private bath. Carved or four-poster beds, floral wallpapers and fabrics, ornate lamps, and other appropriate accessories impart a Victorian look to each room. Of these guest chambers, the Skylight Room is the roomiest, providing space for a desk and a table and chairs. Its sloping ceilings create interesting little nooks.

Although it's hard to imagine that guests would want to gather or just read a good book anywhere other than the Florida room or the game room, the B&B also has a great room with comfortable leather sofas and a large-screen television. A full breakfast can be served in the formal dining room, at poolside, in the courtyard, or in your guest room.

Fairview Inn

734 Fairview Street
Jackson, Mississippi 39202
(601) 948–3429 or (888) 948–1908;
fax (601) 948–1203

E-MAIL: fairview@fairviewinn.com

WEB SITE: www.fairview.com

INNKEEPERS: Carol and Bill Simmons

ROOMS: 8 rooms and suites; all with private bath, telephone with data port and voice mail, TV, VCR, clock radio, hair dryer, robes; some with whirlpool bath and/or fireplace; 1 with wheelchair access

ON THE GROUNDS: Decks, hot tubs, porches, formal gardens

RATES: $115 to $165 double, including full breakfast, snacks, and complimentary wine; $15 for additional guests in the room

CREDIT CARDS ACCEPTED? Yes

OPEN: Year-round

HOW TO GET THERE: From I–55 South, take exit 98A. Go west on Woodrow Wilson Drive and turn left onto North State Street. Go left at the Medical Plaza Building onto Fairview. The inn is on your left. From I–55 North, take exit 96C; go west on Fortification Street to North State Street and turn right. Then turn right onto Fairview as above.

The first thing you'll notice when you drive up the sweeping circular drive is that this big white mansion, flanked by mature magnolias and crape myrtles, bears an uncanny resemblance to Mount Vernon. Owners Carol and Bill Simmons, in whose family the mansion has been since 1930, are quick to tell you, however, that the house (built in 1908) has significant differences with the famous president's house, although the subtleties were lost on us.

Located in Old Jackson near the State Capitol, both the main house and the carriage house are Colonial Revival, a style associated with formality and traditional Southern elegance. Classical detail and ordered proportions popularized by the famous designer and architect Palladio are readily apparent. The long, rectangular two-story, flat-roofed Georgian house is fronted by an immense portico supported by modified Corinthian columns.

Inside, the vast entry foyer seems to us more like a small ballroom, with gleaming floors, crystal chandeliers, and fireplaces. The study, which is virtually unchanged since 1908, features quartersawn oak paneling, Tiffany lamps, a Herschede grandfather clock, an impressive collection of miniature toy soldiers, important oil paintings, and an extensive Civil War library, including many first editions.

Guest rooms and suites are elegantly decorated with antiques and reproductions and given individual character by the use of lavish fabrics, accessories, and collectibles. In addition to all the modern conveniences, the rooms feature queen- or king-size beds as well as extra-special amenities including fine linens and upgraded toiletries. Some guest chambers boast whirlpool tubs and/or walk-in showers. The Hayloft, Tack, and Third Floor Suites offer ample sitting areas, while the Executive Suite has a separate library/sitting room. The Carriage House Suite is popular with honeymooners.

Among the popular places to spend some quiet time are the cheerful garden room with a piano, the porches, two decks with a hot tub, and the formal garden of box hedges and lilies where you can admire a replica of the statue of *La Baigneuse* by French sculptor Jean Baptiste Allegrain, the original of which is found in the Louvre.

A full Southern breakfast of bacon and eggs or French toast, grits, and biscuits is prepared to order and served at your convenience in the sunny Carriage Room, which connects the main house to the carriage house.

Fairview is the proud recipient of AAA's four-diamond designation. It was named *Country Inns* Inn of the Month in October 1994, and one of the magazine's Top Inns for 1994 (keep in mind that these accolades were earned in its first year of operation). It was also selected by the National Trust for Historic Preservation for inclusion in their 1998 calendar.

What's Nearby Jackson

Jackson is the capital city, rich in both history and attractions. Tour local landmarks like the oldest house in Jackson, The Oaks. Other historic sites are the Manship House, the Governor's Mansion and the Old Capitol, which houses the State Historical Museum. Breathe in more history by driving past Belhaven's old gardens and homes. If you're here in early February, check out the Dixie National Rodeo and Livestock Show, which features live performances by today's biggest country musicians.

Millsaps Buie House

628 North State Street
Jackson, Mississippi 39202
(601) 352–0221 or (800) 784–0221;
fax (601) 352–0221

INNKEEPERS: Judy Fenter, on-site inn-keeper; Mary McMillan, Jo Love Little, and Jim Love, owners

ROOMS: 10 rooms and 1 suite; all with private bath, telephone with data port, radio, TV, ceiling fan; some with decorative fireplaces, desks

ON THE GROUNDS: Gardens

RATES: $100 to 170 double, including Southern breakfast; each additional person in the room $15

CREDIT CARDS ACCEPTED? Yes

OPEN: Year-round

HOW TO GET THERE: From I–55, take the High Street exit. Go west to the fifth traffic light and turn right onto State Street. The inn is the fourth building on your left.

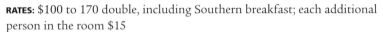

Two of our most indelible memories of the Millsaps Buie House are of the beautiful stained-glass window on the landing between the first and second floors, and of the delicious pralines that are left on your pillow when your bed is turned down at night.

Back in the 1880s when the Millsaps Buie House was constructed, the elite of Jackson built their mansions along State Street near the Capitol. This extraordinary house, with its impressive columned portico, was constructed for the colorful financier and philanthropist Major Reuben Webster Millsaps. A founder of Millsaps College, he was also an officer in the Confederate Army. At his death the mansion passed to his nephew Webster Millsaps Buie, whose widow lived in the house for more than fifty years. After an aborted scheme to sell the house to an oil company for use as its offices and a near-disastrous fire, three Buie heirs (two sisters and a brother) converted the family home into this wonderful inn—stately and formal, yet warm and inviting. You'll have realized from this recitation that the home has remained in the same family throughout its 112-year history—an incredible rarity in these days of far-flung families.

Created with the intent of providing a nineteenth-century urban retreat for twentieth-century travelers, the inn features 14-foot ceilings, hand-molded friezework, bay and stained-glass windows, highly polished newel posts and handrails, and sparkling chandeliers. Guests admire the artistry with which the foyer, library, parlor (with its grand piano), and dining room are furnished. If you're feeling more casual, you may prefer to relax on the screened porches, in the courtyard, or by wandering around the acre-and-a-half grounds.

Ten luxurious guest chambers and one suite are handsomely accoutred with well-chosen period pieces—including the half-tester bed of the founder himself in one—as well as elegant fabrics and rich colors. Rooms on the third floor have a more contemporary decor. Most sport queen- or king-size beds, several have a sleeping porch, one has a balcony, and one even boasts an observatory.

Breakfast is a very special meal that features a generous buffet of casseroles, cheese grits, breakfast meats, cereals, homemade breads and pastries, fresh fruits and juices, and hot beverages. In the late afternoon at social hour, wine and hot hors d'oeuvres are offered.

What's Nearby Jackson

See page 264 for what's nearby Jackson.

The Burn

712 North Union Street
Natchez, Mississippi 39120
(601) 442-1344 or (800) 654-8859;
fax (601) 445-0606

INNKEEPERS: Deborah and Larry Christensen, owners; Layne Taylor, innkeeper/manager

ROOMS: 7 rooms and suites; all with private bath, cable TV, robes, clock radio; some with gas-log fireplace

ON THE GROUNDS: Courtyard, veranda, pool, gardens

RATES: $120 to $200 single or double, including seated plantation-style breakfast, private tour, nightly turndown service, and welcome beverage; additional person $30

CREDIT CARDS ACCEPTED? Yes

OPEN: Year-round

HOW TO GET THERE: From John R. Junkin Drive, take Canal Street 11 blocks to Madison Street. Turn right and go 4 blocks to Union Street. Turn left. The bed and breakfast is in the second block on your left.

Even considering the excess of stunningly beautiful homes in Natchez, we feel The Burn deserves special mention. Built circa 1832 to 1836, it was Natchez's first Greek Revival residence. Originally constructed on one hundred acres within the city limits, The Burn was also the largest private estate in Natchez—and with 3,800 square feet of space on each of its three floors, it qualified as the city's largest private residence. Today the mansion sits on five acres and retains some of its original gardens. (The name, by the way, comes from a brook that once ran through the property and was known as Wee Burn to early Scottish settlers.)

Among The Burn's outstanding original features are its slate roof, leaded-glass windowpanes, interior and exterior walls of slave brick, cypress wallboards and floors, and plaster crown moldings and ceiling medallions. The exterior walls were covered with stucco; the interior were plastered.

The most outstanding interior feature is the free-flying semispiral staircase, made with cypress steps stained to match the mahogany banisters and railing. A cypress spine with ribs running to it supporting each stair tread permits each step below to support the step above until the steps turn back upon themselves, flying free until they attach to a cypress beam in the floor of the third-story hall.

Furnished with exquisite antiques and fine art, The Burn is one of the most visited homes in Natchez. In addition to offering tours, it is also the oldest B&B in Natchez. Superb sleeping accommodations are offered in the main house as well as the guest house, in a detached dependency or *garçonière* where the Walworths lived while The Burn was being built. Of the three bedchambers in the mansion, Sarah is the most romantic and most often-photographed bedroom in Natchez. Its primary attractions are the majestic rosewood full-tester bed draped with bed hangings, separate sitting rooms, and three walls of windows. Lucy, located on the ground floor of the mansion, has pecky cypress ceilings and a cypress tester bed as well as a beautifully carved white marble mantel. Located on the third floor of the mansion, Walworth is a two-bedroom suite with a king-size mahogany rice bed and a gas-log fireplace in one bedroom, a queen-size cherry rice bed in the other. Guest rooms named Douglas, Clara, Renee, and Laura are also elegantly furnished, although they are smaller. Each of these boasts a gas-log fireplace.

Each morning begins with a full plantation breakfast served in a beautiful dining room overlooking the picturesque courtyard and the oldest fountain in Mississippi. The elegant repast might consist of the specialty of the house: grillade and grits (sirloin roast cooked, cubed, marinaded in port and sherry and spices, served over grits) with curried and spiced fruit. This most asked-for menu is typically served on Sunday. Other mornings you might be treated to a ham and egg cup (ham, egg, and cheese boiled in a cup), banana pecan pancakes, or eggs, a breakfast meat, and grits. No matter what the menu, Layne assures us that "everybody cleans their plate." After breakfast, you're invited to join a guided tour of the mansion, then you can spend some leisurely time exploring the five acres of gardens, which include camellias and 125 varieties of azaleas that were planted in the early 1800s. Or perhaps you'd like to take a dip in the swimming pool, or sip a mint julep on one of the verandas while you immerse yourselves in the Old South.

If The Burn is fully booked when you plan to be in Natchez, don't despair. Accommodations are also offered at Myrtle Corner, a town house with four rooms and suites.

What's Nearby Natchez

Natchez is the oldest settlement on the Mississippi River. Before the Civil War, Natchez was home to more than half the millionaires in America. As a result, Natchez is the site of 500 antebellum buildings. Tour some of the opulent homes during the Spring and Fall Pilgrimages. You can also visit the Natchez National Historic Park and see prominent homes like the Melrose, the William Johnson House, and the Longwood. If all the wealth inspires you to spend some of your own money, you'll find great shopping at Canal Street Depot and Market, downtown Natchez, and the Franklin Street Marketplace.

Other Recommended B&Bs in Natchez

Mark Twain Guest House features rooms in an 1830 commercial building at Natchez-Under-the-Hill, close to casino, restaurants, and entertainment; 25 Silver Street, Natchez, MS 39120; (601) 446–8023. *Ravenna,* an 1835 home in the historic district, offers rooms with private baths; walking distance to river and other sites; 8 Ravenna Lane, Natchez, MS 39120; (601) 446–9973. *Ravennaside,* an 1870 mansion with an extensive collection of Natchez Trace memorabilia, offers 5 rooms; 601 South Union Street, Natchez, MS 39120; (601) 442–8015.

The Burn, the Walworths, and the Civil War

Union commander Palmer and Admiral Farragut appeared with gunboats off the Natchez bluffs on May 12, 1862, and demanded that the city surrender. John Walworth replied, "An unfortified city, an entirely defenseless people, have no alternative but to yield to an irresistible force or uselessly imperil innocent blood. Formalities are absurd in the face of such realities." Residents set fire to the bales of cotton stored at the riverside at Natchez-Under-the-Hill rather than have them fall into the hands of the enemy. Thus the city's only currency went up in smoke. Although John's son Douglas had voted against secession, he was elected to the Confederate Constitutional Congress and helped draft the Confederate Constitution. He and his brother Ernest joined the Confederate forces. Upon hearing that New Orleans and Baton Rouge had fallen, he rushed home—only to arrive the day the city surrendered.

Douglas then formed a militia called the Natchez Greys, which fired over the heads of Union soldiers continually raiding ashore from their gunboat. As a result, the gunboat bombarded the city for three hours, destroying or damaging many of the finest mansions and resulting in the death of a three-year-old girl. Blaming himself, Douglas went off to fight in Tennessee.

Indeed, the war caused great heartache for the Walworth family , who also had many relatives in the North, and who lost their homes The Burn and Elmo. The former was used as a Union hospital and was not returned to the family until 1867. Elmo was used as a barracks for a newly formed regiment of confiscated slaves who were forcibly conscripted into the Union Army. It was never returned to the family; it eventually burned.

Barksdale-Isom Bed and Breakfast

1003 Jefferson Avenue
Oxford, Mississippi 38655
(601) 236–5600 or (800) 236–5696;
fax (601) 236–6763

WEB SITE: www.barksdale-isominn.com
INNKEEPER: Susan Barksdale Howorth
ROOMS: 6; all with private bath, TV, alarm clock, telephone, sound machine, robes, Caswell-Massey toiletries; 4 with fireplace; some rooms have wheelchair access

ON THE GROUNDS: Veranda, formal gardens, pergola, off-street parking

RATES: $150 to $190 double, including full breakfast and afternoon refreshments; extra person $50

CREDIT CARDS ACCEPTED? Yes

OPEN: Year-round

HOW TO GET THERE: From Highway 6, exit at South Lamar and go north. At Courthouse Square, merge right and continue to the northern side of the square. Turn right onto North Lamar and go 1 block to Jefferson Avenue. Turn left. The inn is on your right.

It's hard to decide what we love most about the stately house with six slim square columns—the extraordinarily sumptuous interior, the restful veranda and formal gardens, the pampering, or the fabulous food. Together they create one of the most elegant stays in the northern part of Mississippi.

The mansion began as a three-room log cabin built in 1835 by Dr. Thomas Isom, who named the town after Oxford University in England. As his family increased to nine children, the house was expanded again and again. Dr. Isom had his medical office in the house and opened the county's first drugstore there. In fact, at one time the house was known locally as the Isom Place and the Drug Store House. Planning for the University of Mississippi occurred in his dining room, which had to be expanded to accommodate the entire board of trustees. During the Civil War Dr. Isom operated a hospital for both Union and Confederate soldiers on the college campus. As a result, Union troops were ordered to burn the entire town—with the exception of the Isom house, which General Grant had put under his personal protection. It's believed by many that the dilapidated house described in William Faulkner's "A Rose for Emily" was the Isom house after it had fallen on hard times. Faulkner's home, Rowan Oak, is only a few blocks away.

Susan Barksdale Howorth is responsible for the house's present glory. A disillusioned law student, upon graduation she decided to open a bed and breakfast. She bought the house in 1995, gutted it, and in eight months transformed it into the regally appointed showplace that it is today. Furnished with gorgeous eighteenth- and nineteenth-century antiques and adorned with generous swags of imported toile, chintz, and damask fabrics, the house has a nineteenth-century French theme.

Sumptuous accommodations are offered in six spacious guest chambers, which are drenched in comfort. The Barksdale Room, which is where Dr. Isom had his medical office on the first floor, features a full-canopy bed and matching toile wallpaper, canopy, bed hangings, and dust ruffle. Its French doors open onto the veranda. The elegant McDonnel Room features a massive tester bed with bed hangings that match the floral wallpaper. This room boasts a working fireplace. Upstairs, two ornate double beds hand-painted with a bird's-nest and ivy motif are romantically draped with netting. Standard to all the chambers are feathery beds topping excellent-quality mattresses.

You'll be drawn to the oak rockers on the front veranda and to the exquisite peaceful formal garden, which is surrounded by a serpentine brick wall. Enter through the wrought-iron gate, pass through the arbor, and follow the brick pathway past bronze sculptures created by local artists to a pergola festooned with hanging ferns and appointed with wrought-iron tables and chairs and lounge chairs. This is a divine place to sit with a cold drink and a good book.

Silver-service breakfast is served each morning in the formal dining room by the warm glow of a working gasolier, unless you request it in your room. Nancy's fare might include eggs Benedict, cheese grits, ham au gratin, muffins or quick breads, freshly squeezed juices, and hot beverages. Perfect little touches such as soft drinks, ice, and homemade cookies are always available, concealed in an armoire at the foot of the stairs. A formal tea is served in the music room.

What's Nearby Oxford

Oxford is home to "Ole Miss," otherwise known as the University of Mississippi. The heart of Oxford is the town square, the center of restaurants, bookstores, and antiques shops. If you're looking for a peaceful spot to relax, take a break at The Grove, the University's park. While walking around campus, visit the University of Mississippi Blues Archives, the only blues archives in the country.

Spahn House

401 College Street
Senatobia, Mississippi 38668
(601) 562-9853 or (800) 400-9853

E-MAIL: spahn@gmi.net

WEB SITE: www.spahnhouse.com

INNKEEPERS: Daughn and Joe Spahn

ROOMS: 4; all with private bath,
2 with whirlpool tub; cable TV, clock
radio, supersize bath amenities; access to laundry facilities

ON THE GROUNDS: Veranda, landscaped property

RATES: $75 to $125 single or double, including full breakfast and refreshments

CREDIT CARDS ACCEPTED? Yes

OPEN: Year-round

HOW TO GET THERE: From I-55, take exit 265, Highway 4, and go west to Senatobia. After you cross the railroad tracks, go 3 blocks and turn right onto Ward Street. Go 1 block to College. The B&B will be right in front of you.

eautifully restored in 1994, just in time for its ninetieth birthday, this graceful Southern mansion was built in the Neoclassical style with four stately columns supporting a two-story portico. What amazes us is that the venerable structure sat abandoned for twenty-three years without being vandalized. That says a lot about life and folks in Senatobia.

Now decorated with fine antiques, this fine old home features inviting common areas, generously proportioned guest rooms, and every modern convenience the Spahns could think of to ensure a pleasurable stay and a good night's sleep. Among the noteworthy architectural details are windows in arched recesses flanking the formal parlor's fireplace, hardwood floors, tall pocket doors, and rich woodwork, including the carved newel posts on the stairway. All the windows in the house are the original extra-wide glass.

Rich jewel tones, gleaming woodwork, high-back Victorian beds, luxury mattresses, and extra-nice linens characterize the four upstairs guest rooms. Steps allow guests to walk into the whirlpool tub in the Bridal Suite. The Gentleman's Room boasts a whirlpool tub as well.

Some B&Bs have a scrapbook on hand so guests can see before and after pictures of the entire property. The Spahn House is the only one we've run

across that has a scrapbook in each chamber showing the progress of that particular room, as well as describing the style, origin, and history of each piece of furniture and the accessories.

Daughn serves what she calls a "full-blown" breakfast fit for royalty. She says, "Come hungry, skip lunch." Your feast begins with fresh fruit topped with real whipped cream and proceeds to an entree such as Spahn House eggs, 4-inch-high omelettes, German pancakes, or a soufflé accompanied by thick, crisp bacon, country ham, or sausage as well as homemade breads, muffins, or croissants and many other tasty surprises.

When it comes to Christmastime, Daughn is a lady after our own hearts. Among her decorations are twelve Christmas trees, 40,000 lights, a Christmas village, and holiday finery dripping from the formal staircase. Add to all that the strains of Christmas music and the aroma of a thousand cookies baking.

What's Nearby Senatobia

Senatobia offers its own unique local shopping. In addition, it is conveniently located thirty minutes from Memphis. To explore the local area, visit Holly Springs, which is known for its picturesque antebellum homes. You can also take a short ride to the lakes at Sardis and Arkabutla, and even try your luck at the Tunica County Casinos.

Mockingbird Inn B&B

305 North Gloster
Tupelo, Mississippi 38801
(662) 841–0286; fax (662) 840–4158

E-MAIL: sandbird@netdoor.com

WEB SITE: www.bbonline.com/ms/mockingbird/

INNKEEPERS: Sandy and Jim Gilmer and Sharon Robertson

ROOMS: 7; all with private bath, telephone, cable TV, alarm clock; Mackinac Island Room has a separate entrance with a ramp and a handicapped-accessible shower

ON THE GROUNDS: Gazebo, porch swing

RATES: $65 to $125 double, including full breakfast, evening refreshments, and snacks; additional guest on futon in room $10; ask about romance packages

CREDIT CARDS ACCEPTED? Yes

OPEN: Year-round

HOW TO GET THERE: The inn is located on the corner of Jefferson and Gloster; North Gloster is the main thoroughfare through downtown Tupelo.

World travelers Sandy and Jim have brought some of their favorite destinations to Tupelo by decking out guest rooms in the appropriate colors, furnishings, and accessories to re-create each area's distinctive character. For instance, the Mackinac Island Room is done in the style of a whitewashed cottage and sports an old-fashioned porch swing—that's our favorite whimsical touch. A very romantic pewter wedding canopy bed entwined with flowers and greenery sets the scene in the Paris Room. Wicker, floral cushions, a verdigris iron bed, and seashore pastels create a beach mood in the Sanibel Island Room. An Alpine scene, featherbed-topped sleigh bed, knotty pine, and antique wooden skis create an Old World feel for the Bavarian Room. Step into a safari in the Africa Room, which is done in faux zebra and leopard skins, African carvings, and sensuous mosquito netting draped over the bed. The most formal and most traditionally B&B-like room is the Venice Room, where an 1800s tapestry displays scenes of Venetian gondolas, the Doge's Palace, and the city's canals. Shortened Ionic columns serve as night tables in the Athens Room and help create an atmosphere of old Greece. This romantic room features a bed with an upholstered headboard framed by billowing draperies, but its most popular spot is the bathroom, with its L-shaped two-person whirlpool tub. Every room boasts a queen-size bed and all the modern comforts and conveniences.

Built in 1925, the interesting cottage incorporates three architectural styles: Colonial Revival, prairie, and Arts and Crafts. The Gilmers restored it in 1994 and furnished it in an eclectic mix of antiques and found treasures to open as a bed and breakfast. They've been getting rave reviews from guests and travel publications ever since. The small but beautifully landscaped yard is an ideal place to watch for mockingbirds, Mississippi's state bird, for which the bed and breakfast is named.

Breakfast, which is served early on weekdays so business travelers can get off to work, and later on weekends so leisure travelers can sleep in, is a bountiful meal of such entrees as puff pancakes with strawberry preserves, orange French toast, or an egg and croissant casserole. This might be accompanied by hash browns, bacon, ham, or sausage, as well as juices and hot beverages. If hunger strikes during the day, juices, soft drinks, and the fixings for hot beverages are always available. And if you go out for dinner at one of several restaurants located within walking distance, skip dessert so you can enjoy a sweet treat at the bed and breakfast.

Located halfway between Nashville and Natchez on the Natchez Trace Parkway, Tupelo is an excellent base from which to explore northern Mississippi and western Tennessee. Elvis fans will be interested to know that from the Mockingbird Inn they can see the Milam School, where the King attended sixth and seventh grades. Then they can visit the Elvis Presley Birthplace and Museum.

What's Nearby Tupelo

If you're feeling like you're stuck in Heartbreak Hotel, put on your blue suede (walking) shoes and enjoy the city of Tupelo, which happens to be Elvis Presley's birthplace. First stop is the Elvis Presley Birthplace and Museum. Tour Elvis's elementary and junior high schools. And you must stop in Tupelo Hardware, where a young Elvis bought his first guitar.

Anchuca

1010 First East Street
Vicksburg, Mississippi 39180
(601) 661–0111 or (888) 686–0111

E-MAIL: anchuca@cjb.net

INNKEEPER: Loveta Byrne

ROOMS: 6; all with private bath, telephone, TV; 5 with gas-log fireplace

ON THE GROUNDS: Verandas, swimming pool, hot tub, gardens

RATES: $95 to $140 double, including full breakfast, afternoon refreshments, evening turndown service, and tour of home; discount for multinight stay

CREDIT CARDS ACCEPTED? Yes

OPEN: Year-round

HOW TO GET THERE: Take I–20 to Vicksburg and get off at exit 4B, Clay Street. Turn right. Go through eight or nine traffic lights to Cherry Street. Turn right onto Cherry, go 5 blocks to First East Street, and turn right.

Loveta Byrne obviously loves the B&B business—or else she's a glutton for punishment. Until a few years ago, she owned and ran one of the premier bed and breakfasts in Natchez—The Burn. After a major life change, she sold The Burn and moved to New Orleans to live the good life. But she says the good life had its pluses and minuses. After gaining fifteen pounds and suffering some major boredom, she couldn't stand it anymore, moved to Vicksburg, and bought what was left of an 1832 Greek Revival mansion that had been operating as a B&B before being sold.

"The place had been stripped. Even the chandeliers had been sold off," she remembers. This challenge was just what the doctor ordered. She dove into restoring the property to its old perfection.

According to Loveta, she has "partially" restored the property to its original stately elegance, with Empire, Sheraton, Heppelwhite, and Victorian antiques, but she has more on her mind. "There are still some period reproductions in the guest cottage," she explained. And the mansion itself isn't quite up to her exacting standards—although we could see nothing that needed changing. If you're starting to think that this a little too special for you, don't worry. The rooms are comfortable, the beds firm, all have televisions, and five have gas-log fireplaces.

So far Loveta has restored two of the four bedrooms and baths in the main house for guests, and all four rooms and baths in the guest cottages. In addition, she's fixed up and furnished the public rooms and verandas. She has a total of thirteen rooms, but we've seen the property described as having six, seven, or eleven. It actually depends on how you describe the rooms. This book is about bed and breakfasts, so we only count those rooms that are available as bed-and-breakfast rooms. Some are rented as longer-term rooms and do not include breakfast.

Loveta serves a real stick-to-your ribs traditional Southern breakfast of grits, sausage and ham, eggs made to order—or perhaps eggs Benedict—and homemade breads.

Anchuca means "happy home," and hopefully every guest will have a totally joyful experience here. Some have had such a wonderful time that they come back to stay again and again. Gracious comfort and modern conveniences, refined elegance and Southern hospitality—that's what you get at Anchuca.

Of course, most visitors to Vicksburg come to see the historic house museums, the Civil War battlefield, and the Mississippi River—or maybe to gamble. Save some time in your busy schedule, however, to join other guests around the pool—our idea of an ideal spot to crash (or splash)—and the gazebo with a hot tub. You might also want to stroll around the landscaped grounds, or sit in the brick patios and courtyards with a cool drink. All in all, it makes a great package.

What's Nearby Vicksburg

Attention all Civil War buffs. Here's your opportunity to learn about the decisive battle that led to the fall of the Confederacy. Visit the Vicksburg National Military Park and see Civil War markers, statues, and monuments. If you're here in May or June, you can watch the reenactment of the final Civil War battle in Vicksburg during both the Vicksburg Civil War Siege Reenactment and Memorial Day Reenactment. Don't forget to enjoy the historic homes and shopping at the Vicksburg Garden District.

Other Recommended B&Bs in Vicksburg

The Duff Green Mansion Inn, an 1856 mansion, features rooms and suites with fine Palladian architecture; children and pets are welcome; 1114 First East Street, Vicksburg, MS 39180; (601) 636–6968 or (601) 638–6662. *Floweree Cottage* accommodates six in an 1879 cottage; 2309 Pearl Street, Vicksburg, MS 39180; (800) 262–6315.

Annabelle Bed and Breakfast Inn

501 Speed Street
Vicksburg, Mississippi 39180
(601) 638–2000 or (800) 791–2000;
fax (601) 636–5054

E-MAIL: annabelle@vicksburg.com

WEB SITE: www.annabellebnb.com

INNKEEPERS: Carolyn and George Mayer

ROOMS: 8, including 1 suite; all with private bath (1 with whirlpool tub), cable TV with movie channel, telephone; suite has full kitchen

ON THE GROUNDS: Courtyard, verandas, pool, off-street parking

RATES: $80 to $115 single, $93 to $128 double, $83 to $125 suite, including full breakfast, welcome beverage, afternoon refreshments, tour of home; additional person $23; discount for multinight stays

CREDIT CARDS ACCEPTED? Yes

OPEN: Year-round

HOW TO GET THERE: From I–20, take exit 1A, Washington Street. Go north 2.2 miles along the river to Speed Street. Turn left and go to the end of the second block.

The first time we saw charming Annabelle was during a shore excursion from a cruise on the *Delta Queen*. Our thought at the time was that it would make a perfect bed and breakfast, so we were delighted to learn a couple of years later that it had been transformed into an outstanding lodging. Carolyn, a native of New Orleans, and George, a native of Moravia in the Czech Republic who has also lived in Brazil, have spent many years in the hospitality business as owners of award-winning restaurants. Having traveled around the globe themselves, they understand the needs of travelers, which extend beyond a comfortable bed and a clean bathroom. At Annabelle they offer genuine Southern hospitality, luxurious accommodations, outstanding food, and refuge and romance. When you arrive you'll be treated to special lace cookies and iced or hot tea to help you unwind and get into the genteel feeling of a bygone era.

Annabelle is an Italianate residence built in 1868 on a bluff above the Mississippi. John Alexander Klein of Cedar Grove Estate built it for his son Madison Conrad Klein. It's one of five such historic structures in a square block of Vicksburg's historic Garden District. Although modest in comparison to the elder Klein's mansion, this house enjoys the high ceilings, spacious rooms, hardwood floors, elaborate moldings, and tall windows so typical of the era. We particularly liked the bay window tucked behind an archway in the bright, cheerful formal parlor. The Mayers have put everything in shipshape order and decorated the rooms with ornate Victorian furnishings and such accents as Oriental carpets, crystal chandeliers, and interesting art.

Accommodations—seven rooms and one suite—are offered in the main house and the adjacent 1881 guest house. Except for the Natchez Suite, the rooms are named for flowers; all feature extremely comfortable custom-fitted king- and queen-size beds—some with highly carved headboards or full-testers—modern bathrooms, and all the comforts and conveniences discriminating travelers want. Among the most magnificent of these rooms, the Magnolia sports a gas-log fireplace and the Camellia, a whirlpool tub. Several adjoining rooms can be combined to form suites. The Natchez Suite features a separate living room with a queen-size sofabed and can be connected to a fully equipped kitchen.

A pleasant place for guests to relax is the 55-foot gallery in the guest house. This is a divine place to sip your iced tea while overlooking the courtyard paved with old brick. You can listen to the fountain, catch glints of water dancing off the sparkling swimming pool, admire the old magnolias and crape myrtles, and watch the sun set over the Mississippi.

Candlelight breakfast served on china and using silver and crystal in the formal dining room might include the house specialty, eggs Benedict Annabelle, or some other delicacy such as omelettes or French toast. When you arrive you'll be greeted with spiced lemon tea; freshly baked cookies and breads are always available.

What's Nearby Vicksburg

See page 277 for what's nearby Vicksburg.

Belle of the Bends

508 Klein Street
Vicksburg, Mississippi 39180
(601) 634–0737 or (800) 844–2308

WEB SITE: www.belleofthebends.com

INNKEEPERS: Jo and Wally Pratt

ROOMS: 5; all with private bath, cable TV with HBO, VCR; 2 with whirlpool tub

ON THE GROUNDS: Verandas, gardens

RATES: $85 to $150 double, including full country breakfast, afternoon refreshments, tour of house and gardens; additional person $20

CREDIT CARDS ACCEPTED? Yes

OPEN: Year-round

HOW TO GET THERE: From I–20, you can take exit 4B onto Clay Street, then turn left onto Washington and right onto Klein. Or take exit 1A onto Washington, then turn left onto Klein.

Encircled by verandas on two floors, this majestic mansion perched on a bluff in Vicksburg's historic Garden District overlooking the Mississippi River is reminiscent of the steamboats that plied the river for nearly one hundred years. In fact, Jo is the granddaughter of steamboat captain Tom Morrissey, who owned the Morrissey Line, so it seemed only natural to name the magnificent home for one of the finest steamboats in his line.

The Italianate-style manor was built in 1876 by Murray F. Smith and his wife, Kate. At the time Smith was a prosperous young attorney; he later became a Mississippi state senator and U.S. senator. The Smiths flaunted their wealth by pouring money into the front and downstairs of their mansion. Any concessions to economy were hidden. For instance, the front windows are all large single panes of glass. Around the corners, the windows

The Original *Belle of the Bends*

Vicksburg has long been an important port city on the Mississippi River. When it was lost to General U. S. Grant's Union troops on July 4, 1863, the Confederacy's doom was sealed. But in 1876 the mighty Mississippi changed its course, leaving Vicksburg high and dry for more than twenty-five years. In 1903 the Army Corps of Engineers opened a canal between the Yazoo River and the Mississippi, putting Vicksburg back on the river. The *Belle of the Bends*, which was built in 1889 by the Greenville Packet Company to run from Vicksburg to Greenville, served as the flagship that led the parade of boats into the channel. U.S. Senator Murray Smith gave the dedication speech.

In February 1908 the *Belle* sank in a snowstorm at Peelers Landing. She was raised, but sank again. It was at this time that she was bought by Thomas Morrissey, Jo's grandfather. He raised her, refurbished her, and operated her as an excursion boat between Vicksburg and New Orleans. Morrissey sold her to a man in Cairo, Illinois, who operated her for about ten years under a new name—the *Liberty*. Eventually she was dismantled; the only piece of her that survives is the roof bell, now on a plantation near Pine Bluff, Arkansas. Jo hopes to bring it back to the Belle of the Bends someday.

have mullions. Belle of the Bends has been lived in by only four families. The Smiths lived in the house until 1912, the second owner until 1919, the third owner until 1990, and the Pratts since then.

As beautiful as the exterior of Belle of the Bends is, it pales beside the magnificent interior. In addition to the expected attributes of a turn-of-the-century mansion—high ceilings, tall windows, hardwood floors, fireplaces—Belle of the Bends showcases ornate plasterwork moldings and ceiling medallions. In addition, the handsome rooms are elegantly decorated throughout with antiques—many of them handed down from Jo's and Wally's parents and grandparents, others collected throughout their married life, as well as Oriental carpets and steamboat memorabilia. A large bay window and a Carrara marble mantel dominate the sitting parlor, where the furniture is a combination of Victorian and Empire. Take particular notice of the 1870 French player piano (once owned by the previous residents), the Portuguese vases, the Dresden pictures, and the hand-painted summer fireplace screens. These screens, which were used to cover the coal-burning grates in the summer, are found throughout the house, and each is unique. Some of the chandeliers were originally gasoliers.

Among the exquisite guest rooms, the Azalea Room occupies what was the gentlemen's parlor on the first floor. It was here that the gentlemen retired after dinner for private conversation, smoking, and drinks without the ladies. Today, the gracious room is furnished with a Renaissance Revival half-tester bed, armoire, dresser, and Eastlake night tables. A whirlpool tub in the bath beckons you to relax. The 1830 four-poster full-tester bed in the Rose Room is known as a camp bed, because it was designed to be easily dismantled and transported. This room also features a double-size rope bed. Each of the other rooms is just as lovely; each has its own personality and special furnishings. Both the Riverview and Captain Tom's Rooms offer awe-inspiring views of the Yazoo and Mississippi Rivers. Captain Tom's Room has the added bonus of a whirlpool tub.

A full country breakfast is served in the formal dining room on a Chippendale-style table made by Jo and Wally's son, an accomplished artisan woodworker. In addition to china, crystal, and silver flatware, the table is adorned with heavy, ornate serving pieces and candelabra. A converted gasolier hangs overhead.

You'll want to view the river from the first- and second-story verandas that wrap around three sides of the house, and to stroll through the well-kept rose gardens and among the giant shade trees and flowering ornamentals.

For those unable to stay at the Belle of the Bends, tours are offered daily from 10:00 A.M. to 5:00 P.M.

What's Nearby Vicksburh

See page 277 for what's nearby Vicksburg.

Stained Glass Manor—Oak Hall

2430 Drummond Street
Vicksburg, Mississippi 39180
(601) 638–8893 or (888) VICK–BNB; fax (601) 636–3055

E-MAIL: vickbnb@magnolia.net
WEB SITE: www.vickbnb.com
INNKEEPERS: Bill and Shirley Smollen
ROOMS: 4 rooms and 1 cottage; all with private bath (all but 1 with claw-foot tub), cable TV, VCR, telephone jack; all but 1 with working fireplace
ON THE GROUNDS: One-and-a-half-acre property

RATES: $85 to $185, including New Orleans breakfast; additional person $20

CREDIT CARDS ACCEPTED? Yes

OPEN: Year-round

HOW TO GET THERE: From I-20, take exit 1A onto Washington Street and go about a mile to traffic light 29 at the intersection of Washington and Lee Streets. Turn right onto Lee and go 1.3 miles. You'll go past two stop signs and one traffic light; the street changes names to Drummond and then to Monroe. The house is on your left behind a wrought-iron fence. The curved driveway is for tour parking; guests park in the back or along the side.

It doesn't take a rocket scientist to run a bed and breakfast, but in the case of Stained Glass Manor that's what you'll get. Although he's now devoting all his time to innkeeping (and serving as president of the Mississippi B&B association), Bill is a former rocket engineer with thirty-two years at NASA. Bill and Shirley are both native to the Vicksburg area. In fact, when Bill was a kid he delivered newspapers to this very house. Shirley still teaches school in addition to her duties at the bed and breakfast. Bill, who has a very dry sense of humor, told us, "Visiting Stained Glass Manor is kind of like entering a Faulkner novel—we're all crazy."

The National Trust for Historic Preservation describes the magnificent home built by Fannie Vick Willis Johnson—a descendant of Burwell Vick, for whom Vicksburg was named—as "possibly the finest example of mission-style architecture in Mississippi." Built between 1902 and 1908, it is reputed to have been designed by George Washington Maher, an early teacher of Frank Lloyd Wright and one of the architects of the Chicago School. The 10,000-square-foot mansion boasts thousands of board feet of warmly glowing oak paneling and thirty-eight dazzling stained-glass windows in hues of gold, rose, salmon, blue, and green. Thirty-six of the windows have been authenticated as the work of Louis J. Millet, a dean of architecture and the director of the Art Institute of Chicago. The contemporary panels were created by LaMantia of New Orleans.

The handsome entry hall is 16 feet wide by 40 feet deep with oak paneling, a massive fireplace, and a magnificent grand staircase rising to the second floor. A formal parlor, dining room, and library with a coffered ceiling and intricately carved woodwork open off this impressive reception area.

Sumptuous, spacious guest rooms at Stained Glass Manor are named for presidents; all but one boast one or more stained-glass windows. A king-size rice bed romantically draped in netting dominates the Washington Room, which has a working fireplace and access to a sleeping porch as well as a bath with its original claw-foot tub and pedestal sink. The Adams Room is practically a mirror image except for its four-poster bed. Largest of all the rooms is the Jefferson, with its king-size carved bed. A family of four will enjoy the 40-foot-long Polk Room, with its double bed and two twins. Not as sumptuous as the rooms in the main house, but with the advantage of extra privacy, is the Carriage House Suite. This circa-1885 structure boasts a sitting/dining area furnished in 1920s style, a large bedroom, and a kitchen.

Bill describes his breakfasts as "damn good." He offers freshly baked breads, homemade jams and jellies, coffee "imported" from New Orleans, and egg fondue as well as his signature dish, quiche Lorraine. He told us he'd experimented with twenty-two different kinds of sausage until he found the perfect flavor.

If you're not lucky enough to stay at Stained Glass Manor, by all means take the tour—adults $5, children $3, family maximum $15.

What's Nearby Vicksburg

See page 277 for what's nearby Vicksburg.

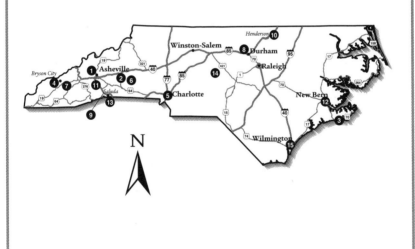

North Carolina

Numbers on map refer to towns numbered below.

1. Asheville,
   The Black Walnut Bed and
      Breakfast Inn and Carriage
      House, 286
   The Colby House, 288
   Flint Street Inns, 289
   Inn on Montford, 290
   The Lion and the Rose Bed and
      Breakfast, 292
   The Old Reynolds Mansion, 294
   The Wright Inn, 296

2. Bat Cave, Hickory Nut Gap Inn,
   298

3. Beaufort, Langdon House, 299

4. Bryson City, Randolph House
   Country Inn, 301

5. Charlotte, The Homeplace, 303

6. Chimney Rock, Dogwood Inn,
   305

7. Dillsboro, Squire Watkins Inn,
   306

8. Durham, Arrowhead Inn, 308

9. Flat Rock, Flat Rock Inn, 310

10. Henderson, La Grange Plantation
    Inn, 312

11. Hendersonville,
    The Claddagh Inn, 314
    Melange Bed and Breakfast, 316

12. New Bern, Harmony House Inn,
    318

13. Saluda, Woods House, 319

14. Siler City,
    Bed and Breakfast at Laurel
       Ridge, 320
    The Inn at Celebrity Dairy, 322

15. Wilmington, Catherine's Inn, 324

The Black Walnut Bed and Breakfast Inn and Carriage House

288 Montford Avenue
Asheville, North Carolina 28801
(828) 254-3878 or (800) 381-3878; fax (828) 236-9393

E-MAIL: -info@blackwalnut.com

WEB SITE: www.blackwalnut.com

INNKEEPERS: Randy and Sandra Glasgow

ROOMS: 7; all with private bath, cable TV, VCR, hair dryer; some with wood-burning fireplace and two-person whirlpool tub

ON THE GROUNDS: Veranda, gardens, mountain bikes

RATES: $95 to $185 double, including full breakfast and afternoon refreshments; additional person $25; two-night minimum on weekends; midweek rates, special promotions throughout the year, corporate rates, gift certificates

CREDIT CARDS ACCEPTED? Yes

OPEN: Year-round

HOW TO GET THERE: From I-240, exit onto Montford Avenue and turn right. Look for the B&B on your left at Waneta and Montford. From I-240 east, turn right onto Haywood Street and then right onto Montford.

Rediscover the peace and quiet of old Asheville at the Black Walnut, a luxurious bed and breakfast located in an 1899 home in the Montford historic district. The shingle-style manor was designed by the supervising architect of the Biltmore Estate, Richard Sharp Smith. As Sandra and Randy put it, they offer "all the comforts of today in the charm of the Biltmore era." The bed and breakfast takes its name from the mature black walnut trees on the property.

Tastefully appointed guest rooms are named for the beautiful shrubbery that surrounds the mansion. Five rooms are located in the main house, and two in the garden carriage house for those who desire more privacy. Special touches include herbal soaps, lotions, shampoo, and lip balm.

Starting at the very tiptop of the house, the entire third floor has been transformed into the Ivy Garden Room—highly sought after for honeymoons and other special occasions. The king-size wrought-iron bed and all the accoutrements are casual French country in style. Tucked into one alcove is a wood-burning fireplace; in another nook is a two-person whirlpool tub surrounded by travertine marble. Coming down to the second floor, the Walnut Room, which was the original master bedroom, features a carved queen-size bed, a wood-burning fireplace, and an oversize claw-foot tub. It can be combined with the Azalea Room to create a suite; the Azalea itself features a queen-size sleigh bed, fireplace, and whirlpool tub. In addition to its queen-size rooster-tail bed and fireplace, some folks choose the Holly Room for its steam bath. The Dogwood Room was indicated on the original architect's drawings as a linen room, however, it's like no other linen room you've ever seen. Although it's smallish compared to other rooms, it's popular because it's in the turret and features a cloud-painted ceiling, a brass bed, and a claw-foot tub. Guests in the Magnolia Cottage enjoy a fireplace, kitchenette, and private deck. They can even request a bedside breakfast. Upstairs, the Cottage Loft has sloped ceilings, skylights, a kitchenette, and a claw-foot tub.

Awaken to the aroma of freshly ground gourmet coffee, a selection of teas, or gourmet hot chocolate (on which you can dollop some freshly whipped cream). Then enjoy a leisurely breakfast served by candlelight in the formal dining room on fine English china. The most requested dish is Belgian waffles with a warmed triberry compote, but the morning feast might consist of any one of several other specialties served with homemade muffins, coffee cakes, fruit strudels, and a selection of seasonal fruit. Special dietary needs can be accommodated with advance notice. Freshly baked goods are offered with afternoon tea; for guests arriving earlier in the afternoon and needing to shake the dust from the road, a complimentary glass of something cold awaits.

Take advantage of the gracious porch during warm weather to sip on some lavender-scented lemonade—a specialty of the B&B. Reminiscent of Monet paintings, the beautifully landscaped gardens invite leisurely strolls. Here's another good idea: Snooze in a hammock under the old black walnut trees.

What's Nearby Asheville

Asheville is an artsy enclave. If you enjoy arts and crafts, visit the Folk Art Center, which sells weaving, pottery, quilts, jewelry, and other handicrafts. On the subject of workmanship, visit the Biltmore Estate, which was once the palatial home of George Vanderbilt. Also, explore the Botanical Gardens at Asheville, which is open year-round. Another interesting attraction is the Thomas Wolfe Memorial, which is the writer's boyhood home and inspiration for much of his writing.

The Colby House

230 Pearson Drive
Asheville, North Carolina 28801
(828) 253-5644 or (800) 982-2118;
fax (828) 259-9479

WEB SITE: www.colbyhouse.com

INNKEEPERS: Bonnie and Peter Marsh

ROOMS: 4; all with private bath, clock
radio, telephone jack; 2 with ceiling fan; 1 with fireplace

ON THE GROUNDS: Porch, gardens

RATES: $115 to $150 double, including breakfast, afternoon refreshments,
and all-day snacks; ask about corporate rates

CREDIT CARDS ACCEPTED? Yes

OPEN: Year-round

HOW TO GET THERE: Take I-240 toward town to exit 4C. If traveling west, at
the end of the ramp turn right onto Montford Avenue. Go about 0.75
mile to Watauga and turn left. Go 1 block to Pearson Drive and turn left.
Go ½ block to Tacoma; the B&B is on the southwest corner of Pearson
and Tacoma. Turn right and enter the parking lot on your left. If traveling east on I-240, at the end of the ramp turn right onto Haywood, then
right onto Montford and follow the preceding directions.

This neat, trim Dutch Colonial home, built in 1924 of North Carolina
blue granite, sits behind a scalloped picket fence on the corner of a quiet,
tree-lined street in Asheville's historic Montford district. Although not
as grandiose as some of its neighbors, it is nonetheless elegant. Listed on the
National Register of Historic Places, the Colby House offers discriminating
travelers a graceful retreat into the past.

Bonnie and Peter are real go-getters. While raising five children, Peter
worked in the health care computer systems field; Bonnie worked as an
administrative assistant, in retail management and sales, and as a volunteer.
During all that time they traveled the world. They loved staying in B&Bs so
much they knew they'd have one someday.

Step into the hospitable foyer and seventy-five years back in time. The
twenty-five years that elapsed between the ostentatious construction preva-
lent at the end of the nineteenth century and the 1920s—when this house
was built—are obvious. Although you'll find burnished hardwood floors
covered by large Oriental carpets and graceful fireplaces, the ceilings are
lower, the rooms smaller, the woodwork trim simpler than in the heyday of

the Victorian era. Still, the house is head and shoulders above most homes constructed today. Flanking the foyer are the formal antiques-filled living room and dining room. In the sitting room comfortable seating is grouped around a lovely fireplace centered between two pairs of French doors that lead out to the side porch. Shaded, cool, and breezy, the rocker-filled porch beckons guests outside and leads to the rear gardens.

Four exquisite guest rooms feature queen-size beds and fine linens. The most spacious is the Williamsburg Guest Room, decorated in eighteenth-century decor and featuring a mahogany four-poster rice bed and sleeper sofa. Colonial American decor defines the Foxfire Guest Room, which boasts not only a mahogany four-poster rice bed but also a wood-burning fireplace. An unusual iron princess canopy bed is the focal point of the Charleston Guest Room.

Bountiful breakfasts feature such specialties as oven-baked pecan French toast, blueberry Belgian waffles, Florentine frittatas, home-baked cranberry scones, and muffins. Come and join your hosts each evening on the porch or before a cozy fire for beverages and before-dinner snacks. For those odd times when hunger strikes, a butler's pantry offers twenty-four-hour "room service" with hot and cold beverages and freshly baked cookies or brownies.

What's Nearby Asheville

See page 287 for what's nearby Asheville.

Flint Street Inns (Best Buy)

100 and 116 Flint Street
Asheville, North Carolina 28801
(828) 253–6723

INNKEEPERS: Rick, Lynne, and Marion Vogel

ROOMS: 8; all with private bath, portable telephone on request, ceiling fan; some with wood-burning fireplace; 6 with claw-foot tub

ON THE GROUNDS: Porches, gardens

RATES: $100, double; $75, single (no single rate on some weekends), including complete Southern-style breakfast and beverages served throughout the day; $25 each extra person; some weekends may require two-night minimum stay

CREDIT CARDS ACCEPTED? Yes

OPEN: Year-round

HOW TO GET THERE: Going north on Haywood Street, keeping the Civic Center on your right and passing over I-240, Haywood becomes Flint Street. The inns are just beyond the corner of Flint Street and Starnes Avenue, on your left. Turn into the driveway for off-street parking. The Vogels will send you a map when you make reservations.

We could smell cookies baking the minute we walked through the door. Lynne said she hoped we wouldn't think she was rude as she excused herself to take them from the oven, and minutes later we were eating warm chocolate chip cookies and sipping hot spiced cider. That's how guests are greeted at the Flint Street Inns. As the years go by, we hear more and more praise for the Vogels' easy, competent style of innkeeping.

The bedrooms, parlors, and dining rooms are all filled with the kind of comfortable, turn-of-the-century furniture that reminds you of visiting a grandparent or favorite aunt in earlier times. Marion made the quilts on the beds, all of which are queen-size. Here and there such novel touches as a collection of hats, some 1920s knickknacks, and a display of 1930s art deco collectibles catch your attention. Carol especially enjoyed Marion's British tea tiles, a collection she's been building for more than twenty years.

A number of working wood-burning fireplaces grace the inns. Sitting in front of one, sipping cider and poring over the menus the Vogels collect from area restaurants to decide where to go for dinner, is our idea of a perfect way to spend an hour late on a chilly fall afternoon.

If you're here in the spring or summer, you'll be enchanted with the way old, old shade trees, old-timey flowers like iris and phlox, bird feeders, and birdbaths that actually attract birds recall the times when yards were treated as places to be rather than green expanses to be mowed.

What's Nearby Asheville

See page 287 for what's nearby Asheville.

Inn on Montford

296 Montford Avenue
Asheville, North Carolina 28801
(828) 254-9569 or (800) 254-9569; fax (828) 254-9518

E-MAIL: info@innonmontford.com

WEB SITE: www.innonmontford.com

INNKEEPERS: Lynn and Ron Carlson

ROOMS: 4; all with private bath and telephone; 3 with whirlpool tub; 2 with TV

ON THE GROUNDS: Veranda

RATES: $145 to $195, including full breakfast; ask about gift certificates

CREDIT CARDS ACCEPTED? Yes

OPEN: Year-round

HOW TO GET THERE: Take I-240 toward town and get off at exit 4C. If traveling west, at the end of the ramp turn right onto Montford; the B&B is the second house on your left past Waneta. If traveling east, at the end of the ramp turn right onto Haywood, then right onto Montford. Follow the previous directions.

When we stepped into this bed and breakfast, which was festively decorated for Christmas, the first thing that caught our eyes was Morris the cat stretched out to his full length on the hearth, luxuriating in the warmth and glow of a cheerily crackling blaze in the stone fireplace. His little paws were dusted with gray ash where he'd scratched about, hinting broadly until Lynn or Ron lit the fire. Well, since we live in a house where even our dogs are dominated by three fabulous felines, we understood the situation immediately. Once we got past paying homage to Morris, we could turn our attentions to the gracious host and hostess, the opulent Victorian decorations, and the magnificent house and guest accommodations.

Like some of its neighbors, the turn-of-the-century mansion was designed by Richard Sharp Smith, who was the supervising architect for the Biltmore Estate. Arts and Crafts in style, it has steeply pitched double gables. Twenty-six mature boxwoods line the front walk leading to the full-length veranda that sweeps across the front, welcoming you to the B&B. On the grounds is the largest Norway maple in North Carolina.

Superb architectural details create a gracious backdrop for English and American antiques dating from 1730 to 1910. Guests have many options for places to gather to get to know each other, to read a good book, or to share some intimate conversation with that special someone. In addition to the formal living room with its double-mantel fireplace, there's a cozy library, and—our favorite—a cheery sunroom. Filled with wrought-iron furniture, palms, and seasonal plants, the garden setting of this window-surrounded getaway makes a perfect place to watch television or listen to music.

Four exquisite guest chambers named for writers, most with an Asheville connection, feature queen-size beds and fireplaces. The highlights of the O. Henry Room are its queen-size four-poster bed, fireplace, and claw-foot tub. An 1840 queen-size mahogany English half-tester bed draped with hangings that complement the linens is the centerpiece of the Fitzgerald Room, but the fireplace and whirlpool tub are equally appealing. An 1870 English half-tester bed with chintz hangings and a whirlpool bath entice guests to the Thomas Wolfe Room. The Edith Wharton Room is furnished with Eastlake furniture. The bed is a brass and iron English half-tester. Its hangings are of Ralph Lauren fabrics, as are the draperies and bed linens. This room also boasts a whirlpool tub.

When you're thoroughly rested and caught up on your reading, take some time for a leisurely perusal of Lynn's collections of silver napkin rings, tea caddies, Staffordshire pottery, antique maps, Baxter prints, and period cut glass.

Get used to being pampered. Coffee or tea is delivered to your room at 8:00 A.M. Breakfast is served family-style in the formal dining room. The three-course meal begins with seasonal fruit dishes, baked peaches, or baked grapefruit. The next course consists of a savory entree such as shirred eggs, eggs continental, eggs in straw, scrambled eggs with Canadian-bacon-filled croissants, or a baked tomato filled with eggs and Brie. It is followed by a sweet course—Bavarian puff pancakes, raspberry French toast, or oven Danish.

What's Nearby Asheville

See page 287 for what's nearby Asheville.

The Lion and the Rose Bed and Breakfast

276 Montford Avenue
Asheville, North Carolina 28801
(828) 255–ROSE or (800) 546–6988;
fax (828) 285–9810

E-MAIL: lion-rose@a-o.com
WEB SITE: http://a-o.com/lion-rose
INNKEEPERS: Lisa and Rice Yordy
and Winston

ROOMS: 5; all with private bath, TV; 2 with gas-log fireplace; iron, ironing board, and emergency toiletries available on request

ON THE GROUNDS: Veranda, gardens

RATES: $135 to $225 double, including full breakfast and afternoon tea; additional person $35; two-night minimum stay weekends from April to December; ask about corporate rates

CREDIT CARDS ACCEPTED? Yes

OPEN: Year-round

HOW TO GET THERE: Take I–240 toward the city to exit 4C. If traveling west, at the end of the ramp turn right onto Montford Avenue. Look for the B&B on the near left corner at Waneta and Montford. From I–240 traveling east, at the end of the ramp turn right onto Haywood Street, then right onto Montford. Follow the previous directions.

Although there are several sculpted lions on the walkways and veranda, the official greeter here is Winston, a regal-looking three-year-old English springer spaniel. He's always available to play a game of catch with apples from trees in the yard or to lie contentedly at your feet while you're watching television. The B&B's star, he's been featured in an article in *Dog Crafts*. And oh yes, there are two human hosts here as well—Lisa and Rice.

The simplified three-story Georgian and Neoclassical mansion was built in 1898 by Charity Rusk Craig, an executive with the local telephone company. Consider what an exalted position this was for a woman at the turn of the century! A few years later the manor house was bought by the Toms family. In *Look Homeward Angel*, a fictional account of Asheville by native son Thomas Wolfe, a character named Tommy French was based on Wolfe's friend Charles French Toms—who lived in this house.

Listed on the National Register of Historic Places and beautifully restored in the 1980s for use as a bed and breakfast, the mansion retains its high embossed ceilings and its classic leaded- and stained-glass windows. Golden oak woodwork includes ornate columns separating the foyer from the inglenook, elaborate moldings, pocket doors, and the grand staircase, which is graced by a 6-foot Palladian stained-glass window. Antiques, Oriental carpets, and period appointments grace the spacious rooms. We visited in winter when there was a charming fire crackling in the foyer and the parlor, but other seasons have their own appeals.

Five tastefully appointed guest rooms feature private baths and queen-size beds. Encompassing the entire third floor, the Craig-Toms Suite has a cottage feel with wicker furnishings and floral wallpaper. The main room of the suite contains a queen-size bed and sitting area with fireplace. A separate dressing room with a daybed is roomy enough to use as a separate bedroom. Outside an oak door with original stained-glass is a private balcony.

But it's the bathroom that kindles most romantic feelings: A garden mural and a skylight serve as a backdrop for a whirlpool tub, complete with candles and bath salts. There's a large, tiled walk-in shower as well.

On the second floor, the Marion Hall Room boasts a high-back tiger-oak bed, a beautiful fireplace, and a sitting area in the bay window. This room can be combined with the Margaret-Grace Room to form a suite. Very light and airy, the latter room features a cherry four-poster bed. In the Fannie Rice Room, a wonderful hand-carved Biltmore Heritage four-poster bed is draped with fabrics made in England. A high antique oak bed, antique Danish plates, and Waverly wallpapers characterize the Holger-Nielsen Room.

A delightful full gourmet breakfast of specially blended coffee, English teas, home-baked breads and pastries, fresh fruit, and various entrees is served using lovely English china and silver in the gracious dining room. On particularly nice days, perhaps you'd rather dine on the wide full-length wicker-filled veranda, an excellent vantage point from which to survey the parklike grounds, hundred-year-old sugar maples, flower gardens, and fountains.

This is a special place run by special people for special guests—a place where you'll be pampered in Victorian style with extras such as fresh flowers in the rooms and evening turndown service with lemon water and chocolates; a place from which you'll depart with memories to cherish always.

What's Nearby Ashville

See page 287 for what's nearby Asheville.

The Old Reynolds Mansion

100 Reynolds Heights
Asheville, North Carolina 28804
(828) 254–0496 or (800) 709–0496

WEB SITE: www.oldreynoldsmansion.com

INNKEEPERS: Fred and Helen Faber

ROOMS: 8 with private bath; 2 third-floor rooms that share one bath; and the one-room Swan Cottage Suite

ON THE GROUNDS: Swimming pool

RATES: $60 to $110, double in house, $125 in cottage, including continental breakfast; single, 10 percent less

CREDIT CARDS ACCEPTED? No

OPEN: Year-round; weekends only in January and February

HOW TO GET THERE: The inn is 4 miles north of downtown Asheville. Take Merrimon Avenue (Route 25 North) past Beaver Lake. Turn right just past the stoplight onto Beaver Street, then turn left up the gravel lane. From Route 19 and 23 North, take Elk Mountain Road, bear to the right, and go left onto Elkwood Avenue at the light. At the next light, turn left and then immediately turn right onto Beaver Street. Turn left up the gravel lane. You cannot see the house from the bottom of the lane.

The Old Reynolds Mansion is a restored brick antebellum mansion sitting in the middle of an expanse of country gardens, yards, and pines on top of a ridge of Reynolds Mountain. From its wraparound verandas, the view makes you feel that nothing else matters. We wonder how Fred and Helen get anything done with that view to tempt them into rocking and contemplating.

Inside, Helen has decorated with what she calls "comfortable antiques." The front parlor has a fireplace and, hidden behind a shelf full of books and games, a refrigerator in which guests are invited to keep their wine and snacks. Helen also keeps a little library there of menus from all the nearby restaurants to help guests choose a spot for dinner. In the winter guests eat breakfast in the parlor. (When it's nice out, of course, they eat on the painstakingly restored veranda.)

All the guest rooms on the second floor have working wood-burning fireplaces. The rooms run along both sides of a wide hall that opens onto the second-floor veranda from which you have the spectacular view of the mountains.

The third-floor rooms have intriguing nooks and crannies that go with alcove windows.

Everywhere you look outside, you see more signs of the work Fred and Helen have done. Their swimming pool, a real, old-fashioned poured-cement pool, measures 25 by 62 feet. But before anybody could swim any laps in it, Fred had to clean out many years' accumulation of gunk and growth, scrub it down, patch it, and paint it. Today, sparkling clean and surrounded by pines and greenery, it's worthy of Hollywood.

Fred saw us admiring the vegetable garden. "Want some zucchini?" he asked. He thought it would be a joke: Nobody he knows wants any more zucchini. When we said yes, he brought a sack full of squash, all as long as our arms. Behind the garden, a well-tended grape arbor promises grapes in nearly as much abundance. Farther back on the property, the Fabers have begun putting benches among rows of pines to create a shady area for sitting in seclusion.

What's Nearby Ashevelle

See page 287 for what's nearby Asheville.

The Wright Inn

235 Pearson Drive
Asheville, North Carolina 28801
(828) 251-0789 or (800) 552-5724;
fax (828) 251-0920

WEB SITE: www.wrightinn.com

INNKEEPERS: Carol and Art Wenczel

ROOMS: 8 rooms and one suite; all with private bath, TV, telephone, hair dryer; 2 with gas-log fireplace

ON THE GROUNDS: Veranda, gardens

RATES: $110 to $155 single or double, including full breakfast and afternoon refreshments; use of bicycles and helmets; additional person $25; ask about seasonal discounts, corporate rates, multinight stay discounts; a two-night minimum may be required on weekends

CREDIT CARDS ACCEPTED? Yes

OPEN: Year-round

HOW TO GET THERE: Take I–240 toward the city to exit 4C. If traveling west, at the end of the ramp turn right onto Montford Avenue. Go 0.8 mile to Watauga Street (1 block past Waneta Street) and turn left. Continue 1 block to where Watauga ends at Pearson Drive; the B&B is on the left corner. Park in front to register and you'll be directed to rear parking. If traveling east on I–240, at the end of the ramp turn right onto Haywood Street. At the next corner, turn right onto Montford. Follow the preceding directions.

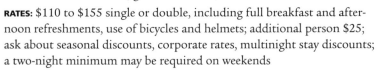

For people who love Christmas as much as we do, nothing beats the opulent decorations festooning the exterior and interior of a grand Victorian mansion. We visited the Queen Anne Victorian Wright Inn in early December when garlands bedecked with tiny lights and intertwined with magnolias draped the veranda and its quaintly charming gazebolike extension. Art was puttering around in the well-manicured gardens. His puttering has earned the bed and breakfast a first-place award in the 1998 Men's

Garden Club and Quality Forward Home Garden Contest. Inside, things were even more dazzling. Ornately decorated trees stood in both the Coleman Parlor and the Willows Drawing Room; other decorations imbued the house with Victorian enchantment. No matter when you visit, however, you'll be guaranteed a memorable experience.

Osella and Leva Wright built this mansion in 1899 and 1900. (Mr. Wright was the prosperous owner of the Carolina Carriage House.) Like many homes of the era, it suffered in modern times; it had become affectionately known by locals as Faded Glory when the Wenczels began to restore it. Now listed on the National Register of Historic Places, the manor house retains the gleaming hardwood floors, graceful wooden mantels and fireplace surrounds, pocket doors, elegant oak moldings, and grand staircase of its former glory days. Period furnishings and family heirlooms, as well as reproductions of wall coverings and fabrics of the era, re-create the turn-of-the-century way of life enjoyed by the upper classes.

Eight lovely guest rooms and a suite are elegantly furnished but afford all the modern comforts and conveniences. Located on the first floor, the Wright Suite features a carved mahogany queen-size bed so high you need a step stool to get into it; there's also a gas-log fireplace and a private breakfast room with its own entrance to the veranda. The remainder of the guest chambers are on the second and third floors. Those on the second floor are spacious and boast high ceilings and tall windows. Of special note, the Green Room has a private balcony, and the Wilkinson Room boasts a gas-log fireplace. All but one feature queen-size beds. On the third floor, as you'd expect, the rooms are cozier and the ceilings lower and sometimes sloping. Three more simply decorated guest rooms lead from this floor's sitting room. The Orr Room has twin beds that can be reconfigured into a king; the other two rooms have double beds. Although each of these rooms has a private bath, two are located off the sitting room, so robes are provided. Fluffy towels and extra-special linens add a touch of pampering to all the bedchambers.

Depending on the weather, the four-course breakfast may be served in the formal dining room or out on the veranda. Freshly squeezed juice, fresh fruit, homemade breads, scones, and muffins, and an entree such as French toast, Bermuda pancakes with blueberry sauce, eggs Benedict, or a strata accompanied by sausage or bacon can carry you all the way to afternoon tea—a delightful break of fresh fruit, cheese and crackers, and cakes or cookies.

In addition to accommodations in the main house, the Wenczels offer a historic carriage house, which is ideal for a family or group of friends. Breakfast, however, is not included for guests in the carriage house.

Hickory Nut Gap Inn

P.O. Box 246
Bat Cave, North Carolina 28710
(828) 625–9108

INNKEEPER: Beau Trammell and Courtney Thompson

ROOMS: 5 rooms and 1 suite; all with private bath

ON THE GROUNDS: Hiking trails

RATES: $80 for rooms, $125 for suite, including mountain gourmet continental breakfast

CREDIT CARDS ACCEPTED? No

OPEN: April through November, weather permitting

HOW TO GET THERE: In Bat Cave, where Highway 64 splits off from Highway 74A and goes west toward Hendersonville, follow Highway 64 for 0.5 mile. On your right, two pillars made of river rock mark the entrance to the inn. A narrow drive winds 0.7 mile up to the bed and breakfast. You'll know you've made the right turn when you see the small sign about 15 feet up the drive.

From this mountaintop inn—elevation 2,200 feet—at the top of Hickory Nut Gorge, you can look out over mountains in all directions and not see another man-made structure. You can sit on the 80-foot screened porch and watch hummingbirds, or look for rainbows, or gaze at a hawk making lazy circles in the sky, or simply do nothing.

This refuge from the insane world was built in 1950 as a mountain retreat by a well-to-do businessman and later inherited by a reconstructed hippie and her husband, who put years of work into refurbishing the place. They concentrated on keeping such features as the cathedral ceiling and stone fireplace of the great room, as well as cleaning up the wood paneling throughout. If you know your wood, you'll recognize maple, cherry, poplar, black walnut, and red and white oak, as well as cedar in the closets.

The decorating grew from their eclectic interests and their respect for history and what was already in the building. For instance, note the eighty-six characters of the Cherokee alphabet mounted high on the walls encircling the recreation room; they were hand-carved in wood by the Cherokee artist Goingback Chiltoskey.

Another former owner was part Native American, and you'll find Native American arts and crafts throughout the B&B, mixed in with such surprising items as a camel saddle used as a footstool, a trunk used as a coffee table, and a honest-to-goodness handwoven hippie dress used as a wall decoration. (It prompts those of us of a certain age to ask, "Remember when everything we wore had to make a statement?")

The eclectic decor works partly because of the obvious care taken in putting things together without overdoing it, and partly because of the spaciousness of the building to begin with. The effect is too sophisticated to call rustic and too comfortable to call exotic.

Beau Trammell, the current owner, tries to see that you have whatever you need and, at the same time, tries to keep out of your hair if what you need most is privacy. We were looking for a word to describe this very special experience, and it finally came to us—laidback.

Beau strongly encourages all of his guests to stay at least three days. "The first day, new guests rush around, trying to see and do everything. It's not until the second day that they start to relax. Finally, on the third day they truly experience what we have to offer—escape."

What's Nearby Bat Cave

You'll be sure to enjoy Bat Cave's local restaurants and crafts and antiques shops. There's plenty of shopping and even golfing to do in the area. And Bat Cave is a short drive to Chimney Rock and Lake Lure, a popular boating spot.

Langdon House

135 Craven Street
Beaufort, North Carolina 28516
(252) 728-5499

E-MAIL: innkeeper@coastalnet.com
WEB SITE: www.langdonhouse.com
INNKEEPER: Jimm Prest
ROOMS: 4; all with private bath
ON THE GROUNDS: Bicycles
RATES: Weekdays: $125 double, with full breakfast; $108 single, with full breakfast; $106 double, with continental breakfast; $94 single, with con-

tinental breakfast; $83 double or single, with morning coffee only. Week-ends in season: two-night minimum stay, $120 to $128 single or double, with continental breakfast; all rates include tax

CREDIT CARDS ACCEPTED? Yes

OPEN: Year-round

HOW TO GET THERE: From Highway 70, take the Morehead drawbridge into Beaufort. Turn right at the first light onto Turner Street, where you'll see a sign for the Historic District. Go 1 block. The house is on the corner of the intersection, facing Craven Street. Park in front of the house or in the side-yard parking area.

The first thing you notice as you walk in is the beautifully restored red-amber heart-pine flooring. Jimm Prest did some of the refinishing him-self, "working way too close to the ground." He has created a comfortable hostelry in this 1732 home, which has verandas on the first and second floors that almost demand some stargazing. The furnishings are comfortably colonial, with bentwood wing-back chairs and an Edwar-dian oak dining table that stretches to 8 feet with all its leaves and can seat fourteen. Many of the antiques, paintings, and musical instruments scat-tered throughout the inn were donated by earlier residents to support his authentic restoration and furnishing of the place.

Jimm says he's functioning as a "glorified storage shed." How else, he asks, can you explain the collection of antique instruments that includes an 1890s pump organ in the parlor, an antique zither, and something called a ukelin from the 1920s?

No matter whom you believe, it happens as it does because this is Jimm Prest's place. The well-restored and -maintained building, the comfortable furnishings and interesting artifacts, are the stage he's created upon which he plays the role of innkeeper with unique style and verve. Take Jimm out of it and it would still be a comfortable place, but it wouldn't be Langdon House.

Consider his list of amenities, for instance. Alphabetically arranged and running to at least a couple of dozen entries, it includes beach baskets, bikes, fishing gear, ice chests, jumper cables, portable gas grills, suntan lotion, and tennis rackets. Nor does he promise anything he can't deliver. He says that the advantage to running so small an inn is that he's able to cater to your whims and provide any service you might need, pretty much one on one.

Or consider his breakfasts. Cooking is a skill he developed in college when he volunteered to cook weekend breakfasts for his housemates and the people who stayed over, because he figured if he cooked, he wouldn't have to clean. He will accommodate any dietary restriction if you warn him ahead of time, but his signature offering is Belgian waffles in such combinations as orange-pecan or cranberry-nut.

Jimm serves breakfast on plain white dishes that won't compete with the appearance of the food, because food "is to be looked at as well as consumed." And that, he figures, is a pretty good use of his college degree in fine arts.

If he went back now, they'd probably give him one in history, or maybe storytelling, too, because he knows the local lore in detail and tells it with wit. He knows about the old burying ground where the oldest, early-1700s graves face east, so the dead will face the sun when they rise on Judgment Morning; he knows about the British Revolutionary War soldier buried standing up, because he swore he would never lie down on foreign soil; he knows the best restaurants and assures you you'll recognize the Net House, because it has a big crab on the front. And he likes to sit on the porch and "trade words."

What it adds up to is that the luster of the heart-pine floors may be the first thing you notice when you arrive, but when you leave, what you'll remember is Jimm Prest.

What's Nearby Beaufort

Once a fishing village, Beaufort is now considered a vacation resort. The downtown area is a National Historic Landmark. See why Beaufort is so historic and find out about the Beaufort Historic Site Tours, which take you to the town jail and courthouse, as well as several historic homes. Some other attractions are the Mattie King Davis Art Gallery and the North Carolina Maritime Museum. At the museum you'll see a great model-ship collection and a wonderful collection of 5,000 seashells from all over the world.

Randolph House Country Inn

223 Fryemont Road
Bryson City, North Carolina 28713
(828) 488–3472 or (800) 480–3472

INNKEEPERS: Bill and Ruth
Randolph Adams

ROOMS: 7; 3 with private bath, some with wheelchair access; separate cottage on Bold Mountain stream

ON THE GROUNDS: Veranda

RATES: $65 to $80 per person, including breakfast and dinner; inquire about cottage rates and arrangements, AAA, senior citizen, and travel agent discounts

CREDIT CARDS ACCEPTED? Yes

OPEN: Mid-April through October

HOW TO GET THERE: From Asheville, take I-40 West to Highway 19/74 to the second Bryson City exit. Turn right off the expressway to the first street on your right, Fryemont Road. Follow the RANDOLPH HOUSE signs.

When you realize how often keepers of historic inns have to answer the same questions and tell the same stories, you appreciate those who can do it without losing their enthusiasm. On that score, Ruth Adams is the best we've seen. Or heard.

She's the niece of the original owner, who built the house in 1895. When we were there she described, in considerable detail, how Amos Frye had owned all the timber in sight but had been forced to sell it when the government decided that it should be national forest land. She said that he'd kept the right to lumber out of those acres for a time and consequently had set to building. It turned out to be the kind of story that gets you involved and carried on by her enthusiasm. We soaked up all the details. Later, we heard her telling parts of the story on the telephone. And that night at dinner, we heard her tell the history twice. Her last telling was as enthusiastic as her first had been.

She radiates the same enthusiasm for the inn itself. As she showed us around, she said, "All the furniture doesn't match. It's just here because it was always here." And she pointed out that one of the rooms has the same furniture with which the Fryes started housekeeping. She showed us the unconventional way that the beds were arranged in some of the rooms, just as they are in any house where you accumulate more furniture than you can accommodate. We admired an old leather chair and a rocker with a needlepoint cushion in the living room. We even got a giggle out of the old-fashioned push-button electric switches in the walls.

Ruth cooks some of the best Southern meals we've ever tasted. When you make a reservation, you have to choose from a list of entrees offered that night, and, for us, the choice was hard because they all sounded so good: Cornish game hens in orange sauce, sautéed shrimp, baked trout, and prime rib of beef. We couldn't pass up the chance for pan-fried trout. It was rolled in cornmeal and then fried in a small amount of fat in an iron skillet. Wonderful! Along with the trout, we had baked spinach Provençal, warm spiced apples, squash casserole, and a baked potato. The vegetables were fresh. They always are.

What's Nearby Bryson City

Bryson City has been called a "mountain getaway." It is a very quiet country town, surrounded by scenic mountains and forests. Bryson City is located between the Great Smoky Mountains National Park and the Nantahala National Forest. You can also explore Fontana Lake, the Museum of the Cherokee Indian, and the Oconaluftee Indian Village. If you're looking for an interesting tour, try the Smoky Mountain Railroad excursion tours.

The Homeplace

5901 Sardis Road
Charlotte, North Carolina 28270
(704) 365–1936; fax (704) 336–2729

WEB SITE: www.bbonline.com/nc/homeplace

INNKEEPERS: Peggy and Frank Dearien

ROOMS: 2 rooms with private bath;
1 suite (sleeps three)

ON THE GROUNDS: Veranda

RATES: $115 per room; suite, $130 for two; third person $25 extra; including full breakfast; two-night minimum stay on holiday and special-event weekends

CREDIT CARDS ACCEPTED? Yes

OPEN: Year-round

HOW TO GET THERE: From I–77, follow Tyvola Road through South Park, where it becomes Fairview Road and crosses Providence Road. Where Fairview crosses Providence, it becomes Sardis Road. The B&B is at the corner of Sardis and Rama. Ask for a map and specific directions from other points when you make reservations.

Don't even think about trying to stay here without making a reservation ahead of time. The Homeplace has become extraordinarily popular and is always busy. It has also become one of the area's most frequently photographed inns, appearing on the covers of travel guides and cookbooks, in television commercials and newspaper articles.

The inn looks like everybody's notion of what a B&B should be. It's a large Victorian farmhouse, painted a creamy color, trimmed in white, with rust-colored shutters. The wraparound porch with rockers looks like a set from *The Waltons*.

The pleasant surprise is that the interior is light and cheerful, with none of the dimness that can be part of the whole Victorian look, especially in the South, where families kept rooms dark in summer to keep them cool.

Furnished with antiques and family treasures, the inn also serves as a sort of gallery for the primitive paintings of Peggy's father, John Gentry. Although he didn't begin painting until he was seventy-nine, his work quickly became popular. For a while the family sold some of it, but since he died at the age of ninety-one, having painted until just six months earlier, no more of his work is for sale. It's just too much a part of the family, and it's not a renewable resource now.

The renewable resource, apparently, is the enthusiasm and energy the Deariens bring to innkeeping. They've withstood all the typical crises of innkeeping as well as some major ones, such as Hurricane Hugo, which ripped up roofs and hundred-year-old oaks in Charlotte, leaving the city without power for about two weeks. The Homeplace not only remained open but also handled two wedding receptions right after the storm hit. Somehow the Deariens managed to convince guests that having Frank cook their breakfasts on an outdoor gas grill under an umbrella was fun, and that candlelight was romantic.

Ordinarily, when electricity is on, the Homeplace smells like the back room of a bakery most of the time, as Peggy makes up a steady supply of homemade breads for breakfast.

The Deariens' involvement with the inn, in decorating, maintaining, hosting, and cooking, makes it a special place. A few words on the telephone, a look around the property, and a whiff of homemade breads are all you'll need to agree—the Deariens aren't going to stop caring.

What's Nearby Charlotte

Charlotte is a great place for museums. First, visit the Mint Museum of Art's collection of Spanish Colonial Art. Next, visit the Hezekiah Alexander Homesite and Museum of History. This history museum exhibits interesting local crafts. Then take the kids to a really neat science and technology museum, Discovery Place, where they can experience hands-on exhibits with computers, fish, and birds.

Dogwood Inn

US 64/74A
(mailing address: P.O. Box 159)
Chimney Rock, North Carolina 28720
(828) 625-4403 or (800) 992-5557; fax (828) 625-8825

E-MAIL: marsha@thedogwoodinn.com

WEB SITE: www.blueridge.net/~dogwoodinn/

INNKEEPERS: Marsha Reynolds and Robert Brooks

ROOMS: 11; 7 with private bath, 4 with shared; 2 with whirlpool tub, 1 with gas-log fireplace; all with ceiling fan, clock radio; 1 with TV

ON THE GROUNDS: Gift shop, patio, porches, river frontage

RATES: $79 to $89 for shared bath, $94 to $105 for private bath, $124 for whirlpool rooms, all double including full breakfast; many special packages; weekends require a two-night minimum stay

CREDIT CARDS ACCEPTED? Yes

OPEN: Closed six weeks from January 1 through mid-February

HOW TO GET THERE: From I-40 or the Blue Ridge Parkway, take US 74 southeast. It goes right through Chimney Rock village. The B&B is on your right. From I-26, take US 64 northeast until it dead-ends into US 74 at the village, then turn right. The B&B is on your right.

An inn has stood on this spot on the banks of the Rocky Broad River and in the shadow of spectacular Chimney Rock for more than a hundred years. In the days before automobiles, a rough road known as the Hickory Nut Gap Turnpike wound through the area, and the Logan Inn offered overnight accommodations for guests traveling through by horse and buggy or stagecoach. The Logan family operated the inn—known for its fine food and good times—through thick and thin for three generations. Challenges along the way included a flood in 1916 and a fire in 1930, which raged through the village and demolished nine buildings, including the inn. Undaunted, the Logans rebuilt this pleasant, simple, white two-story structure, now known as the Dogwood Inn. Today it is operated by Marsha Reynolds and Robert Brooks.

We're talking location, convenience, and casual comfort here. From riverside rooms, you can hear the gurgling of the rushing river and gaze in awe at the gargantuan rock formation that gave the village its name. (Log on to the inn's Web site to hear the river and chirping birds.) Streetside rooms have a view of the village. Four porches and a lovely yard provide many options for enjoying the river and mountain views. The downstairs level provides a comfortable den and a large living/reading/dining room.

Eleven cozy guest rooms, ten of which are upstairs and one of which is on the river level, may be a little tight on space but do provide comfortable bedding and a small seating area. Two special rooms boast whirlpool tubs; one also features a fireplace.

Awaken to a special blend of coffee served every morning in the upstairs hall, followed by breakfast served in the dining room or alfresco on the porch. Guests can choose from a European buffet or the chef's special of the day.

Located in the heart of the hamlet, the B&B is within easy walking distance of restaurants and crafts and antiques shops. A short drive takes you partway up the mountain to Chimney Rock Park, where parts of *Last of the Mohicans* were filmed. Be prepared for some serious climbing the rest of the way; still, you'll be rewarded with spectacular views of the village, valley, and Lake Lure.

What's Nearby Chimney Rock

Chimney Rock is popular for its recreational site, Chimney Rock Park. If you'd rather not hike, take an elevator to the top. On the grounds is Hickory Nut Falls, one of the highest waterfalls in the area. It's a very adventurous park with all of its hiking trails, and it's no wonder that the hit adventure film *Last of the Mohicans* was filmed in this very same park.

Squire Watkins Inn Best Buy

657 Haywood Road
Dillsboro, North Carolina 28725
(828) 586-5244 or (800) 586-2429

INNKEEPERS: Emma and Tom Wertenberger
ROOMS: 4; all with private bath
ON THE GROUNDS: Porches, gardens, lawns
RATES: $68 to $85 double, including breakfast and evening turndown service
CREDIT CARDS ACCEPTED? Yes
OPEN: Year-round
HOW TO GET THERE: From the south, take US 441/23 into Dillsboro. After you cross the bridge, turn left onto Haywood Road/Business 23. The B&B is just a short distance on your left. From the north, turn south off the Great

Smoky Mountain Expressway/US 74 onto US 441. At Haywood Road, turn right.

Our stay at the Squire Watkins Inn was full of laughter and good stories. Emma and Tom provided a warm welcome, spirited conversation, and constant pampering. Their guests added to the hilarity.

The home they've been sharing with guests since 1984 was built by J. C. Watkins and his wife, Flora, in the early 1880s. J. C. was a prosperous merchant and served as the local magistrate, hence the title Squire. Flora was the granddaughter of the founder of the town of Cashiers. To accommodate their growing family, they built this large Queen Anne house on a knoll overlooking the village and the Tuckasegee River. The exterior was characterized by a large square tower sitting at an angle on one front corner, both downstairs and upstairs porches, and a widow's walk (it's no longer there).

Although the interior rooms are capacious, the ceilings high, the windows tall, and the floors hardwood, this was not an ostentatious home with elaborate trimmings. You feel you're in a comfortable home rather than a museum house. The moldings, fireplaces, and stairway are simple. French doors, rather than pocket doors, separate the living and dining rooms. The public rooms are welcoming and cozy. A comfortable blend of inherited family pieces and objects acquired by Emma and Tom on their travels fills the cheerful sitting room and imbues it with a relaxed sense of informality. Light streams in from windows unencumbered with draperies. There's no television and no telephone—nothing obvious to remind you that you're in the late twentieth century.

Not overdone with a high-powered decorator look, the lovely guest rooms reminded us of our grandmothers' houses—dainty floral wallpapers in soft colors, scatter rugs, quilted coverlets, hand-crocheted lace on the pillowcases, sheer curtains, and similar embellishments.

When you arrive in the dining room for breakfast in the morning, the first thing you'll notice is the basket of fresh flowers on the table. Tom calls the contents "the catch of the day" from their gardens. The meal is a masterpiece of such dishes as strawberry crepes with sausage, or sausage and egg casserole with all the accompaniments. Emma promises, "You'll never leave hungry."

Three beautiful, serene acres of gardens and trees invite leisurely strolls. Emma recently told us that they were hosting an increasing number of weddings in the gardens. In fact, she said, the most recent was a young lady who had started coming to the Squire Watkins Inn with her parents when she was a child and decided she couldn't think of anyplace she'd rather have her wedding. From the lower part of the grounds, you can wave to the passengers aboard the Great Smoky Mountains Railway as it chugs slowly by.

The Wertenbergers also offer three cottages where younger children are welcome, but breakfast is not included when staying in one of them, so we don't describe them here.

What's Nearby Dillsboro

Dillsboro will definitely delight you. Downtown, you'll discover crafts, antiques stores, and artist studios. Outdoor options include cross-country and downhill skiing, hiking, white-water rafting, canoeing, tubing, and horseback riding. Dillsboro is convenient to Asheville, where you can take a tour of the Vanderbilt mansion, Biltmore Estate. Finally, take in the vast North Carolina mountains while you drive along the Blue Ridge Parkway.

Arrowhead Inn

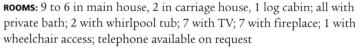

106 Mason Road
Durham, North Carolina 27712
(919) 477–8430 or (800) 528–2207;
fax (919) 471–9538

E-MAIL: info@arrowheadinn.com

WEB SITE: www.arrowheadinn.com

INNKEEPERS: Gloria and Phil Teber

ROOMS: 9 to 6 in main house, 2 in carriage house, 1 log cabin; all with private bath; 2 with whirlpool tub; 7 with TV; 7 with fireplace; 1 with wheelchair access; telephone available on request

ON THE GROUNDS: Four acres for walking

RATES: $98 to $215 double, including full gourmet breakfast; other meals available on request at additional fee; inquire about frequent-stayer program

CREDIT CARDS ACCEPTED? Yes

OPEN: Year-round

HOW TO GET THERE: The bed and breakfast is on US 501, 7 miles north of I–85.

When the Arrowhead Inn opened more than a decade ago, the owners had a problem it's hard to imagine these days—nobody had any idea what a B&B was. But they did such a good job with this first bed and breakfast in Durham that they received an award from the Greater Durham Chamber of Commerce. Moreover, they were the founders and then the president couple of the North Carolina Bed and Breakfast Association. They wrote a column for a journal for innkeepers and taught a seminar on innkeeping for Duke University. The Arrowhead's current owners, the Tebers, were students.

Gloria and Phil Teber had been studying and planning their move into the world of innkeeping for several years. When the chance to buy the Arrowhead came up, they jumped at it.

The eighteenth-century farmhouse has a fascinating history. Two different families bought it and lost it in hard times. The Lipscombe family built the house in about 1775 and had a plantation and slaves here for more than a hundred years before they lost the property. It was then bought at foreclosure by a banker, who lost it in turn at the end of the Great Depression. The son of that family, now in his eighties, still comes to visit.

The original part of the house was exceedingly modest—two rooms down and two up. Nobody is quite sure when the later addition that doubled the house to its present size was built because the records were lost. If you like knowing these kinds of things, you'll also be interested to learn about the original timbers in the attic. You can still read the markings written on them during construction.

And you'll probably be partial to our favorite guest room, a high-ceilinged chamber on the second floor of the original house. It has a brick fireplace (not working, because the old mortar is too soft) topped by an ornately carved Victorian mantel that appears to have been added later. The wainscoting in the room is white and the wallpaper is burgundy with a tiny pattern. The queen-size bed has a burgundy dust ruffle and a tufted, off-white bedcover. It all gives the whole room a comfortable feel.

Gloria and Phil have also made their mark with the addition of a new suite, complete with whirlpool tub (for those whose interests run toward water sports) and fireplace. They have also upgraded the amenities they offer their business clients by installing new data-port telephones and enlarged work areas. Perhaps partly because of the good breakfasts and the gentle tone of the decor, the inn has become popular with businesspeople, especially women. They sometimes bring their work down to sit in the keeping room. They say it's so much nicer than having to lock themselves into a motel room. Also, the four acres of land on which the B&B sits make a nice place to walk at the end of a business day, and, in summer when the old magnolias are blooming, even a workday feels a little like a holiday.

What's Nearby Durham

Duke University is a popular place to visit in Durham. The Duke University Chapel attracts many visitors. The Gothic chapel is widely admired for its eighteenth-century organ, seventy-seven stained-glass windows, and elaborate architectural details. Another campus attraction is the Sarah Duke Memorial Gardens, which has a lovely gazebo and lily pond and rows of flowers. B. Everett Jordan Lake is located right on campus.

Flat Rock Inn

2810 Greenville Highway
Flat Rock, North Carolina 28731
(828) 696-3273 or (800) 266-3996

E-MAIL: fribb@bellsouth.net

WEB SITE: www.bbhost.com/flatrockinn

INNKEEPERS: Sandi and Dennis Page

ROOMS: 3 rooms and 1 suite; all with private bath; 2 with private porches; smoking permitted outside

ON THE GROUNDS: Shaded and sunny lawns, bocce ball, horseshoes, hammock, veranda with swings and Ping-Pong table

RATES: $85 to $145 double, including full breakfast and refreshments; additional person $15; weekends usually require a two-night minimum; ask about romantic getaway, Biltmore, golf, and weekday packages

CREDIT CARDS ACCEPTED? Yes

OPEN: Year-round

HOW TO GET THERE: From I-26 traveling north, take exit 22 west to US 25 South and turn left. You'll pass the Carl Sandburg Home on the right and then see the sign for the inn on your left. From I-26 traveling southbound, take exit 18 and go west into Hendersonville and turn left on US 25 South.

Where shall we start to tell you all about the Flat Rock Inn? It's full of historic ambience, but carries the present comfortably; its hosts, Sandi and Dennis, are genial and the location is terrific. It all adds up to a splendid getaway.

Our first impression, however, was of the gigantic trees shading the large Victorian house with its wraparound veranda. Built in 1888, until 1911 it was the summer retreat of R. Withers Memminger, a minister from Charleston and the son of C. G. Memminger, the first Secretary of the Treasury of the Confederacy. Englishman Thomas Grimshawe and his wife, Elizabeth, then purchased it and made it their year-round residence until 1930, when they gave the house to their daughter Greta Grimshawe King as a wedding present. Pictures of the Grimshawe and King families adorn the walls in the formal dining room.

We checked out the old-fashioned porch swing, comfortable wicker, and the Ping-Pong table on the veranda before we stepped into the grand central hall with an antique clock and a vintage quilt used as a wall hanging—both testaments to another era. A formal parlor with a striking fireplace, a lovely bay window, and comfortable overstuffed sofas and chairs beckon guests to read, relax, and get to know each other.

Upstairs three individually decorated guest rooms and a two-room suite provide elegant accommodations. An extra-large claw-foot tub is the focal point of the bathroom of the Squire Room. What a perfect place for a candlelight bubble bath with your sweetie! Lace, teddy bears, an ornate carved bed from New Orleans' French Quarter, and a private porch characterize the Victoria Room. The Sandburg Room is a tribute to the local resident, poet, and Nobel laureate. The country motif is enhanced with a white iron bed. This room also features a claw-foot tub and a private porch. Perfect for two couples, the Colonial Room is actually a two-room suite with a queen-size carved rice bed in one room and twin beds in the other.

Breakfast begins before you leave your room—when you get the first whiff of the aroma of custom-blended coffee, tea, or hot chocolate. In good weather early risers enjoy a cup out on the veranda. The breakfast bell rings at 8:30 A.M. and beckons guests to the dining room for a family-style meal of such delicacies as baked apples, oranges in poppy seed dressing, Puerto Rican pineapple in vanilla sauce, or succulent Georgia peaches. Entrees range from cherry blintzes to eggs Benedict to Belgian waffles to frittatas or specialty omelettes.

Food figures in the rest of your relaxing day at the Flat Rock Inn. A guest refrigerator is well stocked with complimentary sodas, juices, and wine. Afternoon snacks such as Sandi's Neiman chocolate cookies, walnut brownies, or other goodies are served on the veranda in the afternoon. Nightly turn-down service includes tasty mints on your pillow, but one of the most popular times is in the evening when guests gather to raid the freezer and enjoy ice cream.

Bocce ball tournaments are often held on the lawn and murder mystery weekends occur several times a year. There are also board games and horseshoes for those who like a challenge. If you have little more in mind than reading a good book or taking a nap, there's an oh-so-comfortable hammock.

What's Nearby Flat Rock

The B&B is conveniently located across the street from the restaurant at the Woodfield Inn and live theater performances at the Flat Rock Playhouse and is within easy walking distance of the Carl Sandburg National Historic Site and the antiques and crafts shops of the Village of Flat Rock. Hop in the car and within a few minutes you can be in Asheville or touring the Biltmore Estate, taking a scenic drive on the Blue Ridge Parkway to the Appalachian Folk Art Center, hiking at Chimney Rock Park or in the Pisgah National Forest or Dupont State Forest, taking in a performance at Hendersonville's Brevard Music Center, or touring the nearby Cradle of Forestry Interpretive Center.

La Grange Plantation Inn

NC 1308
(mailing address: Route 3, Box 610)
Henderson, North Carolina 27536
(252) 438-2421

INNKEEPERS: Dick and Jean Cornell

ROOMS: 5; all with private bath, 1 with wheelchair access

RATES: $95 first night, $85 consecutive nights, double; single $10 less; including full breakfast; two-night minimum stay on major holidays

CREDIT CARDS ACCEPTED? Yes

OPEN: Year-round

ON THE GROUNDS: Swimming pool, lakeside fishing, walking trails, croquet, horseshoes

HOW TO GET THERE: From I–85, take exit 214 to NC 39 North and proceed 4.4 miles to Harris Crossroads. There is a state sign pointing right to

Nutbush Creek Recreation Area. Turn right and proceed 0.8 mile to the inn, which is on your left.

There's nothing rural inside La Grange Plantation Inn. The Cornells are sophisticated innkeepers (Jean is English) with exquisite taste. The place is furnished with American and English antiques in what Jean calls "relaxed English country style."

The front parlor has a wonderful fireplace, books ranging from current fiction to history and nature studies, and no television to break the mood. The Cornells, who are great readers, count among their enthusiastic guests the owners of a bookstore in Raleigh, so it's no surprise that one outstanding feature of all the guest rooms is a good bedside reading light at the correct height.

To decorate the guest rooms, Jean made the window treatments and bed coverings herself, different in each room and elegant—made of rich fabrics, full of flowers, in muted colors.

The private baths are clustered in a central location just outside the rooms; Jean provides plush terry robes for guests to move from their rooms to their bathrooms but allows that you don't have to use a robe "if you'd rather streak!"

Turning La Grange into an inn was a major project. The Historic Preservation Foundation of North Carolina described the inn in an issue of its magazine, *North Carolina Preservation,* as a "two-story double-pile Greek Revival house with Italianate brackets," the oldest part of which was built in 1770. When the Cornells bought it in 1985, it was a wreck. Windows rattled, the plaster had big cracks, and the foundation wobbled. It took a lot of time and money as well as the expertise of an architect and an architectural conservator working with a contractor to restore the house to historic preservation standards and also make it comfortable. The Cornells did the interior painting and finished the floors themselves. Today the interior and the hospitality are perfect.

What's Nearby Henderson

If outdoor water sports float your boat, Henderson is the place for you. Choose from a variety of swimming beaches. Practice your water skiing and sailing at Kerr Lake. Take a fishing trip with a guide from Kerr Lake. Closer to home, play some golf, try the local restaurants, and even pack a picnic lunch for an afternoon at one of the state recreation areas.

The Claddagh Inn

755 North Main Street

Hendersonville, North Carolina 28792

(828) 697-7778 or (800) 225-4700; fax (828) 697-8664

E-MAIL: Innkeepers@CladdaghInn.com

WEB SITE: www.CladdaghInn.com

INNKEEPERS: Geraldine and August Emanuele

ROOMS: 16, including a 2-bedroom, 2-bath suite with kitchen; all with private bath, telephone, TV, clock

ON THE GROUNDS: Large wraparound veranda, small lawn and garden

RATES: $99 to $140 double, including full breakfast; additional person $20; children under ten free in the room with parents

CREDIT CARDS ACCEPTED? Yes

OPEN: Year-round

HOW TO GET THERE: From I-26, take US 64 into Hendersonville. Turn right onto US 25. The inn is almost immediately on your left.

One of the first things we wanted to get out of the way when we visited this B&B was the proper way to pronounce the name. As soon as Gerri and Augie told us it's Claw-da, we felt more comfortable. The Claddagh is a Gaelic symbol you've probably seen a million times—two hands holding a heart topped by a crown. It stands for love, loyalty, and friendship and its origin goes back at least four centuries to the Galway Bay region where it appeared on betrothal rings. The original expression that accompanied such a ring was "With these hands I give you my heart and I crown it with my love." Today the Claddagh is often exchanged as a friendship ring.

As you might guess, the ambience here is Irish. The Emanueles aren't Irish themselves; it was a former owner who gave the inn its name and personality, but Gerri and Augie were only too happy to continue the tradition. They had stained-glass windows depicting Irish symbols created for the transoms over the doors to several of the guest rooms. Other touches of whimsy we enjoyed are the fish tank incorporated into the registration counter and an old carousel elephant in the second-floor hall.

How did two longtime New Yorkers became proprietors of an inn in small-town North Carolina? Both Emanueles were air freight forwarders and customs brokers at JFK Airport and were looking for a retirement change of career. They had in mind a golf-related business such as a golf course, restaurant, or shop. They came to the Asheville area to look at properties and as luck would have it, stayed at the Claddagh Inn. Impressed with the inn's charm, they thought innkeeping could be for them. There was a catch, however. Their daughter was a sophomore in high school. She wasn't too keen on moving—especially not giving up her cheerleading. Just to keep the family's options open, she came down to Hendersonville High School to try out for their cheerleading squad and made it, giving her thumbs up to the move. And despite their myriad duties as innkeepers, Gerri and Augie manage to make time to play golf.

The cheerful yellow three-story late-nineteenth-century house, trimmed in green and white, has a welcoming wraparound veranda. Although it was built in 1888 as a single family home for W. A. Smith, Hendersonville's first mayor, it became the Charleston Boarding House in 1906 to house residents from the Lowcountry who escaped to the highlands in the summer for relief from coastal heat and humidity. The stately house has served some type of hospitality function ever since. It became the city's first bed and breakfast in 1985.

Inside are formal and informal parlors, a large dining room, numerous sitting nooks, and sixteen guest rooms ranging in size from a small room perfect for a business person traveling alone to family rooms with several beds and a two-bedroom, two-bath suite with kitchen facilities. Several rooms are on the first floor, so although the inn isn't technically wheelchair accessible, it is user friendly for those who have trouble with stairs. Each room has its own distinct personality and is furnished in a mixture of antiques and reproductions.

The food is Gerri's favorite part of the whole project. She and Augie come from large families and often entertained hordes on holidays, so cooking for large numbers of people doesn't faze her at all. Early risers or those who desire only a light breakfast can enjoy the buffet of fresh fruit, yogurt, granola, and breads. Eggs, a breakfast meat, and grits are on the menu every day as well as a specialty item such as pancakes or rum-raisin French toast with raisin-cinnamon sauce.

What's Nearby Hendersonville

This town features a public park with tennis courts and miniature golf as well as a downtown with antiques shops, boutiques, and restaurants. The Village of Flat Rock,where you can visit the Carl Sandburg National Historic Site or attend a performance of the renowned Flat Rock Playhouse, is only minutes away. The Blue Ridge Parkway, Asheville, Biltmore Estate, and Chimney Rock Park are also nearby, and you'll find plenty of water sports on Lake Lure.

Melange Bed and Breakfast

1230 Fifth Avenue West
Hendersonville, North Carolina 28739
(828) 697-5253 or (800) 303-5253,
fax (828) 697-5751

E-MAIL: melange@brinet.com

WEB SITE: www.melangebb.com

INNKEEPERS: Lale and Mehmet Ozelsel

ROOMS: 4 rooms and 1 suite; all with private bath, TV, VCR, telephone; some with featherbed or whirlpool tub; 1 with fireplace and private porch

ON THE GROUNDS: Porches, extensive lawns and gardens with fountains

RATES: $115 to $185 double, including full breakfast; additional person $25; two-night minimum stay on weekends in season; some holiday weekends require a three-night reservation

CREDIT CARDS ACCEPTED? Yes

OPEN: Year-round

HOW TO GET THERE: From I-26, take US 64 West into town. Turn left onto Church Street and take the second right onto Fifth Avenue West. Melange is 0.8 mile on the left and is identified by a sign.

The word *melange* means medley. It is, therefore, a perfect name for this bed and breakfast where the current owners' Mediterranean background is blended with the French and European decor created by former owners of the house. Lale and Mehmet Ozelsel are a sophisticated international couple who are originally from Turkey, but who lived for many years in Germany. Despite their cosmopolitan background, they decided they wanted to retire in Hendersonville and open a bed and breakfast. The house they chose has an international flair to match their own and the name represents its blend of styles and cultures.

Shielded from the street by towering hemlocks and other century-old trees, the stately federal-style house was designed by architect Erle G. Stillwell in 1920 for the Hobbs family of New England to use as a summer home. The third owners were the Moores of Seattle who were lovers of French culture. They transformed the interior into one of opulent French symmetry with Empire-style wallpapers, marble mantels from Paris, crystal chandeliers from Vienna, and hand-painted porcelain accessories from Italy. The oak parquet floor in the formal parlor was inspired by the floor in the Gallery of Mirrors in the Versailles Palace. Rarely have we seen a relatively simple traditional home that has so much ornate plaster molding on the 11-foot ceilings.

During a two-year restoration, the Ozelsels added contemporary comfort to the rooms and created porches with Mediterranean flair. They enhanced the European decor with marble and tile floors and comfortable seating groups and put considerable effort into creating flower and herb gardens accented with splashing fountains. The gardens and vast velvety lawns serve as the site for weddings and other special events.

Each opulent guest room is designed around a color theme to which antique furnishings, ornate lamps, Oriental carpets, exquisite wall coverings, and striking bed linens and window treatments are added. The signature bedchamber is the very private Cinnamon Room, which has a brass queen-size featherbed and a luxury bathroom with two-person corner whirlpool tub under a skylight. Perhaps the most elegant is the Pearl Room, which features an upholstered king-size featherbed, brocade-covered walls, and bathroom with a pink marble whirlpool tub. Occupying the entire third floor as a romantic and intimate retreat, the Rose Suite boasts a king-size brass bed, a large sitting/dining area with big-screen television and sound system, and a refrigerator and coffeemaker. Two double beds occupy the second bedroom. This suite's bath features a claw-foot tub with an old-fashioned shower.

The most formal of the rooms is the Green Room with its magnificently draped full-tester bed. Its dramatic bathroom is decorated with colorful, intricately designed Turkish tiles. The most popular feature, however, is the working fireplace. A private porch is the main attraction of the Red Room, which features a king-size sleigh bed. The Green and Red Rooms can be combined to create a suite.

Add to the handsome physical surroundings soothing music, fresh flowers, and wonderful culinary delights and you get a total experience. In fact, although Lale is an accomplished cook, Mehmet has enrolled in culinary school to help make your stay an epicurean experience as well as a restful, revitalizing one. In cool weather breakfast is served formally in the turquoise dining room by candlelight using festive china and crystal. In warm weather the morning repast is served outdoors in the rose garden patio under the shade of an old maple tree or on the delightful, secluded west porch. The explosion-of-flavors menu typically includes fresh fruit, a creative egg dish, fresh sourdough bread, and gourmet coffee cake.

To make a romantic getaway even more memorable, you can arrange for fresh fruit, chocolates, roses, a cake, champagne or wine, a five-course candlelight dinner, and/or breakfast in bed at an additional fee.

It's so rare that children are welcome at bed and breakfasts, but they are welcome at Melange. Lale and Mehmet say, "Melange is children friendly; however, parents are expected to support our efforts to watch over family heirlooms and antiques." The Rose Suite, which has two bedrooms, can accommodate up to six people, making it ideal for a family.

What's Nearby Hendersonville

See page 315 for what's nearby Hendersonville.

Harmony House Inn

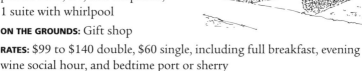

215 Pollock Street
New Bern, North Carolina 28560
(252) 636-3810 or (800) 636-3113

INNKEEPERS: Ed and Sooki Kirkpatrick

ROOMS: 8, including 2 suites; all with private bath, TV, and telephone; 1 suite with whirlpool

ON THE GROUNDS: Gift shop

RATES: $99 to $140 double, $60 single, including full breakfast, evening wine social hour, and bedtime port or sherry

CREDIT CARDS ACCEPTED? Yes

OPEN: Year-round

HOW TO GET THERE: Pollock Street runs 1 block back from Tryon Place Drive, which fronts on the Trent River. Ask for a map when you make your reservations.

For many years this inn was the pride of Diane and Buzz Hansen. In 1994 they sold it to Ed and Sooki Kirkpatrick. Ed had been working in large hotels and was increasingly unhappy with how little control he had over the service offered guests, and how little time he had to spend with them. When he and Sooki learned they were going to have a child, they decided to move into their own B&B so they could spend time with the baby. Not everybody would think having a baby and a new B&B all in the same year was a blessing, but the Kirkpatricks loved it. And the guests have loved the Kirkpatricks as well as the property itself.

The guest rooms are big and comfortable, with good beds and lots of light. They've all been carpeted in colors to match the decor of each room. (The living room has been carpeted, too. The overall effect is warm and cheery.) A section of the B&B has been renovated into a two-room suite. One room is a sitting area with a queen-size sofabed; the other room is a bedroom with a queen-size canopy bed. A family of four fits here comfortably.

Accommodating families is part of the bizarre history of this building. The circa-1850 Greek Revival house was built by a man who had six children. To accommodate them, he made additions to the house about 1860 and again about 1880. The kids grew up, and about 1900 two of the sons, who both wanted to live in the house with their families, sawed it in half and moved one half 9 feet away from the other to add a hallway, front door, staircase, and sitting room. Each family lived in its own half for twenty years. Now it's all one house again, but it has two sets of stairs, halls, sitting rooms, and front doors, side by side. As you can imagine, the effect is very spacious. The Kirkpatricks have used some of the space to open a gift shop offering a small number of items unique to their inn, not things you'll pick up at every gift shop in the state.

What's Nearby New Bern

New Bern, with its antiques shops and attractive historic estates, is a haven for avid antiques collectors and museum-goers. Tour the Tryon Palace Restorations and Garden Complex. Pay a visit to the Attmore-Oliver House Museum, which displays antiques, town artifacts, and Civil War memorabilia. Stop by the Fireman's Museum and see early fireman equipment. If you feel like taking a ride around town, hop on the New Bern Trolley Cars. The trolley tours guide you through downtown New Bern.

Woods House Best Buy

130 Henderson Street
(mailing address: P.O. Box 700)
Saluda, North Carolina 28773
(828) 749-9562; fax (828) 749-9220

INNKEEPER: Dorothy Eargle

ROOMS: 5 rooms and 1 cottage;
all with private bath

ON THE GROUNDS: Porch and rockers

RATES: $75 rooms, $85 cottage, single or double, including continental breakfast; inquire about season rates for cottage

CREDIT CARDS ACCEPTED? No

OPEN: May through October

HOW TO GET THERE: I-26 takes you directly to Saluda's main street, where you will see signs directing you to the Woods House. It is on the corner of Church and Henderson Streets at the top of the hill.

Saluda used to be full of B&Bs and inns, at least a couple of dozen. Now the Woods House is almost the only one left in town. It sits at the top of a steep hill, on a large, shady piece of land, overlooking Saluda's main street. When you're here, you feel that neither the town nor the inn has changed much since it was built just before the turn of the century. Dorothy's late-Victorian and turn-of-the-century antiques contribute to that feeling, as does her collection of old needlework displayed throughout the B&B.

The kitchen is a real country kitchen. We can't think of anything that will make history come alive faster than eating breakfast surrounded by the aromas of homemade bread and brewing coffee.

Dorothy has had an antiques shop for years, even before coming to Saluda. The sure decorating touch of someone who has known and lived with antiques for a long time shows all through the house and in the cottage that once was servants' quarters. The furniture hasn't been here forever, but it seems as though it must have been.

For us, the best part is the wide porch with the obligatory swings and rockers, because you can sit and enjoy the breeze while you watch the activity down on the main street and the birds in the yard. If you're an early riser, you'll find coffee set up in the dining room so that you can enjoy a cup or two on the porch before anyone even thinks about breakfast.

What's Nearby Saluda

Saluda is a small town with a population of less than a thousand people. The downtown area is spotted with antiques and arts and crafts stores. Saluda is known for its local bakery, the Wildflour Bakery, which sells homemade and healthy breads, soups, salads, and sandwiches.

Bed and Breakfast at Laurel Ridge

3188 Siler City-Snow Camp Road
Siler City, North Carolina 27344
(919) 742-6049 or (800) 742-6049

E-MAIL: david@nc.webtel.net or lreynolds@cheerful.com

WEB SITE: www.bbonline.com/nc/laurelridge/ (Look for their upcoming Web site at www.laurel-ridge.com.)

INNKEEPERS: David Simmons and Lisa Reynolds

ROOMS: 2 rooms, 1 suite, and 1 cottage; all with private bath, telephone, clock radio, desk; some with whirlpool tub, ceiling fan, balcony, deck, or screened porch; cottage is fully wheelchair accessible

ON THE GROUNDS: Porches, decks, gardens, walking paths, lawn games, riverfront, forest

RATES: $85 to $125 per room, including full breakfast and afternoon refreshments; additional person beyond a couple $10

CREDIT CARDS ACCEPTED? Yes

OPEN: Year-round

HOW TO GET THERE: From Pittsboro, take US 64 West toward Siler City. Before you get to Siler City, go north on Pearlyman-Teague Road, then turn right onto Siler City–Snow Camp Road. The B&B is on your right.

We were enchanted from the moment we drove up the long winding driveway and saw all the banks of mountain laurel; they reminded us of our childhoods in western Pennsylvania and western Maryland. The resemblance increased as we explored this heavily wooded twenty-six-acre property. Perched on a bluff over the Rocky River, it offers decks, a gazebo overlooking the river (you'll feel like you're in a tree house), and a walking trail down to the river. We arrived at the house just in time for afternoon refreshments served in the gazebo. What a treat to get to know our hosts David and Lisa, savor the scrumptious nibbles, and get right into the peacefulness of the country.

This is definitely a place to relax and recharge your batteries. The rustic timber-framed, tin-roofed house, built in 1983 by local craftsmen, blends in perfectly with the natural surroundings. Inside, large exposed beams and paneled walls are featured throughout. The rusticity is blended with touches of luxury.

Romantic draped fabric swoops down from the ceiling over the iron canopy bed in the Rose Suite, an elegant chamber that boasts a whirlpool tub, private balcony, and skylight. Twin beds flank a window under the sloping eaves of the Pine Room. A brass bed is the focal point of the Jewel Room. Nestled next to the house is the Carolina Cottage, which features a whirlpool tub and a private screened porch.

The outstanding food is prepared by David, an accomplished chef. Served on pottery created by the area's exceptional potters, the morning meal is an anticipated delight. David might serve any one of his seven renowned specialty pancakes (poppyseed or pumpkin basil are the most popular), cheddar and sun-dried tomato soufflé, or his own version of huevos rancheros, accompanied by fresh juices, locally roasted coffee, homemade sausage, and freshly baked breads or pastries. David uses fresh edible flowers and herbs from the gardens to garnish his specialties.

What's Nearby Siler City

Get away from it all and visit the Body Therapy Institute. Then use that rejuvenated source of energy to tackle a busy day of shopping at Siler City's crafts galleries and studios. The area also offers golf, horseback riding, water sports, biking, and hiking.

The Inn at Celebrity Dairy

2106 Mount Vernon-Hickory Mountain Road
Siler City, North Carolina 27344
(919) 742-5176 or (877) 742- 5176;
fax (919) 742-1432

E-MAIL: theinn@celebritydairy.com

WEB SITE: www.celebritydairy.com

INNKEEPERS: Fleming and Brit Pfann

ROOMS: 7; 5 with private bath, 2 with shared; all with clock radio, desk; 1 ground-floor room and bath is fully wheelchair accessible, the other has limited wheelchair access

ON THE GROUNDS: Porches, farm buildings, 200 acres, one hundred goats

RATES: $60 to $120 double, including full farm breakfast; additional person $15

CREDIT CARDS ACCEPTED? Yes

OPEN: Year-round

HOW TO GET THERE: From the Pittsboro Courthouse, go 10.2 miles west on US 64 and turn right onto Mount Vernon-Hickory Mountain Road. Go 2 miles north and turn right into the farm drive at the CELEBRITY DAIRY sign. From the US 64 and US 421 Bypass at Siler City, go 4 miles east and turn left onto Mount Vernon-Hickory Mountain Road. Follow the preceding directions.

etting away from it all and indulging in informal comfort and simple pleasures are the specialties at this farm. Enjoy a goat's affection, a moonrise undimmed by city lights, the relaxation of an evening fire,

deer grazing at dusk, the soothing call of whippoorwills or owls, a substantial farm breakfast after the morning's milking. Although we only watched, guests may join in the morning and evening chores and learn the art of milking. We were too busy taking precious pictures of the goats that make this bed and breakfast unique.

Someone once told Fleming and Brit that "nobody intends to get into goats—it's always an accident." When the Pfanns moved back to North Carolina from Florida in 1987, they purchased a farm that had been unworked for twenty-five years and bought some goats to eat down the brush. One of the goats was in milk and it turned out that Fleming, who is intolerant of cow's milk, had no trouble digesting goat's milk. So the goats were bred and multiplied. So much milk was produced, the Pfanns didn't know what to do with it all, so they made a trip to the library for a book on cheese making. As they describe it, "Some of the cheese tasted okay. Other people tried and liked it. And nobody died." In 1989 they decided to build a dairy and make cheese commercially. Following time-honored French techniques, they transform the milk from their Alpine and Saanen goats into fresh chèvre. Their cheese is renowned in the area and sold directly to restaurants and at farmers' markets and specialty grocery stores.

Located on 200 acres, the farm's original 1820s log cabin, log hay barn and granary, 1880s smokehouse, and 1940s tobacco barn survive. Sheltered on a knoll under 250-year-old oak trees is a simple Colonial Revival farmhouse with first- and second-story porches. So naturally does this residence fit into the farm picture that we'd have sworn it dated from the last century as well. We were surprised to learn that it is of recent construction. The goat barn and microdairy are new, too.

Accommodations are offered in the big house and the log cabin, which are connected by an atrium. The B&B's six guest rooms and the log-cabin suite, each of which has a private bath, are comfortably furnished in country charm and named for a family member who might have lived there a century ago. Bedding ranges from two twins that can be made into a king to doubles and queens. Lauren's Room sports a two-person whirlpool tub. The log cabin boasts a sitting area, dressing room, private entrance, and separate porch.

On a farm, breakfast is the most important meal of the day; at Celebrity Dairy it is a communal meal served to both guests and farmhands in the atrium after the morning milking—about 8:30 A.M. The chèvre is featured in omelettes, frittatas, and other dishes using fresh eggs from their free-range chickens as well as in creamy condiments sweetened with preserves. The meal is accompanied by home-baked pastries, scones, or quick breads as well as seasonal fruits and preserves created from the bounty of their neighbors' gardens.

A fully stocked weaving studio spills over into the B&B, and a spinning wheel and loom invite you to try your hand at spinning or weaving a rag rug. The atrium and porches provide ideal places to sit and watch the farm animals and wildlife, read a book or magazine from the library, or do nothing.

What's Nearby Siler City

See page 322 for what's nearby Siler City.

Catherine's Inn

410 South Front Street
Wilmington, North Carolina 28401
(910) 251-0863 or (800) 476-0723;
fax (910) 772-9550

E-MAIL: catherin@wilmington.net

WEB SITE: www.catherinesinn.com

INNKEEPERS: Catherine and Walter Ackiss

ROOMS: 5; all with private bath, TV, telephone with data port, TV in parlor

ON THE GROUNDS: Porch, lawn, sunken garden, horseshoes, croquet, bicycles

RATES: $80 to $115, single or double, including full breakfast and evening sherry; ask about corporate rates

CREDIT CARDS ACCEPTED? Yes

OPEN: Year-round

HOW TO GET THERE: Cross the Cape Fear Memorial Bridge on Highway 74/76/17. Exit right on the Front Street North exit. Drive 3 short blocks. Number 410 will be on your left past Church Street. From I-40, take Highway 17 (Market Street) south into the historic district. Proceed to Front Street and turn left. The inn is 4 blocks south on your right.

A few years back Catherine had an inn in the historic district called the Inn on Orange. Later, she called it Catherine's Inn on Orange. Now she's moved to a gorgeous waterfront house, and her inn is simply Catherine's Inn. The way the name changes to fit her situation tells you something about the depth of her involvement in the hospitality business. She decided to become an innkeeper because, as she told her husband, Walter, she wanted to be a hostess. And she felt that her own travel experience had taught her what people value in small lodgings.

The B&B is in an Italianate house built in 1883. It has wrought-iron fences and gate, a Colonial Revival wraparound front porch, and a two-story, screened rear porch. Impressive as the structure is, Catherine's hospitality is still more important than the building.

As she sees it, when you walk through the door, you become part of her family. The feeling is not one way. One young businesswoman who stays here regularly mentioned at breakfast that, as she was driving toward Wilmington, she found herself thinking, "I can't wait to see Catherine and tell her about the new guy I went out with last weekend." She and Catherine sat up together talking long after we'd drifted off to sleep.

Catherine says that, like a good family member, she tries to know when guests want to talk and when they want to be left alone.

The family sense comes also from the B&B's being furnished with many antiques and family pieces that Catherine has refinished herself, including a stunning piano that once belonged to her mother and a cedar chest her mother gave her when she was twelve. Several dolls that belonged to Catherine's grandmother fit right in.

On an upstairs screened porch, you'll find the comfort of a well-stocked refrigerator from which you can help yourself to wine, beer, and soft drinks, just as you might at home (if you could keep the refrigerator that well stocked). Also, from the porch you can enjoy the sunset and the views of a 300-foot private lawn that overlooks a sunken garden and the Cape Fear River.

In the morning Catherine's breakfasts are a delight, featuring everything from French toast to blueberry muffins and an opportunity for some casual conversation. It's like the kind of laughing breakfast conversation we fantasize about enjoying just as soon as our own families become perfect.

What's Nearby Wilmington

Learn all about Historic Wilmington District by taking the Wilmington Adventure Walking Tour. Along the way, you'll visit historic houses, churches, gardens, and fountains. You can also take the Springbrook Farms sight-seeing tour through the historic district. Another attraction worth seeing is the St. John's Museum of Art, which displays original color prints by Mary Cassatt, and Impressionist painter. No need to fear, there's still more to do, like take a cruise on the Cape Fear River. Don't miss the specialty shops and restaurants in Chandler's Wharf on the Cape Fear River.

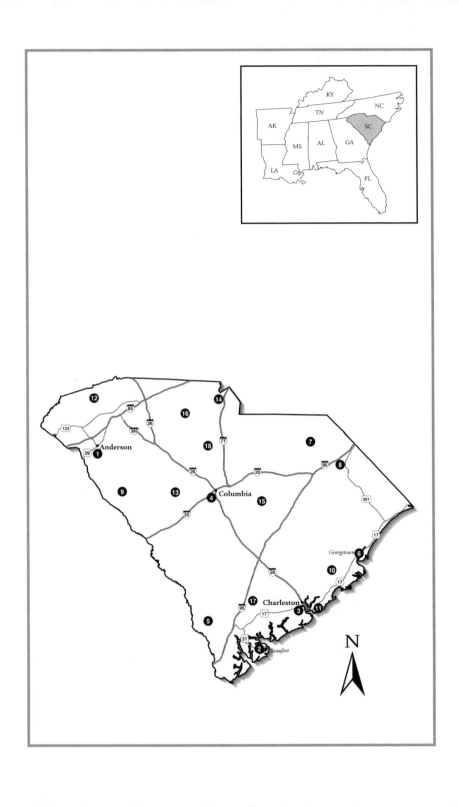

South Carolina

Numbers on map refer to towns numbered below.

1. Anderson, Anderson's River Inn Bed and Breakfast, 328

2. Beaufort,
   The John Cuthbert House B&B, 329
   Old Point Inn, 331
   TwoSuns Inn, 333

3. Charleston,
   The Ashley Inn Bed and Breakfast, 334
   Belvedere, 336
   Cannonboro Inn, 337
   Hayne House, 339

4. Columbia,
   Chestnut Cottage Bed and Breakfast, 341
   Richland Street B&B, 342

5. Estill, John Lawton House, 344

6. Georgetown,
   1790 House Bed and Breakfast, 346
   The Shaw House, 348

7. Hartsville, Missouri Inn Bed and Breakfast, 350

8. Latta, Abingdon Manor, 351

9. McCormick, Fannie Kate's Country Inn, 353

10. Moncks Corner, Rice Hope Plantation, 356

11. Mount Pleasant, Guilds Inn, 358

12. Pickens, The Schell Haus Bed and Breakfast, 359

13. Ridge Spring, Southwood Manor, 361

14. Rock Hill, East Main Guest House, 362

15. Sumter,
    The Bed and Breakfast of Sumter, 364
    Calhoun Street Bed and Breakfast, 365
    Magnolia House, 367

16. Union, The Inn at Merridun, 360

17. Walterboro, Bonnie Doone Plantation, 370

18. Winnsboro, Songbird Manor, 372

Anderson's River Inn Bed and Breakfast

Best Buy

612 East River Street
Anderson, South Carolina 29624
(864) 226–1431

E-MAIL: andersonsin@carol.net

WEB SITE: www.bbonline.com/sc/andersons

INNKEEPERS: Pat Clark and Wayne Hollingsworth

ROOMS: 3; all with private bath, telephone, TV, jacks for computer connection, wood-burning fireplace

ON THE GROUNDS: Large backyard, hot tub

RATES: $85 double, including full breakfast, afternoon refreshments

CREDIT CARDS ACCEPTED? Yes

OPEN: Year-round except Christmas

HOW TO GET THERE: From I–85, take exit 19A, Clemson Boulevard, south to Main Street. Just past the courthouse, turn left onto East River Street.

This lovely two-story federal-style home was constructed in 1914 by Dr. Archer LeRoy Smethers, who used it as his home and office. Inside the style is Arts and Crafts of the Stickley period. We appreciated the warmth of the walnut-stained woodwork, 10-foot beamed ceilings, crown moldings, and built-ins produced by craftsmen whose skills and materials are no longer available. Although much of the front yard was usurped by highway widening, a commodious backyard invites guests to relax in the shade of the large old trees.

Still, it's the warm and personal hospitality of the owners, which is manifested in so many ways, that sets this bed and breakfast head-and-shoulders above many others. Interesting folks who enjoy sharing their lives with others, Pat and Wayne seem like old friends within minutes. We sat down with them over early-evening wine and cheese and ended up talking till after midnight. Pat and Wayne's varied interests range from collecting raccoons and lanterns to their love of bluegrass and jazz. Christmas was rapidly approaching, so Pat sent us home with a huge bunch of holly from the yard with which to decorate our own house.

Three beautifully decorated guest rooms are appointed with comfort and convenience in mind. On the first floor the Roy Nance Smethers Room, which has a private entrance from the side porch, features a whitewashed and stenciled floor and a fireplace, as well as a 1930s bath with a black and white ceramic-tile floor. The centerpiece of the Laurie Ligon Room is the coal fireplace with an ornate cover imported from Italy by Dr. Smethers's daughter. Its large private bath, formerly a dressing room, overlooks the garden and the outdoor hot tub. Named for a schoolteacher and author who once roomed there, the Alice Humphries Room readily sleeps four with an additional trundle daybed. Its large bath features a large shower and a dressing table.

Part of the hearty traditional Southern breakfast is grits, and Pat explains, "You get them whether you eat them or not." This is just fine with us. I like them; Dan doesn't, so I never fix them at home. It's a treat to get my helping and his, too.

What's Nearby Anderson

Anderson is the place for water sports. The town is located near five major lakes and the Chattooga National Wild and Scenic River, which is perfect for white-water rafting. You'll come across the Chattooga Scenic River when you travel the Cherokee Foothills Scenic Highway. The highway takes you through the Blue Ridge Mountains, Raven Cliff Falls, and Sassafras Mountain. The mountain peak of Sassafras is the highest point in the state.

The John Cuthbert House B&B

1203 Bay Street
Beaufort, South Carolina 29902
(843) 521–1315 or (800) 327–9275

E-MAIL: cuthbert@hargray.com

WEB SITE: www.cuthbert-bb-beaufort.com

INNKEEPERS: Sharon and Gary Groves

ROOMS: 7; all with private bath, in-room refrigerator, telephone, cable TV; 1 with whirlpool tub; wheelchair access only to the first-floor suite

ON THE GROUNDS: Piazzas, use of bicycles

RATES: $145 to $215 single or double, including full breakfast and sunset refreshments

CREDIT CARDS ACCEPTED? Yes

OPEN: Year-round

HOW TO GET THERE: As you enter Beaufort on SC 21, take Business 21 to Bay Street. Turn left and go 5 blocks to Church Street. Turn right and then immediately left into the parking area for the inn.

One of the most striking antebellum homes along Beaufort's waterfront, the stately federal-style John Cuthbert House was built in 1790 by a successful rice and cotton planter as a wedding present for his bride. To the classical style he added British West Indies touches such as the verandas on both floors. In the typical Beaufort tradition, the mansion is constructed on a raised foundation, with central hallways on both floors that run front to back. From its piazzas we looked through bobbing moored sailboats and watched the tide retreat—an incredibly romantic sight. It was hard to tear ourselves away from the mesmerizing view to go indoors, but we were glad we did.

Inside, we admired the heart-pine floors and rare hand-carved rope molding in the hall and parlors, as well as the Civil War signatures discovered scratched into the black marble fireplace during a renovation. Union brigadier general Rufus Saxton commandeered the house as his headquarters after Beaufort fell, and General Sherman spent the night of January 23, 1865, here during his march from Savannah to Columbia. Public and guest rooms are filled with mid-nineteenth-century cherry and mahogany heirloom furniture and accented with glamorous fabrics, Oriental carpets, period-inspired wallpapers, and rich wall colors. Appealing to cultivated travelers, the inn is refined and elegant without being stiff or fussy. Sharon and Gary made us feel like friends in their home.

You Say Porch, I Say Piazza

It seems so mundane to say that a grand mansion has a *porch*—even if it's an extensive wraparound affair supported by highly decorative pillars. In the South vast porches are more likely referred to as *verandas*. In the Lowcountry of South Carolina, however, porches are referred to in an even more grandiose manner. Here in the stereotypical Old South around Charleston and Beaufort, they're known as *piazzas*. If you slip up and use the word *porch* around locals, you'll get a haughty, down-the-nose contemptuous look, and probably a shudder.

Beautifully appointed guest rooms feature reproduction plantation-style king-size rice beds or authentic antique beds converted to queen size. Three rooms feature claw-foot tubs. The rich patina of nineteenth-century furnishings combines with all the modern amenities to create a blissful haven. The crown jewel of the guest chambers is the luxury Parlor Suite, which boasts a sitting room with a spellbinding bay view, an adjoining bedroom with an antique cherry Eastlake bed, and an upscale traditional bathroom with a 6-foot-long soaking tub.

Guests look forward to breakfast with great anticipation. The meal begins with a fruit course and progresses to an entree such as Belgian waffles with pecans or orange pancakes with Grand Marnier sauce accompanied by a breakfast meat.

Park your car at the Cuthbert House for the duration of your visit in Beaufort and walk everywhere—to shops, restaurants, nightlife, the marina, museums, and other diversions.

What's Nearby Beaufort

What do actors Matthew Broderick, Glenn Close, Tom Hanks, and Barbara Streisand all have in common? They all filmed movies in Beaufort. Why Beaufort? Well, find out for yourself and tour the town by foot or horse-drawn carriage. There are dozens of historical sites, including the George Elliott Museum and famous Bay Street Bookstore. You can always rent a video, namely *Glory*, *The Big Chill*, *Forrest Gump*, or *Prince of Tides*. All were filmed right in the middle of Beaufort.

Old Point Inn

212 New Street
Beaufort, South Carolina 29902
(843) 524-3177

WEB SITE: www.oldpointinn.com

INNKEEPERS: Joan and Joe Carpentiere

ROOMS: 4; all with private bath, ceiling fan

ON THE GROUNDS: Verandas, garden, hammock

RATES: $75 to $125, including full breakfast, afternoon refreshments; additional person $15

CREDIT CARDS ACCEPTED? Yes

OPEN: Year-round

HOW TO GET THERE: As you enter Beaufort on SC 21, take Business 21 and follow it to Bay Street; turn left. At the end of the block, the road makes a sharp left and becomes New Street. The inn is the first house on your left.

Known locally as the Wedding Gift House, this Victorian-era, Beaufort-style house was built by William Waterhouse in 1898 as a wedding gift for his new bride, Isabelle Richmond. Pretty nice gift. The distinguishing exterior architectural feature is the two-story wraparound veranda. Not as grandiose as some of Beaufort's historic homes, the Old Point Inn is nonetheless alluring in its intimacy.

Delightful public rooms and cozy guest rooms are decorated with lace and Victorian-era antiques without looking so stiff and formal you can't relax. We visited in early December a couple of years ago, and the house was beautifully decorated to represent a Victorian Christmas. In fact, the opulent, eye-catching way Joan bedecked the stairway with garland, beads, and ornaments provided the inspiration for the way we've decorated our own staircase ever since.

Guest chambers are named for nineteenth-century literary figures. Although we loved them all, Joan tells us that the most popular room is the Jane Austen—a bright, cheerful, raspberry room with English garden rose accents. A unique "eyelash" window (a kind of skylight) perches above the white wicker king-size bed. We certainly agree that it's a charmer, but so are the others. The Molly Bloom, which overlooks the garden, features a queen-size pencil-post canopy bed with a crocheted canopy as well as a single sleigh bed and a separate dressing room. Romantic violets and an antique white iron double bed characterize the Lucy Honeychurch Room. Paisley and stripes create an eye-pleasing decor in the Nicholas Nickleby Room, with its queen-size mahogany bed and single sleigh bed.

You're sure to get your day off to a good start with Joan's ample breakfast. The entree might consist of yummy walnut pancakes with strawberries and whipped cream, French toast, a casserole, or almond quiche accompanied by grits, fruit, juices, and hot beverages. She always tries to offer something sweet and something savory in order to satisfy every taste. Although the breakfast buffet is generally available beginning at 8:30 A.M., Joan sets up a lighter buffet for early risers.

Shaded by ancient trees, the two-level patio and fetching gardens make a great place to nap in a hammock or watch the sailboats gliding silently by. On chilly or inclement days, guests enjoy the inviting library/game room. Located in the downtown historic district, the bed and breakfast is within easy walking distance of all Beaufort's many attractions.

TwoSuns Inn

1705 Bay Street
Beaufort, South Carolina 29902
(843) 522-1122 (phone and fax) or
(800) 532-4244

E-MAIL: twosuns@islc.net

WEB SITE: www.twosunsinn.com

INNKEEPERS: Carrol and Ron Kay

ROOMS: 6; all with private bath, TV by
request, telephone; 1 with wheelchair access

ON THE GROUNDS: Gift area, bicycles

RATES: $105 to $151 single and double, including full breakfast and
afternoon tea or sherry; inquire about special discounts

CREDIT CARDS ACCEPTED? Yes

OPEN: Year-round

HOW TO GET THERE: US 21 becomes Carteret, which runs directly into Bay
Street in downtown Beaufort. As you drive along Bay Street, with the
water on your left, the inn is on your right.

When you walk into TwoSuns, you see a homey living room with a white
brick fireplace to your left and Carrol's weaving studio with two functioning looms to your right. And unless the world turns upside down
and goes black tonight, you'll quickly find Ron Kay, brimming with excite-
ment and ready to tell you the story of the inn, even if he has to stop in the
middle of something else to do it.

The place is worth talking about. For one thing, it is not an antebellum
mansion. It's a restored and renovated Neoclassical Revival home, built in
1917 and used for some years in the 1940s as a communal home (called "the
Teacherage") for local female schoolteachers.

Since its complete restoration between 1990 and 1994, it has been designated a Certified Historic Building by the U.S. Department of the Interior
and won a 1998 South Carolina Honor Award for Historic Preservation. It
was the first home in the community to be built with indoor plumbing. An
interesting aspect of that is the brass "full body shower" in one of the

upstairs rooms, patented in Philadelphia in 1916 as the "Combined Needle and Shower Bath." It's original to the home. This thing has nozzles to squirt you from both sides and several heights all at once. It's fully operational in the bathroom of Chamber D.

Each guest room has its own theme and exhibits touches of Carrol's creativity in unusual window treatments, wall hangings, and such decorating touches as a stuffed parrot high up in a corner. Two of the upstairs rooms have access to the screened porch facing the bay.

The dining room, where breakfast and afternoon tea are served, could get by without much decorating from anybody, because it has windows on three walls looking out on a yard full of camellias and greenery. Like the room, breakfast is special, featuring an entree of the day along with fruits, cereals, and hot baked goods. If you have any dietary restrictions or special breakfast requests, just ask.

It wouldn't do to forget "tea and toddy hour," either. From about 5:00 to 6:00 P.M., guests mingle over tea or sherry, brandy, or wine, chatting about what they've discovered in and around Beaufort. This is definitely the kind of place where guests spend time getting to know each other. And Ron and Carrol are on hand with lots of stories about the house and community, and suggestions for good restaurants and interesting side trips.

If you've thought you might like to try innkeeping yourself, you'll be interested to learn that Ron, who was founding president of the South Carolina Bed and Breakfast Association, offers workshops and consulting services for prospective innkeepers and inn-sitters.

One of the most pleasurable trips for people who enjoy the beach is a picnic on Hunting Island, a beautiful, unspoiled spot. The Kays will prepare a picnic basket for you.

What's Nearby Beaufort

See page 331 for what's nearby Beaufort.

The Ashley Inn Bed and Breakfast

201 Ashley Avenue
Charleston, South Carolina 29403
(843) 723-1848 or (800) 581-6658;
fax (843) 765-1230

E-MAIL: Ashley@cchat.com

WEB SITE: www.charleston-sc-inns.com

INNKEEPERS: Bud and Sally Allen

ROOMS: 6 rooms and 1 suite; all with private bath, TV

ON THE GROUNDS: Piazza, touring bicycles

RATES: $69 to $170, depending on room and season, double or single; $130 to $190 suite; $25 per person extra if more than two in room; all rates include full breakfast and afternoon tea

CREDIT CARDS ACCEPTED? Yes

OPEN: Year-round

HOW TO GET THERE: From I–26, exit at the MEETING STREET VISITOR INFORMA-TION sign onto Meeting Street. Turn right onto Calhoun Street and right again onto Ashley Avenue to the inn. It is just off the crosstown express-way at the intersection of Bee Street and Ashley Avenue, next to the Med-ical University of South Carolina. Park in the driveway off Bee Street.

If your grandmother was right about cleanliness being next to godliness, here's heaven on earth. This inn is spotless, from chandeliers and ceiling fans to hardwood floors, which are mopped with vinegar every day. The Ashley's owners, Sally and Bud Allen, believe that if a place is clean, every-thing else will be first rate. They didn't just make this up.

Bud and Sally stayed at inns around the world, taking notes and plan-ning for when they'd apply what they'd learned in their own inn. First they rescued and restored the Cannonboro, which has become a popular inn in Charleston. Then, a few years ago, they bought and restored an 1832 Charleston house, furnished it with antiques and good reproductions, and essentially gave the Cannonboro a sister. The Ashley retains the 13-foot ceil-ings, Victorian crown moldings and medallions, and brass chandeliers orig-inal to the house. This represents a triumph of restoration!

In the cream-colored sitting room, furniture is upholstered in cranberry, deep green, blue, and gold—elegant in the traditional Charleston mode.

Small touches—floral arrangements in crystal vases, a tapestry bell pull, and the caned rocker by the fireplace—make you feel you're visiting the home of a well-heeled local who's just stepped out for a minute. Or, as the innkeeper at the Cannonboro likes to say, "Staying at the Cannonboro is like visiting your grandmother; staying at the Ashley is like staying at your rich aunt's."

The guest rooms have reproduction rice beds and televisions hidden in built-in armoires.

Nice as the rooms are, you'll probably be willing to leave yours for breakfast on the piazza, which features Lowcountry specialties such as savory sausage soufflé with zucchini and cheddar biscuits, crunchy French toast with hazelnut-peach syrup, and Southern-style grits casserole with white cream gravy.

What's Nearby Charleston

Charleston will make you feel like dancing. There's just so much to do. For starters, you can visit the Dock Street Theatre, one of the oldest continuously running theaters in the country. If it's the last week in May or first week in June, you're right in time for the Spoleto Music and Art Festival held at the theater and around town. Perhaps you'd like to take a trip to the Battery, a famous Civil War memorial park. Stroll through Middleton Place, America's oldest landscaped garden. See Boone Hall, the plantation that served as a model for the Tara from *Gone with the Wind*. And if you like mansions, you'll love the Calhoun Mansion, a Victorian estate open for tours.

Belvedere

40 Rutledge Avenue
Charleston, South Carolina 29401
(843) 722-0973

WEB SITE: www.belvedereinn.com

INNKEEPER: David Spell; Rick Zender, manager

ROOMS: 3; all with private bath and TV

ON THE GROUNDS: Piazza

RATES: $150 to $175, single or double, including continental breakfast and evening sherry; two-night minimum stay on weekends

CREDIT CARDS ACCEPTED? No

OPEN: Year-round except December and January

HOW TO GET THERE: The inn is between Queen and Beaufain Streets on Rutledge. Ask for a map when you make reservations.

We think of David Spell as Charleston's Innkeeper. For years he kept Two Meeting Street, generally acknowledged as one of the best and most stable inns in Charleston. Recently, his niece Karen took over as innkeeper there and David "retired" to Belvedere, a new, smaller lodging owned by his nephew, Jim Spell.

When we say the inn is new, we're not exactly accurate. Its use as an inn is new, but the building is old, and—try to follow this—the interior woodwork is older than the exterior by about a hundred years. The building itself is a huge white mansion in the Colonial Revival style, built about 1900 and bought by a local physician in 1925. But much of its interior is woodwork of the late eighteenth century, salvaged from nearby Belvedere Plantation, which was destroyed in the 1920s to build a golf course and navy officers' club. The physician, whose passion was woodworking, rescued the fine Adams-style woodwork from the plantation and had it installed in his mansion. The mansion then became the inn that is called Belvedere, after the original plantation.

Enough of the history lesson. How about your creature comforts, the things we all care about? Each of the guest rooms has a high ceiling with a ceiling fan, an ornamental fireplace, antiques, queen-size poster canopied beds, and Oriental rugs.

Evening sherry and breakfast are served in an 18-foot-wide central hall upstairs that has been furnished as a living room for guests. It opens out onto a piazza that overlooks Colonial Lake and the Ashley River. Potted plants bend gently in the breeze and the white wicker furniture sparkles against the white columns and ceiling of this semicircular porch. It is the obvious place to take your breakfast on a nice morning.

Downstairs, you'll see that David has brought his fine china, brass, silver, and crystal with him to Belvedere, so in the formal rooms you can enjoy not only the transplanted woodwork, but also his museum-quality collections.

What's Nearby Charleston

See page 336 for what's nearby Charleston.

Cannonboro Inn

184 Ashley Avenue
Charleston, South Carolina 29403
(843) 723-8572 or (800) 235-8039;
fax (843) 723-8007

E-MAIL: cannon@cchat.com
WEB SITE: www.charleston-sc-inns.com
INNKEEPERS: Bud and Sally Allen

ROOMS: 6 rooms and 1 suite; all with private bath and TV; suite with kitchen and sitting room; telephone available

ON THE GROUNDS: Touring bikes

RATES: $69 to $170, depending on room and season, single or double, including full breakfast and afternoon tea; $25 per person extra if more than two in room

CREDIT CARDS ACCEPTED? Yes

OPEN: Year-round

HOW TO GET THERE: From I–26, take the Meeting Street exit, turn right onto Calhoun Street, then right again onto Ashley Avenue. The inn is 2 blocks down on Ashley between Calhoun and Bee Streets, across the street from the Medical University of South Carolina. Park in the driveway off Ashley Avenue.

One word: breakfast. Guests staying here who couldn't remember where they'd eaten the night before recounted in delicious detail every breakfast they'd eaten here. Here are some of the offerings: bread pudding, freshly squeezed orange-papaya juice, a homemade grind of special coffees, and a soufflé of eggs, grits, ham, and cheese.

One guest had a simple breakfast while everyone else was dipping into the scone-and-cinnamon-swirl bread pudding, fruit, bacon, and the like. She said that she had to follow a special diet and was happily surprised that the staff asked if she had any dietary restrictions when she made her reservation.

Yes, but you don't visit Charleston just to eat breakfast. When you stay at the Cannonboro, you're staying in an award-winning restored home.

Outside, it has curb appeal. It's dark tan with cream trim and Charleston-green shutters. (The preservation people in Charleston are very strict about paint colors in historic neighborhoods.) Piazzas on the first and second floors provide places to sit at wrought-iron tables and chairs. A tiny formal garden with a stone cherub fountain in a goldfish pond provides a zenlike focal point.

Inside, you hear classical music playing softly. The formal parlor is furnished with antique reproductions, and the polished hardwood floors showcase Oriental rugs. The guest rooms are in keeping with the rest of the house; they have rice canopy beds. Throughout the house Bud and Sally Allen, the owners, have kept the colors light—pale blues, greens, and mauves. And they have avoided shrouding the large windows with excessively heavy drapes, so lots of light comes in. The overall feel is spacious and bright.

At the top of the house, an inviting two-bedroom suite furnished with antiques has a kitchen, a skylight, and a comfortable sitting room.

We think it's important to mention that people who stay here are delighted with the little kindnesses and extra, unexpected services the staff provide. Whether it's help planning a bike route or a handful of warm cookies sneaked from the kitchen before tea, these little things tell you that nobody at the Cannonboro has gotten jaded and bored with receiving guests. In any tourist town, that's a prize.

What's Nearby Charleston

See page 336 for what's nearby Charleston.

Hayne House

30 King Street
Charleston, South Carolina 29401
(843) 577-2633

E-MAIL: brmcgre@ibm.net

WEB SITE: www.haynehouse.com

INNKEEPERS: Jane and Brian McGreevy

ROOMS: 3 rooms and 3 suites; all with private bath; 4 with fireplace, (2 gas-log and 2 decorative), and/or whirlpool tub

ON THE GROUNDS: Piazza with swing, garden

RATES: $135 to $295 single or double, including full breakfast, turndown service; additional person $15; babysitting available with advance reservations

CREDIT CARDS ACCEPTED? Yes

OPEN: Year-round

HOW TO GET THERE: From I–26, which ends in Charleston, take the Meeting Street/Visitor Center exit and continue through about fourteen traffic lights. After passing the last light at Broad Street (now you're South of Broad), continue and take the third right onto Ladson Street. The Hayne House is the last house on your right and the entrance is on King Street.

Before your visit to Charleston, make sure that you understand that SOB is a badge of pride, not a slur. It stands for South of Broad (Street)—the most desirable part of the historic district near the Battery where the Ashley and Cooper Rivers meet. Anyone who lives or is staying in this exclusive enclave is therefore an SOB.

The Hayne House, owned and operated by an old Charleston family, is located South of Broad. Built in 1755, the house is associated with the

Revolutionary War hero Isaac Hayne and was later the home of U.S. Senator Robert Hayne, famed for his fiery Senate debates with Daniel Webster, and of Paul Hamilton Hayne, one of the poets of the Confederacy. Brian and Jane say, "Lord Cornwallis, Lord Rawdon, and General Beauregard all loved our neighborhood—and so will you!"

Imagine being pampered in this quiet historic home filled with elegant family antiques and artwork while you hear the clip-clop of horses' hoofs and the squeak of wooden wheels outside. You'll hear the bells at nearby St. Michael's Church chime as they have for more than 200 years. It's easy to imagine yourself transported back a hundred years or two. We visited in December when the public rooms were especially gussied up for an Old South Christmas.

Brian has preservation in his blood. He grew up in Charleston and worked for both the Historic Charleston Foundation and the National Trust for Historic Preservation. What could be more natural than for him and his wife Jane to operate a historic bed and breakfast in one of America's most historic cities?

Each of the lovely guest rooms and suites, which are found in the main house or the kitchen house, has its own special charm created with family antiques, important art (and lots of it), historical-inspired fabrics, Oriental carpets, and perfect accessories. Of particular interest is the collection of memorabilia related to *Gone with the Wind* author Margaret Mitchell's years at Washington Seminary, which she attended at the same time as the owner's great aunt, Amy Whitfield Potts. Several bedchambers feature ornately carved antique four-poster rice beds or sleigh beds that have been modified to accommodate queen-size mattresses. Twin beds in the Wicker Room can be transformed into a king. Extremely popular, the Ginkgo and Cypress Suites, located in the kitchen house, feature a whirlpool bath and a kitchenette. The king among the guest chambers is the Cypress Suite because it also boasts a reproduction king-size bed, a sitting room, and a private garden balcony. As impressive as each room is, little touches set the Hayne House apart: hand-ironed all-cotton Ralph Lauren and Laura Ashley sheets, Turkish cotton bathrobes, fresh flowers, turndown service with sherry and chocolates.

Breakfast is a meal of Southern specialties served in the dining room using sterling silver, Waterford crystal, and English porcelain.

In your spare time, you can gather with other guests in the grand drawing room with its selection of good books and music (but no television) and enjoy the garden and the small piazza with its old-fashioned swing.

Chestnut Cottage Bed and Breakfast

1718 Hampton Street
Columbia, South Carolina 29201
(803) 256–1718

E-MAIL: ggarrett@logicsouth.com

WEB SITE: www.bbonline.com/sc/chestnut/

INNKEEPERS: Diane and Gale Garrett

ROOMS: 5; all with private bath, TV, telephone; some with footed tubs; 3 with whirlpool tubs; VCR on request; computer with Internet access available by the hour

ON THE GROUNDS: Porch, garden, bicycles

RATES: $75 to $200 double, including breakfast and afternoon refreshments; discount for stays of three days or longer

CREDIT CARDS ACCEPTED? Yes

OPEN: Year-round

HOW TO GET THERE: From I–26, take exit I–26/Downtown, which becomes Elmwood Street. When Elmwood dead-ends at Bull Street, turn right. At Hampton Street, turn left. The inn is 2½ blocks on your right. From I–20 or I–77, take exit 277/Downtown, which becomes Bull Street, then follow the directions above.

tay where history was lived and made and recorded. As we watched Ken Burns's *The Civil War* on PBS, we became intimately acquainted with Mary Boykin Chestnut, wife of Confederate general James Chestnut, through quotations from her *Diary from Dixie*, which was published after her death in 1886. Having also read C. Vann Woodward's voluminous revised edition—for which he won the Pulitzer Prize—we were fascinated to be able to see one of her homes. Confederate President Jefferson Davis gave a speech to the citizens of Columbia from the front porch in October 1864.

Although the Chestnuts owned Mulberry Plantation in Camden, this federal-style cottage, which was built around 1850, was their town house. During the war they spent time in Charleston, Richmond, and here. Among the period antiques are a sofa and chair in the parlor that belonged to the

Chestnuts. Guests feel at home curled up with a book by a blazing fire or mingling with other visitors.

Of the five lavishly decorated period guest rooms, naturally two are named for the Chestnuts. The cozy and delightful Mary Boykin Chestnut Room features a queen-size four-poster bed and a soft, feminine touch. The more masculine General James Chestnut Room is tastefully decorated with a queen-size cannonball bed and accessorized with Civil War memorabilia. Overlooking the piazza and garden, the President Jefferson Davis Room features a king-size pencil-post bed. The incredibly romantic Carriage House Bridal Suite boasts an opulently draped canopy bed. A breakfast nook allows romantic couples to enjoy a secluded breakfast. Although the Carriage House Two Room is smaller than the Bridal Suite, its tub is bigger. The latter three rooms all boast whirlpool baths.

Among the amenities enjoyed by guests in all the rooms are luxurious robes, nightly turndown service, and a hearty breakfast of eggs, French toast, or pancakes, a breakfast meat, and all the accompaniments. It's served on the porch or in the parlor or, for guests in the whirlpool suites, in the privacy of their room.

What's Nearby Columbia

The lively city of Columbia is home to the University of South Carolina. Visit the new Columbia Museum of Art, which offers one of the best collections of Impressionist and Baroque art in the region. Then stop at the South Carolina State Museum, which exhibits hands-on science displays. Take the kids to the Riverbanks Zoological Park, which is ranked in the country's top ten zoos. Or visit Five Points, a popular college hang-out and bustling downtown neighborhood.

Richland Street B&B

1425 Richland Street
Columbia, South Carolina 29201
(803) 779-7001

WEB SITE: www.inns.com/south/ai-sc.htm

INNKEEPERS: Naomi and Jim Perryman

ROOMS: 7 rooms and 1 suite; all with private bath, telephone, TV, in-room desk and modem, clock radio, hair dryer, bath amenities, robes; some wheelchair access

ON THE GROUNDS: Verandas

RATES: $79 to $140 single or double, including deluxe continental breakfast, complimentary beverages, afternoon refreshments, nightly turndown service; additional person $20

CREDIT CARDS ACCEPTED? Yes

OPEN: Year-round

HOW TO GET THERE: From I–77, take I–277, which becomes Bull when it crosses Elmwood. Continue 2 blocks on Bull and turn right onto Richland. The B&B is on your right. From I–26, take exit 108 onto SC 126, which becomes Elmwood. Turn right onto Bull and follow the previous directions.

So perfectly does this Victorian-style house with its turret, upstairs and downstairs verandas, and gazebo blend in with its neighbors in a downtown historic district that we were astounded to learn that it had been built in 1992. Naomi, a former nurse and interior designer, saw a need and decided to fill it. She realized that businesspeople are getting tired of cookie-cutter accommodations and looking for something more personal, so she decided to open an inn custom-designed for discerning businesstravelers. Unfortunately, she couldn't find just the right historic house to meet her needs. Never mind—it was Jim to the rescue. They found a lot in the historic district and he produced the plans to transform Naomi's envisioned bed and breakfast into reality. As a bonus, although it was created with the businessperson in mind, this bed and breakfast is romantic enough for those wanting to get away together for some R&R.

The handsome entrance introduced us to the inn's ribbon motif. Custom-designed and created by a North Carolina artist, the stained-glass transom features a lavender Victorian bow with streamers gracefully cascading down each sidelight. We stepped inside to an extraordinarily stylish and comfortable place with the high ceilings, spacious rooms, and grand staircase you'd find in eighteenth-century homes.

Guest rooms, which are named for South Carolina governors, are beautifully appointed with an eclectic mixture of fine antiques and traditional reproductions, Oriental carpets, handmade quilts, and extra touches such as fine linens, sacheted closets with quilted hangers, and cozy comforters for chilly nights. For the business traveler, the rooms are outfitted with an ample workspace, good lighting, a modem, and a telephone.

There's no better way to get the day off to a good start than with Naomi's health-conscious, low-cal breakfasts, served in the dining room. These sit-down meals might include a hot casserole, Belgian waffles, French toast, and freshly baked breads. When you come in from a hard day's work, you can relax with complimentary beverages and fresh cookies. Icy-cold lemonade on the veranda is a perfect antidote to a hot day.

Whether you're looking for a place to get some work done or to prop up your feet, Richland Street Inn has what it takes.

What's Nearby Columbia

See page 342 for what's nearby Columbia.

John Lawton House

118 Third Street East
Estill, South Carolina 29918
(803) 625-3240;
fax (803) 625-3240+*51

E-MAIL: lcocain@internetx.net

INNKEEPER: Lawton Clarke O'Cain

ROOMS: 2; both with private bath, telephone, TV, gas-log fireplace, ceiling fan

ON THE GROUNDS: Verandas, gardens, courtyard

RATES: $85 to $105, including full breakfast and afternoon refreshments

CREDIT CARDS ACCEPTED? Yes

OPEN: Year-round

HOW TO GET THERE: Located 1½ blocks east of US 321 on SC 3.

Presided over by feisty sixth-generation descendant Lawton (female) O'Cain, the tin-roofed, turn-of-the-century house was once the town home of John Lawton Jr. He was the son of "Steamboat" John Lawton Sr., owner of several steam-driven side-wheeler riverboats that plied the Savannah River from Augusta to Savannah, stopping at all the bluffs along the way. Although generations of the Lawton family lived at nearby Jericho Plantation in Old Lawtonville, John Jr. thought the horse-and-buggy ride to school in town was too strenuous, for his two daughters so he had the town house built with lumber and materials brought from the plantation by mule-drawn wagon.

Lawton is a gracious hostess in the Southern tradition, but not the syrupy sweet kind—she qualifies as a genuine character. She welcomed us with a drink and some of her tasty homemade cheese crackers, then regaled us with fascinating stories. A fount of knowledge about the surrounding area, small towns, plantations, cemeteries, and of course, the Civil War, she can tell you an amazing amount about the Yankees who invaded South Carolina by crossing the Savannah River and coming up the Old Orangeburg Road. There's absolutely no doubt where her loyalties lay in the "Recent Unpleasantness." She also told us this story about modern-day Yankees. "Honey," (she always calls you Honey) "Yankees are so infatuated with the South, one of 'em even asked me if I still had slaves. I said yes, there's one. And that's me."

The home is appointed with family antiques, lovingly cared for. The mood is quiet, with muted colors, dark rich woods, Oriental carpets, hand-painted porcelains, and original family oil portraits. Sit down with Lawton in the friendly kitchen or in the comfortable den with its arched fireplace and dark wainscoting below floral wallpaper and get her to tell you more stories.

Each of the guest rooms has its own personality and special touches including period reproductions of fabrics and wallcoverings. Both are warmed by coal-burning fireplaces adapted for gas. Either European or American bathing accommodations are available. Modern tiled baths are equipped with adjustable shower massages, and for the lady's luxury you'll find lighted makeup mirrors. Shutters shade each room and slow-moving overhead fans provide a cooling breeze (although there is air-conditioning for the most sizzling days).

Century-old live oaks dripping with silver-grey Spanish moss shade the house and yard. The courtyard boasts magnolias, camellias, azaleas, roses, jessamine, and an array of perennials, annuals, and herbs for a flamboyant visual display in all seasons. Guests love sitting on the veranda or in the courtyard to watch the antics of a parade of birds.

A morning repast that might include venison sausage, sourdough bread, and banana and raisin fritters is served wherever strikes your fancy: the dining room, den, or garden. Be sure to try Lawton's Steamboat Mustard with the sausage; it's available at gift shops around the state.

What's Nearby Estill

Estill is a good central location from which to explore the small towns of South Carolina's Lowcountry. The remnants of several Civil War sites are near the tiny town. Visit the Hampton Museum and Visitors Center as well as the Hampton County Museum in nearby Hampton, South

Carolina's largest producer of watermelons and home of the annual Hampton County Watermelon Festival. Don't miss the South Carolina Artisans Center or the Edisto River Canoe and Kayak Trail in Walterboro. The beaches and golf courses of Hilton Head Island are just a short drive away as is historic Savannah, Georgia; Augusta, Georgia; and Charleston, South Carolina.

1790 House Bed and Breakfast

630 Highmarket Street
Georgetown, South Carolina 29440
(843) 546–4821 or (800) 890–7432

E-MAIL: jwiley5211@aol.com

WEB SITE: www.1790house.com

INNKEEPERS: Patricia and John Wiley

ROOMS: 6; all with private bath and sitting area, telephone, clock radio; some with decorative or gas-log fireplace, ceiling fan; some have wheelchair access

ON THE GROUNDS: Veranda, gardens, gazebo, tea room, gift shop

RATES: $75 to $115 double, including full breakfast and evening refreshments

CREDIT CARDS ACCEPTED? Yes

OPEN: Year-round

HOW TO GET THERE: From Myrtle Beach, take US 17 south to Georgetown, cross over the bridge, and go about 0.25 mile to St. James Street; turn left. Continue 2 blocks to Highmarket Street and turn right. The B&B is ahead 3 blocks at the corner of Highmarket and Screven. From Charleston, take US 17 North to Georgetown, cross over the bridge, and continue to the third traffic light. Turn right onto Highmarket and go 7 blocks to the B&B. From I–95, exit at Manning and take US 521 into Georgetown, where it becomes Highmarket Street. Continue to number 630.

The first thing that caught our eye was the gracious double stairway leading from the street up to the full-length veranda on this imposing three-story home. It's no wonder that staircases such as these are known as "welcoming arms." We weren't disappointed; the Wileys' welcome and hospitality were just as warm as we'd hoped.

The 1790 House is a meticulously restored West Indies–style Colonial house named after the year it was built by the Allstons, one of the most prominent families in South Carolina history. Rice planters, they owned many of the plantations in the coastal area. In 1812 their daughter Martha married John Pyatt, owner of four rice plantations; the couple moved into this house, where they raised three children. The house remained in the Pyatt family until 1896.

The attractive frame house, with its hip roof and five hip-roofed dormers, has a foundation laid in English bond brick except for the porch foundation, which is Bermuda coral. These large pieces of coral were used as ballast in early cargo ships coming from the British West Indies to Georgetown and then appropriated for building material.

Hardwood floors, 11-foot ceilings, elegant detailed cornices, original chair rails, wainscoting, fluted mantels, and hand-carved dental molding characterize the generously proportioned public rooms and guest chambers. Whether you want to socialize with other guests and your hosts or spend some time alone, there are numerous attractive, tastefully decorated places to indulge your desires. Curling up by the fire in the formal parlor is popular on chilly evenings. A television, VCR, books, games, and refreshments in a guest refrigerator draw guests to the keeping room, which was created by enclosing a veranda. While you're relaxing there, take note of the unusual ceiling plaster. In nice weather rocking chairs and wicker furniture beckon you to the veranda, where you can survey the handsome historic district. Brick paths meander through the formal gardens; here you can sit on a stone bench to watch the birds, or relax in the gazebo.

You'll get a wonderful night's sleep in one of the spacious guest rooms in the main house or in the cottage. A gracious guest room located on the first floor in the old library sports lovely built-in bookcases and a Victorian-era queen-size iron and brass bed, but the best feature is the gas-log fireplace. Created from old servants' quarters, Captain Quarters has a wood-beam ceiling, a comfortable sitting area with a television, and a game table and chairs. A twin-size sleigh bed in addition to the king-size pencil-post bed makes the Indigo Room ideal for those traveling with an additional person. A fireplace and a desk complete the picture. Romance abounds in the Rice Planters Room, which is dominated by a queen-size rice-carved canopy bed and a fireplace. Tucked up under the eaves, the Prince George Suite features an antique iron and brass bed, a separate sitting room with an additional daybed, and a bathroom with a square-foot tub. A whirlpool tub is just one of the attractions at the Dependency Cottage, which boasts a patio overlooking the garden and a separate sitting room.

Taking tea is quintessentially English—a social event and a culinary delight. The Wileys operate the Angel's Touch Tea Room, where a proper English tea is served to the public at 12:30 and 2:30 P.M. Tuesday, Thursday, and Saturday. Reservations are required. Handmade tea cozies, Christmas ornaments, angels, note cards, and jewelry pouches are among the gifts sold in the tearoom's gift shop.

The Wileys offer numerous special packages. Ask them about their off-season specials, Valentine special, and packages created for the weekends of plantation tours and ghost walks (Georgetown claims to be the Ghost Capital of the South).

What's Nearby Georgetown

Georgetown, the third oldest city in South Carolina, offers a number of interesting attractions. Let's start at the Harborwalk, a boardwalk running along the Sampit River. Enjoy the Front Street shops and restaurants on the boardwalk. Located on Front Street is the Town Clock/Old Market, which now houses the unusual Rice Museum. To explore more of Georgetown's history, take a walking tour of the city, which covers forty-four historic sites.

The Shaw House Best Buy

613 Cypress Court
Georgetown, South Carolina 29440
(843) 546-9663

INNKEEPER: Mary Shaw

ROOMS: 3; all with private bath, TV, and telephone; 2 with dressing room

ON THE GROUNDS: Bicycles, bird-watching

RATES: $60 to $70 single or double, including full breakfast; $15 per person extra if more than two in room

CREDIT CARDS ACCEPTED? No

OPEN: Year-round

HOW TO GET THERE: US 17 goes through town. Turn away from the business district onto Orange Street. Make a quick jog left. You will see the street signs for Cypress.

When a reader is disappointed by a B&B we have recommended, we hear about it; we seldom hear when guests enjoy an inn. The Shaw House is a notable exception. We've heard repeated praise for Mary Shaw and her little inn. It has two outstanding features: a spectacular location overlooking Willowbank Marsh, and Mary Shaw.

First, the marsh. It's a bird-watcher's dream. Any birder would be pleased to slog around out here, identifying one hard-to-find bird after another. But from the Shaw House, on a little bluff overlooking the marsh, you can sit at the breakfast table by the great picture windows in the corner and see more birds than you would right out in the grasses. Guests who are serious about bird-watching bring their binoculars and books and notepads right to the table.

Now, Mary, a tiny, perky woman who favors bright-colored clothes, is a natural-born Southern storyteller who also has the knack of hospitality. The house is full of antiques. She can lead you on a tour of the rooms, telling stories about when and how she and her husband, Joe, acquired or inherited each piece. In the telling, the rice bed, the Eastlake chair, the English dressing table from the early 1800s, the rare petticoat mirror—all take on reality as furniture that living people used over generations.

Mary enjoys her guests. In the evening she offers wine and cookies and snacks. In the morning she prepares a mammoth breakfast and gives you your own pot of coffee. Her casserole of grits, cheese, and sausage is so popular that she has had copies of the recipe printed for all who ask. If you stay several days, you'll see that Mary sets the table with different dishes and linens each morning.

The Shaw House is an easy place to be. You can come and go without ceremony and rely on Mary for whatever advice you need about local historic sites and restaurants.

On her recommendation, we tried the River Room Restaurant, an easy walk from the inn. It's a small place, with a tiny bar and a nice variety of wines. Iced tea is served in widemouthed Ball jars. People dress casually. We had a fine crab salad and some of the best fried onion rings ever. The onions were cut into thick slices, and the breading was not the typical heavy cornmeal bomb, but a crispy, tempuralike batter. If you go there, try to be early. Because the dining room is so small, no reservations are accepted.

What's Nearby Georgetown

See page 348 for what's nearby Georgetown.

Missouri Inn Bed and Breakfast

314 East Home Avenue
Hartsville, South Carolina 29550
(803) 383–9553

INNKEEPERS: Kyle and Kent Segars

ROOMS: 5; each with private bath,
desk, telephone, TV, clock radio,
electric blanket, heated towel rack, hair dryer, robes; smoking is allowed
in the public rooms; 1 room has wheelchair access

ON THE GROUNDS: Screened porch, landscaped property

RATES: $75 single to $85 double, including breakfast, snacks, and beverages; ask about business rates

CREDIT CARDS ACCEPTED? Yes

OPEN: Year-round

HOW TO GET THERE: From I–95, take exit 164, Florence, and proceed on US 52. Take SC 151 toward Hartsville and go about 12 miles to Business 151, which will take you into town. Turn right when it dead-ends. The B&B is 2 blocks ahead on your right at the traffic light.

We're always suckers for innkeepers with a sense of humor. When we stepped onto the front porch here and saw the paunchy carved bear with the silly grin, straw hat, and big welcome sign, we knew we were in for a good time. (Kyle picked up this cheerful fellow in Stowe, Vermont.) The name of the inn also reflects the innkeepers' droll wit. In 1947 Kent's grandparents F. E. and Emily Fitchett bought and redesigned the turn-of-the-century house. Kent's father sometimes called his mother Missouri, because he said she was as stubborn as a Missouri mule. Kent chose to name the inn in her honor. Emily's 1920s bridal portrait sits on the living room mantel, where she plans to stay put.

Located on a quiet, tree-lined street of stately homes in one of Hartsville's oldest neighborhoods, the bed and breakfast is across the street from the well-landscaped Coker College campus. Enormous ornamental shrubs and giant trees share the grassy four acres with the house and give guests an attractive place to stroll. A substantial house with a hip roof, the Missouri Inn's wraparound porches have been enclosed to provide more living space.

Five individually decorated, bright, airy guest rooms are designed for comfort. Three of them boast decorative fireplaces. The Segals have thought of everything: We don't know of many inns that provide electric blankets—

much less ones with dual controls—heated towel racks in the bathroom, or soap/lotion/shampoo/conditioner dispensers in the shower.

Guests on the go enjoy the refreshment nook in the upstairs hall. A mini refrigerator stocked with complimentary beverages, a coffeemaker with a selection of coffees, teas, and hot chocolates, and a basket of munchies keep unexpected hunger pangs at bay. When you awaken in the morning, you'll find freshly brewed coffee here as well to imbibe while getting ready for breakfast or to enjoy in bed.

A graduate of the Culinary Institute of New York, Kyle once operated a popular restaurant and now runs a catering business, so you can be sure that breakfasts are special. Whatever her mood, you can expect fresh juices and fruits, homemade granola, and a variety of homemade breads. On weekdays breakfast is a deluxe continental meal; on weekends it's more substantial with the inclusion of a breakfast casserole. When the weather is nice, afternoon refreshments are served on the wicker-filled screened porch. If there's a nip in the air, tea will be served fireside in the paneled library. There are so many reasons to linger at the Missouri Inn, it will take more than a Missouri mule to drag you away.

What's Nearby Hartsville

Ranked a 1996 All-America City, Hartsville is a traditional, small city. The heart of the city is its pretty downtown with shopping, a movie theater, restaurants, and local museum, surrounded by lots of trees and historic homes. Hartsville is the site of Coker College. The botanical gardens, Kalmia Gardens of Coker College, adjoins a large nature preserve. In addition, the campus borders Prestwood Lake, which is popular among students for sailing and canoeing.

Abingdon Manor

307 Church Street
Latta, South Carolina 29565
(843) 752–5090 or (888) 752–5090

E-MAIL: abingdon@southtech.net

WEB SITE: www.bbonline.com/sc/abingdon/

INNKEEPERS: Patty and Michael Griffey

ROOMS: 4 rooms and 1 suite; all with private bath, gas-log fireplace, featherbed, color cable TV, VCR, clock, robes

ON THE GROUNDS: Porches, hot tub, bicycles

RATES: $105 to $140 double, including full breakfast and evening refreshments; additional person $25; a minimum stay may be required for holidays and special events

CREDIT CARDS ACCEPTED? Yes

OPEN: Year-round

HOW TO GET THERE: From I–95, take exit 181. Go east and follow Route 917, which becomes Main Street. At the first light, turn left onto Marion Street. At the Methodist church, take the right fork onto Church Street and follow it to the end. Abingdon Manor is on your left. From Route 301/501 going north, go past Main Street to the next light. Turn left onto Academy Street and go 3 blocks. Abingdon Manor is on the corner of Church and Academy Streets.

Abingdon Manor, a grand 1902 estate in the manner of the English country house, now operates as an exquisite small luxury hotel, but what really sets it apart are owners Patty and Michael Griffey, who know what service with a smile is all about. In just a short time, they've earned a well-deserved four-diamond rating from AAA.

It's hard to say which is more appealing—arriving at the B&B in the daylight to enjoy the stunning architecture and the vast lawns peppered with ancient trees, or approaching at night when warm, welcoming lights blaze from the many windows. One of the most outstanding exterior architectural elements of the Greek Revival mansion is the circular two-story entry porch supported by massive columns centered on wraparound verandas.

Inside, a grand entry hall that seems to stretch endlessly from the front to the back is flanked by matching sumptuously furnished formal parlors, a dining room, and an informal sitting room. Many original architectural features created with Old World craftsmanship—counterweighted shutters, ornate mantels, intricate moldings of maple and mahogany, enormous arched pocket doors, hardwood floors, and pier mirrors—have been restored to their former grandeur. Although filled with antiques and collectibles, the house isn't pretentious or stuffy.

Upstairs, the elegant two-room suite and four spacious guest rooms feature private baths and gas-log fireplaces. Each of these rooms is developed around a color theme and boasts a king, a queen, or two double beds as well as luxurious furnishings and perfect accent pieces.

A full gourmet breakfast of fresh fruits and juices, muffins and breads, and such main dishes as baked French toast or cheese omelettes with garden-fresh herbs is served in the formal dining room, next to a blazing fire if the weather warrants. Early-evening refreshments, which might include herbed breadsticks and hot crab dip, are served in one of the formal parlors or outdoors under the pecan, black walnut, and chestnut trees. Just-baked goodies may miraculously appear at bedtime.

Patty and Michael know how to pamper their guests—big things like featherbeds on top of a firm mattress and their delicious breakfasts; little things like fresh flowers in your room, high-thread-count ironed sheets, plush robes, high-quality bath amenities, early-morning coffee and tea service on the guest level, afternoon hors d'oeuvres, sherry, evening turndown service, and sending a bag of freshly baked cookies along on your day trip. On Friday evening you can enjoy dinner with the innkeepers for $30 per person.

What's Nearby Latta

Latta itself is a little gem of a town, still considered off the beaten track although it's only 6 miles from I-95. It has three National Register historic districts encompassing ninety-three significant residential and commercial properties. The Dillon County Museum, recognized as one of the best small-town museums in the state, is within easy walking distance, as is the downtown where antiques shops offer everything from fine English furniture to South Carolina collectibles at significant savings. And the town is developing into an active artists' colony; the Main Street Art Center and several galleries display works of nationally recognized local painters and other artisans.

Fannie Kate's Country Inn

Best Buy

127 South Main Street
McCormick, South Carolina 29835
(864) 465–0061 or (800) 965–0061;
fax (803) 465–3238

E-MAIL: fanniekate@wctel.net

INNKEEPERS: Barbara and Lou Roberts

ROOMS: 9; all with private bath, ceiling fan, telephone, alarm clock; 1 room has wheelchair access; dogs of less than fifteen pounds allowed

ON THE GROUNDS: Porches, patio

RATES $40 to $45 single, $65 to $75 double, including full breakfast and afternoon refreshments; additional person $10

CREDIT CARDS ACCEPTED? Yes

OPEN: Year-round

HOW TO GET THERE: From I-85, take SC 187 to SC 81 into the center of McCormick. From I-20, take SC 28 to US 221 into McCormick. From I-26 in Columbia, take I-126 west to US 378 and follow it west into McCormick.

In the booming railroad days at the end of the nineteenth century, McCormick supported several hotels. One was the McCormick Temperance Hotel, built in 1882, which provided safe lodgings for railroad passengers and "sample rooms"—places designated for drummers (traveling salesmen) to display their wares to local shopkeepers. In 1905 Mrs. J. M. Marsh bought the hotel. All her children, including seven-year-old Fannie Kate, assisted her with her duties at the hotel. Years later, when Mrs. Marsh died, an adult Fannie Kate took over the operation of the hotel and continued to run it in the family tradition. Locals began to refer to the hotel affectionately as "Fannie Kate's." During the Great Depression several McCormick residents boarded at the hotel for $3.00 a week, including room and board—and complained that the price was too high. During the 1940s business looked up with the construction of nearby Clarks Hill Dam. Fannie Kate used her newfound prosperity to brick the exterior of the heretofore frame structure, and she added modern heating and plumbing as well as the second-story porch. New rooms with tile baths were added, and furniture and decor were upgraded.

Who says you can't go home again? Barbara was born in McCormick, but left when she married. Forty years later she and Lou returned from Miami, looking for a project to keep them busy in their retirement. What should they find but the old abandoned hotel that she remembered so fondly? They purchased it for $10,000 and renovated it for use as a bed and breakfast and restaurant. In a stroke of luck, Fannie Kate's furniture remained and has been refurbished to give the hotel the ambience it had during its heyday—with lots of modern conveniences added, of course. It seemed only natural to Barbara and Lou to name the establishment after Fannie Kate, and longtime locals enthusiastically concur.

Cozy rooms are simply furnished and accessorized with quilts and other country accents. Hardwood floors, high ceilings, and tall windows create a light, airy look. Soft colors, braided rag rugs, ceilings fans, and 1930s iron beds original to the hotel complete the comfy, country ambience. The five largest rooms feature both a queen-size and a double bed; three boast a gas-log fireplace. The four smaller rooms have queen-size beds.

We're Sitting on a Gold Mine

One of the most astounding historical events in McCormick was William "Billy" Dorn's discovery of gold in 1852. Although he was considered a fool by many, his initial investment of $1,200 yielded him more than $900,000 in just seven years. When fifty-six-year-old Dorn married sixteen-year-old Martha Rutledge, guests were disappointed by the apparently inexpensive gift of gloves he presented to the minister. Each finger of the gloves, however, was stuffed with $500 worth of gold. Dorn reputedly financed an entire troop of the Confederate Army. "Fool" Billy had the last laugh, too—gold is still being mined.

In 1871 Cyrus H. McCormick, inventor of the reaper and founder of International Harvester, purchased Dorn's gold mine as well as the surrounding area; he also purchased stock in two railroads, which he persuaded to come to town, and donated the land for the town named for him, although he never set foot there. The town, which is constructed over a labyrinth of 5 miles of mine tunnels, claims to be the origin of the saying, "We're sitting on a gold mine." Fannie Kate's sits over some of the mine tunnels.

B&B guests enjoy a full breakfast of grits, potatoes, omelettes or French toast, fruit, juices, and hot beverages. The restaurant, where you can dine inside in cool weather or outside when the climate warrants, serves lunch Monday through Friday and dinner Monday through Saturday. Oak tables and chairs are original to the hotel. Also be sure to admire the old brass dinner bell that used to be rung on the porch to summon guests who had strolled away from the hotel. At dinnertime the gas lights are dimmed and classical music plays softly in the background as guests dine on a wonderful blend of traditional Southern dishes and cosmopolitan fare.

The newest addition since we visited is Fannie Kate's Pub—a British-style tavern open Monday through Saturday. Located below street level, it opens out onto the patio for alfresco drinks and pub grub. Inside the lower portions of the walls is the original stone foundation. Antique signs and old paintings give the decor flair. Come for local entertainment on weekend evenings.

Guests like to gather to relax in the formal parlor, where there's a gas-log fireplace and the piano is original. When the weather's good, rocker-filled first- and second-story porches cooled by ceiling fans are peaceful places to watch the slow-paced world of McCormick through a screen of oaks and azaleas.

McCormick offers something for everyone. If you enjoy the theater, get a ticket to see a play at the McCormick Arts council at the Kenturah. If you're feeling nostalgic for the past, visit McCormick's old-fashioned soda fountain and antiques shops. And if you're looking for an outdoor challenge, visit the Sumter National Forest, Clarks Hill Lake, and Lake Thurmond for hiking, biking, and water sports.

Rice Hope Plantation Best Buy

206 Rice Hope Drive
Moncks Corner, South Carolina 29461
(843) 761–4832 or (800) 569–4038

E-MAIL: doris@ricehope.com

WEB SITE: www.ricehope.com

INNKEEPER: Doris Kasprak

ROOMS: 5; 3 with private bath; all with robes, TV, alarm clock, ceiling fan

ON THE GROUNDS: Tennis court, hot tub, dock, canoe, mountain bikes, lawn games

RATES: $60 to $95 single or double, including breakfast and afternoon refreshments

CREDIT CARDS ACCEPTED? Yes

OPEN: Year-round

HOW TO GET THERE: From Moncks Corner, take US 52 west. Turn right onto SC 402 and proceed 1.9 miles. Turn right onto Dr. Evans Road and go 8 miles until it ends; there, turn right onto Rice Hope Drive.

Rice Hope Plantation has existed since 1696. Today only eleven acres remain, but oh, what acres they are. Two-hundred-year-old formal azalea and camellia gardens terrace down to a sweeping lawn and the scenic Cooper River. Sixty massive live oaks and swaying Spanish moss shade the "new" house (it was built in the 1840s), perched grandly above the gardens and the river. The first house was destroyed, probably by fire; its surviving chimney serves as the brick wall in the present dining room. Constructed of cypress with a slate roof, the rambling federal-style mansion was remodeled to its present appearance in 1929. Its shutters have a cutout crescent moon in the upper portion to represent the one on the South Carolina state flag. A depiction of a sheaf of rice etched into the glass of the front door pays homage to the plantation's past. The house is beautiful in its simplicity—not as ostentatious as town houses in Charleston. Some scenes from the movie *Consenting Adults* were filmed here.

Although the lovely parlor and magnificent dining room, bounded on three sides by windows and French doors, are inviting, from the moment we saw the grounds, we knew we'd want to spend most of our time outdoors. That's one of the blessings of the Lowcountry—the weather's usually divine. The dock is a perfect place to get some sun, watch eagles and wading birds, try your hand at some fishing, or catch the sunset, which is almost always spectacular. A tennis court and bicycles beckon Type-A personalities. Since we visited, we understand that a garden hot tub has been added. Sounds full of romantic possibilities to us. As Doris says, "We aren't close to anything except nature, comfort, and warm hospitality."

Simple, cozy guest rooms furnished with antiques and reproductions are named for birds indigenous to the area: Owl, Spoonbill, Osprey, Canadian Goose, and Heron. Several of them boast ornately carved four-poster rice beds—as is only appropriate on a rice plantation—as well as colorful Oriental carpets and seating areas. A porch overlooking the river is an added attraction to the Owl Room. You might want to spend some private time there with your sweetie.

A continental-plus or full breakfast is served buffet-style or cooked to order. When the weather's chilly, there'll be a crackling fire in the fireplace. Complimentary refreshments are offered each afternoon in the parlor or out on the patio. Lunch and a four-course candlelight dinner are available by reservation at an additional fee. If you're lucky, one of these meals might include the signature dessert—an apple torte with cream cheese filling topped with apples and almonds.

What's Nearby Moncks Corner

Cypress Gardens is a terrific getaway. The swamp garden offers nature trails and guided boat tours. You may also rent a canoe. On your journey you'll meet alligators, woodpeckers, owls, and otters, and you'll have a great opportunity to bird-watch. Another interesting spot is the Francis Biedler Audubon Swamp Garden, which is a short ride away in Harleyville. this garden is home to the world's largest bald cypress and tupelo gum trees.

Guilds Inn

101 Pitt Street
Mount Pleasant, South Carolina 29464
(843) 881–0510 or (800) 331–1510

INNKEEPER: Lou Edens

ROOMS: 6; all with private bath with whirlpool tub, telephone, TV, ceiling fan

ON THE GROUNDS: Courtyard, restaurant

RATES: $85 to $135 double, including continental breakfast

CREDIT CARDS ACCEPTED? Yes

OPEN: Year-round

HOW TO GET THERE: Take I–26 to exit 221B, US 17N Mount Pleasant. Cross the river on US 17N. After crossing the river, bear right on Highway 703. Go to the fifth traffic light and turn right onto Mill Street immediately after crossing the Shem Creek bridge. Go 1 block and turn left onto Church Street. Go 3 blocks to Venning Street where Church becomes Pitt Street. The inn is on the corner of Venning and Pitt.

Nestled in the heart of Mount Pleasant's historic Old Village is a luxuriously restored 1888 building that was built by German immigrants, the Lundens, as a grocery store with their residence in the floors above. With its white clapboards, green shutters, neat row of dormers, and flower-filled window boxes, it is a fine example of Colonial Revival architecture. For ninety-seven years it served as the cornerstone of the village. Even after it ceased serving as a grocery store, it became a hardware store, a boarding house, and the offices of the Mount Pleasant Waterworks. Expertly restored in 1985, today it operates as a bed and breakfast with two restaurants, Captain Guild's Cafe, a popular lunch spot, and Supper at Stacks, an exclusive place to go for dinner.

The care with which the venerable building has been restored is evidenced by the furnishings in the guest rooms. These bedchambers are individually appointed with antiques, reproductions, and South Carolina Lowcountry pieces of rare craftsmanship. Exceptional cabinetry was, after all, a hallmark of early-day Mount Pleasant. On the other hand, modern conveniences have not been neglected. All rooms have everything you could want for a luxurious, comfortable stay including a whirlpool tub. Don't miss a peek at the outstanding doll collection.

Guilds Inn beckons you to take your ease as if you were in the home of a dear friend. While away some time in the sunroom or in the courtyard.

What's Nearby Mount Pleasant

Mount Pleasant is only fifteen minutes away from downtown Charleston. What's more, Mount Pleasant is just ten minutes away from Charleston's finest sandy beaches, Isle of Palms and Sullivan's Island. For more information, see "What's Nearby Charleston" on page 336.

The Schell Haus Bed and Breakfast

117 Hiawatha Trail
Pickens, South Carolina 29671
(864) 878–0078

E-MAIL: schellhs@bellsouth.net

WEB SITE: www.bbonline/sc/schellhaus/

INNKEEPERS: Sharon and Jim Mahanes

ROOMS: 5 rooms and 1 suite; all with private bath, coffeemaker, TV; some with whirlpool tub

ON THE GROUNDS: Verandas, pool

RATES: $80 to $160 single or double, including breakfast and afternoon refreshments; discount for three or more nights; minimum stay on weekends during the September through November leaf season

CREDIT CARDS ACCEPTED? Yes

OPEN: Year-round

HOW TO GET THERE: From I–85, take Scenic Highway 11 North. Turn right onto Hiawatha Trail.

A woodland paradise tucked away on four acres in the foothills of the Blue Ridge Mountains off the Cherokee Foothills Scenic Highway in extreme northwestern South Carolina, the Victorian-style Schell Haus is a perfect getaway for rest and relaxation. From the verandas and some rooms you can see Table Rock, a natural wonder. With no cities nearby, this is a place to get away from it all and to enjoy nature and numerous outdoor activities.

When we pulled up the winding driveway through the woods and into the manicured clearing and spied the turret and wraparound veranda, we had to remind ourselves that the Schell Haus is a modern reproduction of a turn-of-the-century house, not the real thing. Accented with leaded glass, the front door and sidelights feature decorative shells, a motif continued throughout the house. The Schell Haus was built by George and Sherry Schell in 1991 to operate as a bed and breakfast. Current owners Sharon and Jim Mahanes bought it in 1996 and continue the fine tradition of hospitality begun by the Schells.

Antiques and carefully chosen reproductions continue the turn-of-the-century illusion inside. The parlor, for instance, features an ornate Victorian sofa and chairs grouped around a working fireplace, a marble-topped coffee table, a grand piano, hardwood floors, and appropriate art and accessories—all of which make it a perfect gathering place for guests. A cozy sitting nook in the entrance hall affords more privacy for those who desire it.

All but one of the comfortable guest rooms, each with its own personality, features antiques and reproductions; a canopy, mansion, four-poster, or sleigh queen-size bed; a seating area; and all the modern conveniences. Among the guest rooms, some standouts are the Carrick Creek Room, which features a king-size bed; the Table Rock Room, which boasts a whirlpool tub and a wet bar; and the Oolenoy Suite, which has a whirlpool tub and a separate sitting room with a wet bar. Its semiprivate deck overlooks the swimming pool.

Sharon serves light hors d'oeuvres in the late afternoon and early evening; nuts, pretzels, and soft beverages are always available. On chilly days enjoy a snack by pulling up a rocker beside a blazing fire in the fireplace; in the summer relax in or around the pool.

Breakfast is an event, served in the formal dining room to a background of soft music. Sharon prepares orange juice, an entree such as eggs olé with homemade salsa or apricot casserole, accompanied by grits, homemade cheese muffins, and hot beverages. Dinner can be prepared for guests with prior arrangement and at an additional fee.

What's Nearby Pickens

There's plenty to do at Pickens. Just take your pick. You can go antiques shopping downtown or amble through any of four state parks—Table Rock, Caesars Head, Jones Gap, and Devils Fork. Don't forget the fishing at lakes Keowee and Jocassee. The Pickens area offers a little something for everybody—boating, hiking, swimming, biking—even guided nature walks.

Southwood Manor

100 East Main Street
Ridge Spring, South Carolina 29129
(803) 685-5100 or (888) 806-9898

E-MAIL: sothent@pbtcomm.net

INNKEEPERS: Judy and Mike Adamick

ROOMS: 4; 3 with private baths; 1 suite with shared bath; all with TV and gas-log fireplace

ON THE GROUNDS: Pool, tennis court, airstrip, stable

RATES: $65 single or $75 double ($125 during the Master's Golf Tournament in nearby Augusta, Georgia), including full gourmet breakfast and afternoon refreshments

CREDIT CARDS ACCEPTED? Yes

OPEN: Year-round

HOW TO GET THERE: From I–20, take exit 22 and go north on US 1 for 9.2 miles. Turn left onto SC 392 into Rock Spring. Turn right onto SC 23. The B&B is 0.5 mile on your left.

Sitting well back from the road on the outskirts of small Ridge Spring and surrounded by century-old pecan trees, this Georgian Colonial mansion with its impressive two-story, six-columned portico is the epitome of the Southern plantation. It's hard to imagine that a lady in her early twenties without any architectural training designed this house eighty-odd years ago. When an earlier home burned, John Calhoun Watson, gentleman farmer, acquired this estate for a cotton plantation. During World War I, he got a government contract to grow as much cotton as he could; it was in demand for parachute uniforms and plane seats. The cotton was processed at a cotton gin located right across the road, then shipped out by rail. (Still in operation, it is the oldest cotton gin in South Carolina.) The wealth Watson amassed permitted him to build this grand mansion. It was his sister who designed it.

Judy and Mike are the fourth owners of the property. Judy is a talented watercolor artist, and many of her works adorn the house; some are for sale. An aviation buff, Mike provided open-cockpit biplane rides in Myrtle Beach before the Adamicks resettled in Ridge Spring. He retains his plane, however, and spends many enjoyable hours tinkering with and flying it. In fact, this is one of the few bed and breakfasts we know of that have a private airstrip—2,000 feet of grass, enabling guests with small planes to actually fly in. It's also one of only a few we've visited with "horse motel" accommodations for guests traveling with horses. Among the most exciting events in the area are the fox hunts held from November to February; guests can participate in a hunt breakfast and ride along on the tally-ho wagon. The Adamicks' horses can be seen nibbling in the pastures beyond the paddock while handsome peacocks strut their stuff on the grounds. An oversize swimming pool and a tennis court provide even more entertainment for guests who simply want to get away from it all.

Large, comfortable guest rooms feature four-poster beds and gas-log fireplaces. We stayed in the beautiful hunter green and pink Land of Cotton, which boasts a four-poster king-size bed and floral balloon draperies. Since it was a chilly December night, we particularly enjoyed our cozy fire. This room connects with the Beachstormer, a twin-bedded room, to form a suite for four.

The sumptuous breakfast might include broiled grapefruit, apricot crepes, an omelette with unusual herbs from Judy's garden, homemade sourdough English muffins, and muscadine jams. Accompanied by a background of classical music, breakfast is served in the formal dining room, from which you can enjoy woodsy views.

We particularly enjoyed chatting with Judy in her wonderful kitchen, where she actually cooks on an antique stove.

What's Nearby Ridge Spring

If you're staying in Ridge Spring, you have ample opportunity to enjoy the outdoors. First visit Lake Murray, a popular spot for water sports. Then head out to Dreher Island State Park. To explore more options, visit nearby Aiken's horse country. The Aiken County Historical Museum is a pleasant attraction, and you'll enjoy their turn-of-the-century furnishings and agricultural displays.

East Main Guest House

Best Buy

600 East Main Street
Rock Hill, South Carolina 29730
(803) 366–1161

WEB SITE: www.bbonline.com/sc/
eastmain/ or through
www.bedandbreakfast.com

INNKEEPERS: Melba and Jerry Peterson

ROOMS: 3; all with private bath, TV, telephone; 2 with gas-log fireplace; 1 with whirlpool tub

ON THE GROUNDS: Patio, terraced garden

RATES: $59 to $79 single or double, including breakfast

CREDIT CARDS ACCEPTED? Yes

OPEN: Year-round

HOW TO GET THERE: From I–77, take exit 79, Dave Lyle Boulevard, and go west to Main Street. Turn left onto Main and go through downtown for approximately 6 blocks to a two-story gray-blue brick home on your right with a white picket fence and matching porch railings.

Carol's grandmother always used to say, "Good things come in small packages"—which certainly is true of the East Main Guest House. The modest turn-of-the-century Craftsman-style bungalow disguises the charms within. The entire downstairs, which contains the formal parlor and dining room, features original heart-pine flooring, French doors, and wide moldings. What was an unfinished attic has been transformed into three gracious guest rooms and an informal sitting room outfitted with comfortable seating, a game table, cards, games, puzzles, a refrigerator stocked with drinks, cable television, and a VCR. The Petersons' restoration effort earned them a Historic Rock Hill Renovation Award in 1992. Melba and Jerry are so personable, you'll feel like lifelong friends within minutes. They're a big part of the charm.

We luxuriated in the Honeymoon Suite, which features stained-glass windows, a queen-size canopy bed with an upholstered headboard, a gas-log fireplace with a custom-made surround, and a whirlpool garden tub—over which hung a crystal chandelier, no less. Who says decadence is bad? The East Room, with beautiful designer window treatments, matching headboard on the queen-size bed, and gas-log fireplace, is no less popular. Two adults traveling together might be more comfortable in the twin beds of the Garden Room. Corner windows make this bedchamber especially bright and cheerful.

An extended continental breakfast of homemade croissants, muffins, fruit, and sometimes waffles or a casserole is usually served in the cheery dining room, but when the weather's just right, it can be enjoyed on the brick terrace or underneath the pergola in the garden.

Rock Hill is named for a cut made through white flinty rock during construction of the Columbia-to-Charlotte railroad. Four captivating 13-foot female statues representing the cornerstones of life and prosperity and two 60-foot Egyptian Revival columns surrounded by terraced gardens create the gateway into this charming small city.

What's Nearby Rock Hill

Rock Hill is the attractive backdrop for Winthrop College. Stroll through the pretty campus, and don't miss seeing the original school building called the Little Chapel. A quick ride from Rock Hill is Paramount Studio's Carowinds, a water and theme park. Enjoy the Hollywood-inspired rides and shows.

The Bed and Breakfast of Sumter

6 Park Avenue
Sumter, South Carolina 29150
(803) 773–2903 or (888) SUM–TERB

WEB SITE: www.bbonline.com/sc/sumter/

INNKEEPERS: Charles, Joyce, and Kathryn Thielman

ROOMS: 4; all with private bath; some with fireplace

ON THE GROUNDS: Verands

RATES: $75 double, including gourmet breakfast, complimentary beverages; discount for multiple-night stays

CREDIT CARDS ACCEPTED? Yes

OPEN: Year-round

HOW TO GET THERE: From I–95, take exit 135 West onto Route 378 to Route 763. Turn left and go 2 miles to a dead end. Turn left onto Liberty and proceed through eight traffic lights, then turn right onto North Washington. Turn left onto Hampton Street and go 4 blocks. Turn right onto Park. The B&B is the second house on the left.

In 1896 Colonel B. C. Wallace built this spacious prairie-style home in a quiet residential neighborhood; more than a hundred years later, much of the original architecture and charm remain. Surrounded by venerable old trees, the house showcases a large front porch with rockers and an old-fashioned swing facing lush, green, quiet Memorial Park.

Step through the front door into a bygone era. High ceilings, hardwood floors, elaborate moldings, and antique furnishings grace the spacious public and guest rooms. French doors frame the formal parlor, which is accented by a European soapstone fireplace with turned columns topped by a magnificently hand-carved mirror reaching to the 10-foot ceiling.

Among the four guest rooms, the Plantation Rice Room, named for the elaborately carved, queen-size cherry rice bed and featuring lace curtains, a crocheted bedspread and pillow covers, an ornamental fireplace, and a hanging antique quilt, is the favorite. The working fireplace in the Peach Room makes it a close second in cool weather. The Sumter Room has a historical motif with a king-size walnut and iron bed; the Veranda Room features two three-quarter-size antique rope beds. Little touches such as fresh flowers make guests feel at home.

Your gourmet breakfast, which might include freshly squeezed orange juice, fruit, an entree such as eggs Benedict, Belgian waffles, or artichoke soufflé, and home-baked breads and muffins, can be served in the dining room, the privacy of your room, or out on the veranda in good weather.

What's Nearby Sumter

Sumter is a charming town with many attractions, but one is especially deserving of a visit. The Swan Lake and Iris Gardens is home to all eight species of swans that exist in the world. More than 30,000 irises bloom around Memorial Day and set the stage for the Iris Festival.

Calhoun Street Bed and Breakfast

Best Buy

302 West Calhoun Street
Sumter, South Carolina 29150
(803) 775–7035 or (800) 355–8119

E-MAIL: calhnbb@mindspring.com

WEB SITE: calhnbb.home@mindspring.com

INNKEEPERS: Mackenzie and David Sholtz

ROOMS: 4; all with private bath and portable telephone; 1 with telephone jack

ON THE GROUNDS: Front and back porches, rose gardens

RATES: $65 to $75 per room, including full breakfast and evening refreshments; $10 for additional cot; ask about corporate rates

CREDIT CARDS ACCEPTED? Yes

OPEN: Year-round

HOW TO GET THERE: From Columbia, turn right off US 378 onto Broad Street. Turn right onto North Salem, then right onto West Calhoun. The B&B is at the corner of North Salem and West Calhoun. From Camden, US 521 becomes Broad Street. Follow the preceding directions.

This early-1890s home, built by current owner Mackenzie's great-uncle, has always been a congenial place in which to meet and converse with family and friends. That's just as true today as it was more than one hundred years ago.

Public rooms and four eclectically decorated guest rooms are richly appointed with family antiques and an outstanding collection of medieval, nineteenth-century, and contemporary art. The Audubon Room has large windows on three sides overlooking the garden, a queen-size canopy bed with crocheted canopy, two cozy Victorian armchairs, and an ample desk. A favorite with sun lovers, the Heron Room has a large bay window—early-morning light floods the room in a warm glow—as well as a four-poster queen-size bed. The view from the Iris Room's bay window is of the quince garden and bird feeders. This room features a queen-size Empire poster bed, a marble-topped dresser, and an armoire original to the house. All three of these rooms have private baths. The Monterey Room has a treetop view into the stately magnolias and overlooks the side garden. Furnished with twin beds, this room is perfect for friends traveling together. Robes are provided for the short trip down the hall to this boudoir's private bath.

Breakfast is a hearty meal served in the dining room or on the screened back porch overlooking two old rose gardens. Guests choose from a menu the night before; options range from various omelettes to hot cereal and pancakes.

A recent addition is an exercise room in the back; for those who don't want to expend that much energy, the front porch has an old-fashioned swing and a joggling board.

What's a Joggling Board?

A joggling board, which is most often found in the Lowcountry of South Carolina, is a bench-size board suspended between two supports. When you sit on it, the board bounces up and down or "joggles." The longer the board, the more it joggles.

There are various stories about the origin and use of the joggling board. The most mundane is that it was simply the forerunner of the porch swing, but we like the one that says it was used as a courting device. Proper young couples, often under the watchful eye of a chaperone, would sit at each end of the board; as they bounced up and down on it, they'd drift closer and closer together.

Joggling boards originated in Scotland and got to South Carolina by way of one Mrs. Huger from Sumter County, who sent for the plans because she believed the joggling motion would help her rheumatism.

Magnolia House

230 Church Street
Sumter, South Carolina 29150
(803) 775–6694 or (888) 666–0296

E-MAIL: magnoliahouse@sumter.net

WEB SITE: www.bbonline.com/sc/
magnolia/

INNKEEPERS: Carol and Buck Rogers

ROOMS: 3 rooms and 1 suite; all with private bath, telephone, TV, ceiling
fan; 2 with fireplace, 1 with VCR; pets are welcome

ON THE GROUNDS: Porches, garden

RATES: $85 to $135 double, including breakfast and afternoon refreshments; single $10 less

CREDIT CARDS ACCEPTED? Yes

OPEN: Year-round

HOW TO GET THERE: Exact directions will be given at the time of booking.

We hit it off instantly with Carol and Buck (maybe it's a Carol thing).
You'd think we'd been friends for years. That's what it takes to run a
successful bed and breakfast—owners who genuinely love people, who
treat all their guests like long-lost friends. After getting our hosts' suggestions of places to go for dinner, we opted to order in and had an enjoyable
dinner with them, telling each other our life stories.

Of course, having an outstanding property doesn't hurt, either. Four soaring columns support the pediment of this stately Greek Revival mansion,
named for the mature magnolia trees surrounding it. The epitome of the Old
South, it boasts front and back wraparound porches and tall, shapely chimneys. Built by G. A. Lemmon in 1907, it has been home to only four families.
You almost expect to see ladies in flowing gowns and gentlemen in evening
dress floating down the stairs and drifting from room to room.

Among the interior architectural details of note are five fireplaces—
three of them gas-coal and two decorative—stained-glass windows, and
inlaid oak floors. Furnished and decorated in antiques from different
eras, the public and guest rooms are equally inviting. Delightful vignettes

make you smile at every turn—a doll bed filled with old bears and well-used dolls, a Heim carousel horse, bookshelves packed to the gills with everything from miniature volumes to copious tomes, a musical corner with a fife, drum, and dulcimer.

Among the guest rooms, Luta's Salle (room) is very French. Decorated around a massive three-door mirrored wardrobe, it features a carved head-board on the extra-long double bed, a stuffed French couch, and a fireplace. Its bath features a footed tub, pillbox toilet, and pedestal sink. The more masculine British Safari Room has two three-quarter-size colonial beds, kangaroo and New Zealand opossum pelts, and animal pictures gracing the painted chamois leather walls. As always-working, never-on-vacation writers, we loved the writing desk in our Victoria's Retreat, which also features a high-back Victorian double bed and a comfy sofa. Its bath is 1930s vintage.

The two-room Sunflower Suite has a high-back queen-size oak bed in one room and a wonderfully carved Eastlake suite in the other. Upholstered chairs, rockers, and a carved oak lounge offer plenty of opportunities to relax or put your feet up.

A full breakfast that might include shrimp and grits, eggs béarnaise, quail and dilled potatoes, or country ham and eggs is served in the formal dining room, which is dominated by some of the most massive French antiques we've ever seen outside of a castle. They look perfectly natural and not a bit overpowering in these spacious, high-ceilinged rooms. And there are afternoon refreshments—how about on one of the verandas or in the formal walled English-style backyard garden?

What's Nearby Sumter

See page 365 for what's nearby Sumter.

The Inn at Merridun

100 Merridun Place
Union, South Carolina 29379
(864) 427–7052 or (888) 892–6020

E-MAIL: merridun@carol.net
WEB SITE: www.bbonline.com/sc/merridun/
INNKEEPERS: Peggy and Jim Waller and J. D. (Jefferson Davis or Just Darn cat)
ROOMS: 5; all with private bath, TV, telephone, clock radio, hair dryer; 2 with whirlpool tubs, 1 with claw-foot tub; 1 room is wheelchair accessible

ON THE GROUNDS: Veranda, lawn games

RATES: $89 to $129 single or double, including breakfast, beverages and snacks, evening refreshments

CREDIT CARDS ACCEPTED? Yes

OPEN: Year-round

HOW TO GET THERE: In Union, take the SC 176 Bypass to Rice Avenue, turn right onto Rice and go about 0.75 mile. Turn right onto Hicks and make an immediate right into the driveway.

Although the Inn at Merridun is located in town, we'd have sworn we were at a country plantation. Nestled in the center of nine wooded acres rich with azaleas, magnolias, and wisteria, the inn occupies a serene world of its own—a world where the graciousness of the Old South lives again. Peggy and Jim describe Merridun's setting as "city close and country quiet."

Scarlett O'Hara would have been perfectly comfortable in this grand Greek Revival mansion where first- and second-story verandas are supported by massive soaring Corinthian columns. The mansion boasts 7,900 square feet of living space and an astounding 2,400 square feet of verandas.

Despite the villa's size, Peggy and Jim make it cozy and inviting. We stepped into the immense entrance hall and our breath was taken away by the stunning curved staircase. We could easily imagine Scarlett or some other pampered Southern belle sweeping down those stairs, skirts rustling. And what an entrance a bride would make! We considered ourselves especially fortunate to be seeing the inn at Christmastime, when a sumptuous Victorian-bedecked tree was framed by the staircase, itself trimmed with garland.

We hardly knew where to look next—admiring in turn the 14-foot ceilings; the frescoed ceilings in the music and dining rooms; the mosaic tiles, turn-of-the-century stenciling, and faux graining in the foyer; and the raised designs in the fireplace tiles. All the while we were beguiled by the aromas of freshly cut pine and baking cookies, and the soft strains of classical music.

No matter which of the five distinctively decorated guest rooms becomes your home away from home, you'll enjoy a private bath and all the modern conveniences, including a king- or queen-size bed. The only downstairs guest room, the romantic Senator's Chamber, features a king-size French Quarter bed, a sitting area, and a double-size whirlpool tub as well as a separate shower. A touch of whimsy in Lucy's Garden Retreat, which also boasts a whirlpool tub, is a picket-fence headboard. The Sisters' Boudoir boasts a queen-size bed with a feather mattress and a claw-foot tub. The focal point of the Governors' Gallery is the king-size rice bed.

Whether you're a honeymoon couple sharing your first breakfast together at a candlelight table in the ladies' parlor or joining the other guests at the 18-foot table in the dining room, you'll be in for a memorable culinary experience. Jim writes a "Cooking—Inn Style" column for the local newspaper, and both Wallers have taught cooking classes on the radio and for local colleges. Breakfast begins with juice and fruit and proceeds to an egg dish with meat, a starch, and breads, then culminates with "dessert": coffee cake, French toast, or blueberry pancakes. (Check your calorie counter at the door!) Lunch and dinner can be arranged in advance for an additional fee. As if being full-time innkeepers and chefs isn't enough, Peggy and Jim sponsor many special events throughout the year: murder mystery weekends, wine tastings, Sunday brunches, cooking retreats, Sunday-afternoon teas, and romantic weekend packages, to name just a few.

Although the inn is only a five-minute walk from downtown and within a short driving distance of numerous historical sites and outdoor activities, had we been there in warmer weather, all we'd have wanted to do was spend the afternoon in a hammock or get our exercise by rocking on the veranda—perhaps exerting ourselves to play croquet or horseshoes or explore the property: There's a brick wing that used to house the servants' kitchen, laundry house, servants' smokehouse, well, and carriage house containing one of the original owners' carriages.

What's Nearby Union

There's a little of everything in the Union area: museums, art galleries, historic homes, fishing, golf, and hiking. A pleasant way to spend the afternoon is a visit to the Rose Hill Plantation State Park. Another option is to explore nearby historic Brattonville. If you're interested in Brattonville's history, tour the restored eighteenth- and nineteenth-century homes of the Bratton family, the town's namesake.

Another Recommended B&B in Union

JUXA Plantation, an early-1800s Greek Revival plantation house, offers rooms with private baths; tours of the house and extensive grounds; Wilson Road, Union, SC 28379; (803) 427-8688.

Bonnie Doone Plantation

5878 Bonnie Doone Road
Walterboro, South Carolina 29488
(843) 893-3396 or (888) 317-6799; fax (843) 893-2479

E-MAIL: bonniedoone@lowcountry.com

INNKEEPERS: Kelly and Robbie King

ROOMS: 18; with private and shared baths; 1 room has wheelchair access

ON THE GROUNDS: Porch, gardens, extensive lawns, no smoking or alcohol

RATES: $85 to $120 double, including continental-plus breakfast

CREDIT CARDS ACCEPTED? Yes

OPEN: Year-round

HOW TO GET THERE: From I–95 heading south, take exit 57 and go south on SC 64 to County Road 458. Follow the discreet signs to the plantation. If you are traveling north on I–95, take exit 53 onto SC 64 and follow it north to County Road 458. The total distance from I–95 is 16 miles.

Truly out in the country, Bonnie Doone Plantation is a place to come and do nothing. The land was once a grant from England; it became a major rice producer. Located at the headwaters of the Ashepoo River in Colleton County, the secluded and tranquil site is characterized by a long avenue of century-old oaks, abandoned rice fields, woodlands, and marshlands. The original mansion house met the fate of many others during the Civil War—it was burned to the ground by Sherman's troops in 1865 and lay in ruins for more than sixty-five years. The present Georgian-style mansion was built in 1931. At the same time, a formal camellia garden was designed and planted next to the house. The name Bonnie Doone came from an adjacent plantation that was added to the estate.

Today the house and the remaining 131 acres of the plantation are owned and operated by the Charleston Baptist Association and used for various purposes—as a conference center, a site for Elderhostel classes, and a special-events facility—in addition to offering bed-and-breakfast accommodations. The present ballroom was included in Helen Comstock's book, *The One Hundred Most Beautiful Rooms in America*.

This is a place to relax in a world of peace and tranquillity free of televisions, telephones, and radios. Because of its church affiliation, it won't surprise you to learn that alcohol and smoking aren't permitted. Guest accommodations are offered in the elegant mansion or the authentic caretaker's cottage. Because so many groups use Bonnie Doone, guest rooms primarily offer two beds—either two twins, two doubles, or two queens. Among the rooms in the main house, seven have private bath and the remainder have shared; the rooms in the caretaker's cottage share as well.

A generous continental-plus breakfast of quiche or eggs Bonnie Doone is accompanied by cereal and fruit. You can spend hours sitting on a porch with a good book or wandering through the gardens and the grounds.

What's Nearby Walterboro

Walterboro is a quiet country town. You'll be charmed by the local sights, like the Colleton Museum, Little Library, and courthouse. The town is filled with historic homes and churches. To sample some local art, visit the South Carolina Artisans Center. In addition, you can enjoy the outdoors at the Edisto River Canoe and Kayak Trail.

Songbird Manor Best Buy

116 North Zion Street
Winnsboro, South Carolina 29180
(803) 635-6963 or (888) 636-7698

E-MAIL: s.yenner@gte.net

WEB SITE: www.bbonline.com/sc/songbird

INNKEEPER: Susan Yenner

ROOMS: 5; all with private bath, cable TV, VCR, telephone, ceiling fan, clock radio, hair dryer, full-length mirror, flashlight, smoke alarm, extinguisher

ON THE GROUNDS: Verandas, use of bicycles

RATES: $65 to $110 double, including full breakfast, afternoon refreshments, evening turndown service; many packages for special occasions

CREDIT CARDS ACCEPTED? Yes

OPEN: Year-round

HOW TO GET THERE: From I-77, take either Highway 200 or Highway 34 to Business 321, which becomes Congress Street in town. At the Clock Tower, turn east and go 1 block. Turn left onto Zion Street. Songbird Manor is the fourth house on your right.

Located in the heart of Winnsboro's historic district, Songbird Manor is surrounded by other venerable turn-of-the-century homes. The mansion at 116 North Zion Street was built in 1912 by Marcus W. "Big Daddy" Doty in the William Morris style. A showcase of Southern craftsmanship, the mansion features elaborate plaster ceiling moldings and woodwork. Original beveled glass greets you in the front door and parlor windows. Among the other outstanding interior features are oak and chestnut pocket doors, extensive dental moldings, wainscoting, coffered ceilings, and imported scenic fireplace tiles. Fine oak columns separate the front and back of the foyer.

Both guest and public rooms are named for birds. Breakfast is served in the Cardinal Dining Room, which is painted a deep shade of rose and further warmed by an oak mantel and wainscoting. Guests like to gather in either of two parlors for board games, cards, puzzles, reading, television, movies, or easy conversations with new friends. The Mallard Room, known as the gentlemen's parlor in Big Daddy's day, is more informal. Painted hunter green, it features an oak-mirrored mantel and comfy overstuffed furniture. The formal Peacock Room struts its stuff like a proud peacock. Although the floral wallpaper and elaborate floral rug get your immediate attention, do take time to notice the imported ceramic tiles around the fireplace and the inlaid Honduran mahogany design in the oak floor.

Comfortably appointed guest rooms are painted colors similar to the plumage of the birds for which they are named. Each is spacious and light with several windows. Three baths have footed tubs original to the house. We liked the king-size four-poster bed, the sitting area in the bay window, and the soft blue and navy accents in the Indigo Bunting Room. Civil War buffs like to peruse the volumes of Civil War history in the Blue Jay Room, which features a queen-size four-poster cannonball bed, a bay window, and a beige and blue color scheme. Honeymooners like the French influence of the furnishings in the Hummingbird Room, which boasts a king-size bed and is decorated in burgundy, rose, pink, and gold. Rich emerald greens and gold, a queen-size wrought-iron and wood four-poster bed, brass plates displayed on a picture rail, and a window seat in the bay window characterize the Carolina Warbler. Two extra-long wicker beds in the Carolina Paroquet Room can be converted to a king. This room, decorated in violets against hunter green, can be combined with the Mockingbird Porch—an enclosed sunporch with a daybed and a trundle—to create a suite.

While Susan is serving a breakfast of homemade breads, gourmet coffees, and regional and specialty delights using pecans and fruits grown on the grounds, get her to tell you about visits from the ghost of Big Daddy.

What's Nearby Winnsboro

Winnsboro is famous for its town clock, the oldest continuously working town clock in the country. If you have the time, visit the Fairfield County, South Carolina Railroad Museum in Rockton. Take a ride back in time and enjoy the museum's great collection of old steam engines and cabooses.

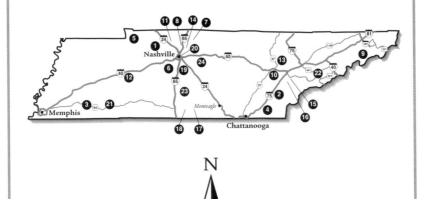

N

Tennessee

Numbers on map refer to towns numbered below.

1. Ashland City, Birdsong Lodge at Sycamore Creek, 376

2. Athens, Woodlawn Bed and Breakfast, 378

3. Bolivar, Magnolia Manor, 380

4. Cleveland, Rose Hill Inn, 382

5. Dover, Riverfront Plantation Inn, 384

6. Franklin, Namaste Acres Farm, 385

7. Gallatin, Hancock House, 387

8. Goodlettsville, Crocker Springs Bed and Breakfast, 389

9. Greeneville, Big Spring Inn, 391

10. Harriman, Bushrod Hall Bed and Breakfast, 393

11. Hendersonville, Spring Haven, 395

12. Jackson, Highland Place Bed and Breakfast, 396

13. Kingston, Whitestone Country Inn, 398

14. Lebanon, Cedarvine Manor, 400

15. Lenoir City, The Captain's Retreat, 402

16. Loudon, The Mason Place Bed and Breakfast, 404

17. Lynchburg, Lynchburg Bed and Breakfast, 406

18. Mulberry, Dream Fields Country Bed and Breakfast Inn, 408

19. Murfreesboro,
Byrn-Roberts Inn, 410
Carriage Lane Inn Bed and Breakfast, 412
Clardy's Guest House, 414
Simply Southern B&B Inn, 416

20. Nashville,
Apple Brook Bed, Breakfast and Barn, 418
Carole's Yellow Cottage, 419
Hillsboro House Bed and Breakfast, 421
Linden Manor Bed and Breakfast, 423

21. Savannah, White Elephant B&B Inn, 424

22. Sevierville, Von-Bryan Inn, 426

23. Shelbyville, The Old Gore House Bed and Breakfast, 428

24. Watertown, Watertown Bed and Breakfast, 430

Birdsong Lodge on Sycamore Creek

1306 Highway 49 East
Ashland City, Tennessee 37015
(615) 792-1767

E-MAIL: robpilling@nashville.com

WEB SITE: www.birdsonglodge.com

INNKEEPERS: Rob and Bett Pilling,
innkeepers; Elizabeth and George
Trinkler, owners

ROOMS: 2 rooms, 1 suite, 1 cottage; all with private bath, telephone, cable TV

ON THE GROUNDS: Screened porch, patio, gardens, trails

RATES: $175 to $195 double, including full breakfast and afternoon
refreshments; additional person $25; ask about corporate rates

CREDIT CARDS ACCEPTED? Yes

OPEN: Year-round

HOW TO GET THERE: From I-24, take exit 24 and go left on TN 49 for 6 miles.
When you see the sign for the Girl Scout camp and just before you get to
the green bridge, turn left into the driveway.

Log cabin. Elegant and sophisticated. Oxymorons, right? Wrong. Well,
first let's establish that this isn't just any log cabin. Built in 1912, it was
the summer getaway of Nashville's fabulously wealthy Cheek family, of
Maxwell House coffee fame. In fact, they lived in it full time while Cheek-
wood, their in-town mansion, was being built. Knowing the cabin's origins
should alert you to the fact that this rambling home is something very special. In fact, it gets a solid 10 in our book.

The lodge was recently purchased by Elizabeth and George Trinkler.
Elizabeth is the great-granddaughter of E. C. Lewis, who ran the Sycamore
Mill in the late 1800s, inspired and engineered the building of Nashville's
Parthenon and Union Station, and owned this property at one time. Elizabeth was naturally anxious to get it back into the family. Busy with careers
in Nashville, however, the Trinklers have teamed up with the delightful Bett
and Rob Pilling, who act as innkeepers. Together, the two couples have renovated Birdsong Lodge as a luxurious and exclusive retreat.

The long, sprawling, one-story lodge hugs the hill on which it sits above
Sycamore Creek. Huge, dark cedar logs chinked together with startling
white plaster are visible from both outside and inside. We entered through
the screened porch and saw a magnificent porch swing—it's as large as a
twin bed—plumped up with animal-print pillows. Then we stepped into the

great room, a wonderful haven with gleaming hardwood floors, a beamed ceiling, a built-in bench along one side, and a huge stone fireplace. Gone are ceiling fans, rustic furniture, and country accents; they've been replaced with fine antiques, striking contemporary pieces, dramatic pieces of art, brass or crystal chandeliers, and soothing music that all combine to create a warm and romantic ambience. Bett's hand is evident everywhere, especially in her flower arrangements.

Only four guest accommodations—two rooms, a two-bedroom suite, and a cottage—assure guests as much privacy and pampering as they want. The three main bedrooms in the lodge all boast four-poster beds and opulent bathrooms. Fabrics strewn with violets and a dramatic green and white bathroom with an unusual art deco chandelier characterize the Cheek Suite. Its second bedroom contains twin beds, making this suite ideal for family members or friends traveling together. Blacks and creams in the bedroom, blacks and whites in the bath (both of which even sport crystal chandeliers), create a sexy look in the King Charles Room. We were partial to the animal-print accents in the comfortable, elegant cream and white Queen Anne Room. For those very special occasions when you and your beloved want an extra dose of privacy, choose the Lewis Cottage. Pickled floors, light floral fabrics in the bedroom, a separate sitting room, a claw-foot tub in the bath, both front and back porches, and a hammock slung between two trees all strike a sentimental mood.

Dining at Birdsong Lodge is an intimate experience complimented by the use of candlelight, a fire in the fireplace when it's chilly, fresh flowers, and antique china, crystal, and silver, some from the Lewis estate. Bett makes everything from scratch using organic vegetables and herbs, many from her gardens. The description of crusted French toast in a boysenberry pool made our mouths water, as did Rob's salmon and wild rice omelette.

When you're not cuddled up on the swing or stretched out in the hammock, there are gardens and grounds to explore, including a trail down to the creek. And just one more thing—there's a resident standard-size white poodle named Happy, who's a delightful companion whenever you want her to be.

What's Nearby Ashland City

Ashland City offers a lot of different kinds of activities. You can go horseback riding at the city's Girl Scout camp. You can also go biking or hiking on the Rails-to-Trails in Ashland City. There are a number of Civil War battle sites and monuments to visit, or you can browse the city's antiques shops. If you really dig archaeology, check out the city's prehistoric Indian mounds. Another option is the Cheatham Wildlife Management Area. If you miss the sounds and sights of the big city, Nashville is only twenty-five minutes away.

Woodlawn Bed and Breakfast

Best Buy

110 Keith Lane
Athens, Tennessee 37303
(423) 745–8211 or (800) 745–8213

WEB SITE: www.woodlawn.com

INNKEEPERS: Susan and Barry Willis

ROOMS: 4; all with private bath, TV, clock radio

ON THE GROUNDS: Verandas, gardens, pool

RATES: $75 to $110 double, including full breakfast, snacks, and beverages; ask about corporate rates

CREDIT CARDS ACCEPTED? Yes

OPEN: Year-round

HOW TO GET THERE: From I–75, take TN 30 East to downtown. At intersection 6, turn right onto County Road 39/Washington Street, which is one way at that point. In a few blocks it merges into Madison Avenue, which is two way. Follow Madison to Keith Lane, the last street before you get into open countryside, and turn left. Woodlawn is the first house on your right.

Truly an estate, majestic Woodlawn perches on a hill on five acres at the edge of Athens. Formerly known as the Keith Home, the redbrick Greek Revival mansion is one of the oldest masonry structures in McMinn County. Built in 1858 by Alexander Humes Keith, it was used as a hospital for wounded Union soldiers during the Civil War. When the Willises purchased it, they changed the name to Woodlawn to honor Susan's grandfather's home. Much of the acreage is in velvety lawns shaded by ancient trees.

All the elements of a classic Greek Revival structure are here in the mansion: a temple pediment supported by four tall columns, creating a first-floor veranda and shading a second-story balcony. We swept (at this type of house, you can't simply climb) up the front stairs to be greeted at the door by Oh No, a friendly miniature poodle, and Ima Jean King, the housekeeper. She told us that when Susan brought the dog home, Barry said, "Oh no!" The name stuck.

Once we were ushered inside, we immediately fell under the spell of Woodlawn's grace and charm. Thirteen-and-a-half-foot ceilings downstairs, tall windows, burnished hardwood floors, working fireplaces—some of them with elaborate marble mantels—and ornate moldings have been lovingly restored. To this elegant and serene backdrop, Susan and Barry have added antiques original to the house, such as the 1800s rosewood square piano, other carefully chosen period pieces, Oriental carpets, art, gilt-framed mirrors, and accessories. Opulent silk floral arrangements are everywhere. Paintings and photographs of family members give the house some of the personality and intimacy missing in many bed and breakfasts. A partially completed puzzle awaits your attention in the music room. A portrait of Susan smiles down from above the mantel in the sunny yellow parlor.

Guest chambers are graciously decorated and well appointed. Several have sleeping options other than the usual one bed for a couple. The elegant downstairs bedroom features twin beds, a square bathtub, and a crystal chandelier. Upstairs, the bedrooms are named for colors. Central to the Green Room is a four-poster bed and an additional twin bed. In addition to a pretty double bed with an unusual headboard, the Rose Room offers a twin bed as well. Our favorite, however, was the Red Room, which features a four-poster queen-size bed, a gas-log fireplace, a chaise longue, and a claw-foot tub with a shower. An informal sitting room in the upstairs hall also offers access to the second-floor balcony.

Despite how enchanting all this is, more attractions await behind the house. A small back porch—a pleasant place to while away some time—leads into a small formal garden, and then through a brick wall and picket fence into the swimming area. The inviting pool is surrounded by umbrella tables, an arbor, and a covered area with comfortable wicker seating. In good weather, you'll want to spend lots of time out here.

After a divine night's sleep, drift into the blue and white formal dining room for a full country breakfast that might consist of orange French toast, quiche, or an egg dish along with fresh fruit and homemade muffins served at the Chippendale dining table under a crystal chandelier.

Pretty little Athens is located halfway between Chattanooga and Knoxville, making it an ideal base from which to explore the area, perhaps venturing over to the Great Smoky Mountains National Park.

Tennessee Wesleyan College is located right in Athens. The oldest building on the college campus, known as "Old College" building, served as a hospital during Civil War. Athen's McMinn County Living Heritage Museum is an interesting destination, with its permanent display of nineteenth- and twentieth-century quilts. Take a tour of the Mayfield Dairy and treat yourself to fresh ice cream at the dairy bar. If you visit in September, check out the annual Arts in the Park festival. The arts and crafts show is held on the campus of Tennessee Wesleyan.

Magnolia Manor

418 North Main Street
Bolivar, Tennessee 38008
(901) 658–6700

INNKEEPERS: Elaine and James Cox

ROOMS: 4; 1 with private bath; 3 with ceiling fan

ON THE GROUNDS: Veranda, extensive grounds

RATES: $85 for rooms, $95 for suite, double, including continental or full breakfast

CREDIT CARDS ACCEPTED? Yes

OPEN: Year-round

HOW TO GET THERE: From US 64, turn north onto Main Street. Magnolia Manor is 4 blocks ahead on your right.

Lovely old magnolias shield and shade antebellum Magnolia Manor, a Georgian-style mansion located in one of Bolivar's historic districts. (Although the town is named for Simon Bolivar, citizens pronounce it *Bolliver*.) The house was completed in 1849 using slave-made, sun-dried red brick—its walls are 13 inches thick. Judge Austin Miller, one of two men given credit for putting Memphis in Tennessee rather than Mississippi when they helped set the state boundary, not only designed the house but supervised its construction as well. The symmetrical design features wide front-to-back halls on both floors separating spacious rooms with 15-foot ceilings on both sides. Only three families have ever lived in this house. Although the Millers had five children, none of them had children of their own, so once the last daughter died, the house went out of their family. Elaine and Jim have owned it since 1981.

It's not surprising that a house as old as this has its share of stories to tell. One is that when General Grant attempted to commandeer the mansion for his headquarters, Mrs. Miller used her delicate health as an excuse to stay in at least part of the house herself. (She was a true steel magnolia!) Although she tried to act as a gracious hostess to Grant and his generals—Sherman, Logan, and McPherson—Sherman eventually drove her to tears when he declared that all Southern women and children should be exterminated. Grant demanded that Sherman apologize, which he did but with such ill grace that he struck out in anger with his saber; the slash mark is still visible. You might be surprised to know that these four generals still inhabit the manor. Portraits of the four unwelcome visitors hang in the front hall and up the stairway.

As soon as we met gracious, soft-spoken Elaine Cox and saw what she has re-created in this house, we could imagine her in the role of Mrs. Miller defending her home and Southern womanhood from the Yankee generals. Elaine's stick-to-itiveness stood her in good stead during the restoration process, when she tried, as much as was practical, to keep the mansion's architectural integrity intact. Although the virgin-pine random-width floorboards and simple mantels are original and only needed to be refinished, Elaine found such challenges as twenty-five layers of wallpaper to be stripped and irreplaceable antique French wallpaper to be installed without tearing. Original colors are used throughout.

Massive Victorian antiques, dramatic period window treatments, and Oriental carpets add to the authentic flavor of the public and guest rooms.

What's Nearby Bolivar

Bolivar is home to one of the oldest original courthouses in the state. Referred to as the Little Courthouse, it holds the county museum. Bolivar is also known for its historic estate, The Pillars, which was owned by one of the state's original settlers.

Rose Hill Inn

367 Horton Road Southeast
Cleveland, Tennessee 37323
(423) 614–0700

E-MAIL: rosehill@bellsouth.net

WEB SITE: http://earth.vol.com/~rosehill

INNKEEPERS: Ann and Richard Rosenberg

ROOMS: 4; all with private bath, clock radio; 1 with dedicated telephone with data port

ON THE GROUNDS: Porch, courtyard, swimming pool, stocked pond

RATES: $89 to $139 double, including breakfast, snacks, and beverages; $5.00 less for single occupancy; additional person $5.00; ask about corporate rates

CREDIT CARDS ACCEPTED? Yes

OPEN: Year-round

HOW TO GET THERE: From I–75, take the Cleveland Bypass around to the US 64 exit. Turn east onto US 64 and travel approximately 4 miles east on US 64 to Kinzer Road; turn right. Go 1 mile to Bates Pike and turn left. Travel 1.3 miles to Horton Road and turn right. The B&B is 0.5 mile ahead on your left.

A pretty setting, congenial hosts, attractive and comfortable rooms, and great food: We added it all up and decided that what we had here was a recipe for a very pleasant getaway. When we turned off the country road, the first thing we saw was the pond, then the split-rail fence as we traveled up the hill to the house. Located on nine wooded acres, the lovely "old" saltbox was actually built in 1986. Next, we met Ann and Richard, bustling from kitchen to dining room to serve a group holding a meeting there. Without skipping a beat, Ann continued serving and Richard whisked us around to see the rooms. Afterward, when they had a breather, we sat down in the kitchen to chat and sample some of the goodies.

The Rosenbergs told us that a couple of years ago they'd gotten tired of the rat race and decided to open a bed and breakfast. Although they were living in Florida at the time, they had somewhere else in mind. They'd visited in this area of southeastern Tennessee before and liked it. They looked for more than a year before they found this appealing property, which they opened as a bed and breakfast two years ago. The colorful climbing roses gave their name to the new enterprise.

Continuing the theme, the four guest rooms are named for roses as well. The royalty among these rooms is the Rose of Sharon. Located on the ground floor and decorated in shades of hunter green and rose, this palatial accommodation boasts a king-size bed, a sitting area, a private entrance, and the pièce de résistance—a deluxe bilevel bathroom with a sunken whirlpool tub and a separate shower. Candles and music make this a perfect haven for the incredibly romantic.

Upstairs, we got a kick out of the pure whimsy in the yellow and blue Cottage Rose Room. First we had to open the picket-fence gate in the doorway to enter. Then we noticed the picket-fence headboard of the queen-size bed, the birdhouses painted on the walls, and the hand-painted furniture. Battenburg lace, floral wallpaper, and a view of the pond add up to romance in the Tapestry Rose Room. Beautiful hardwood floors, patchwork quilts, antiques, primitives, and collectibles enhance the hunter, plum, and ecru color scheme in the Prairie Rose Room, which offers a king-size bed and a daybed.

And now for the icing on the cake. Tucked behind the house and the garage and completely enclosed on the other sides by a wall is a gem of a brick-paved courtyard with an inviting free-form pool and umbrella tables. We know that's where we'd spend endless hours. That is, when we weren't relaxing in the screened porch, napping in the hammock, strolling the grounds, fishing in the stocked pond, or eating.

Richard is the chief cook, with Ann's able assistance, and his specialty is a breakfast casserole made with eggs, bread, milk, sausage, cheese, and dry mustard. This and other delicacies are served in the big dining room beside a stone fireplace, where you'll find a blazing fire in cold weather. A built-in buffet at one end of the room is always supplied with the makings for tea and coffee, as well as cookies or other treats.

What's Nearby Cleveland

Cleveland has a rich Native American heritage. Take a walking tour of the Downtown Historic Greenway and Johnson Park, and see twenty different historic sites. Then try the Cherokee Heritage Wildlife Tour and visit Red Clay and the Ocoee River. At Red Clay, follow the Trail of Tears State Historic Route. The Cherokees were forced to march from Red Clay to Oklahoma on the Trail of Tears in 1838.

Riverfront Plantation Inn

190 Crow Lane
(mailing address: P.O. Box 349)
Dover, Tennessee 37058
(931) 232-9492; fax (931) 232-5267

E-MAIL: flcombs@ibm.net

WEB SITE: www.bbonline.com/tn/
riverfrontplantation (coming soon)

INNKEEPERS: Lynn and Fulton Combs

ROOMS: 5; all with private bath and private porch, TV, clock, luggage rack

ON THE GROUNDS: Veranda, gazebo, views

RATES: $95 to $115 double, including early-morning coffee service to the room, full breakfast, evening turndown service; lunch and dinner are available by reservation at an additional fee

CREDIT CARDS ACCEPTED? Yes

OPEN: Year-round, except Christmas Day

HOW TO GET THERE: From TN 79/Donelson Parkway, cross the Cumberland River and in a few blocks turn right (west) onto Church Street. Go 0.3 mile west and turn right onto Crow Lane. Follow it past a cemetery and some new houses to its end at the B&B.

Not to take anything away from the stately historic home, but the stars here are the sweeping grounds and the stunning view of the Cumberland River. And that's not to mention the convenience for Civil War buffs of being right next door to Fort Donelson. The simple but imposing white-columned house sits majestically near the highest point of the property, which slopes down gently over a long distance of manicured lawns and isolated stands of trees to the riverfront. A gazebo placed halfway between the house and the water is conveniently outfitted with lounge chairs. We could imagine reclining here with a cool drink, some binoculars, and maybe a good book. But no, reading would probably be out—we'd never be able to tear our eyes away from the view.

The original portion of the substantial two-story house was probably a four-over-four floor plan, with giant chimneys at both ends and a large two-story veranda stretching across the entire front. To this a large wing was added out the back, making the structure T shaped. We saw pictures of the place taken when the Combs acquired it, and it was in pretty derelict condition; they certainly chose a daunting task for themselves! Although they rehabilitated the exterior pretty much as it was, the interior was gutted, so all that remains of any architectural detailing from the period when it was built is the fireplaces. What's been added, however, is very pleasing to the eye.

Just inside the front door, a central staircase rises to the second floor. To one side is the pleasant formal sitting room with a wood-burning fireplace and lots of comfortable seating, making this an ideal place to gather on a less-than-perfect day. Behind this is the dining room, where a sumptuous breakfast that might feature an omelette or waffles and strawberries is served by a gas-log fireplace along with three breakfast meats, hash brown potatoes, and fruit.

Elegant guests rooms, which feature brass or four-poster beds and decorative fireplaces, are located on both the first and second floors. The most popular is the Gold Room, which boasts a king-size bed, a sitting area, a private screened porch, and beautiful views of the river.

But it is in the area of customer service and pampering that the Riverfront Plantation Inn excels.

You're greeted with a special gift basket and taken on a personal tour of the inn. In the evening your bed will be turned down and ice, water, and chocolates left in your room. In the morning you'll find coffee service outside your door, complete with juice, homemade pastries, and the newspaper to enjoy in your room or on a porch before the main breakfast meal. The staff will be happy to pack a picnic lunch for you before you set off for a day's exploration of the area.

What's Nearby Dover

Visit the Land Between the Lakes, a peninsula between Kentucky Lake and Lake Barkley. The area offers hiking, trails, water sports, and paved biking trails. Also on the site is the Homeplace, a nineteenth-century historic museum. Or you might visit the city of Clarksville, with its unique architecture in the downtown area, including the headquarters of the Clarksville-Montgomery County Historical Society.

Namaste Acres Farm

5436 Leipers Creek Road
Franklin, Tennessee 37064
(615) 791–0333; fax (615) 591–0665

E-MAIL: namastebb@aol.com
WEB SITE: www.bbonline.com/tn/namaste/
INNKEEPERS: Lisa, Bill, and Lindsay Winters

ROOMS: 4; all with private bath, private entrance, gas-log fireplace, telephone, TV, VCR, videos, CD/cassette player, clock radio, coffeemaker, mini refrigerator; some with private deck

ON THE GROUNDS: Decks, swimming pool, hot tub, horseshoe pit, fire ring, gas grill, tree house, swing, stables, trail riding

RATES: $75 to $85 double, including continental or full breakfast; additional person $15; guest horse boarding $5.00 for pasture, $10 for stalls; horse trailer shuttle service $25 to $50

CREDIT CARDS ACCEPTED? Yes

OPEN: Year-round

HOW TO GET THERE: Take TN 96 west from Franklin to the caution light at County Road 46. Turn left and drive 7.3 miles through Leipers Fork. Namaste Acres is on your left and is well identified by a ranch-style entrance.

When we drove up we were a bit surprised: The modest cream and brick 1980 Dutch Colonial house sitting below the road isn't unlike our own home. But oh, what surprises and pleasures awaited within! *Namaste*, an Indian word, is the highest form of greeting—an honorable tribute from one person to another. This type of welcome is reflected in the warmheartedness Lisa, Bill, and their daughter Lindsay bestow on the guests to their working horse farm. And as pet lovers, we were delighted to immediately make the acquaintance of the four resident pooches and two felines. (They're either outside or in the Winterses' living quarters, so you can be as friendly or aloof from them as you wish. Those with allergies don't need to worry.) And your hosts have facilities for horses as well as two-legged guests.

The Winters live on the upper two floors, while the guest accommodations are cleverly arranged in the walk-out lower level overlooking the pool, hot tub, rock garden, stables, and riding ring with pastures and forest beyond. An early-frontier theme runs throughout the guest chambers. The Winters made many of the furnishings and accessories that reflect their passion for the lifestyles of Indians, cowboys, and pioneers. A fireplace in each room adds to the nostalgic ambience. Even so, you'll enjoy all the modern conveniences, including queen-size beds (in all but one room) topped with down comforters.

In the Frontier Cabin you can enjoy the feel of pioneer living with all the modern comforts. It's a spacious yet cozy backwoods retreat. Rough-sawn lumber walls and 12-foot beamed ceilings set the scene for the handcrafted timber bed, chairs, benches, and other furnishings. The room is accented with wrought iron, rag rugs, and animal pelts. The Cowboy Bunkhouse is for those looking for a taste of the Old West. Here again rough-sawn lumber walls create the backdrop for massive handcrafted timber bunk beds and ranch furniture and accessories. This is probably not the room for honeymooners, although it does sport a romantic claw-foot tub. The Indian Lodge is decorated with a Native American motif, with numerous artifacts and paintings that complement the Southwestern color scheme. The Franklin Suite, the most traditional of the rooms, features a four-poster cannonball bed and is embellished with Confederate memorabilia and art.

As befits a working ranch, a hearty country breakfast starts the day. It's likely to include eggs and ham, French toast, or pancakes, with grits, fruits, juices, and hot beverages. Stoke up for an active day.

There's lots of room to romp and play here, both on the property and adjacent to it. Swim in the pool, soak in the hot tub, pitch horseshoes, or simply rock contentedly on the swing in the tree house. From the B&B you're within walking distance of a 24½-mile hiking and bridle trail that's part of the original Natchez Trace. The Winterses offer a half-day 2½-mile Western Escape and full-day 5-mile Western Adventure trail ride.

What's Nearby Franklin

Franklin is a dream for antiques collectors. In the downtown area, there are dozens of antiques and crafts stores. What's more, the city is also home to the Franklin Antique Mall, occupied by fifty different antiques dealers. It's no surprise that Franklin has been declared the state's "antiques capital." The town also has significant Civil War history.

Hancock House

2144 Nashville Pike
Gallatin, Tennessee 37066
(615) 452–8431; fax (615) 452–1616

WEB SITE: www.bbonline.com/tn/hancock/

INNKEEPERS: Roberta and Carl Hancock

ROOMS: 5, including 1 two-level cabin;
all with private bath, fireplace; some with whirlpool tub; TV and telephone in common area

ON THE GROUNDS: Private courtyard

RATES: $90 to $200 double, including full country breakfast, afternoon tea, various beverages, and fruit in season; gourmet dinner can be arranged with prior notice at an additional fee

CREDIT CARDS ACCEPTED? Yes

OPEN: Year-round

HOW TO GET THERE: From I–65, take exit 95, Vietnam Veterans Boulevard East. The B&B will be on your left.

When we visited the Hancock House, we were on a press tour and Roberta and Carl were hosting the group for brunch. Travel writers can eat more than just about any other group of people, except maybe for travel agents, when it's free. We sat down at about 10:00 A.M. and began to eat. An hour and a half later, when we were supposed to be at our next stop, we were still eating and there was no indication that there was any bottom to the barrel. Through it all, Roberta still had time to tell us all about her historic stagecoach inn and tollhouse, and encourage us to have "just one more" fried biscuit or pancake with her wonderful hot fruit compote.

The highway department didn't do the Hancocks any favors when they put in the new Vietnam Veterans Boulevard—the new highway cuts very close to the front of the old building. Luckily, the view isn't obstructed and it wasn't long before we forgot all about the highway.

The B&B began life as a fifteen-room Colonial Revival log inn sometime before 1878. It served as a stagecoach stop and tollgate house known as Avondale Station on the Avery Trace. For more than fifty years before Roberta and Carl bought it, the old inn was owned by Felice Ferrell and run as a nationally known antiques establishment. In 1978 the Hancocks bought the old stage stop and returned it to its roots as a B&B.

The building is a real log house with wide hardwood-plank floors covered with area rugs, exposed beams, lots of nooks and crannies where period antiques can be found, large wood-burning fieldstone fireplaces, and interior log walls. Together, it makes for a comfortable visit to a bygone era. For overnight guests, there are four bedrooms in the main building as well as a two-story cabin across the lawn. The first-floor Chamber Room is a guest room when it's needed, but when there's a large special event planned, the antique Murphy bed folds up into the wall. The second-floor Bridal Suite contains an antique four-poster bed, fireplace, and whirlpool tub for two, and the Felice Ferrell Room offers an antique elevated bed and a large wood-burning fireplace. The fourth room is located half a floor off the dining room and features period antiques, another large fireplace, and bath with claw-foot tub.

Roberta's five-year-old granddaughter showed us the cabin, turning on and off all of the lights, appliances, and faucets; opening and closing every door; and even flushing the toilet to show us that it worked. The only thing she didn't demonstrate was the whirlpool tub and shower combination. Obviously, she has a future in the hospitality industry or real estate! The cabin can sleep up to six and has a fully stocked kitchen. There are also two rooms in the stone house, which are rented occasionally as B&B rooms.

What's Nearby Gallatin

Gallatin is noted in the National Register of Historic Places. The downtown area has dozens of restored buildings that predate the Civil War. Try visiting the Sumner County Museum in Gallatin. This history museum features an interesting display of fossils. Next to the museum, you'll find Trousdale Place, which is a restored historic home. Trousdale was built for one of Tennessee's governors, William Trousdale. Lovely antiques and a historical library are some of the sights of the home tour.

Crocker Springs Bed and Breakfast

2382 Crocker Springs Road
Goodlettsville, Tennessee 37072
(615) 876–8502; fax (615) 876–4083
(call first)

E-MAIL: crockersprings@juno.com

WEB SITE: www.bbonline.com/tn/crockersprings

INNKEEPERS: Bev and Jack Spangler

ROOMS: 3 (1 can be a suite); all with private bath, clock radio, ceiling fan

ON THE GROUNDS: Deck, stream, hiking trails, fish pond

RATES: $100 rooms, $135 suite, double, including full breakfast and refreshments; additional person $15; ask about corporate rates

CREDIT CARDS ACCEPTED? Yes

OPEN: Year-round

HOW TO GET THERE: From Nashville, take I–24 North to exit 40, Old Hickory Boulevard. Turn left and go 1.1 mile to Lickton Pike. Turn right and go 2.2 miles to the third left-hand turn, which is Crocker Springs Road. Turn left and go 0.9 mile. Crocker Springs Bed and Breakfast is on your right and identified by a sign.

We could see the attraction right away. No pretensions here; just a simple farmhouse in a bucolic setting, a gurgling stream running past the deck, easygoing innkeepers, a great old dog, horses in the pasture. What more could you ask for in a get-away-from-it-all hideaway? Located on fifty-eight acres, the old house was built in the 1880s. Bev and Jack, who are the third owners, made some tasteful additions—the garage, an apartment for themselves, a cheery sunroom and deck overlooking the stream, and dormers to create space for private baths.

This is a place to relax and be casual, a place where your grandparents might have lived—not a grand mansion with museum-quality furnishings and art. Cozy rooms are furnished in modest country charm. The living room features overstuffed seating grouped around an electric fireplace, the dining room a humble oak table and chairs near a woodstove, but it's the sunroom where guests are most likely to gather. Surrounded on three sides by windows, the pleasant room contains wicker seating and a dining area, where you can partake of early-morning coffee, breakfast, or afternoon beverages.

The two upstairs guest rooms are named for the Spanglers' grown children. An antique double bed in Stefanie's Quilt Room is topped with not only a quilt, but a featherbed mattress as well. Jack's use of wainscoting, an old door, an antique glass doorknob salvaged from an old house in Pennsylvania, and a pedestal sink make you believe that the bathroom was original to the house or an early addition, rather than a recent one. A queen-size iron bed is the focal point of Todd's Paisley Room. Downstairs, the Rose Room features a queen-size bed and a youth bed that doubles as a daybed. Its bathroom boasts a claw-foot tub. This room can be combined with the den to create a suite.

Bev prepares several substantial morning repasts that are well worth getting up for. If you stay five days, you'll feast on different treats every day, and be served on different china as well. She's best known for her Farm Extravaganza—an egg, bacon, and sausage casserole served with tomato pudding and orange biscuits that Jack isn't afraid to tell you are "to die for." Other favorites include French vanilla French toast and a Dutch/Scandinavian meal of breads, open-faced meat and cheese sandwiches, a soft-boiled egg, and jams and jellies.

One of the appeals of the Crocker Springs Bed and Breakfast is its proximity to Nashville. Although it is truly located in the country, the B&B is only 14 miles from downtown, so you can have the best of both worlds. Zip into town for country music and numerous other sights as well as casual or fine dining and entertainment, then return to the country to listen to the crickets and watch the fireflies before retiring for a uneventful night's sleep.

What's Nearby Goodlettsville

See what's nearby Nashville, page 419.

Big Spring Inn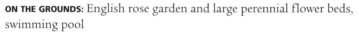

315 North Main Street
Greeneville, Tennessee 37745
(423) 638-2917

INNKEEPERS: Marshall and Nancy Ricker

ROOMS: 5; all with private bath, telephone, computer modem, cable TV; 2 with fireplace

ON THE GROUNDS: English rose garden and large perennial flower beds, swimming pool

RATES: $80 single, $86 double, including full breakfast and afternoon refreshments

CREDIT CARDS ACCEPTED? Yes

OPEN: April through October

HOW TO GET THERE: The inn is 75 miles northeast of Knoxville. From the south, leave I-81 at exit 23, Greeneville–Bulls Gap. Follow Business 11E to Main Street, and turn left. After the third stoplight, the inn is the seventh house on your left. From the north, turn right onto North Main and continue to the corner of Nelson. Turn right onto Nelson and then left into the drive.

The Rickers have taken over this inn from earlier owners Jeanne Driese and Cheryl Van Dyck. Nancy likes to say that she's kept all the special touches Cheryl and her mother started, such as fresh flowers in the rooms and dining room, and a full gourmet breakfast with home-baked goods and juices and fruits along with the main entree. Then, as you'd expect, the Rickers added touches of their own.

For instance, they provide afternoon refreshments and place treats such as cookies in your room. Maybe the best addition of all is a tea cart with coffee set outside the guests' rooms for early risers.

This inn is housed in an old three-story Greek Revival building in remarkably good shape. It's furnished with both antiques and reproductions, comfort being the main consideration. Our room was especially restful, with the blue of the walls and carpet echoed in the shades of a woven coverlet and in the bouquet of blue miniature irises on the oak library table. At bedside were leather-bound editions of *Jane Eyre* and *Stories of Edgar Allan Poe*.

Just outside the room, a library for guests invites browsing. Also, the Rickers' Civil War library continues to grow. This seems logical, given how divided Greeneville was between Union and rebel sympathizers during that war. (Greeneville has the only county seat with a monument to both northern and southern soldiers.)

The Civil War collection is now set up in the recently restored front parlor. It's a bright, cheery room, not at all reminiscent of war, with pale peach paint, period and reproduction furniture, and French doors that open onto a sunporch that is filled with plants all winter.

Outside the inn, new perennial gardens flourish and will get better and better as the plants mature. On the lawns you can play croquet or badminton.

While you're romping about outside, you may be joined by Mel, the Rickers' "pound dog," who is mostly golden retriever and, of course, loves to run. Nancy says guests are usually quite fond of him. Mel now has a new friend, Higgins, a Siamese-mix cat.

Big Spring Inn has traditionally offered various special vacation and honeymoon packages as well as special picnic arrangements. Be sure to ask about current offerings.

What's Nearby Greenville

Greenville was once home to our country's seventeenth president, Andrew Johnson. You can visit the Andrew Johnson National Historic Site and see Johnson's tailor shop, where he once set up his own business. Greenville's Tusculun College houses the state's largest presidential library, the Andrew Johnson Library and Museum. Johnson's papers and manuscripts are kept here, as well as a collection of original Civil War–era newspapers.

Bushrod Hall Bed and Breakfast

422 Cumberland Street Northeast
Harriman, Tennessee 37748
(423) 882-8406 or (888) 880-8406

E-MAIL: bushrodbb@aol.com

WEB SITE: www.bbonline.com/tn/bushrod/

INNKEEPERS: Nancy and Bob Ward

ROOMS: 3; all with private bath and clock radio

ON THE GROUNDS: Enclosed veranda

RATES: $75 to $115 double, including early coffee, full breakfast, snacks; single $10 less; additional guests $20; gift certificates available; ask about corporate rates

CREDIT CARDS ACCEPTED? Yes

OPEN: Year-round

HOW TO GET THERE: From I–40, take exit 347 and turn north onto US 27/TN 61 to Harriman. Follow the signs into the historic downtown area. Turn right at traffic light 6 onto Walden Avenue. Go 3 blocks and turn left onto Cumberland Avenue. The B&B is in the middle of the block on your right. Parking is in the rear.

Legend has it that S. K. Paige, president of the S. K. Paige Lumber and Manufacturing Company, built this attractive Queen Anne Victorian mansion (for the incredible sum—in 1892—of $18,000) in a contest with Frederick Gates to see who could build the most elaborate home. Mr. Paige's house was reported to be handsomely finished, incorporating electric wiring, hydrant water attachments, closets, lavatories, and furnace heating. Among the outstanding original features was a magnificent, highly carved stairway, which was ordered from Sweden for the princely sum of $3,000. Eight different woods were used for the floors and trim. Despite all this finery, Mr. Gates won the contest with his home, Cornstalk Heights.

Still, Mr. Paige had the last laugh. Cornstalk Heights was later demolished to make way for Harriman Middle School, while the Paige home not only survives, but enjoys a new life as a bed and breakfast. In between, it has had an interesting life. In 1895 it became the Bushrod W. James Hall of Domestic Science for young ladies, a division of the American Temperance University. Some years later it was subdivided into apartments, and the wraparound porch and a small upstairs porch were enclosed to create more rooms.

Nancy and Bob, who met in Alaska where they were both working before coming to Harriman, bought Bushrod Hall in 1996 and have been restoring it ever since. Guests are encouraged to use the public rooms, of which there are many—a formal parlor and sunroom on the first floor, and an informal sitting room and guest kitchen on the second floor. Ask Nancy and Bob about their Alaskan mementos, which are displayed in the parlor and dining room.

Among the guest rooms, all of which have private baths, the one on the first floor is small and plain and would perhaps be more appropriate for a businessperson or a handicapped traveler. The upstairs room are larger, fancier, and more appealing to romantics. A bay window with a built-in love seat, a sleigh bed in the bedroom, and a beautiful stained-glass window in the bathroom characterize the large Front Room. Although smaller, the Back Room is very romantic with its pencil-post bed, crocheted bedspread, brocadelike wallpaper, and lace curtains.

A bountiful gourmet breakfast is served in the formal dining room. Nancy's specialty is caramel French toast topped with strawberries from the Wards' backyard strawberry patch, but the morning meal might consist of a baked egg casserole. Either is accompanied by fruits, juices, and hot beverages.

Harriman's Cornstalk Heights neighborhood, named for Gates's house, was established as a residential district for the families of industrial leaders. By 1892 it had more homes in the $3,000 to $10,000 range than any comparable city in America. In 1990 the entire neighborhood was named to the National Register of Historic Places. It has 135 significant homes, sites, and structures. Architectural styles include Queen Anne, folk Victorian, Southern Revival, Colonial Revival, Craftsman bungalow, Tudor, Dutch Colonial Revival, and San Francisco painted lady. The streets were planted with rows of red and yellow maples, many of which survive today.

What's Nearby Harriman

Harriman offers a historic district with museums and antiques shopping and plenty of recreation areas. Visit the Temperance Building and Heritage Museum, the Roane County Museum of History and Art, and the Fort Southwest Point and Museum. Some nearby recreation areas are the Watts Bar Recreation Area, Frozen Head State Park, and Big South Fork Recreation Area. You can also hike at Walden's Ridge, and fish on the Obed and Little Emory Rivers.

Spring Haven

545 East Main Street
Hendersonville, Tennessee 37075
(615) 826–1825; fax (615) 826–1623

WEB SITE: www.bbonline.com/tn/
springhaven/

INNKEEPERS: Celia and Curtis Ellis

ROOMS: 5 (3 in the main house, 2 in the cabin);
all with private bath, TV, VCR

ON THE GROUNDS: Veranda, three acres with spring, springhouse, original
plantation dairy barn, stone stillhouse, and woods

RATES: $95 to $250, including full country gourmet breakfast, snacks,
beverages, and dessert; candlelight dinners available by special request at
an additional cost

CREDIT CARDS ACCEPTED? Yes

OPEN: Year-round

HOW TO GET THERE: From I–65, take exit 95, Vietnam Veterans Boulevard,
6 miles to exit 7, Calendar Lane. Turn right and go 1.2 miles to the traffic
light at US 31 East. Turn left. Follow US 31 East 1 mile to Carrington
Road and turn right. When it dead-ends, turn right into the gravel drive
that leads to the main house.

There we were, driving along a typical commercial street lined with strip
malls, fast-food outlets, and car dealerships; then we made one turn,
drove a couple of hundred feet into a wooded area, and found ourselves
in another time and place. The original 640-acre tract was purchased via
grant in 1797, but was not occupied until Edward Sanders purchased 250
acres of it and built the original house (a log cabin), which can be seen as
part of the structure today. Over the years the cabin grew into a six-room
main house, and various outbuildings were constructed. In 1996 Celia and
Curtis Ellis bought the house and the three acres that remained of the original farm and began its transformation into an elegant bed and breakfast.

We loved the rich luster of the original Louisiana heart-pine floors, the
seven original fireplaces, and all the original woodwork. The detached slave
kitchen and smokehouse have been connected to the main house, and we're
waiting to see what Celia comes up with for these two great rooms. All the
rooms in the main house are meticulously decorated with period antiques
and authentically copied period wallpapers and paints. For those who like
classic elegance, the main house will suit you to a T.

On the other hand, if you're more comfortable in less formal surroundings but still want real quality, try the two new rooms in the original cedar cabin. If you're traveling with friends or other family members, you can take the entire cabin or just take one room. Either way you have your own private bath. What we particularly like about the cabin are its exposed old cedar-log walls and more casual decor.

Breakfast can be served in the formal dining room, in the main house, or in your room, but we prefer having it on the screened porch looking out into the backyard toward the stream and woods. If you're lucky, Celia will be serving her cranberry-orange muffins when you're there. If you're planning to stay, let us suggest that you also talk to Celia about preparing a candlelight dinner for you and your special someone. It really sets the mood for a wonderful getaway.

What's Nearby Hendersonville

Hendersonville offers antiques shopping and outlet malls, golf, horseback riding, and fine dining. You can also venture to Nashville, and explore Nashville attractions, like Music Row and the Opryland Hotel.

Another Recommended B&B in Hendersonville

Morning Star Bed and Breakfast, a newly constructed Victorian-style house on extensive grounds, offers rooms with whirlpool tub and fireplace; 460 Jones Lane, Hendersonville, TN 37075; (615) 264-2614.

Highland Place Bed and Breakfast

519 North Highland Avenue
Jackson, Tennessee 38301
(901) 427-1472

E-MAIL: relax@highlandplace.com
WEB SITE: www.highlandplace.com
INNKEEPERS: Janice and Glenn Wall
ROOMS: 3 rooms and 1 suite; all with private bath, clock radio, telephone

ON THE GROUNDS: Verandas, patio, landscaped yard

RATES: $80 to $135 double, including full breakfast, afternoon refreshments, and beverages; ask about corporate rates

CREDIT CARDS ACCEPTED? Yes

OPEN: Year-round

NOTE: Transitional neighborhood

HOW TO GET THERE: From I–40, take exit 82A, Highland Avenue. Go south 3.3 miles. Parking is behind the house, accessible from the alley, so go past the house, then turn right onto King and right again into the alley.

At Highland Place the decor is stunning, the service is great, the rooms are spacious and comfortable, the chairs are easy, and you'll be pampered in just the right ways. The stately, dark redbrick Classical Revival house, built in 1911, features a portico supported by imposing columns. After the Walls bought the property, they had a great stroke of luck: Highland Place was chosen as the 1995 Designer Showhouse for West Tennessee. Janice and Glenn put their personal belongings into storage while twenty-five interior designers and three landscape artists spent three months and their best creative talents giving the mansion a face-lift and complete body overhaul. The walls were stripped down to the bare plaster for the transformation. When the house was presented to the public, it had a fresh look while retaining its character and reputation. More than 7,000 people toured the newly refurbished house.

You've probably heard the old saying, "Back-door friends are best"; well, it's apt for Highland Place. Because there's no on-street parking in front of the house, guests enter from the rear. As soon as you get settled into your abode, go for a tour of the house. Beginning in the central hall, we first noticed the leaded glass surrounding the oversize front door, the gleaming hardwood floors, the beautiful border on the ceiling, and the striking Oriental carpet. To the right, we stepped into the front-to-back formal parlor, the focal point of which is the marble fireplace. Gathering with fellow guests, examining interesting mementos from Glenn's aviation career, or watching television or a movie on the VCR are pleasant diversions in this lovely room. Opposite the parlor is what has been described as the architectural crown jewel of the house, the library. This rich room is encased in warm cherry cut from the farm of the original owner. The ½-inch-thick tongue-and-groove paneling covers not only the walls but the ceiling as well, with cherry beams giving the final touch of elegance. A mirror image of the grand entrance foyer, the upstairs hall serves as an informal sitting room and gathering place for guests.

Naturally, potential guests are most concerned with their sleeping accommodations, and those at Highland Place are well above average. Three spacious, Old World–style guest chambers are located on the second floor;

a more contemporary suite is located on the bottom level. Starting upstairs, the Hamilton Suite boasts a crochet-covered canopy queen-size bed, a working fireplace, and a tub for two. The Butler Suite features a featherbed on top of its firm queen-size mattress, while the Louis Room has a king-size bed that can be reconfigured into two twins, as well as an authentic claw-foot tub with sold brass plumbing and a handheld shower. We loved staying in Rachel's Atrium Suite. This spacious lower-level accommodation includes a traditional bedroom, a roomy bathroom with a shower for two that boasts a waterfall shower head, and a sitting room that has a skylight that runs its entire length, as well as ample workspace for business travelers.

Little touches mean so much. There were fresh flowers in the room, mints on a velvet pillow on the bed, fresh fruit and cheese served in the afternoon in our room, and stamped postcards with pictures of the bed and breakfast. Each morning before breakfast a silver tea tray was delivered to our room with dainty china cups, a selection of teas, sugar cubes, and lemon slices. Every breakfast got an A for presentation as well as for taste.

What's Nearby Jackson

Feeling nostalgic for your childhood train set? Then visit Jackson's local railroad museums, the N.C. & St. L Railroad Depot, and the Casey Jones Home and Railroad Museum. Jackson also has several antiques shops in its Main Street historic district. In addition, Jackson is halfway between Graceland and Opryland.

Whitestone Country Inn

1200 Paint Rock Road
Kingston, Tennessee 37763
(423) 376-0113 or
(888) 247-2464;
fax (423) 376-4454

E-MAIL: moreinfo@whitestones.com

WEB SITE: www.whitestones.com

INNKEEPERS: Jean and Paul Cowell

ROOMS: 16 rooms and suites; all with private bath, fireplace, whirlpool tub, TV, VCR, telephone with data port, desk, iron and ironing board, coffeemaker

ON THE GROUNDS: Verandas, tennis, lawn games, gift shop, conference facilities, wedding chapel, walking trails, boating facilities, restaurants

RATES: $105 to $200, including country breakfast

CREDIT CARDS ACCEPTED? Yes

OPEN: Year-round

HOW TO GET THERE: From I-75 South, take exit 72, TN 72, and travel west 9 miles. When you get into the crossroads village of Paint Rock, bear right onto Paint Rock Road. Follow it 9 miles to the inn. Signs clearly indicate where to go.

Not just a B&B, not just an inn, this elegant and delightful place is a destination in itself. Far out in the country, the hilly, tree-covered, 360-acre estate affords sweeping vistas of Watts Bar Lake on the Tennessee River and is surrounded by a wildlife and waterfowl refuge. We'd seen pictures of the attractive main inn, but weren't prepared for the vastness of the property, the collection of other buildings, or the variety of things to do. Obviously, Jean and Paul have a vision, and we probably haven't seen the scope of it yet.

Our introduction began by driving through a big red barn that serves as the entrance. Registration is in the little red schoolhouse next door, which also serves as a gift shop. From there we could look down over the hill to see charming gazebos and a bandstand, the main inn with Watts Bar Lake behind it, and, in the distance on the next hill, the newly constructed wedding chapel and adjacent conference center. We just simply couldn't resist whipping out the cameras—this is a photographer's paradise.

Checking out the inn was next on our agenda. Traditionally Southern looking, it is a two-story structure covered in white clapboard and topped with a green roof from which five dormers poke their heads. An almost full-length, one-story veranda is supported by columns and topped with a railing. The rear of the building features another veranda and a patio, both overlooking the lake.

Inside, although the style is traditional, the look is sleek and elegant. We entered into a small foyer with a white and black marble fireplace, which turned out to be double sided: The other side faces into the great room. Vast windows overlook another veranda and the lake in the distance. Next door is the cheery restaurant with tables in a big bay window; downstairs is a huge recreation room with kitchenette facilities. We stepped outside and found a sauna on the covered patio. The cozy third-floor sitting room also has a fireplace and is filled with books and videos.

Every one of the nine guest rooms, named for birds, is a work of art. The Mallard Suite, for instance, boasts a king-size four-poster bed carved with acanthus leaves; beyond, a large sitting area in the bay window overlooks the lake. The bathroom—as large as many hotel rooms—sports a huge whirlpool tub in a bay window, a separate corner shower, a vanity, and two sinks. We got a kick out of the birdhouse headboard in the Blue Heron Room (this room is handicapped accessible) and the picket-fence headboard in the Blue Bird Room. There are six more accommodations in the main inn, three more suites in the barn, and one in the schoolhouse. The Victorian conference center has three suites upstairs—one with the prize view of them all.

Breakfast is a substantial meal that might consist of an egg casserole or blueberry pancakes served along with fried potatoes, sausage, biscuits, fruit, and juice. Lunch and dinner are available by twenty-four-hour advance reservation at an additional fee. Iced tea and cookies are always available if you get an attack of the munchies.

For those who want to do more than just stay and play in their room or rock on one of the verandas, there are 8 miles of walking trails and 8,000 feet of lake frontage with canoes, kayaks, and paddleboats. Fishing and bird-watching are popular pastimes, a chapel is the perfect site for weddings, and tennis courts, a regulation croquet lawn, and stables are under construction.

What's Nearby Kingston

We wouldn't do Kingston justice unless we mention the historic Roane County Courthouse. Inside you'll find the Old Courthouse Museum, as well as free maps and brochures. Then head out to Fort Southwest Point, which overlooks Watts Bar Lake. You can also go horseback riding, bird watching, and hiking in the Kingston area.

Cedarvine Manor

8061 Murfreesboro Road
Lebanon, Tennessee 37090
(615) 443-2211 or (800) 447-9155; fax (615) 443-2123

E-MAIL: mail@cedarvine.com

WEB SITE: www.cedarvine.com

INNKEEPER: Debbie Hancock

ROOMS: 11, including 1 suite; all with ceiling fan, clock radio; some with private outside entrance and/or porch; 8 with gas-log fireplace, some with whirlpool tub; telephone jack in each room; all rooms are wheelchair accessible

ON THE GROUNDS: Porches, courtyard, pond, covered bridge, special-events barn, helipad

RATES: $125 to $265 single or double, including full breakfast; lunch and dinner can be arranged with prior notice at an additional fee

CREDIT CARDS ACCEPTED? Yes

OPEN: Year-round

HOW TO GET THERE: From I–40, take I–840 South toward Chattanooga. Take exit 67 and turn left (east) onto Couchville Pike; drive 4.5 miles to US 231 South. Cedarvine Manor is directly across the highway. From I–24, take I–840 North toward Lebanon. Take exit 67 and turn right (east) onto Couchville Pike. Follow the directions above.

What began as a two-story log home in 1865 has had many incarnations: private home, hospital, convalescent home, and now this fine 8,000-square-foot bed and breakfast with all the modern conveniences. The grounds were originally purchased through a Revolutionary War land grant in 1832 and the two-story home was begun, although it wasn't completed until 1865. During the Civil War the home was commandeered as a hospital to treat the thousands of soldiers wounded at the Battle of Stones River. There was even a secret tunnel running from the kitchen to a cave across what is now US 231. Previous owners tell stories of soldiers escaping through the tunnel and of valuables and cattle being hidden there when the Yankees came looking for them. After the war it continued to serve the survivors as a convalescent home for veterans.

Four years ago a group of investors purchased the old home and began to turn it into a state-of-the-art resort property. *Modern*, however, doesn't mean "sterile" or "uninteresting." The new building incorporates and surrounds the original house—you can see its brick walls, fireplaces, and old beams in the master bedroom, front room, and dining room. The modified structure offers 5,000 square feet of guest rooms and common rooms with all the creature comforts and a definite country feel. The hobbies and interests of the new owners can be found throughout the inn.

What impressed us were the little details we kept discovering all around the house. There's a button box full of hundreds and hundreds of odd buttons in the second-floor sitting room, a hand-painted mural on the wall going up the fine old black walnut staircase, a 9-foot harvest table that dates to the 1800s. Somehow it all fits together into a comfortable mix of relaxed country elegance.

On the other hand, the property is completely up to date with many of the amenities you'd expect to find in a five-star country inn. Our favorite room is the Honeymoon Suite, with its giant king-size bed and double whirlpool tub and shower combination, which should get any newlyweds off to a swimmingly great start. There is also a more rustic honeymoon suite located in the 1832 reconstructed log cabin that sits in the courtyard—perfect for those who want a little extra privacy. Take it from us, you don't have to be just-married to enjoy either.

Breakfast is served in the breakfast room, where you can enjoy watching the horses next door graze peacefully in the pasture that they share with the local deer and wild turkeys. The manor's idea of a country breakfast is a bit more glorious than those Dan remembers being served as a child on his uncle's farm: Here you'll find fresh fruit, freshly baked breads, muffins, biscuits, and croissants, smoked pork chops, scrambled eggs, a potato-cheese casserole, tomato provincial, juice, and coffee or tea.

The Barn is a large special-events facility being built for family reunions, weddings, conferences, and the like; it was still under construction when we visited. We saw the property as it was just opening and the grounds were still a little raw; all the ingredients, however, are here—gazebo-type covered bridge, small pond, pastures with horses happily cavorting, hidden verandas and porches, and a great double hammock.

What's Nearby Lebanon

Lebanon is dangerous territory for antiques collectors. With more than a dozen antiques stores and malls, it's possible to find just about anything. The highlight of Lebanon, though, is the Wilson County Fair held in August. As a youngster, Vice President Al Gore showed animals at the fair. Another annual treat is the Wildflower Pilgrimage in April, which is held at the Cedars of Lebanon State Park.

The Captain's Retreat Best Buy

3534 Lakeside Drive
Lenoir City, Tennessee 37772
(423) 986-4229; fax (423) 986-7421

E-MAIL: cretreat@icx.net

WEB SITE: www.bbonline.com/tn/ captains

INNKEEPERS: Kelley Honea and Alice Clayton

ROOMS: 4; all with private bath, whirlpool tub, clock radio, ceiling fan; 3 with private porch; limited wheelchair access

ON THE GROUNDS: Porches, hot tub, lakefront on Fort Loudon Lake

RATES: $95 double, including full breakfast, snacks, and beverages; $10 less for single occupancy; additional person $15; ask about mid-week corporate rates

CREDIT CARDS ACCEPTED? Yes

OPEN: Year-round

HOW TO GET THERE: Take I-75 to US 321 to US 11, and follow it north into Lenoir City. Look for the Dairy Queen on your right, and turn right between it and the Tilley Lane Chrysler/Plymouth dealership onto Oak Street. Go 1 block to the stop sign and turn left onto Martel; follow this 1.4 miles to the second road on the right, which is Lakeview Road. Turn right, cross over the railroad tracks, and follow Lakeview 1.6 miles to where it dead-ends. Turn right onto Beals Chappel Road and continue 0.4 mile down a hill and across a small bridge, then immediately turn right onto Lakeside. Follow it 1 mile. The B&B is on your right and is identified by a sign.

Lakefront cottages are always a big hit with us. We love sitting on a porch or dock, gazing out on the ruffled or glassy water, watching the sun rise and set over it casting reflections on the surface, catching glimpses of ducks and other birds or the occasional fish leaping out of the water. So imagine our anticipation when we went to visit the Captain's Retreat. Would it be a rustic old-timey cabin or a slick contemporary cottage? We were delighted to find that it is a little bit of both—an old house updated with modern creature comforts. But what first caught our eye was a small sternwheel riverboat moored at the dock. The restored *John H. Agee* is the owners' permanent residence.

Alice's stepdaughter Kelley, who acts as the innkeeper, lives in the lower level of the lake house, leaving the entire main level for guests. The original part of the long, low-slung house, painted forest green to blend in with the natural surroundings, was built in the 1920s or 1930s and occupied by a teacher with seven children. The very thought boggles the mind. Considering that the house was so much smaller then, what did she do with all of them? In fact, they all slept at one end of what is now the great room, in two sets of built-in double-size bunk beds enclosed with curtains. One set of these beds has been retained for present-day guests' amusement. It's a great place to curl up with a good book on a cool day.

Every effort has been made to make the most of the lake setting. Large windows in the great room and breakfast room overlook the lawn and lake. A rocker-filled front porch and a covered dock allow you to get even closer to nature. But probably the most popular outdoor diversions are the hammock and the hot tub. On inclement days you can snuggle up in front of the fireplace in the cathedral-ceilinged great room and enjoy a cup of coffee or hot cider. A coffeemaker, refrigerator, and microwave are conveniently on hand for guests' use.

Guest rooms, though small, are nicely decorated in different themes and well appointed. Each boasts a whirlpool tub, and several have private screened porches. A picket-fence headboard sets the tone in the Garden Room, where twin beds can be reconfigured as a king. This room features a screened porch as well. The Creel Room has a fly-fishing theme. Its screened porch has a camp daybed to accommodate another person. Kelley made the rustic bed frame in the Pine Room from saplings and found similar end tables to complete the woodsy picture. This room's screened porch has a Pawleys Island hanging chair. Most popular with honeymooners is the Oak Room, which sports a sleigh bed and a big garden tub situated in the bedroom rather than in the bath.

Guests are treated to a full or continental breakfast, according to their desires. Kelley always puts out homemade granola, yogurt, and fruit, but for those who want more, she'll fix something hot. In the afternoon she'll fix lemonade or hot beverages and her famous granola chocolate chip cookies. At the end of a perfect day, there's nothing like moonlight on the water, fresh air, and blessed quiet to ensure sleeping like a log.

What's Nearby Lenoir City

Lenoir City is another haven for antiques and specialty shops. The area includes Cedar Hills Golf Course, two wineries, and Tellico Lake, where you can enjoy water sports and serene peace and quiet.

The Mason Place Bed and Breakfast

600 Commerce Street
Loudon, Tennessee 37774
(865) 458-3921; fax (865) 458-6092

E-MAIL: mpbb@altum.net

WEB SITE: www.bbonline.com/tn/masonplace/

INNKEEPERS: Donna and Bob Siewert

ROOMS: 4 rooms and 1 honeymoon getaway cottage; all with private bath, gas-log or gas-coal fireplace, clock radio, luggage rack; some with phone lines

ON THE GROUNDS: Verandas, pool, gardens

RATES: $96 and $120 for rooms, $135 for the Smoke House, including full breakfast and afternoon refreshments

CREDIT CARDS ACCEPTED? Yes

OPEN: Year-round

HOW TO GET THERE: From I–75, take exit 81, 76, or 72 onto US 11 and follow it into the center of Loudon at the courthouse and fountain. Turn north onto Grove and go 2 blocks and turn left onto Commerce.

"Romantic, relaxing, and revitalizing." "First-class accommodations, and what a breakfast!" That's what some guests have said about the Mason Place. Donna and Bob Siewert promise all this and more, and boy, do they deliver.

Construction of the house began in 1861 when Thomas Jefferson Mason, a colorful riverboat captain, decided to build on his land grant property. A quarter of a million bricks had been handmade by slaves, the basement dug, a foundation five bricks thick laid, and chimneys set in place when the Civil War broke out. Construction ceased immediately, and the bricks were confiscated to build fortifications overlooking the Tennessee River. General Longstreet crossed the river behind the house, and 30,000 troops marched across the yard. After the war Mr. Mason was anxious to finish the house, but he didn't want to go to the time and expense of replacing all those bricks, so he decided on heart-pine construction. Mason Place remained in the family until 1986, when the Siewerts purchased it. They spent six years restoring the 7,000-square-foot mansion, doing most of the work themselves as a labor of love.

As soon as we saw the stately home with its upstairs and downstairs porches and its shaded and landscaped setting, we looked at each other and said, "Wouldn't this be a perfect place for weddings?" In fact, Donna tells us, they do several dozen weddings a year both inside and out.

Large enough to be grand yet small enough to be intimate, Mason Place provides a perfect escape from city lights and traffic. We could feel Donna's love and pride as she greeted us at the double front doors and began our tour, pointing out the ten fireplaces converted to gas-log use, original hand-blown window panes, chandeliers (once gasoliers) original to the house, and designer wallpaper. Delightful antiques-filled public rooms include a formal parlor, an informal keeping room, and a garden room from which French doors lead out onto the patio. In the well-appointed guest rooms, authentic featherbeds top firm mattresses, and working fireplaces add to the romantic ambience.

Although we were charmed by all the guest rooms in the main house, the best was yet to come. A very ordinary old smokehouse contains one delightful and very private accommodation. Brick walls and exposed beams set a perfect backdrop for romance. One of the things we liked best about this room was the claw-foot tub with its oak rim set in the bedroom rather than in the bathroom (purportedly used in the Mel Gibson/James Garner movie *Maverick*). Others were the carved high-back bed and the Franklin stove. A tight little stairway leads upstairs to a loft sitting room.

Adjacent to the smokehouse is a delightful pool area surrounded by brick walls, a picket fence, brick pool deck, gazebo, and wisteria-covered arbor in which hangs a hammock. Pool towels are rolled up in a basket on the porch.

A bountiful candlelight full breakfast, served in the dining room, is always delectable. Although menus vary with the whims of chef Donna, typical is waffles with whipped cream, strawberries, and toasted almonds.

The public rooms and pool area are delightful places to gather with other guests, but if you and that special someone want to be alone, there are several romantic porches with wicker seating and old-fashioned porch swings, as well as a fern garden with a fish pond, waterfall, and stone benches on which to sit. Three acres make plenty of places for an arm-in-arm stroll.

What's Nearby Loudon

Loudon is a short ride away from The Lost Sea, a "bottomless" underground lake. The Lost Sea is listed in the Guinness Book of World Records as "America's largest underground lake." Tour the lake and see why it's such a phenomenon. The Lost Sea is also a Registered Natural Landmark. You can also visit the Tennessee Valley Authority Lakes. Loudon also offers antiques stores, wineries, museums, and Civil War sites.

Lynchburg Bed and Breakfast

107 Mechanic Street
(mailing address: P.O. Box 34)
Lynchburg, Tennessee 37352
(931) 759–7158

E-MAIL: lynchburgbb@cafes.net
WEB SITE: www.bbonline.com/tn/lynchburg/
INNKEEPERS: Virginia and Mike Tipps

ROOMS: 2; both with private bath, clock radio, TV; 1 with ceiling fan

ON THE GROUNDS: Porches, patio

RATES: $68 to $75 double, including full breakfast and afternoon refreshments; additional person $5

CREDIT CARDS ACCEPTED? Yes

OPEN: Year-round

HOW TO GET THERE: From I-24, take TN 55 into Lynchburg. You'll pass the Jack Daniel's Distillery on your left and cross over Mulberry Creek. At the traffic light, turn right onto Mechanic Street. The bed and breakfast is on your left in the second block.

Lynchburg is synonymous with the Jack Daniel's Distillery, home of great sippin' sour mash whiskey. Virginia and Mike won't argue with that. They're intimately tied to the distillery themselves. Mike, who was born and raised in Lynchburg and educated at Tennessee Technological University, has worked for many years as the quality control specialist at Jack Daniel's. Virginia worked there as well but saw the need for accommodations in Lynchburg and left the distillery to open a bed and breakfast in 1985—Lynchburg's first and still the closest to the distillery. Since then they've had guests from all fifty states and more than thirty different countries.

Their simple home was built in 1877 for Lynchburg's first sheriff. From its upstairs and downstairs porches, you can see steam rising from the oldest registered distillery in the United States, as well as several of the whiskey-aging warehouses. In fact, you can easily walk over to the distillery for the fascinating tour.

The Tippses offer two cozy, simple bed-and-breakfast rooms furnished with antiques. The focal point of the Floral Room is a carved high-back queen-size bed. The other room offers two double beds. For your convenience, the upstairs hall is equipped with a small refrigerator in which you can find soft drinks or store your own beverages. We were charmed by the small upstairs porch with its view of the distillery through an archway. This is also a great place from which to watch the antics of the squirrels and hummingbirds. When the weather is less than ideal, guests like to gather around a fire in the sitting room.

Virginia's breakfasts include fruits and juices, hot beverages, and a variety of homemade breads, muffins, and jellies. (One of her recipes appears on page 50 of the latest Jack Daniel's cookbook.) The meal is served at your convenience in your room or on the porch.

What's Nearby Lynchburg

Lynchburg is most famous for its Jack Daniel's Distillery. The whiskey king, Jack Daniel, spent his entire life in Lynchburg. The village today is known for its charming square of gift shops, arts and crafts outlets, and, of course, stores selling Jack Daniel souvenirs. Tims Ford Lake and Tims Ford State Park are great getaways.

Dream Fields Country Bed and Breakfast Inn

Best Buy

9 Backstreet
Mulberry, Tennessee 37359
(931) 438–8875

E-MAIL: gantry@vallnet.com
WEB SITE: www.bbonline.com/tn/dreamfields/

INNKEEPERS: Rickie and Chris Cedzick

ROOMS: 3; all with private bath, working fireplace, clock radio; first-floor room is wheelchair friendly

ON THE GROUNDS: Porches, lawns, animals

RATES: $65 for the upstairs rooms, $75 for the downstairs room, including full breakfast and refreshments; additional person $10

CREDIT CARDS ACCEPTED? Yes

OPEN: Year-round

HOW TO GET THERE: From Lynchburg, follow TN 55 South out of town. About 2 miles out of town, it becomes TN 50 West. Continue south to Mulberry. Turn left into the town square on Mulberry Road, then right. Look for the small white signs with a silhouette of a horse and buggy; turn in the direction the horse is headed. Turn into the lane before the last house on the street (this isn't it), and follow the lane well back into the fields.

During a recent trip to Middle Tennessee and southern Kentucky in which we saw about three dozen B&Bs, this was one of our favorites. Tucked away down a dirt road on the outskirts of the minuscule town of Mulberry, the 260-acre farm and old white farmhouse have tons of character. The owners are pretty great as well.

Maybe our enchantment had something to do with the kittens Chris was feeding on the porch of an old outbuilding, the very friendly Lab-mix dog named Sweetie who begged us to toss her a ball to chase, or the horse and foal watching nearby. Surely we attuned ourselves right away to the beauty and peacefulness of the surroundings. This is a place for simple pleasures: rain drumming on the red tin roof, sunshine splashing through the windows, the sweet smell of freshly mown hay, deer tentatively emerging from the nearby woods, or jumping into the old swimming hole like Tom and Huck.

We loved hearing the stories about the 1860s farmhouse. For one thing, it belonged to Jack Daniel's oldest brother, Wiley Butler Daniel, and it remained in the Daniel family for generations. The farm is just 7 miles from the distillery, so it isn't too hard to envision lots of rollicking sippin' and samplin' going on. Rickie told us that the house had sat vacant for more than fifteen years before she and Chris bought it; they had to evict the groundhogs and other critters before they could start renovating and move in.

We were pleased to see that the Cedzicks hadn't renovated to the point of making the interior unrecognizable or stripping it of its personality. Nor has it been gussied up to pass for an in-town tart. Clapboard walls and ceilings and hardwood floors—some stained, some painted—give the house a primitive flavor. The simple antiques with which the house is furnished are completely in character. Overstuffed sofas pulled up around the fireplace create a pleasant conversation area in the intimate common room, which has everything you could wish for a relaxing afternoon or evening—a television, game table, small refrigerator, and always-available soft drinks, water, and iced tea or lemonade.

A working fireplace and a carved high-back, queen-size bed dominate the first-floor guest room. This room can be provided with a television on request. Upstairs under the eaves are two simple bedrooms, one with a brass bed, the other with a simple wooden bed. All three boast private baths.

After sleeping like a baby, lulled by birdsongs and rustling leaves, awaken to the aromas of a big country breakfast in the dining room or on the porch. Rickie will start you off with some freshly squeezed orange juice and coffee followed by fresh fruit, and then rustle up some bacon and eggs. You'll feel fortified for such strenuous activities as sitting on one of the porches or strolling around the grounds visiting the animals.

And just one other thing: You might recognize unassuming Chris under his professional name, Chris Gantry. A songwriter and performer who has written more than 1,000 songs for artists including Roy Clark, Johnny Cash, Wayne Newton, Robert Goulet, Gary Puckett, and Reba McEntire, he penned Glen Campbell's hit "Dreams of the Everyday Housewife," which earned him three BMI Awards, the Nashville's Songwriters Award, and the

Millionaire's Award (for more than two million performances). Currently he's a staff songwriter for Warner/Chappell Music and works in Nashville during the week. And in his spare time, he's also a playwright.

What's Nearby Mulberry

Mulberry is quite small, but it still has its own antiques stores, historic sites, and hiking and biking trails. After sampling the town's offerings, you might drive to the neighboring town of Lynchburg and perhaps tour the Jack Daniel Distillery.

Byrn-Roberts Inn

346 East Main Street
Murfreesboro, Tennessee 37130
(615) 867-0308 or (888) 877-4919;
fax (615) 867-0280

E-MAIL: byrnrobert@aol.com

WEB SITE: www.byrn-roberts-inn.com

INNKEEPERS: Julie and David Becker

ROOMS: 4; all with private bath (2 with whirlpool tub), cable TV, VCR, private-line telephone with data port, clock radio; some with ceiling fan

ON THE GROUNDS: Tandem bike, verandas, screened porch

RATES: $100 to $140 double on weekends, including full breakfast and afternoon refreshments; 15 percent discount for weeknights; ask about corporate rates

CREDIT CARDS ACCEPTED? Yes

OPEN: Year-round

HOW TO GET THERE: From I-24 North, take exit 81, Church Street, to the town square. Turn right onto East Main. The B&B is on the corner of East Main and Maney. From I-24 South, take exit 78 to Northwest Broad and turn right, then left onto West Main. Continue around the courthouse to East Main.

It's a small world and a festive one. When we arrived a family reunion of guests was enjoying the afternoon social hour, and we learned that one of the couples was from just a mile or two up the road from us in Atlanta. Besides the guests, we met our charming hosts Julie and David and their three Shelties—Lady, Annie, and Misty. It was instantly apparent that this bed and breakfast was a fun place to be. The Beckers have incorporated what they know from experience a business traveler wants with what they like in a romantic getaway for themselves to successfully create the perfect combination to delight their guests—1900 atmosphere with 1999 amenities.

The impressive redbrick Queen Anne Victorian mansion was built in 1903 by Charles and Allie Byrn at a cost of $30,000. It contains an astounding 12,000 feet of space including the attic and basement, although the Beckers are using only 5,700 square feet on two floors at present. Radiant heat was new at the time and the Byrns weren't sure they trusted it, so although the house had a furnace and radiators, it also boasts eleven coal fireplaces, now converted to gas-log use. The original owners weren't sure they trusted electricity either, so the house was fitted with gas and electric combination light fixtures, just in case. These lovely chandeliers remain, but the gas is no longer connected. Another innovation of the time was the marble sink in each bedroom; these survive as well. After Mr. Byrn's death in the 1920s, Mrs. Byrn continued to live here with their daughter Anne, her husband Earl Roberts, and their three children—hence the name Byrn-Roberts House. It remained in their family until 1996.

Downstairs public gathering rooms include an informal reception hall, formal parlor, and cozy library with a big-screen television, as well as the dining room. Also downstairs, the Four Season Room has been faux-finished in three shades of creamy white for a soft marble look; accessories change with the season. A massive king-size four-poster bed carved with acanthus leaves and an extra-large shower for two make this a popular choice.

Upstairs, spacious guest rooms have 12-foot ceilings, tall windows, and all the modern conveniences. The bird's-eye maple woodwork determined the Maple Room's name. In the Sunrise Room, so named because you can watch the sun come up if you're awake that early, you can play in the two-person garden-style whirlpool tub or the king-size Victorian-style bed. The first thing you see when you step into the Candle Light Room is the claw-foot whirlpool tub with a European handheld shower—the first we've ever seen—prominently placed in front of the turret windows. The rest of the room is lovely, too, and sports a king-size bed. Created from a sleeping porch, the sunny on-site fitness center boasts a stationary bike, cross-country machine, weights, a television, and small refrigerator.

We mustn't neglect mentioning breakfast, which one guest described as "almost too pretty to eat." Served in the dining room on earthenware specially created by a friend of the Beckers, the meal begins with a fresh fruit platter or grapefruit in a vanilla bean sauce, and might move on the buttermilk pancakes with strawberry sauce and whipped cream, or stuffed French toast with strawberry liqueur sauce. Julie will, however, cater to any dietary restrictions with prior notice.

What's Nearby Murfreesboro

You'll enjoy Murfreesboro's historic district and local antiques shopping. For a taste of local history, tour the Oaklands Mansion. For a good workout, try hiking or biking on the Stones River Greenway. You can also visit the Stones River National Battlefield. If you're longing for the big city, Nashville is only twenty minutes away.

Carriage Lane Inn
Bed and Breakfast

411 North Maney Avenue
Murfreesboro, Tennessee 37130
(615) 890–3630 or (800) 357–2827;
fax (615) 890–9324

E-MAIL: sharonpetty@mindspring.com

WEB SITE: www.bbonline.com/tn/
carriagelane/

INNKEEPERS: Sharon and Ted Petty

ROOMS: 3; all with private bath; 1 with fireplace, whirlpool tub, TV, VCR, telephone

ON THE GROUNDS: Veranda, patio, off-street parking

RATES: $80 to $100, including full breakfast, snacks, and beverages

CREDIT CARDS ACCEPTED? Yes

OPEN: Year-round

HOW TO GET THERE: From the courthouse square, go east on East Main to Maney. Turn left. The B&B is on your left in the fourth block.

ute as a button is how we describe the Carriage Lane Inn. The exterior of the hundred-year-old Queen Anne Victorian cottage and its grounds are meticulously cared for, as is the interior. Painted a soft gray with white trim around the windows and the columns supporting the wraparound porch, the inn exudes serenity. Hanging ferns and geraniums provided a jaunty welcome. Although it looks petite from the outside, the house is surprisingly roomy inside. Still, we remember it fondly as a perfect little dollhouse. With its location only a few blocks from the town square, we were surprised to learn that when the houses in this neighborhood were built, this area was considered Murfreesboro's first suburb.

Although Sharon and Ted were out of town, Sharon's mother was inn-sitting and told us that Sharon loves to restore old houses. That's obvious from the care and attention to detail we saw everywhere. Like bigger houses of the period, the cottage shows off high ceilings, heart-pine floors, gra-cious proportions, and lovely fireplaces, all beautifully refurbished. To this backdrop Sharon has added Oriental carpets, antiques, dramatic window treatments, brass or crystal chandeliers, art, and period accessories to create exquisite rooms. Both the formal parlor, a peaceful place to unwind, and the dining room feature corner fireplaces that have been converted to gas-log use. We can envision how cozy that would make these rooms on a chilly day. Also downstairs for guest use are a small sunroom, the front veranda with wicker and rockers, and a delightful back porch with an old-fashioned porch swing.

When it comes to guest rooms, Sharon has created enchanting havens with antiques and all the modern conveniences. The downstairs bedcham-ber, often requested as a honeymoon suite, boasts everything needed for a romantic getaway: a queen-size bed topped with a featherbed and featuring a draped effect at its head, a gas-log fireplace, a whirlpool tub with candles and bath oils, and a private entrance onto the veranda. Just picture soaking in the tub by candlelight, then slipping between the featherbed and the comforter! This room also has a telephone and television, although we can't imagine that you'll need them.

Upstairs under the eaves, there's a pleasant guest sitting room with a chintz sofa and chair, a bistro table and chairs, television, games and puz-zles, and a coffeemaker, toaster, and small refrigerator cleverly concealed in an old armoire/dresser. There's a phone here for the convenience of upstairs guests as well. Each of the upstairs guest rooms has its own distinctive per-sonality. We particularly liked the animal-print fabrics in one, and the gar-den scene in the bathroom of another.

When morning comes, you have several options for breakfast. You can join your fellow guests in the formal dining room or, if this is a special romantic occasion, dine privately on one of the porches or in the garden. The meal always includes a hot dish, fruit, muffins, juice, and hot beverages.

What's Nearby Murfreesboro

See page 412 for what's nearby Murfreesboro.

Clardy's Guest House Best Buy

435 East Main Street
Murfreesboro, Tennessee 37130
(615) 893-6030

E-MAIL: rdeaton@bellsouth.net

WEB SITE: www.bbonline.com/tn/clardys/

INNKEEPERS: Barbara and Robert Deaton

ROOMS: 2; both with private bath

ON THE GROUNDS: Porch, garden

RATES: $65, including tax and breakfast; special rates for seven-day or more stay

CREDIT CARDS ACCEPTED? No

OPEN: Year-round

HOW TO GET THERE: From Chattanooga, take exit 81 onto US 231 North and go all the way to the town square. Turn right in front of the courthouse onto East Main Street. After you pass the third traffic light, Clardy's is the fifth house on your left. From Nashville, take I–24 East to exit 78-B, TN 96 East. Turn right onto US 41 South. Turn left at the next light onto West Main.

The guest houses of the 1940s and 1950s have gotten a bad rap. They're often thought of as dumpy rooming houses in seedy neighborhoods. But think again. Clardy's, which has been open since 1948 and operated by the same family since 1954, is located in an opulent Richardson Romanesque mansion in Murfreesboro's historic district. Its longevity makes it one of the oldest continuously operating bed and breakfasts in the country.

The mansion was built in 1898 for J. T. Rather, a former mayor of Murfreesboro. At a cost of $14,000, it was one of the most elaborate homes in town. Romanesque architecture, which was most often used for churches and public buildings, is characterized by massively proportioned, fortresslike elements. The most readily identifiable characteristics are wide rounded arches on porches, above entryways, and around windows. The arches rest on squat columns, which sometimes have ornamented capitals. Roofs are hipped and have one or more cross gables; dormers are common as well. Stone or brick laid in patterns across asymmetrical facades creates texture and decoration. Take a look at Clardy's and you'll see all these elements. In fact, the mansion is Murfreesboro's only surviving Romanesque home.

J. T. Rather was from a family of masons, so it's no surprise that he choose this imposing style for his home. The house has been known around town as the "firecracker house," because it was rumored that Rather had such a fear of fire that he had giant firecrackers built into the walls to serve as an early fire alarm. Fortunately, his precaution has never been tested. He spared no expense on the interior of his twenty-room home. Just a few of the outstanding architectural details are eleven fireplaces—each with a different mantel—elaborately carved moldings and mantels, interior columns with Corinthian capitals, and a stunning staircase with a nautical motif. At the landing is a magnificent 8- by 8-foot stained-glass window. It is reported that Rather and his wife had bought the magnificent window on a European trip ten years before they built the house. They were able to design the perfect spot to make the window a focal point.

Barbara's parents bought the home at auction in 1954. Her father liked massive walnut Victorian furniture and it was easy and cheap to get at the time, so he filled the house with beautiful pieces that remain today. Although Barbara grew up here and she and Bob were married in the parlor, she never intended to operate it as a guest house or bed and breakfast. When her parents died in the 1980s, however, she decided to carry on the family tradition.

Barbara's great-grandparents' antiques are used to furnish the first-floor guest room. The focal point of this chamber is the massive, high-back bed whose ornate carvings match those around the mirror on the marble-topped dresser. Another antique bed makes the room ideal for family members or friends traveling together. Other special features in this room are the mantel, bay window, and claw-foot tub. Upstairs, a guest room located in a rounded tower features a brass bed and a high-back bed. If we stayed in this room, we'd leave our door open whenever possible so we could look through the three arches in the hall overlooking the stained-glass window.

Enjoy television, movies, reading, and good conversation in the formal living room, or while away some time on the tiled front porch or in the gardens. Breakfast is a satisfying meal with an entree such as French toast with fruit topping or an egg casserole.

When we told Barbara she should be charging a lot more, she shrugged and said she was just following in the tradition of her parents.

What's Nearby Murfreesboro

See page 412 for what's nearby Murfreesboro.

Simply Southern
B&B Inn

211 North Tennessee Boulevard
Murfreesboro, Tennessee 37130
(615) 896–4988 or (888) 723–1199

E-MAIL: InnSouth@aol.com

WEB SITE: www.bbonline.com/tn/simplysouthern/

INNKEEPERS: Georgia and Carl Buckner

ROOMS: 4 rooms and 1 suite; all with private
bath, TV, telephone, clock radio, ceiling fan; some have desks, data ports

ON THE GROUNDS: Verandas, patio, garden

RATES: $85 to $145 double, including full breakfast, snacks, and beverages; additional person $25; ask about corporate rates

CREDIT CARDS ACCEPTED? Yes

OPEN: Year-round

HOW TO GET THERE: From I-24, take exit 81, South Church Street, and go to the courthouse square. Turn left onto East Main Street, go 1 mile to Tennessee Boulevard, and turn left. The B&B is the third house on your left and is identified by signs.

We've all played with a kaleidoscope at some time in our lives. Come on, now; admit it. Even as an adult, you'll play with these toys any chance you get. Why are we so fascinated with them? Because they're ever changing and have infinite possibilities. Georgia and Carl use the kaleidoscope as their theme—ever-changing phases, ever-changing events, ever-changing guests. They have dozens of unusual and very fine kaleidoscopes in their bed and breakfast to serve as ice breakers and entertainment for their guests.

Georgia and Carl have traveled a lot and know what they like in accommodations. They've obviously gone to a lot of effort to make sure their guests are comfortable and enjoying themselves. We usually don't talk about recreation rooms first, but theirs deserves special mention. Located in the basement, this immense room is a place to play pool, sing along with the karaoke machine, choose from one of the dozens of rolls to play on the player piano, put together a puzzle, play cards, buy a Coke for a dime from the vintage Coke machine, or gather around the fireplace. As a matter of fact, Simply Southern is loaded with places to play or simply relax: the formal main living room and adjacent parlor, the upstairs sitting room, the

sunroom, the large front porch, the rear courtyard and garden, and the out-door hot tub. Several of these rooms sport a television, VCR, and CD player. An upstairs and a downstairs refrigerator are stocked with soft drinks and ice. Hot beverages and popcorn are available as well. But we're getting ahead of ourselves.

One of Murfreesboro's finest old homes, the redbrick four-square house with Dutch influences was built in 1907. Over its long life, it has often welcomed guests. Because it is directly across the street from Middle Tennessee State University, former owners offered part of the second floor and all of the third floor and basement to students. Today, the B&B is a perfect place for visiting parents and people doing business with the university.

The finely restored interior was constructed in the Craftsman style with beamed ceilings, lots of built-in bookcases, cabinets, window seats, and benches, and less ornamentation than some houses of the period. To this backdrop Georgia and Carl have added bright colors, period wallpapers, fine antiques, comfortable reproductions, and showy art and accessories.

Each of the guest rooms, most of which are named for Tennessee plants, is comfortable and tastefully decorated. Each has its own bath—some with footed tubs, others with marble showers or tub/shower combinations, and all with cute little yellow rubber duckies. Three feature king- or queen-size beds; the fourth has twin beds. In winter guests are kept cozy with down comforters on the beds. Every detail has been planned with your comfort and pleasure in mind. Deserving of special note is the Azalea Room, which can be combined with the sunroom to create a suite.

In the South food reigns supreme, and it's an integral part of any stay at Simply Southern. Georgia even has her own cookbook, *A Kaleidoscope of Recipes*. Early risers can enjoy a continental breakfast, but if you can wait until later, you'll be in for a special treat. Served in the formal dining room, the morning repast might consist of eggs in a nest, scrambled eggs with tomatoes and chives, or a breakfast casserole with all the appropriate accompaniments.

What's Nearby Murfreesboro

See page 412 for what's nearby Murfreesboro.

Apple Brook Bed, Breakfast, and Barn ⬤ Best Buy

9127 Highway 100
Nashville, Tennessee 37221
(615) 646–5082 or (877) 646–5082

INNKEEPERS: Cynthia and Don Van Ryen

ROOMS: 4; all with private bath

ON THE GROUNDS: Swimming pool, brook, five acres, barn

RATES: $95 double, including full breakfast; extra charge for horses

CREDIT CARDS ACCEPTED? Yes

OPEN: Year-round

HOW TO GET THERE: From Nashville's ring highways I–265 or I–440, take West End Boulevard South. When it splits, stay on Highway 100. After you pass Old Hickory Boulevard and the Natchez Trace Parkway, Apple Brook is on your left.

We were intrigued when we learned that there was a bed and breakfast practically within the city limits of Nashville where guests can bring their horses. We had to check it out for ourselves, even though we don't travel with any equine friends. When we arrived, we did indeed find a rustic one-hundred-year-old barn next to a gussied-up turn-of-the-century farmhouse, but we were met first not by horses but a strutting rooster, a friendly dog, and a kitten just begging us to play. The four-pawed critters would have cheerfully followed us inside, but just then Don appeared and said they weren't allowed. Such crestfallen looks we got! If we'd been able to stay longer and lounge around the pool or take long walks in the pastures, we'd have shared with the pets some of the pampering the two-legged creatures get at this down-home place.

Apple Brook offers the best of both worlds—a country getaway just minutes from all the attractions of the city. Despite its proximity to Nashville, geese make their home in the pond and deer often wander across the lawn.

While Don and Cynthia were showing us around, they told us about how they'd chosen a name for their retirement home on what was originally Beechgrove Plantation. A babbling brook fed by a natural stream runs through the property, and it seems that long-ago teacher Sally Morton would send students through the apple orchards from the nearby one-room schoolhouse to get fresh water. The Van Ryens thus named their farm to honor the apple orchard and brook.

The onetime clapboard two-story farmhouse with its white-pillared front porch had a brick facade put on at some time in its long history, giving it a substantial and more citified air. Inside, the house speaks of its simple origins. Lacking here are the high ceilings and ornate woodwork found in so many town houses of the same period. Cynthia and Don have furnished it in country casual antiques and pieces of their own. Four comfortable bedrooms—Peach, Tea Rose, Cardinal, and Blue—are individually decorated in upscale country charm and feature queen-size beds and private baths. Every room is supplied with books and magazines and even a flashlight.

When we heard about the breakfast, we were really sorry we weren't spending the night. In addition to apple pancakes with real Wisconsin maple syrup, Don serves bacon specially cured and smoked over applewood chips. The eggs used are from their own guinea hens. Don says that when he starts cooking and the aromas start drifting through the house, "We don't have to wake the guests."

What's Nearby Nashville

Music lovers will have a ball in Nashville. Check out the music scene at Opryland USA and Nashville Palace. In the evening, go clubbing in The District and hear live jazz, bluegrass, country, or rock 'n' roll. Don't miss Music Row, where you can shop at souvenir shops of the stars and see the recording studios. You can also stop at the Country Music Hall of Fame. There's still more to do, so take note. You can visit the Tennessee State Capitol, Batman Building, the Hermitage, Centennial Park, and much much more.

Another Recommended B&B in Nashville

End o' the Bend Lodge and Landing, located on a bend in the Cumberland River, offers rooms with country French furniture in a log cabin; 2523 Miami Avenue, Nashville, TN 37214; (615) 883-0997.

Carole's Yellow Cottage

Best Buy

801 Fatherland Street
Nashville, Tennessee 37206
(615) 226-2952

WEB SITE: www.bbonline.com/tn/yellowcottage/

INNKEEPER: Carole Vanderwal

ROOMS: 2; both with private bath, ceiling fan, clock radio

ON THE GROUNDS: Porch, deck, garden

RATES: $85 to $95 single, $95 to $105 double, including full breakfast and beverages; two-night minimum stay required (Carole prefers you to reserve two weeks or more in advance.)

CREDIT CARDS ACCEPTED? Yes

OPEN: Year-round

HOW TO GET THERE: From downtown Nashville, go across the Woodland bridge to Eighth Street and turn right. The B&B is on the corner of Eighth and Fatherland.

This bed and breakfast, located in a 1902 neoclassical Queen Anne Victorian cottage in the historic Edgefield neighborhood, is an urban sanctuary for the weary traveler. As was common in the day when it was built, the Yellow Cottage features specialty millwork. We took special notice of the sunburst design in the temple pediment on the porch roof that frames the front door—it's painted lavender to complement the summer crape myrtles—and the sunburst fretwork in the main hall.

Although the house has 12-foot ceilings, hardwood floors, and beautiful woodwork, it is understated compared to some of the more flamboyant homes of the era. Carole herself is understated as well; she won't wear you out the way some innkeepers can. She has decorated her house in soothing colors and furnished it with simple antiques and interesting artwork from various periods, all with the idea of creating a restful retreat.

You'll want to spend as much time as possible on the front porch, where you can catch gentle breezes and admire the various styles of architecture in the neighborhood, or on the deck appreciating the lilies, antique climbing roses, lavender, peonies, yucca, begonias, coneflowers, herbs, and annuals. When the weather doesn't permit, Carole has outfitted her sitting room with lots of books, and there's a television and sound system to keep you entertained. One of the books you'll want to look at is *Growing Up in Edgefield*, an account (with wonderful old pictures) of life in the turn-of-the-century neighborhood.

Two sleeping rooms are simply furnished and offer private baths. One of the things we noticed and appreciated was the provision of large bottles of shampoo and other toiletries in the bathrooms. Although it has an antique bed, the art, bed and window treatments, and sofa created from a futon mattress and frame all give the Blue Room (actually done in blue and plum) a contemporary look. The Yellow Room is more historical. Its focal point is an antique bed delicately painted with garlands and cameos. An octagonal table matches the bed. Pegs for hanging your clothes and a quilt hanging over a quilt stand also impart a look of the past to this room.

Breakfast is a casual meal served in the kitchen. Carole will prepare you just about anything you want; she's especially into healthy cooking and uses a lot of whole grains. If you're on a diet, you can request a light breakfast.

What's Nearby Nashville

See page 419 for what's nearby Nashville.

Hillsboro House Bed and Breakfast

1933 20th Avenue South
Nashville, Tennessee 37212
(615) 292-5501 or (800) 228-7851

E-MAIL: hillsboro@acelink.net

WEB SITE: www.bbonline.com/tn/hillsboro/

INNKEEPER: Andrea Beaudet

ROOMS: 3; all with private bath, queen-size featherbed, cable TV, telephone

ON THE GROUNDS: Veranda, gardens, patio

RATES: $100 single, $110 double, including breakfast and refreshments; additional person $20; two-night minimum stay on weekends

CREDIT CARDS ACCEPTED? Yes

OPEN: Year-round

HOW TO GET THERE: From I–440, take the 21st Street exit. Stay on 21st Avenue South through three traffic lights from I–440 East, or two traffic lights from I–440 West. After crossing Blair Boulevard, Portland is the second street. Turn right onto Portland. Turn left onto 20th Avenue South. The Hillsboro House is the first house on your left.

When we arrived at dusk, Andrea was out tending her herb, ornamental vegetable, and perennial garden, accompanied and "helped" by Bonnie, the Westie, and Maggie, the cat (short for Magnolia). So we stepped through the arbor entwined with clematis and roses and let her take us on a little tour of the grounds behind the neat picket fence. Then we went inside to tour the cottage and retired to the pretty drawing room for some good conversation.

Located on a corner in the historic Belmont-Hillsboro district, the picture-pretty and neat-as-a-pin Victorian cottage is convenient to both Vanderbilt and Belmont Universities, the trendy Hillsboro Village—site of popular eateries and quaint boutiques—and Music Row. When you're sitting out on the front porch or in the side garden, you can hear the angelus morning and evening chimes of Belmont's carillon.

Andrea's an interesting person. She's from Maine, but her ancestry is Acadian. She's worked in retail, marketing, and as a music teacher. Because she's bilingual, she's worked at both the Montreal and Knoxville World's Fairs and has lived in Paris. She was the first person to apply for a B&B license in Nashville, back in 1993. Andrea told us that the 1904 cottage had been condemned and was slated for demolition when she rescued it. Looking at its wonderful hardwood floors, original moldings, ornate mantel, and leaded-glass windows, among other architectural features, we'd have found it hard to believe if she hadn't shown us the pictures. In her spare time she serves as president of the Tennessee Bed and Breakfast Innkeepers Association.

Guest accommodations are provided in three lovely rooms—Fairfax, Acklen, and Magnolia—one on the first floor, two on the second. Each restful room boasts a queen-size bed topped with a featherbed as well as a private bath, one with a claw-foot tub. With romance in mind, one bedchamber features a four-poster bed, another an iron bed. With the business traveler in mind, Andrea has thoughtfully provided workspace in each bedroom, and private telephone lines as well.

Our mouths were watering as she described a breakfast of peaches and cream French toast made with homemade bread. Other breakfast delights might include omelettes, sausage, fruit, and biscuits. Andrea's recipe for carrot-pecan pancakes is found in Gail Greco's *Recipes for Romance*. We can well believe the many notes former guests have written in Andrea's guest books, stating that by the end of breakfast, strangers leave the table as friends.

Be sure to check out her Web site to see live action at the B&B via Web cam.

What's Nearby Nashville

See page 419 for what's nearby Nashville.

Linden Manor Bed and Breakfast

1501 Linden Avenue
Nashville, Tennessee 37212
(615) 298–2701 or (800) 226–0317

E-MAIL: LindenB&B@aol.com

WEB SITE: www.bbonline.com/tn/linden/

INNKEEPERS: Catherine and Tom Favreau

ROOMS: 3; all with private bath,
ceiling fan, clock radio, telephone,
cable TV, fresh flowers; 1 room with desk

ON THE GROUNDS: Porch

RATES: $95 to $135 double, including full breakfast and afternoon
refreshments; no additional guests in room; military discount, corporate
rates

CREDIT CARDS ACCEPTED? Yes

OPEN: Year-round

HOW TO GET THERE: From I–440, take exit 3, Hillsboro Pike/21st Street. Turn
north and look for Linden on your right four to five streets from the exit.
Follow Linden to the bed and breakfast. (*Note:* When Linden appears to
dead-end, turn left, then immediately right, and you'll be back on Linden.)

We'd like to bottle some of Catherine's boundless energy to use when
we're flagging! Renovating and decorating this 1893 Victorian cottage
(with Tom's help, of course) to operate as a bed and breakfast is the
fulfillment of a twelve-year dream, and it doesn't seem to have tired her out
at all.

During their married life, Tom has been in the Coast Guard, and they've
lived and traveled around the world. All the while, it was their goal to open
a bed and breakfast when his enlistment was up, so during their travels
they've picked up some wonderful pieces with which to furnish their dream
house—Asian carpets, interesting screens, wall hangings, even a table with
three huge carved fish serving as the pedestal. Guests can entertain themselves just locating and examining these fabulous finds.

Located in the historic Belmont-Hillsboro district, the B&B is close to
Belmont and Vanderbilt Universities, so it's an attractive place for visiting
parents or those doing business with the schools to stay, as well as for
leisure travelers. Three guest rooms are surprisingly spacious gems painted
in rich jewel colors. For instance, the muted plum tone in the Tennessee
Suite is called royal velvet. This romantic suite also features an elegant

carved high-back bed as well as a whirlpool tub in the marble bathroom. A gas-log fireplace and a four-poster rice bed make the Vanderbilt Room an attractive alternative. The Belmont Room has an iron bed. Old houses are notorious for poor water pressure and limited hot water, but the Favreaus have made sure their guests will always have plenty of both by installing a seventy-five-gallon water heater and ¾-inch lines.

Breakfast, served in the dining room by a corner fireplace that's lit in cool weather, is a sumptuous feast that might begin with a granola fruit cup and proceed to an entree such as stuffed French toast, or creamed sherry gravy with mushrooms served over English toast. Honeymoon guests in the Tennessee Suite can request breakfast in their room. If you're not out sightseeing till all hours, Catherine serves refreshments in the afternoon, in good weather on the wraparound porch.

What's Nearby Nashville

See page 419 for what's nearby Nashville.

White Elephant B&B Inn **Best Buy**

304 Church Street
Savannah, Tennessee 38372
(901) 925-6410

WEB SITE: www.bbonline.com/tn/ elephant/

INNKEEPERS: Sharon and Ken Hansgen

ROOMS: 3; all with private bath (1 bath is adjacent to the room), ceiling fan, clock radio

ON THE GROUNDS: Porches, no smoking

RATES: $65 to $95 single, $75 to $105 double, including full breakfast and welcome refreshments; discount for weeknights and multiple-night bookings

CREDIT CARDS ACCEPTED? Yes

OPEN: Year-round

HOW TO GET THERE: US 64 goes right down Savannah's Main Street. Two blocks east of the Hardin County Courthouse, turn north onto Church Street. Go 1½ blocks and look for two white elephants sitting in front of a big white house on your right. The driveway is in the rear so continue past the house, turn right onto College Street, right onto North Pickwick Street, and right again into Elephant Alley. Park on the southeastern side of the house.

"Going to see the elephant" was an old-fashioned phrase used to describe a particularly daunting task. We, however, didn't find the White Elephant daunting at all. In fact, it's rather whimsical. Sharon ancestors were from Hardin County; she and Ken thus visited from California to do some genealogical research and so that Ken, a Civil War buff, could visit nearby Shiloh National Military Park. While they were in town, the handsome Welch-Nesbett House, a 1901 Queen Anne, caught their eye. When they contacted a Realtor about it, he said, "What do you want that old white elephant for?" They knew exactly what they wanted it for—a bed and breakfast. Sharon was working in the B&B industry on the state level in California at the time and had aspirations to own and operate one of her own; she just didn't envision it being outside California. The white elephant name stuck, however, and you'll find amusing elephant accents around the house.

From the outside the focal point of the house is the circular tower with its conical roof; also note the towerlike dormer and wraparound porch. Three circular bow windows—one each in the formal parlors and one in the upstairs tower room—high ceilings, hardwood floors, and oak moldings characterize the interior, which is furnished primarily in oak antiques. An oak staircase leads to the second floor, where there are three individually decorated guest rooms—all with antique beds modified to accommodate queen-size mattresses.

The central motif of the Poppy Room is the golden California poppy. A floral tapestry-print comforter and draperies coordinate with a wallpaper border. The massive bed of the matching oak bedroom suite has an ornately carved headboard. A soaking-size 1900 claw-foot tub dominates the bathroom. Variegated ivy covers the comforter and entwines the draperies and accessories in the Ivy Room, which features an iron bed and a daintier claw-foot tub. Peacocks and paisley provide the Far East ambience in the Peacock Room. Although this room features a carved-oak bed, the Victorian fainting couch is the perfect place to relax with a good book. This room's private bath is reached via the hall. To preserve the turn-of-the-century mood, telephones and televisions are absent from the guest rooms, but they do have clock radios in case you have to get up at a certain time in the morning. A full breakfast, which might include quiche, a fruit salad, and homemade breads along with juice and hot beverages, is served in the formal dining room.

Both Civil War enthusiasts, Sharon and Ken were active in the National Civil War Association in northern California; Sharon was a civilian reenacter, and Ken portrayed an infantryman in Company A, 71st Pennsylvania. Sharon is a member of the Ladies Soldiers Friends Society and United Daughters of the Confederacy. Ken is a board member of the Friends of Shiloh National Military Park, where he gives guided tours. He's also a step-on guide for the Hardin County Tourism Board, Hardin County Chamber of Commerce, and the Delta Queen Steamboat Company. In their "spare time," they're also involved in little theater.

Just a note: Although few bed and breakfasts allow smoking in the house, most agree to let guests smoke on the porches. At the White Elephant, smoking is not permitted anywhere on the premises.

What's Nearby Savannah

Besides the local shopping and restaurants, Savannah also offers a number of water excursions. Visit the Tennessee River and Tennessee River Museum. Pack a picnic for an afternoon at Pickwick Lake. Go canoeing on Indian Creek. Outdoor activities in the area include golf, fishing, hiking, and water sports.

Von-Bryan Inn

2402 Hatcher Mountain Road
Sevierville, Tennessee 37862
(865) 453-9832 or (800) 633-1459;
fax (865) 428-8634

INNKEEPERS: D. J. and Jo Ann Vaughn

ROOMS: 6 in main house and 1 three-level suite; all with private bath, some with whirlpool; separate chalet with whirlpool, 3 bedrooms, kitchen, living room, fireplace, decks, hot tub

ON THE GROUNDS: Swimming pool, hot tub

RATES: In main house, $110 to $145, double, $25 each additional person, including full breakfast and afternoon refreshments; in chalet, $220 for up to four people, $20 each additional person (two-night minimum stay in chalet and on weekends)

CREDIT CARDS ACCEPTED? Yes

OPEN: Year-round

HOW TO GET THERE: From Highway 321, turn onto Hatcher Mountain Road (the inn's sign marks the turn) and follow inn signs all the way to the top of the mountain. Ask for a map and more detailed instructions when you make reservation.

Von-Bryan Inn is on top of a mountain near the Great Smoky Mountains. Not near the top, on it. The view includes the Smokies and Wears Valley and treetops in the clouds. The inn is set up to make the most of the view, especially the garden room, a room on three levels with a reading loft and many windows from which you can look out over the hills and watch the sunset. The outdoor pool seems to float above clouds and mountains, and from there the view is panoramic. And the large hot tub by the pool is a great place to relax while you watch the stars at night. While we were here, we saw men stand in the yard looking across the valleys and deciding, without even going inside, that this was a place to which they must bring their wives.

We could've told them that it's nice inside, too. The living room has a stacked-stone fireplace and attractive, unobtrusive furniture grouped for conversation.

The suite is interesting. It has lots of glass, a pine floor, a queen-size canopy bed, and a reading loft. Each of the other guest rooms has a special delight, a special view or an unusual bed, for example, but the Red Bud Room is unlike anything we've ever seen. It has a king-size four-poster bed against a natural paneled wall, windows along another wall, a sitting area with a love seat, and a big cherry-red hot tub in the corner. Red simply dominates the room. Jo Ann says that it's one of the most requested rooms and theorizes that folks who would find a red hot tub just too racy at home get a kick out of it on vacation.

Speaking of Jo Ann, if personable innkeepers are important to you, you'll enjoy this inn. Jo Ann is thoroughly competent and produces a gourmet breakfast without a flick of the eyelid, but she's easy, chatty, and comfortable, all at the same time. D. J. has a green thumb and also is a good conversationalist. We lingered much too long over breakfast because we got to talking about everything from food and plants to our earlier careers, and couldn't make ourselves leave.

Among the nice little treats you can arrange for yourself if you stay here are helicopter pickup and delivery to the inn. We didn't experience the helicopter trip, but given the view and the height of the mountain, we think it would be a sensational experience.

One treat you don't have to arrange. Jo Ann unobtrusively sets out lemonade, tea, and desserts each evening for all who want them.

The Old Gore House Bed and Breakfast

Best Buy

410 Belmont Avenue
Shelbyville, Tennessee 37160
(931) 685–0636

E-MAIL: garyashley@hotmail.com

WEB SITE: www.bbonline.com/tn/gorehouse/

INNKEEPER: Gary Ashley

ROOMS: 3; all with private bath, telephone, ceiling fan, TV, clock radio, luggage rack; ask about pets; limited wheelchair access

ON THE GROUNDS: Veranda, gardens

RATES: $50 to $75 double, including full breakfast and afternoon refreshments; minimum ten-day stay during the Tennessee Walking Horse Celebration

CREDIT CARDS ACCEPTED? Yes

OPEN: Year-round

HOW TO GET THERE: Take US 231 into Shelbyville to the town square. Follow Main Street around the square by taking a right and then a left. Go straight at the light to get onto Depot Street. Follow Depot to the first red light (the depot will be on your right). Bear to the left onto Belmont Avenue. The B&B is the second house on your right and is identified with a sign.

Gary makes a mean bread pudding—one of our favorite decadent desserts of all time—and he had some hot and waiting for us when we arrived. It was divine and we were in hog heaven. Gary's a great host with lots of energy and a good sense of humor.

Of course, we had to ask the obvious question—did the house have any connection with Tennessean Vice President Al Gore? Gary told us it did: Although the house was built in between 1884 and 1890 for Henry Clay Ryle and owned from 1899 to 1927 by George Evans, it was bought in 1927 by James K. Gore, a cousin of Al Gore Sr. James acted as the elder Gore's campaign manager. For many years the Gore House operated as a boardinghouse or as apartments.

Although the stately two-story house has a full-length veranda supported by white columns, we're not talking about a grandiose mansion here. Spacious as it may be, it was built as an upper-middle-class home, not a palace for the very wealthy. Still, it features the high ceilings, hardwood floors, numerous fireplaces, and gracious mantels we've come to expect in houses of the era. Beautifully restored, it is decorated with period colors and wallpapers and furnished with antiques, gilt-framed mirrors, and Oriental carpets. We particularly liked the gingerbread brackets in the doorjambs and the variety of quilts hanging throughout the house.

You'll want to get to know Gary and your fellow guests, and your options for doing so are many. Gas-log fireplaces in both parlors and the dining room make appealing spots to cozy up to on a chilly day, but by far the most popular place to gather is the huge sunroom, comfortably furnished with wicker pieces. A black and white tile floor, walls of windows, ceiling fans, and plenty of lush greenery give this room a real conservatory look. And do take time to examine the small but picture-perfect garden, with its fountain, statuary, and fish pond.

Like many Southerners, Gary has a thing for *Gone with the Wind*, and you'll find many rooms here named for the characters as well as *GWTW* memorabilia on display. Double parlors are named for Scarlett and Rhett, the dining room for Mammy, and the guest rooms for Melanie, Ashley, and Aunt Pitty Pat. Each of these bedchambers is blessed with a carved high-back antique bed modified to accommodate a queen-size mattress.

You'll never go hungry here. Gary serves a huge breakfast that might include bacon and eggs or an egg casserole with fruit, biscuits and gravy, juice, and hot beverages. Whether you eat in Mammy's Dining Room or the sunroom, an added attraction is musical accompaniment from an old crank-operated Edison Victrola. You can also dine in your bedchamber on request. In the afternoon Gary serves tea and cookies or some other treat. And if you're really lucky, he just might make that famous bread pudding.

What's Nearby Shelbyville

Shelbyville is called Tennessee's horse country. It's home to the Tennessee Walking Horse Celebration, a competition to earn the title of World Grand Champion. The event is held at the Calsonic Arena, where you can tour the Tennessee Walking Horse Museum. The rural area also consists of farms, antiques malls, crafts shops, and fine restaurants. Also, try fishing at Normandy Lake and Tims Ford Lake.

Watertown Bed and Breakfast

116 Depot Avenue
Watertown, Tennessee 37184
(615) 237-9999 or (615) 237-9434

E-MAIL: mccomb28@earthlink.net

INNKEEPERS: Sharon and Bob McComb

ROOMS: 5, including 1 suite; all with private baths; some with decorative fireplace and whirlpool tub

ON THE GROUNDS: Hammock on upper veranda, porch swing on downstairs porch

RATES: $55 to $ 125 double, including full breakfast; $5 less for single, $10 more for each extra person in room; six-course gourmet dinner for $25 per person extra with advance reservations (BYOB—this is a dry town.)

CREDIT CARDS ACCEPTED? Yes

OPEN: Year-round

HOW TO GET THERE: From I–40, exit onto US 70 East and follow it to Watertown. The B&B is ½ block off the square on Depot Street. If you're flying, Bob or Sharon will pick you up from the nearby Lebanon airport.

"You don't come to Watertown to do, you come to undo," explains Sharon McComb, innkeeper of the Watertown Bed and Breakfast. About seven or eight times a year, an excursion train comes to town from Nashville and the economy gets an infusion of cash; the rest of the year, the pace remains a nice comfortable crawl.

We ate lunch at the cafe—fried green tomatoes, some very good barbecue, homemade dinner rolls, and a piece of very rich pecan pie. The tablecloths were green oilcloth, the knife, fork, and spoon wrapped in a paper napkin, a model railroad train ran in endless circles on a shelf around the wall, and everyone spoke to each other. By the time we left the cafe, just about everyone in town knew who we were, where we were staying, and that we were writing a book about bed and breakfasts. In return we knew which shops had the best antiques; when the train was next coming to town; that

one shopkeeper's daughter had just had a baby, and if we wanted to see her shop someone would have to run over to her house and get the key from her son, who was home from college; and that we could just pay Sharon for anything we wanted to buy, and she'd make sure the owner got the money.

When we finally got to the B&B, Sharon greeted us with a glass of iced tea and showed us around. Each room is named for a place where the McCombs have lived; they range from the Watertown Room on the first floor with the bathroom across the hall to the Tennessee Suite with its queen bed, sitting room with gas-log fireplace, and large bath with a two-person whirlpool tub. We immediately homed in on the second-floor veranda with its two-person hammock and—after a short stop at the paperback swap library—proceeded to do a little "undoing."

A major part of any successful B&B is the personality of the innkeepers. Sharon and Bob are our kind of people. We first suspected they would be when we saw the black and white Mona Lisa wallpaper in the Watertown bathroom. It displays eighteen poses that Leonardo da Vinci never imagined. Of course the toy airplane/weather vane that resides on the top of a 15-foot-tall stump in the front yard should have given us some idea of what to expect. (If you're wondering—yes, Sharon's husband, Bob, is a pilot.) The house is furnished with antiques that have been in their families for years. The grandfather clock was actually built by Sharon's grandfather. The windup Victrola in the upstairs hall still works, and the McCombs have a great collection of old 78 rpm records that you can play on it.

Some time later we did rouse ourselves to check out the swing on the front porch. That's when we discovered the garden area in the side and backyard that is used for family gatherings, baby showers, weddings, or whatever other occasion might be appropriate.

When you return to the B&B in the evening after dinner, you'll find your bed turned down and GooGoos (which originated here and went on to become an internationally known confection) set out on each pillow as a late-night treat.

What's Nearby Watertown

Watertown is a quiet old farming and railroad town that time seems to have passed by. Today, the town square is populated with an assortment of crafts and antiques shops and a fine small-town cafe, with the original name of the Watertown Cafe. Relax and enjoy!

About the Authors

Carol and Dan Thalimer have been associated with the travel industry for eighteen years, and for seven of them they owned travel agencies. They've inspected dozens of cruise ships and hundreds of hotels, inns, and bed and breakfasts and reported on them for travel agent publications and guides such as *Travel Agent Magazine* and *ABC Star Service*. For the past twelve years they have written about travel for fifty magazines and newspapers and for guidebook publishers. They are the authors of *Quick Escapes from Atlanta, Fun with the Family: Georgia, Romantic Days and Nights in Atlanta,* and *Recommended Country Inns: The South,* all from The Globe Pequot Press.

Indexes

Alphabetical Index to B&Bs

(* denotes a historic property)

Especially Family-Friendly B&Bs

B&Bs with Wheelchair Access

B&Bs That Allow Unrestricted Smoking

B&Bs with a Pool or Hot Tub

B&Bs in Scenic Areas

B&Bs on the Shore

B&Bs in Rural Locations

B&Bs in Urban Areas

indulge in some southern comfort

Hiking South Carolina Trails
North Carolina Is My Home
North Carolina Curiosities
Fun with the Family™ in North Carolina
Short Bike Rides® in North Carolina
The Outer Banks
Romantic Days & Nights® Savannah
Romantic Days & Nights® Atlanta
Quick Escapes® Atlanta
Georgia: Off the Beaten Path®
Romantic Days & Nights® New Orleans
Quick Escapes® Florida
Fun with the Family™ in Florida
Choose Florida for Retirement: Discoveries for Every Budget
Guide to Sea Kayaking Southern Florida
Great Family Vacations: South
Southeastern Lighthouses
Gulf Coast Lighthouses
Choose the South: Retirement Discoveries for Every Budget
The Best Bike Rides® in the South
Dixie: A Traveler's Guide

And an *Off the Beaten Path*® guide for every state in the South!